D1736419

REHABILITATION
for
TRAUMATIC
BRAIN INJURY

REHABILITATION
for
TRAUMATIC
BRAIN INJURY

Edited by
Walter M. High, Jr.
Angelle M. Sander
Margaret A. Struchen
Karen A. Hart

OXFORD
UNIVERSITY PRESS
2005

OXFORD
UNIVERSITY PRESS

Oxford University Press, Inc., publishes works that further
Oxford University's objective of excellence
in research, scholarship, and education.

Oxford   New York
Auckland   Cape Town   Dar es Salaam   Hong Kong   Karachi
Kuala Lumpur   Madrid   Melbourne   Mexico City   Nairobi
New Delhi   Shanghai   Taipei   Toronto

With offices in
Argentina   Austria   Brazil   Chile   Czech Republic   France   Greece
Guatemala   Hungary   Italy   Japan   Poland   Portugal   Singapore
South Korea   Switzerland   Thailand   Turkey   Ukraine   Vietnam

Copyright © 2005 by Oxford University Press, Inc.

Published by Oxford University Press, Inc.
198 Madison Avenue, New York, New York 10016

www.oup.com

Oxford is a registered trademark of Oxford University Press

Library of Congress Cataloging-in-Publication Data
Rehabilitation for traumatic brain injury / edited by Walter M. High, Jr. . . . [et al.].
  p. ; cm.
Includes bibliographical references and index.
ISBN-13 978-0-19-517355-0

1. Brain damage—Patients—Rehabilitation.
[DNLM: 1. Brain Injuries—rehabilitation.   2. Evidence-Based Medicine.   WL 354 R345205
2005]   I. High, Walter M.
RC387.5.R426 2005
617.4'810443—dc22   2004030357

The science of medicine is a rapidly changing field. As new research and clinical experience broaden our
knowledge, changes in treatment and drug therapy do occur. The authors and publisher of this work have
checked with sources believed to be reliable in their efforts to provide information that is accurate and
complete, and in accordance with the standards accepted at the time of publication. However, in light of the
possibility of human error or changes in the practice of medicine, neither the authors, nor the publisher, nor
any other party who has been involved in the preparation or publication of this work warrants that the
information contained herein is in every respect accurate or complete. Readers are encouraged to confirm
the information contained herein with other reliable sources, and are strongly advised to check the product
information sheet provided by the pharmaceutical company for each drug they plan to administer.

Printed in the United States of America
on acid-free paper

Foreword

Over the past 25 years, the significant growth of clinical research and applied knowledge in the field of traumatic brain injury (TBI) has supported the development of specialty rehabilitation services for TBI and the expansion of clinical practice. The interdisciplinary framework of rehabilitation has lead to rich research findings in the diagnosis, assessment, treatment, and service delivery for persons with traumatic brain injuries. With the advent of such findings, it has become clear that TBI is a far-reaching problem that affects the survivor, family members, and the community. As such, the research that has emerged from this clinical picture has extended beyond the individual with a brain injury to systems that have a direct impact on advocacy and policy.

In September 2003, the Rehabilitation Research Training Center at The Institute for Rehabilitation and Research (TIRR), funded by the National Institute on Disability and Rehabilitation Research (NIDRR), hosted a conference on the State of the Science in TBI research. This conference gathered the nation's experts in TBI rehabilitation research to present empirical findings in specific areas of TBI research, to describe what is known and what has yet to be determined with respect to treatment interventions. This edited volume evolved from that event. The breadth and depth of the chapters in *Rehabilitation for Traumatic Brain Injury* highlight the vast knowledge that we have gained over the last 100 years, as noted in Dr. Boake's chapter on the history of TBI, as well as the many types of treatment that have yet to be refined and validated empirically. A quick glance at the chapter titles will reveal the broad nature of TBI research. Although many of the chapters focus on traditional topics such as medical and neuropsychological treatment intervention, they extend to other areas including community integration, family functioning, environmental factors, and working with specialty populations such as older adults with brain injury. Because rehabilitation is a complex process that involves multiple determining factors, *Rehabilitation for Traumatic Brain Injury* attempts to comprehensively address the numerous aspects of TBI rehabilitation that affect functional independence and recovery following TBI.

Despite the wide variety of topics, a common theme emerges throughout the book: Although significant strides have been made in acute and post-acute rehabilitation of persons with TBI, the majority of treatment interventions that are currently in use or are being proposed have yet to be validated. As such, this text also focuses on identifying the research required to empirically validate such treatments and discusses how this research must reach the standards of evidence-based medicine. An objective and comprehensive evaluation of the state of the science in TBI rehabilitation research clearly indicates that we should be proud of the research outcomes that have benefited quality of life for so many survivors and their family members. However, we need to set the ambitious goal of raising the standard to the point at which we have Level I evidence for the majority of rehabilitation research.

ROBIN HANKS, PH.D., ABPP (CN)
Chief of Rehabilitation Psychology and Neuropsychology
Project Director, Southeastern Michigan Traumatic Brain Injury System
Assistant Professor, Wayne State University School of Medicine
Detroit, Michigan

Preface

The move toward evidence-based medicine has affected many areas of medicine, including rehabilitation for traumatic brain injury (TBI). In the past, rehabilitation interventions for TBI have been guided by common sense and a "best-practices" approach. Persons with TBI generally get better during rehabilitation, and it was natural to attribute much of their improvement to rehabilitation interventions. However, as health care costs have continued to rise at a rate greater than the general rate of inflation, there has been increasing pressure to reel in the costs of health care, particularly the costs associated with catastrophic injury. Health care providers now find that they need to justify expenditures. To be reimbursed, they must document improvement in participants' health status and quality of life which is the direct result of rehabilitation. Third party payers increasingly will only pay for therapies which have been shown to be effective and cost-efficient.

As practitioners, payers, and participants looked to the scientific literature to identify therapeutic interventions that worked for persons with TBI, evidence for many interventions was not always easy to identify. This problem led the National Institutes of Health (NIH) to hold a Consensus Conference on Rehabilitation of Persons With Traumatic Brain Injury in October of 1998. The panel of experts assembled by NIH concluded that, "Although studies are relatively limited, available evidence supports the use of certain cognitive and behavioral rehabilitation strategies for individuals with TBI. This research needs to be replicated in larger, more definitive clinical trials. Well-designed and controlled studies using innovative methods are needed to evaluate the benefits of different rehabilitation interventions."[1]

These events highlighted the need to bring into one volume a concise and authoritative account of what is currently known in the field of traumatic brain injury rehabilitation. To that end, the editors of this volume asked leading experts from various aspects of brain injury rehabilitation to write a "state-of-the-science" review of their particular research area. The authors were asked to (1) write a concise summary of what is currently known in that specific area of brain injury rehabilitation; (2) critique the methodological difficulties with current studies and identify gaps in knowledge; (3) delineate the most pressing research questions that remain unanswered; and (4) recommend directions for future research priorities.

Rehabilitation for Traumatic Brain Injury is the end product of this effort. The first section of the book begins with an historical perspective on brain injury rehabilitation. The general effectiveness of programs of rehabilitation is then reviewed. The second section of the book reviews the rehabilitation of specific cognitive impairments in awareness, memory, executive functioning, social communication, and emotion and motivation. The third section examines special topics in traumatic brain injury rehabilitation: rehabilitation of persons with alcohol and drug problems, interventions for caregivers, and vocational rehabilitation. The fourth section explores the rehabilitation of specific populations with TBI: children, older adults, and persons from diverse backgrounds. The final section considers topics in medical inventions for persons with TBI, including interventions for spastic hypertonia and disorders of consciousness. The role of neuroimaging in rehabilitation is also considered.

It is hoped that this book will serve as a resource and guide for both researchers and practitioners in the field of brain injury rehabilitation. It is anticipated that this volume will serve not only as a reference for what is known about brain injury rehabilitation, but also as a guide for researchers concerning the most important areas for future study.

The authors are grateful to the National Institute on Disability and Rehabilitation Research (NIDRR), U.S. Department of Education, grant H133B990014, Rehabilitation Research and Training Center on Rehabilitation Interventions for TBI, for support of this work.

W. M. H
A. M. S.
M. A. S.
K. A. H.

NOTE

1. National Institutes of Health. (1998, October 26–28). Rehabilitation of persons with traumatic brain injury. *NIH Consensus Statement 1998, 16*(1): 1–41.

Contents

Contributors

CORWIN BOAKE, PhD, ABPP-ABCN
Department of Physical Medicine and
  Rehabilitation
University of Texas Medical School
  at Houston
Neuropsychologist
The Institute for Rehabilitation and
  Research
Houston, Texas

KEITH D. CICERONE, PhD
Department of Neuropsychology
JFK–Johnson Rehabilitation Institute
Edison, New Jersey

JOHN D. CORRIGAN, PhD
Professor
Department of Physical Medicine and
  Rehabilitation
The Ohio State University
Columbus, Ohio

LEONARD DILLER, PhD
Department of Rehabilitation Medicine
New York University School of
  Medicine
Rusk Institute of Rehabilitation
  Medicine
New York, New York

GERARD E. FRANCISCO, MD
Department of Physical Medicine and
  Rehabilitation
University of Texas Health Science
  Center at Houston
Brain Injury and Stroke Program
The Institute for Rehabilitation and
  Research
Houston, Texas

JOSEPH T. GIACINO, PhD
Associate Director of
  Neuropsychology
JFK Medical Center/New Jersey
  Neuroscience Institute
Edison, New Jersey
Department of Neuroscience
School of Graduate Medical
  Education
Seton Hall University
South Orange, New Jersey

FELICIA C. GOLDSTEIN, PhD
Department of Neurology
Emory University School of Medicine
Atlanta, Georgia

WALTER M. HIGH, JR, PhD
Department of Physical Medicine and
  Rehabilitation
Baylor College of Medicine
Brain Injury Research Center
The Institute for Rehabilitation and
  Research
Houston, Texas

HARVEY S. LEVIN, PhD
Department of Physical Medicine and
  Rehabilitation
Departments of Psychiatry and
  Behavioral Science, Neurosurgery,
  and Pediatrics
Baylor College of Medicine
Houston, Texas

JAMES F. MALEC, PhD, ABPP-ABCN,
  ABRP
Department of Psychology
Mayo Clinic and Medical School
Rochester, Minnesota

GEORGE P. PRIGATANO, PhD
Department of Neuropsychology
Barrow Neurological Institute
St. Joseph's Hospital and Medical
  Center
Phoenix, Arizona

ANGELLE M. SANDER, PhD
Department of Physical Medicine and
  Rehabilitation
Baylor College of Medicine
Brain Injury Research Center
The Institute for Rehabilitation and
  Research
Houston, Texas

RANDALL S. SCHEIBEL, PhD
Department of Physical Medicine and
  Rehabilitation
Baylor College of Medicine
Houston, Texas

MARK SHERER, PhD, ABPP-ABCN
Department of Neuropsychology
Methodist Rehabilitation Center
Departments of Neurology and
  Psychiatry
University of Mississippi Medical
  Center
Jackson, Mississippi

McKAY MOORE SOHLBERG, PhD
Department of Communication
  Disorders and Sciences
University of Oregon
Eugene, Oregon

MARGARET A. STRUCHEN, PhD
Department of Physical Medicine and
    Rehabilitation
Baylor College of Medicine
Brain Injury Research Center
The Institute for Rehabilitation and
    Research
Houston, Texas

JAY M. UOMOTO, PhD
Department of Graduate Psychology
Seattle Pacific University
Seattle, Washington

MARK YLVISAKER, PhD
School of Education
College of Saint Rose
Albany, New York

I

OVERVIEW

History of Rehabilitation for Traumatic Brain Injury

CORWIN BOAKE AND LEONARD DILLER

While the occurrence of traumatic brain injury (TBI) in some ancient myths implies that TBI was recognized before recorded history (Courville, 1967), the resulting high fatality rate made rehabilitation generally impossible until the twentieth century. As shown by Gurdjian's (1973) compilation of statistics of brain wounds suffered in wars, most penetrating brain wounds before the 1900s were fatal. For example, during the U.S. Civil War, the fatality rate from penetrating brain wounds was about 70%. When advances in neurotrauma care during World War I led to improved survival, rehabilitation of TBI victims became a possibility.

CREATION OF DEDICATED BRAIN INJURY REHABILITATION PROGRAMS DURING WORLD WAR I

During and after World War I, programs for rehabilitation of wounded veterans were created in several countries (Camus, 1917/1918; Harris, 1919). Most of these programs were dedicated to orthopedic injuries or blindness, and their descriptions do not mention brain injury. The first rehabilitation programs dedicated to brain injury were probably created during World War I in Germany and Austria (Poser et al., 1996). The programs were based on earlier legislation creating a social security system, introduced during the nineteenth century by Bismark. The system supported rehabilitation by pension funds in order to reduce premature retirement by the working-age population (Schönle, 2000).

The activities at the brain injury rehabilitation centers located in Frankfurt and Cologne are better known because the writings of the centers' directors, Kurt Goldstein (1942) and Walther Poppelreuter (Poppelreuter, 1917/1990), have been translated into other languages. It is possible to credit these centers for major innovations followed by the field of brain injury rehabilitation since that time. First, it was recognized that neuropsychological impairments were a major cause of disability after brain injury. To address this problem, Goldstein and Poppelreuter arranged for patients to undergo detailed evaluations to identify impairments that could be targeted in rehabilitation and that might cause permanent disability. Domains assessed in these evaluations included memory, vigilance, and visual perception in addition to speech and language. Tests of visual-spatial perception and reasoning developed during the post–World War I period continue in use today. For example, a sorting test used at the Frankfurt center is probably the origin of the Wisconsin Card Sorting Test (Weigl, 1927/1941). Much of the work was based on the principles derived from Gestalt psychology, which stressed the importance of perception. It was thought that brain-injured persons suffered from a disturbance in attention so that perceptions could not be stable. Hence, perceptual tests such as tests of figure-ground, the Bender-Gestalt test, and the Rorschach test were commonly used to assess the presence of brain damage. The World War I rehabilitationists recognized that their tests had important limitations as predictors of later functioning. Goldstein and Poppelreuter stressed the need for clinical assessments combined with direct observation in vocational workshops.

A second contribution, described in greatest detail by Goldstein, was the teaching of strategies to use preserved skills in order to compensate for impairments. Goldstein's writings include specific recommendations about therapy for impairments of speech, reading, and writing (Goldstein, 1919, 1942). For example, a strategy used with patients who could not make certain speech sounds was to elicit a similar movement (e.g., puffing out tobacco smoke) and then to shape this movement into the desired speech sound.

A third innovation was the focus on employment as the primary outcome of brain injury rehabilitation. The vocational emphasis may have been due to the fact that the wounded veterans were all working-age males. Follow-up studies after the war gave special attention to employment outcomes (Credner, 1930; Goldstein & Reichmann, 1920). Figure 1.1 is a reproduction of a bar chart from the review of brain injury rehabilitation by Goldstein and Reichmann (1920) that may be the first graphic presentation of statistics on the outcome of TBI. As the figure shows, the rate of employment was lower in veterans who had been employed as laborers and miners before the war.

In the United States, the development of brain injury rehabilitation following World War I was much less extensive. A report from the single hospital dedicated

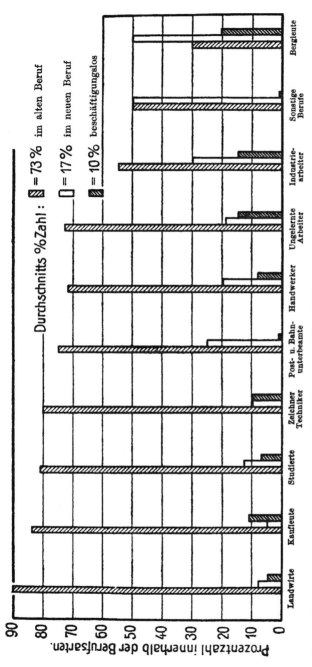

Figure 1.1. Return to work in German brain-injured veterans of World War I as a function of preinjury occupation. Each group of bars represents the percentages of veterans in a given preinjury occupation who resumed their former occupation (*im alten Beruf*), changed occupation (*im neuen Beruf*), or were unemployed (*beschäftigungslos*). Occupations are ranked in order of the percentage of veterans who resumed their former jobs. The best vocational outcome was in farmers (*Landwirte*) and shopkeepers (*Kaufleuter*), and the worst was in miners (*Bergleute*). (Reproduced by permission from Goldstein, K., & Reichmann, F. [1920]. Über praktische und theoretische Ergebnisse aus den Erfahrungen an Hirnschußverletzten. *Ergebnisse der inneren Medizin und Kinderheilkunde, 18,* 453. figure 4. Copyright Springer-Verlag, 1920.)

to veterans with head wounds, located in Cape May, New Jersey, mentioned that speech teachers had been recruited from public schools in order to provide "daily individual instruction and exercise in conversation, reading and writing adapted to the needs of the patient and the character of his language disturbance" (Frazier & Ingham, 1920, p. 31). Given the limited understanding of the consequences of brain injury, it is likely that many brain-injured veterans in the United States received little information, services, or support after discharge. The neurosurgeon Harvey Cushing (1919) complained that many veterans with brain wounds had been awarded pension that were inadequate for their degree of disability and then discharged home without further rehabilitation. A national rehabilitation institute for veterans with nervous system injuries was proposed but never funded (Franz, 1917). Rehabilitation services were set up under the direction of medicine and outpatient services within vocational systems operated under state control (Diller, 2000). This decision influenced service delivery systems until World War II. The joining of these two systems following World War II created the structure of postwar rehabilitation in civilian settings.

BRAIN INJURY REHABILITATION FOLLOWING WORLD WAR II

After World War II the development of brain injury rehabilitation was resumed with the establishment of centers in the United Kingdom (Babington, 1954; Hern, 1946; Zangwill, 1945), the Soviet Union (Luria, 1979), and other countries. Earlier research on compensatory training, functional prognosis, and medical complications was carried forward. The Russian neuropsychologist Alexander Luria, assigned to a special hospital for brain-wounded veterans, elaborated a rehabilitation model based on compensatory approaches (Luria, 1979). He developed strategies for motor planning, visual perception, and executive functions in addition to language disorders (Christensen & Caetano, 1996). Some of Luria's important writings on rehabilitation are available in English (Luria, 1948/1963, 1947/ 1970). In the United Kingdom, W.R. Russell (1971) identified the duration of posttraumatic amnesia as a predictor of return to work after TBI. Follow-up studies described the prevalence and risks of post-traumatic epilepsy (Russell & Whitty, 1952; Walker, 1949) and other TBI complications.

An important innovation in the post–World War II brain injury rehabilitation programs was the multidisciplinary team approach, in which psychologists and speech-language pathologists took responsibility for cognitive and communication disorders. Writings from this period (e.g., Butfield & Zangwill, 1946; Granich, 1947) acknowledge the influence of Goldstein, who escaped the Holocaust, went to the United States, and published in English an updated review of TBI rehabilitation (Goldstein, 1942). For the first time, the effectiveness of aphasia therapy was evaluated in group studies. In Edinburgh, Edna Butfield and Oliver Zangwill carried out a study of the outcome of aphasia therapy, using therapy techniques that they described as adaptations of Goldstein's work. Their design was an uncontrolled pre- to post-treatment comparison, with outcomes measured by global ratings of improvement. While concluding that the results showed that patients' speech "was judged to be much improved after re-education," they acknowledged that, by not including a no-treatment comparison group, "we possess no definite standards whereby to assess spontaneous recovery of cerebral function as opposed to the effects of re-education" (p. 75). However, they attempted to control for the effect of spontaneous recovery by analyzing separately the outcomes of patients who had started therapy at least 6 months after the onset of illness, "when relatively little further spontaneous improvement was to be expected" (p. 79).

A similar study was carried out in California by Joseph Wepman (1951) at one of a group of brain injury centers established in the United States to provide specialist medical and rehabilitation services to brain-wounded veterans (Spurling & Woodhall, 1958). An innovation of Wepman's study, which also used the uncontrolled pre- to post-treatment design, was to measure the outcome by means of standardized psychological tests. Figure 1.2 shows the distribution of IQ scores at the time of induction, before treatment, and after treatment. As the figure shows, IQs improved after treatment to a level below the preinjury baseline.

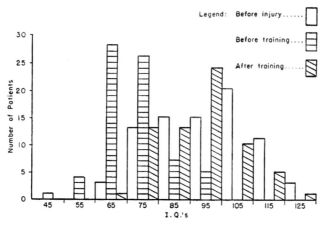

Figure 1.2. Pre- and post-treatment IQ test scores of American brain-injured veterans of World War II. This histogram chart shows the distribution of IQs of 68 veterans with posttraumatic aphasia who were treated in a specialized aphasia rehabilitation program at Dewitt General Hospital and Letterman General Hospital, both in California. Treatment was provided 6 hours per day, 5 days per week, for 18 months. IQs were measured before and after treatment with the Wechsler-Bellevue Intelligence Scale. Preinjury IQs were estimated from induction test scores. (Reproduced by permission from Wepman, J.M. [1951]. *Recovery from aphasia*. New York: Ronald Press.)

The positive experiences with wartime brain injury rehabilitation encouraged the postwar development of rehabilitation services. After the war, physiatry, occupational therapy, physical therapy, psychology, speech-language pathology, and vocational rehabilitation counseling underwent rapid professional development in order to meet the needs of veterans with disabilities (Gritzer & Arluke, 1985). These disciplines collaborated throughout the 1950s and 1960s to create rehabilitation centers that treated patients with stroke, amputation, and other disabling conditions.

BRAIN INJURY REHABILITATION AFTER THE 1970s

The 1970s witnessed rapid growth of interest in TBI. With the increase in high-speed highways came an increase in head injuries caused by vehicle crashes, along with growing recognition of TBI as a public health problem. Neurosurgeons became concerned about the follow-up of their patients, and a series of outcome studies focused on disability in addition to survival (Jennett & Teasdale, 1981). This increasing interest spurred the growth of rehabilitation programs devoted to TBI (Evans, 1981; Höök, 1972; Walker et al., 1969). A particular development was the creation and expansion of organized outpatient programs that had been neglected.

In TBI rehabilitation a major innovation was introduced by Yehuda Ben-Yishay (1996), who realized that domain-specific training was useful but not sufficient to meet the needs of a population with major problems associated with frontal lobe damage. Ben-Yishay, who had studied under Kurt Goldstein in the late 1950s and early 1960s, began to adapt some of the methods he had learned during the 1960s in working with stroke patients to TBI. A watershed experience took place in the Yom Kippur War of 1973 in Israel, when Ben-Yishay had an opportunity to set up the first holistic program for brain-injured soldiers (Ben-Yishay et al., 1978). Recognizing the absence of such a program in the United States, he developed a research program for civilians, funded by federal grants from 1978 to 1983. On termination, the program continued as a clinical service, although research remained part of its mission. In a series of workshops in the 1970s and 1980s, specific procedures were presented to ameliorate cognitive deficits as well as neurobehavioral and psychological problems resulting from TBI. The basic model of Ben-Yishay's program has been emulated in many countries (Christensen et al., 1992; Prigatano et al., 1986; Scherzer, 1986). A survey of outpatient programs (Mazmanian et al., 1993) reported that cognitive rehabilitation was offered in 93% of outpatient medical rehabilitation facilities. Additional important new models supported employment in vocational rehabilitation and neurobehavioral interventions (Wehman et al., 1995), as in the United Kingdom's Brain Injury Rehabilitation Trust (Wood et al., 1999).

CURRENT TRENDS IN BRAIN INJURY REHABILITATION

Beginning in the 1990s in the United States, a major shift in health care occurred through the ongoing industrialization of rehabilitation services. The major shift was toward efficiency, reduced costs, and shorter rehabilitation periods. A direct impact on research is seen in the fact that the development of perceptual retraining for visual neglect, which took place in a research program 30 years ago, involved retraining of stroke inpatients who typically stayed for 60 days or more, permitting extended periods of treatment (Weinberg et al., 1977). Today, lengths of stay are so much shorter that such a study could probably not be conducted. In addition, third-party payers now require more precise definitions of service recipients, refinement of measures for judging outcomes, and the generation of databases to enhance clinical decisions.

One effect of this shift has been the development of functional rating scales to capture the concerns in clinical management that are more specific to a TBI population than to a general medical rehabilitation population (Johnston & Miklos, 2002). The rating scales evolved from global outcome measures, such as the Glasgow Outcome Scale and the Disability Rating Scale, to more limited, narrow measures that reflected actual targets of treatment, such as the Community Integration Questionnaire. Assessments also began to discribe the diverse emotional and neurobehavioral sequelae of TBI together with role demands facing individuals returning to society. The proliferation of scale development led to a plethora of measures, to the point where investigators have had to co-calibrate scales. One emerging trend in assessment has been the recognition that the subjective experiences of patients must be considered along with objective measures of functional limitations (Johnson & Miklos, 2002).

Another effect has been that professional groups have moved to create paths toward levels of evidence for interventions that work. Professional services have grown in sophistication. Along with the development of the Committee for Accreditation of Rehabilitation Facilities (CARF), there has been an articulation of practice standards, respect for individual patients' rights, and ethical guidelines, which generate questions subject to empirical study (Kirschner et al., 2001). The major lesson from all of this may be that research on TBI rehabilitation is an empirical quest to answer questions stemming from substantive developments of a field of studies and market forces with multiple stakeholders.

Despite the wide acceptance of cognitive rehabilitation among TBI professionals, it has aroused a great deal of skepticism and controversy. As a result of such criticisms and the heavy investment of resources in unproven procedures, cognitive rehabilitation has been one of the most controversial and most thoroughly researched areas of TBI rehabilitation. Several reviews have been presented over the past 5 years. A National Institutes of Health (NIH) consensus conference that examined all publications from January 1988 through August 1999 (including 11 randomized trials) noted that evaluating treatment effectiveness was limited by the heterogeneity of subjects, interventions, and outcomes (Chestnut et al., 1999a, 1999b; NIH Consensus Development Panel on Rehabilitation of Persons with Traumatic Brain Injury, 1999). A task force of the American Congress of Rehabilitation Medicine (Cicerone et al., 2000) reported that a Medline search yielded 655 pertinent articles, 171 of which qualified for consideration as treatment outcome studies for stroke and TBI. A report by a task force on cognitive rehabilitation of the European Federation of Neurological Societies (Cappa et al., 2003), taking into account review panels and recommendations of the Cochrane Review, proposed guidelines to evaluate the level of scientific evidence for cognitive rehabilitation. Review panels apply variations of level-of-evidence scales and then base recommendations on the level of evidence. The highest level of recommendation then translates into a standard of practice. For example, Cicerone et al. (2000) provide three levels of recommendation: standards of practice, practice guidelines, and practice options. *Standards of practice* should include specific interventions for functional communication deficits, including pragmatic conversational skills and compensatory memory strategy training for persons with mild memory impairments. Comprehensive holistic programs provide a standard of practice to reduce cognitive and functional disability. A *practice guideline* includes attention training, including varied stimulus modalities, levels of complexity, and response demands; cognitive interventions for specific language impairments; and programs for problem-solving strategies and their application in everyday life situations. A *practice option* consists of memory notebooks or other aids to compensate for memory problems in persons with severe or moderate TBI, along with verbal self-monitoring and self-instruction to promote self-regulation for persons with executive function deficits.

BACK TO THE FUTURE

The three evidence-review panels agree that more rigorous studies evaluating cognitive rehabilitation in TBI are needed. Evidence appears increasingly promising as more class I studies are beginning to appear. The existing evidence base is useful to provide concrete reference points to guide decision making. However, gaps between research findings and clinical practices may be difficult to close. While researchers focus on theory-driven studies with narrow outcomes, rehabilitationists are confronted with patients who seldom show single impairments and have cognitive deficits in the absence of emotional problems. While research proceeds more certainly when focused on narrow problems, rehabilitation must come to grips with issues of people who have multiple or layered difficulties. Multiple-modality interventions are the rule rather than the exception. A major issue for the future of brain injury rehabilitation may be how to translate evidence-based standards into practice. Once a standard has been set, delivery of brain injury rehabilitation is actually highly idiosyncratic. Clinical practice often must be molded to fit individual needs.

ACKNOWLEDGMENTS
The authors are grateful to Dawn Carlson and Manfred F. Greiffenstein for help in translation.

REFERENCES

Babington, A. (1954). *No Memorial: The Story of a Triumph of Courage Over Misfortune and Mind Over Body*. London: W. Heinemann.
Ben-Yishay, Y. (1996). Reflections on the evolution of the therapeutic milieu concept. *Neuropsychological Rehabilitation, 6*, 327–343.
Ben-Yishay, Y., Ben-Nachum, Z., Cohen, A., Gross, Y., Hofien, A., Rattok, Y., & Diller, L. (1978). Digest of a two-year comprehensive clinical rehabilitation research program for out-patient head injured Israeli veterans (Oct. 1975–Oct. 1977). In *Working Approaches to Remediation of Cognitive Deficits in Brain Damaged Persons (Rehabilitation Monograph No. 59)* (pp. 1–61). New York: New York University Medical Center Institute of Rehabilitation Medicine.
Butfield, E. & Zangwill, O.L. (1946). Re-education in aphasia: A review of 70 cases. *Journal of Neurology, Neurosurgery, and Psychiatry, 9*, 217–222.
Camus, J. (1917/1918). *Physical and Occupational Re-education of the Maimed*. London: Bailliere, Tindall & Cox.
Cappa, S.F., Benke, T., Clarke, S., Ross, B. Stemmer, B., & van Heugen, C.M. (2003). EFNS guidelines on cognitve rehabilitation: report of an EFNS Task Force. *European Journal of Neurology, 10*, 11–23.
Chesnut, R.M., Carney, N., Maynard, H., Mann, N.C., Patterson, P., & Helfand, M. (1999b). Summary report: Evidence for the effectiveness of rehabilitation for persons with traumatic brain injury. *Journal of Head Trauma Rehabilitation, 14*, 176–188.
Chesnut, R.M., Carney, N., Maynard, H., Patterson, P., Mann, N.C., & Helfand, M. (1999a). *Rehabilitation for Traumatic Brain injury. Evidence Report No. 2* (Contract 290-97-0018 to Oregon Health Sciences University). Rockville, MD: Agency for Health Care Policy and Research. Online: http://www.ahcpr.gov/clinic/tp/tbitp.htm
Christensen, A.L., & Castano, C. (1996). Alexander Romanovitch Luria (1902–1977): Contributions to neuropsychological rehabilitation. *Neuropsychological Rehabilitation, 6*, 279–303.
Christensen, A.L., Pinner, E.M., Møller-Pederson, P., Teasdale, T.W., & Trexler, L.E. (1992). Psychosocial outcome following indivdualized neuropsychological rehabilitation of brain damage. *Acta Neurologica Scandinavica, 85*, 32–38.
Cicerone, K.D., Dahlberg, C., Kalmar, K., Langenbahn, D.M., Malec, J.F., Bergquist, T.F., Felicetti, T., Giacino, J.T., Harley, J.P., Harrington, D.E., Herzog, J., Kneipp, S., Laatsch, L., & Morse, P.A. (2000). Evidence-based cognitive rehabilitation: Recommendations for clinical practice. *Archives of Physical Medicine and Rehabilitation, 81*, 1596–1615.
Courville, C.B. (1967). *Injuries of the Skull and Brain: As Described in the Myths, Legends and Folk-Tales of the Various Peoples of the World*. New York: Vantage.

Credner, L. (1930). Klinische und soziale Auswirkungen von Hirnschädigungen. *Zeitschrift für die gesamte Neurologie und Psychiatrie, 126,* 721–757.

Cushing, H. (1919). Some neurological aspects of reconstruction. *Transactions of the Congress of American Physicians and Surgeons, 11,* 23–41.

Diller, L. (2000). Cognitive rehabilitation during the age of industrialization. In A.L. Christensen & B.P. Uzzell (Eds.), *International Handbook of Neuropsychological Rehabilitation* (pp. 315–326). New York: Kluwer Academic/Plenum.

Evans, C.D. (Ed.). (1981). *Rehabilitation After Severe Head Injury.* Edinburgh: Churchill Livingstone.

Franz, S.I. (1917). Re-education and rehabilitation of cripples maimed and otherwise disabled by war. *Journal of the American Medical Association, 69,* 63–64.

Frazier, C.H., & Ingham, S.D. (1920). A review of the effects of gunshot wounds of the head: Based on the observation of two hundred cases at U.S. General Hospital No. 11, Cape May, N.J. *Archives of Neurology and Psychiatry, 3,* 17–41.

Goldstein, K. (1919). *Die Behandlung, Fürsorge und Begutachtung der Hirnverletzten. Zugleich ein Beitrag zur Verwendung psychologischer Methoden in der Klinik.* Leipzig: F.C.W. Vogel.

Goldstein, K. (1942). *Aftereffects of Brain Injuries in War: Their Evaluation and Treatment; The Application of Psychologic Methods in the Clinic.* New York: Grune & Stratton.

Goldstein, K., & Reichmann, F. (1920). Über praktische und theoretische Ergebnisse aus den Erfahrungen an Hirnschußverletzten. *Ergebnisse der inneren Medizin und Kinderheilkunde, 18,* 405–530.

Granich, L. (1947). *Aphasia: A Guide to Retraining.* New York: Grune & Stratton.

Gritzer, G., & Arluke, A. (1985). *The Making of Rehabilitation: A Political Economy of Medical Specialization.* Berkeley: University of California Press.

Gurdjian, E.S. (1973). *Head Injuries From Antiquity to Be Present with Special Reference to Penetrating Head Wounds.* Springfield, IL: C.C. Thomas.

Harris, G. (1919). *The Redemption of the Disabled: A Study of Programmes of Rehabilitation for the Disabled of War and of Industry.* New York/London: D. Appleton.

Hern, K.M. (1946). *Physical Treatment of Injuries of the Brain and Allied Nervous Disorders.* London: Balliere, Tindall & Cox.

Höök, O. (Ed.). (1972). International symposium on rehabilitation in head injury, Göteborg, 1971 [special issue]. *Scandinavian Journal of Rehabilitation Medicine, 4*(1).

Jennett, B., & Teasdale, G. (1981). *Management of Head Injuries.* Philadelphia: F.A. Davis.

Johnston, M.V. & Miklos, C.S. (2002). Activity-related quality of life in rehabilitation and traumatic brain injury. *Archives of Physical Medicine and Rehabilitation, 83,* S26–S38.

Kirschner, K.L., Stocking, C., Wagner, L. B., Foye, S.J., & Siegler, M. (2001). Ethical issues identified by rehabilitation clinicians. *Archives of Physical Medicine and Rehabilitation, 82,* S2–S8.

Luria, A.R. (1948/1963). *Restoration of Function After Brain Injury* (B. Haigh, Trans.). New York: Macmillan.

Luria, A.R. (1947/1970). *Traumatic Aphasia: Its Syndromes, Psychology, and Treatment* (M. Critchley, Trans.). The Hague: Mouton.

Luria, A.R. (1979). *The Making of Mind: A Personal Account of Soviet Psychology* (M. Cole & S. Cole, Eds.). Cambridge, MA: Harvard University Press.

Mazmanian, P.E., Kreutzer, J.S., Devany, C.W., & Martin, K.O. (1993). A survey of accredited and other rehabilitation facilities: Education, training and cognitive rehabilitation in brain-injury programmes. *Brain Injury, 7,* 319–331.

NIH Consensus Conference on Rehabilitation of Persons with Traumatic Brain Injury. (1999). Rehabilitation of persons with traumatic brain injury. *Journal of the American Medical Association, 282*, 974–983. On-line: http://consensus.nih.gov/cons/109/ 109_intro.htm

Poppelreuter, W. (1917/1990). *Disturbances of Lower and Higher Visual Capacities Caused by Occipital Damage; with Special Reference to the Psychopathological, Pedagogical, Industrial, and Social Implications* (J. Zihl, Trans.). New York: Oxford University Press.

Poser, U., Kohler, J.A., & Schönle, P.W. (1996). A historical review of neuropsychological rehabilitation in Germany. *Neuropsychological Rehabilitation, 6*, 257–278.

Prigatano, G.P., Fordyce, D.J., Zeiner, H.K., Roueche, J.R., Pepping, M., & Wood, B.C. (1986). *Neuropsychological Rehabilitation After Brain Injury*. Baltimore: Johns Hopkins University Press.

Scherzer, B.P. (1986). Rehabilitation following severe head trauma: Results of a 3-year program. *Archives of Physical Medicine and Rehabilitation, 67*, 366–373.

Schönle, P.W. (2000). Neurological rehabilitation in Germany: The phase model. In A.L. Christensen & B.P. Uzzell (Eds.), *International Handbook of Neuropsychological Rehabilitation* (pp. 327–338). New York: Kluwer Academic/Plenum.

Spurling, R.G., & Woodhall, B. (1958). *Neurosurgery (Medical Department, United States Army: Surgery in World War II, vol. 1)*. Washington, DC: Office of the Surgeon General.

Russell, W.R. (1971). *The Traumatic Amnesias*. London: Oxford University Press.

Russell, W.R., & Whitty, C.W.M. (1952). Studies in traumatic epilepsy: Factors influencing incidence of epilepsy after brain wounds. *Journal of Neurology, Neurosurgery, and Psychiatry, 15*, 93–98.

Walker, A.E. (1949). *Posttraumatic Epilepsy*. Springfield, IL: C.C. Thomas.

Walker, A.E., Caveness, W.F., & Critchley, M. (Eds.). (1969). *The Late Effects of Head Injury*. Springfield, IL: C.C. Thomas.

Wehman, P.H., West, M.D., Kregel, J., Sherron, P., & Kreutzer, J.S. (1995). Return to work for persons with severe traumatic brain injury: A data-based approach to program development. *Journal of Head Trauma Rehabilitation, 10*(1), 27–39.

Weigl, E. (1927/1941). On the psychology of so-called processes of abstraction (M.J. Rioch, Trans.; C. Landis & K. Goldstein, Eds.). *Journal of Abnormal and Social Psychology, 36*, 3–33.

Weinberg, J., Diller, L., Gordon, W.A., Gerstman, L.J., Lieberman, A., Lakin, P., Hodges, G., & Ezrachi, O. (1977). Visual scanning training effect on reading-related tasks in acquired right brain damage. *Archives of Physical Medicine and Rehabilitation, 58*, 479–486.

Wepman, J.M. (1951). *Recovery from Aphasia*. New York: Ronald Press.

Wood, R.L., McCrea, J.D., Wood, L.M., & Merriman, R.N. (1999). Clinical and cost effectiveness of post-acute neurobehavioural rehabilitation. *Brain Injury, 13*, 69–88.

Zangwill, O.L. (1945). A review of psychological work at the Brain Injuries Unit, Edinburgh, 1941–1945. *British Medical Journal, 2*, 248–250.

2

Effectiveness of TBI Rehabilitation Programs

WALTER M. HIGH, JR.

As in many areas of medicine, rehabilitation following traumatic brain injury (TBI) has historically been guided as much by compassion and common sense as by hard scientific evidence. If persons were too injured or weak to feed themselves, the community fed them. If they were too injured or weak to stand by themselves, the community helped them up. If they could not bathe themselves, the community bathed them. If they could not go to the bathroom, the community helped them. If they could not work, the community supported them. Helping people after they have become injured or sick no doubt precedes recorded history. People who have become incapacitated from brain injuries have been helped since before hospitals existed, and some people in the community have been better than others at helping injured and sick people longer than medical schools have been granting medical degrees.

So much of what happens in brain injury rehabilitation seems so obviously necessary that it is little wonder that 20 years ago the question of whether rehabilitation was effective or necessary was not asked. Persons came into the rehabilitation hospital totally or almost totally dependent and left in a clearly more independent state. They were taken care of by specialists in rehabilitation. The specialists knew more about the rehabilitation process than anyone else. Persons with brain injury and their families were usually very grateful for the assistance they were given. The rehabilitation professional helped and did a better job than anyone else could have done.

Times have changed. This is the age of managed care. Catastrophic injuries seem inherently unpredictable, outliers on the accountants' balance sheets. Physicians and case managers spend significant portions of their days justifying to insurance companies why a person with brain injury needs rehabilitation services. Each day of service has become a point of negotiation. Is it absolutely necessary that the person remain in the hospital or can he or she be moved to a less expensive nursing facility, or home where the family will provide care? Is it really necessary for a person to participate in a comprehensive outpatient program before attempting to return to work?

The questions imposed on rehabilitation by outside payers have resulted in rehabilitation professionals asking themselves these same questions. How can they demonstrate that their programs are necessary and effective? In this chapter, we will review some of the methods that rehabilitation professionals have used to try to answer these questions.

EFFECTIVENESS OF INPATIENT PROGRAMS OF REHABILITATION

Studies of the effectiveness of inpatient rehabilitation following TBI have been previously reviewed (Chesnut et al. 1999; Cope, 1995; High et al., 1995; NIH Consensus Development Conference on the Rehabilitation of Persons with Traumatic Brain Injury, 1999; Rice-Oxley, 1999). Most of the reviews cautiously concluded that the available evidence supported the effectiveness of inpatient rehabilitation. However, each reviewer pointed out that no randomized clinical trials (RCTs) of the effectiveness of acute inpatient rehabilitation have been performed. The reasons for this are clear. An RCT testing the effectiveness of inpatient rehabilitation would be enormously complex. If the complexities could be worked out, the costs might be staggering if the cost of treatment has to be borne by the study itself. It would likely require a partnership of payers. If these hurdles could be overcome, it would still be necessary to determine what the alternative treatments would be. Would these treatments be rehabilitation services delivered in a nonintegrated fashion on a general rehabilitation unit not specializing in brain injury? Would going home (or to a nursing facility) with minimal rehabilitation services be an alternative treatment? In an informed consent procedure, who would consent to be possibly randomized to such alternative treatments? These obstacles have proved daunting to researchers interested in RCTs. The problems have led some to look to well-controlled observational studies (Type II studies) as alternatives to RCTs for showing the effectiveness of rehabilitation (Whyte, 2002). Other researchers (Powell et al., 2002) have questioned the ability of nonrandomized studies to determine the effectiveness of different services. Nonetheless, the majority of effectiveness studies have been nonrandomized observational studies.

Research attempting to show the effectiveness of programs of inpatient rehabilitation have generally been of four types: (1) studies demonstrating functional gains made by persons participating in inpatient rehabilitation programs, (2) studies demonstrating that earlier rehabilitation interventions are better than those delivered later, (3) studies showing that more intense rehabilitation services are better than less intense services, and (4) studies comparing persons who received services in an integrated rehabilitation program to those who received less integrated (and usually less intensive) services. The evidence will be considered in each of these categories in turn.

Studies Demonstrating Functional Gains

One of the earliest modern reports of the gains made by persons with TBI who participated in rehabilitation was by Rusk et al. (1969a). They reported on a series of 157 patients with disabilities caused by severe traumatic brain injury who were admitted to the Institute of Rehabilitation Medicine at New York University Medical Center. The patients were well characterized with respect to severity of injury. The report does not detail their functional level at admission other than to say that "admission to the rehabilitation program was dictated by the severity and complicated nature of the residua of trauma." However, it presents discharge data on functional outcome concerning ambulation, toileting, dressing and feeding, hand function, and speech and language that presumably implicitly represent gains from admission. It also presents data showing the maintenance of those gains 5–15 years later.

Tobis et al. (1982) examined the functional gains made by 75 patients with severe head injury treated consecutively on an inpatient service. Criteria for severity of injury were not specified. However, a large proportion of patients were noted to have major neurological deficits. For example, 59 of 75 patients were said to have aphasia. Criteria for aphasia were not defined. Perhaps more importantly, all patients were clearly impaired in at least one area of functional independence including feeding, personal hygiene, grooming, bowel and bladder continence, bed activities, dressing, transfers, wheelchair use, and walking on admission to the rehabilitation program. The number of patients who were independent in these areas increased two to four times by the time of discharge.

A large-scale study was conducted by Carey and colleagues (1988). These investigators studied 429 persons with head injury as part of a study of 6194 patients with various principal diagnoses. The head injuries were not characterized with respect to severity of injury. The sample made significant gains on the LORS American Data System (LADS) from admission to discharge. Patients made gains in communication, activities of daily living (ADLs), and mobility.

Sahgal and Heinemann (1989) evaluated the functional improvement of 189 patients with TBI who participated in a comprehensive rehabilitation program. The initial severity of injury was not characterized. Functional ratings by therapists in nine disciplines were made at admission and at discharge. Improvements were observed in mobility and self-care, as well as communicative, family, nursing, psychological, and recreational functions.

A similar study was reported by Heinemann et al. (1990). Sixty-six patients with TBI were included. Average Glasgow Coma Scale (GCS) scores (Teasdale and Jennett, 1974) were reported be 14.1. However, the GCS was assessed on admission to the rehabilitation program rather than on admission to acute care. An ADL score was computed based on the Barthel Index (Mahoney & Barthel, 1965), as modified by Granger et al. (1979). The ADL scores improved an average of 50% from admission to discharge.

The functional outcome of patients with low-level TBI following rehabilitation was studied by Whitlock (1992). The patients were well characterized with respect to severity of initial injury using the GCS score during the first 24 hours following injury. They were also characterized with respect to initial level of functioning using the Rancho Los Amigos level (Hagen et al., 1972) on admission to rehabilitation. A total of 23 patients were included. All were completely dependent in all functional areas, as measured by the Functional Independence Measure (FIM) (Hamilton et al. 1987), having a FIM of 19 or less on admission. All but three patients had made significant functional improvements on the FIM by the time of discharge.

Cowen et al. (1995) examined the effect of severity of injury on FIM scores during acute inpatient rehabilitation. Severity of injury and demographic variables were well characterized. Both motor and cognitive FIM scores improved from admission to discharge. The FIM scores improved for mild, moderate, and severe injuries.

Functional improvement has also been reported by the National Institute on Disability and Rehabilitation Research's TBI Model System program (Hall et al., 1996). A total of 133 cases were studied with FIM and Disability Rating Scale (DRS) scores (Rappaport et al., 1982) at admission to rehabilitation, at discharge from rehabilitation, at 1 year, and again at two years postinjury. Patients showed significant improvement from admission to discharge and from discharge to 1 year following injury. Little change was seen from year 1 to year 2 following injury. Severity of injury and level of initial disability were well characterized.

In general, the above studies show that functional independence improves for patients with TBI following acute inpatient rehabilitation. However, the evidence is not as persuasive as it could be. One problem with some of the studies is the lack of uniformity in using well-validated measures of functional independence. A second problem is the general lack of rigor in specifying the case mix of the sample. Criteria for characterizing severity of initial TBI are well established (Levin et al. 1990). If more uniform measures and more uniform characterizations of severity of injury and demographic characteristics were used across studies, it would be clearer whether the gains reported for one program of rehabilitation were comparable to the gains made in another program. Even within the National Institute on Disability and Rehabilitation Research's TBI Model System program, individual programs vary widely on these characteristics (High et al., 1996). A larger problem is the lack of a comparison group. Without a comparison group, it is impossible to separate the effects of rehabilitation from spontaneous recovery (High et al., 1995).

Early versus Later Intervention

Another strategy that investigators have used to try to demonstrate the effectiveness of programs of inpatient rehabilitation has been to compare persons with TBI who began rehabilitation early in the recovery process with persons who started rehabilitation relatively later. The rationale for such studies is that delivering rehabilitation services early is better than delivering them later. Rusk et al. (1969b) reviewed 102 cases in which rehabilitation was delayed an average of 20 months postinjury. They found large numbers of patients with frozen shoulders, major decubiti, and major joint deformities, conditions that were potentially treatable.

Cope and Hall (1982) used the study by Rusk et al. (1969b) and findings from animal studies as a rationale for studying patients admitted to rehabilitation before ($n = 16$) or after ($n = 20$) 35 days postinjury. Patients were matched for length of coma, age, level of disability, and neurosurgical procedures required. No difference was found between the two groups on the DRS at admission, at discharge, or at 2 year follow-up. However, the late admission group required twice as much acute rehabilitation as the early group. Careful reading indicates that the late group had significantly greater incontinence and cognitive impairment. While the small number of subjects resulted in no significant differences between the groups in terms of number of surgeries, the late group had 60% more neurosurgeries, three times as many other surgeries, four times as many seizures, seven times as many tracheotomies ($p < .05$), and 50% more bilateral cerebral contusions.

Rappaport et al. (1989) also compared early (<60 days postinjury) and late (>60 days postinjury) patients admitted to rehabilitation. Patients were not matched for severity of initial injury. They were matched on severity of disability on the DRS at admission to rehabilitation. There was no demonstration that delay in admission to rehabilitation was not completely confounded with severity of initial injury.

Spettell and colleagues (1991) found a small but significant relationship between duration of acute hospitalization and outcome as measure by the Glasgow Outcome Scale (GOS) (Jennett & Bond, 1975) at least 6 months postinjury. Length of acute hospitalization explained additional variance beyond that explained by duration of coma. In predicting rehabilitation length of stay, acute length of stay was a more powerful predictor than severity of injury. While the authors concluded that their results were consistent with those of Cope and Hall (1982) and Rappaport et al. (1989), they acknowledged that the question of what independent effect acute length of stay has on long-term outcome remains unanswered.

Mackay et al. (1992) compared 17 patients with TBI who received acute care in a single hospital with a formalized brain injury program to 21 patients who received acute care in one of 10 hospitals without a formalized program. In the formalized program, patients began receiving therapy while still in a coma, an average of 2 days postinjury. Patients who received their acute care in a nonformalized program started therapy an average of 23 days following injury. All patients were admitted to the same rehabilitation facility. Despite lower initial GCS scores, patients treated in the formalized program had shorter coma durations. In addition, they had shorter rehabilitation lengths of stay and less residual impairments on discharge from rehabilitation. The results are compelling. However, the 38 patients were accrued over a 6-year period, which brings into question the representativeness of the samples.

The primary flaw in all of these studies is the implicit assumption that patients delay in seeking rehabilitation for some reason other than the obvious: that they are more severely injured or sicker than patients who make it to rehabilitation early. High et al. (1996) have shown that low initial GCS scores, especially when coupled with low FIM scores on admission to rehabilitation, are associated with longer lengths of stay in both acute care and rehabilitation settings.

Effect of More Intense Intervention

The third way investigators have tried to demonstrate the effectiveness of programs of inpatient rehabilitation has been to show that more intense rehabilitation interventions result in improved outcomes or shorter lengths of stay. If rehabilitation is good, surely more is better.

Blackerby (1990) retrospectively examined the effect of increasing rehabilitation intensity from 5 to 8 hours per day. Different cohorts of patients were studied before and after the program change. No significant differences were found between the groups on age, education, time since injury, or level of functioning on admission to rehabilitation. Length of stay decreased 31% when the intensity of the program was increased. What is impossible to know from this study is whether the increase in intensity caused the decreased length of stay.

Spivack et al. (1992) assigned patients to high-intensity and low-intensity groups based on a median split of the total number of treatment hours. At discharge, the high-intensity group surpassed the low-intensity group on higher-level cognitive skills. However, it is unclear why one group received more treatment. The possibility exists that the less impaired patients were capable of participating in more hours of therapy than the more impaired patients.

Putnam and Adams (1992) published provocative results suggesting that more intense treatment might be associated with worse outcomes. They studied 100 randomly selected persons with TBI from a catastrophic claims office in Michigan and concluded that the patients receiving the most costly treatment with the greatest duration had the worst outcomes. Shorter duration of treatment was associated with modest improvements in outcome. These results were due to the confounding of treatment duration and severity of initial injury.

Studies Comparing Persons Receiving Integrated Rehabilitation Services to Other Groups

Finally, researchers have attempted to demonstrate the effectiveness of inpatient rehabilitation by comparing the outcomes of persons who were treated in an integrated comprehensive inpatient rehabilitation program to persons who received other treatments.

Aronow (1987) studied two groups of patients with TBI. One group consisted of patients from a comprehensive inpatient rehabilitation program in a rehabilitation hospital. The other group was drawn from across the country from a general neurosurgery unit of a large teaching hospital with no comprehensive rehabilitation. Patients were included if they had loss of consciousness for an hour or more or altered consciousness for 24 hours or more. Ages ranged from 5 to 80 years. The acute hospital stay had to be at least 15 days, and patients had to be noncomatose at the time of discharge from the acute care hospital. From the rehabilitation program, 68/104 subjects met criteria for inclusion, whereas only 61/1400 from the general neurosurgery unit met criteria due the preponderance of milder TBI. The procedure resulted in two groups grossly mismatched for severity of injury. Injury severity information and demographic information were not shown separately for each group, so it is difficult to tell how comparable the groups were. The effect of rehabilitation on outcome was computed, adjusting for age, sex, race, and several injury severity parameters. Outcome was measured using an unpublished outcome index of unknown reliability and validity. Rehabilitation accounted for less than 3% of the variance in the model. No interactions were included in the model.

Semlyen et al. (1998) published a study using a quasi-experimental design comparing patients with TBI who received a coordinated multidisciplinary rehabilitation service ($n = 33$) to patients who received services provided by district hospitals using a single-discipline approach ($n = 18$). The group that received coordinated services made significant gains on the FIM and maintained the treatment effect over time. The comparison group did not demonstrate equivalent gains. However, the group receiving comprehensive services had nearly double the coma duration and more than double the length of stay in acute care. This suggests that the group receiving comprehensive services was more severely injured. Only change scores on the FIM are reported for each group. It is impossible to know whether the lack of gains reported for the comparison group was due to ceiling effects.

Powell et al. (2002) have questioned the ability of nonrandomized studies to determine effectiveness. In their study, 365 consecutive patients were discharged to inpatient rehabilitation and/or home. One year following injury, discharge to rehabilitation was associated with poorer functioning on the GOS, Sickness Impact Profile (SIP), and Perceived Quality of Life (PQOL) scale. Longer lengths of rehabilitation were associated with worse outcomes. The authors concluded that typical severity indices were inadequate to control for injury severity and recovery for groups so inherently disparate in their initial severity of injury and severity of resultant disability.

High et al. (in preparation) studied 53 patients with moderate to severe TBI admitted to a comprehensive inpatient rehabilitation program and 59 moderately to severely injured patients who received acute care at the county hospital but did not receive comprehensive rehabilitation services. The two groups were comparable in age. Patients from the county hospital had less education, lower socioeconomic status, and a greater representation of minorities. Patients from the rehabilitation hospital were somewhat more severely injured but not significantly so. The latter patients also had somewhat longer lengths of stay in the acute care hospital and somewhat greater levels of disability at the time of discharge. The effect of rehabilitation on outcome, as measure by the DRS at 1 year, was evaluated by computing a regression model using a backward elimination procedure. Demographic and injury severity variables and a number of interactions were included in the model. Overall, 48% of the variance in the DRS at 1 year postinjury was explained. Rehabilitation accounted for about 4% of the variance in the DRS at 1 year. The effect of rehabilitation interacted significantly with severity of injury and socioeconomic status. Whether rehabilitation was provided had a greater effect on more severely injured persons and on persons with higher socioeconomic status. Rehabilitation and its interactions with severity of injury and socioeconomic status accounted for about 13% of the variance in the DRS at 1 year postinjury.

EFFECTIVENESS OF POSTACUTE PROGRAMS OF REHABILITATION

Studies of the effectiveness of postacute programs of rehabilitation have been primarily observational cohort-type studies (Class II). One RCT was conducted by Salazar et al. (2000). Although this took place in a hospital setting, it was essentially a test of the effectiveness of programs more typically delivered in an outpatient setting. The Class II studies will be considered first, and then the trial by Salazar et al. will be discussed.

The outcomes of persons who have participated in postacute brain injury rehabilitation (PAR) have been compared to outcomes following natural recovery after TBI in a review by Malec and Basford (1996). They compared the follow-up vocational outcomes for 856 patients from 15 PAR studies to those 796 patients who received no, unspecified, or inpatient only rehabilitation. Independent work, training, or homemaking was found for 56% of the patients who participated in PAR compared to 43% of those with no or unspecified PAR. Unemployment was 29% following PAR compared to 47% for those with no or unspecified PAR. Of the 15 PAR studies reviewed by Malec and Basford, several will be considered in more detail below.

Cope et al. (1991a, 1991b) examined the outcomes of 145 subjects participating in a PAR program. The subjects were of mixed etiology, severity, and chronicity. Persons with TBI comprised 79% of the sample. Initial severity of TBI was not characterized; however, the severity of the initial disability was well characterized. Twenty-nine percent of patients were admitted within 3 months of injury, and 24% were admitted more than 1 year following injury. Overall, competitive employment or academic involvement increased from 6% to 35%. Nonproductive activity decreased from 92% to 28%. When the results for the TBI group were considered separately, they were found to be essentially identical to those for the larger group. The group that began PAR more than 1 year following injury is of particular interest. Since they reached a plateau in neurological recovery, the confounding of improvement due to PAR with spontaneous recovery is much less of a factor. For this chronic group, competitive employment rose from 6% to 23%.

Very similar study was conducted by Johnston and Lewis (Johnston, 1991; Johnston & Lewis, 1991). This study examined 82 subjects, 71% of whom had sustained closed head injury. As in the Cope et al. study, severity of TBI was not specified. The median onset to admission interval was 451 days but ranged from 31 days to 13 years. Only 2% of the patients were working prior to admission. Participants were evaluated 1 year following discharge. At that time point, 10% were working full-time, 14% were working part-time, 21% were in unpaid vocational training, and 10% were students.

Ben-Yishay et al. (1987) studied 94 patients with primarily severe injuries (mean coma duration 34.4 days; range 1–20 days). The participants were primarily in a chronic stage of recovery (mean time postinjury 36.5 months; range, 4–207 months). All were judged to have reached a neurological plateau, and all were deemed unemployable or unable to pursue academic studies in any capacity by the investigators. The average educational level was 14 years. Following participation in comprehensive day treatment, 84% were able to engage in productive endeavors, 63% at a competitive level and 21% at a subsidized level.

Prigatano and colleagues (1984) compared 18 patients who participated in their comprehensive holistic rehabilitation program to 17 historical controls studied at the same hospital prior to the development of the program. The investigators re-

ported modest improvements in neuropsychological functioning but more substantial reductions in emotional distress. Following participation in the program,
50% of the treated group were productive 75% or more of the time compared to
only 36% of the untreated group. The treated group tended to be older, better
educated, and with more chronic injuries. The differences did not reach statistical
significance, but given the small sample size, the investigators cautiously adjusted
for age and education in their analysis anyway.

In a follow-up to the above study, Prigatano et al. (1994) examined 38 patients
with TBI who participated in their neuropsychologically oriented milieu rehabilitation program and 38 historical controls who did not receive this form of treatment. The patients were matched on initial GCS score, age at injury, and gender.
As in the above study, the historical comparison group was less well educated (12
vs. 13.6 years). In addition, the comparison group had less chronic injuries (33.5
compared to 43.3 months). Comparison of the two groups revealed that 87% of
the treated patients were productive (workers, students, or both) compared to only
55% of the comparison group. The investigators emphasized that a good working
(therapeutic) alliance with the staff was significantly related to productivity.

The outcome following PAR has also been studied by Malec et al. (1993). These
investigators examined functional outcomes before and after participation in a
comprehensive-integrated PAR. They studied 29 individuals, 20 with TBI and 9
with other neurological conditions. On average, participants had 13.3 years of
education. The TBI sample was composed mainly of persons with severe injuries
but included some with milder injuries (average loss of consciousness 13.4 days;
range 0–60 days). A majority of the participants ($n = 18$) were more than a year
post-onset when they began the program. The investigators reported that following PAR, living with supervision decreased from 41% to 7%. Unemployment
decreased from 76% to 31%, and transitional or competitive work placements
increased from 7% to 59%. The gains made during PAR were maintained at
1-year follow-up. Eighty-six percent of these patients were living without supervision, and 48% were competitively employed.

High et al. (2002) reported on 212 persons who participated in a comprehensive PAR. Subjects were assessed at the time of admission and at discharge. Long-
term follow-up (6–12 months postdischarge) was available for 167 subjects. There
was no difference between the groups with and without follow-up data on age,
ethnicity, education, coma duration, or best GCS score in the first 24 hours following injury. Participants were divided into three groups based on the interval
between their injury date and when they entered the PAR program: <6 months
since injury ($n = 115$), 6–12 months since injury ($n = 23$), and >12 months since
injury ($n = 29$). The groups did not differ on age, education, gender, or marital
status. The most chronic group was more severely injured. They took longer to
follow simple commands, had a longer duration of posttraumatic amnesia (PTA),
and had longer acute and rehabilitation lengths of stay. The 6–12-month group

generally fell between the other two groups with respect to severity of injury and length of stay. All three groups improved significantly on the DRS and Community Integration Questionnaire (CIQ) (Willer et al., 1993) from admission to discharge. The gains were maintained at long-term follow-up. Similar findings have been reported by Sander et al. (2001). These results have been replicated for the CIQ in a postacute residential treatment setting (Seale et al., 2002).

The study of Salazar et al. (2000) stands out as the single RCT of the effectiveness of a program of rehabilitation following TBI. This study is sometimes referred to as a study of the effectiveness of inpatient rehabilitation. The confusion is understandable since the main intervention was delivered in an inpatient setting. In this study, funded by the Department of Veterans Affairs, 120 subjects with moderate to severe TBI were randomly assigned to participate in either an inpatient milieu-oriented cognitive rehabilitation program or a home-based program involving education, structured exercise, and recreational activities. The report does not explicitly state how long postinjury participants entered the program. Presumably, they entered after acute care and any acute inpatient rehabilitation they might have received. To be randomly assigned to a home-based intervention, subjects must have been capable of living at home. The in-hospital rehabilitation program was modeled on Prigatano's milieu-oriented approach (Prigatano et al., 1994). This program was designed to be delivered as a PAR program. For these reasons, we consider it an RCT of the effectiveness of PAR.

In this study, moderate to severe TBI was defined as a GCS score of 13 or less *or* PTA of at least 24 hours *or* focal findings on computed tomography or magnetic resonance imaging. An important inclusion criterion was that participants had to be on "active military duty, not pending medical separation." The investigators reported that no differences in rate of employment were found. In fact, over 90% of the subjects in each group returned to work. Furthermore, there was little evidence of neuropsychological impairment in either group. It is unclear whether these subjects are comparable to those with severe injuries reported in other studies.

CONCLUSIONS AND METHODOLOGICAL CONSIDERATIONS

Overall, it may be concluded that persons with TBI make functional gains while participating in either inpatient rehabilitation or comprehensive PAR programs. The functional gains made in rehabilitation are largely retained over time. Determining the contribution of spontaneous recovery to the functional gains made by persons with TBI remains problematic. The issue is somewhat less problematic for studies of PAR, several of which have demonstrated that persons starting PAR more than a year postinjury show significant functional gains.

Attempts to demonstrate the effectiveness of inpatient rehabilitation programs by examining early versus late admission to such programs have largely been unsuccessful and inherently flawed due to faulty assumptions. The same may be said of studies attempting to use intensity of services within a rehabilitation program to measure effectiveness. Unless subjects are randomized, these approaches to evaluating the effectiveness of rehabilitation should probably be abandoned.

The usefulness of studies using cohorts of patients who receive different types or levels of services is still to be determined. Opinions within the research community are still somewhat mixed. Whether a person receives rehabilitation is not a random event. Access to rehabilitation depends on severity of injury and socioeconomic factors. Within a single system where decision rules are based on severity of injury, groups receiving or not receiving rehabilitation are likely to be essentially nonoverlapping (Powell et al., 2002). In this case, no amount of analysis of covariance will be able to solve the problem. Researchers who study systems of care where different decision rules are operating (High et al., in preparation) may find more overlap with respect to severity of injury. However, groups may then differ on other characteristics (e.g., socioeconomic status) that may be just as problematic.

Comparing cohorts of patients who have received different types or intensities of treatment can be informative only if we understand the ways in which the cohorts are similar or different. The case mix needs to be adequately defined, including information on age, gender, socioeconomic status, initial GCS score, duration of impaired consciousness, duration of PTA, radiological findings, level of disability/impairment at admission and discharge, acute length of stay, and rehabilitation length of stay. All of these factors may affect the outcome and must be controlled in some fashion if the effects of rehabilitation are to be dissentangled.

DIRECTIONS FOR FUTURE RESEARCH

Randomized clinical trials of treatment versus no treatment are probably not feasible for programs of acute inpatient rehabilitation. However, randomized trials to examine the timing and the intensity of interventions should be considered. For example, many patients now go to subacute facilities after acute care before going to inpatient rehabilitation. The effect of this practice on outcome is essentially unknown. Thus, RCTs that systematically vary the timing and intensity of interventions in subacute settings may be feasible. This would likely require the cooperation of hospitals, payers, and research funding agencies.

The study of Salazar et al. (2000) has demonstrated that RCTs of PAR, while difficult, are possible. However, the level of services must be appropriate to the level of disability for the studies to be meaningful.

Finally, other methods of demonstrating effectiveness need to be considered. Clinical practice improvement models (Horn, 2001) may hold particular promise for research in TBI rehabilitation.

ACKNOWLEDGMENTS
Preparation of this chapter was supported by Grant No. H133B990014 from the National Institute
on Disability and Rehabilitation Research, U.S. Department of Education.

REFERENCES

Aronow, H.U. (1987). Rehabilitation effectiveness with severe brain injury: Translating research into policy. *Journal of Head Trauma Rehabilitation, 2,* 24–36.

Ben-Yishay, R., Silver, S.L., Piasetsky, E., & Rattok, J. (1987). Relationship between employability and vocational outcome after intensive holistic cognitive rehabilitation. *Journal of Head Trauma Rehabilitation, 2,* 35–40.

Blackerby, W.F. (1990). Intensity of rehabilitation and length of stay. *Brain Injury, 4,* 167–173.

Cary, R.G., Seibert, J.H., & Posavac, E.J. (1988). *Archives of Physical Medicine and Rehabilitation, 69,* 337–343.

Chesnut, R.M., Carney, N., Maynard, H., Mann, N.C., Patterson, P., & Helfand M. (1999). Summary report: Evidence for the effectiveness of rehabilitation for persons with traumatic brain injury. *Journal of Head Trauma Rehabilitation, 14,* 176–188.

Cope, D.N. (1995). The effectiveness of traumatic brain injury rehabilitation: A review. *Brain Injury, 9,* 649–670.

Cope, D.N., Cole, J.R., Hall, K.M., & Barkan, H. (1991a). Brain injury: Analysis of outcome in a post-acute rehabilitation system. Part 1: General analysis. *Brain Injury, 5,* 111–125.

Cope, D.N., Cole, J.R., Hall, K.M., & Barkan, H. (1991b). Brain injury: Analysis of outcome in a post-acute rehabilitation system. Part 2: subanalyses. *Brain Injury, 5,* 127–139.

Cope, D.N., & Hall, K. (1982). Head injury rehabilitation: Benefit of early intervention. *Archives of Physical Medicine and Rehabilitation, 63,* 433–437.

Cowan, T.D., Meythaler, J.M., DeVivo, M.J., Ivie, C.S., Lebow, J., & Novack, T.A. (1995). Influence of early variables in traumatic brain injury on functional independence measure scores and rehabilitation length of stay and charges. *Archives of Physical Medicine and Rehabilitation, 76,* 797–803.

Granger, C.V., Albrecht, G.I., & Hamilton, B.B. (1979). Outcome of comprehensive medical rehabilitation. Measurement of PULSES and the Barthel Index. *Archives of Physical Medicine and Rehabilitation, 60,* 145–154.

Hagan, C., Malkmus, D., Durham, P., et al. (1972). *Levels of Cognitive Functioning. Original Scale.* Los Angeles: Communication Disorders Service, Rancho Los Amigos Hospital.

Hall, K.M., Mann, N, High, Jr., W.M., Wright, J., Kreutzer, J.S., & Wood, D. (1996). Functional measures after traumatic brain injury: ceiling effects of FIM, FIM+FAM, DRS, and CIQ. *Journal of Head Trauma Rehabilitation, 11,* 27–39.

Hamilton, B.B., Granger, C.V., Sherwin, F.S., et al. (1987). A uniform national data system for medical rehabilitation. In M.J. Fuhrer (Ed.), *Rehabilitation Outcomes: Analysis and Measurement* (pp. 137–147). Baltimore: Paul H. Brookes.

Heinemann, A.W., Sahgal, V., Cichowski, K., Ginsgurg, K., Tuel, S.M., & Betts, H.B. (1990). Functional outcome following traumatic brain injury. *Journal of Neurological Rehabilitation, 4,* 27–37.

High, W.M., Jr., Boake, C., & Lehmkuhl, L.D. (1995). Critical analysis of studies evaluating the effectiveness of rehabilitation after traumatic brain injury. *Journal of Head Trauma Rehabilitation, 10,* 14–26.

High, W.M., Jr., Hall, K.M., Rosenthal M., et al. (1996). Factors affecting hospital length of stay and charges following traumatic brain injury. *Journal of Head Trauma Rehabilitation, 11,* 85–96.

High, W.M., Jr., Hannay, H.J., Sander, A.M., et al. (in preparation). The effect of rehabilitation on long-term outcome following traumatic brain injury.

High, W.M., Jr., Roebuck, T., Sander, A., Struchen, M., Atchison, T., & Sherer, M. (2002). Acute versus chronic admission to post-acute rehabilitation: Impact on functional outcome. *Journal of the International Neuropsychological Society, 8,* 289.

Horn, S.D. (2001). Quality, clinical practice improvement, and the episode of care. *Managed Care Quarterly, 9,* 10–24.

Jennett, B., & Bond, M. (1975). Assessment of outcome after severe brain damage: A practical scale. *Lancet, 1,* 480–484.

Johnston, M.V. (1991). Outcomes of community re-entry programmes for brain injury survivors. Part 2: Further investigations. *Brain Injury, 5,* 155–168.

Johnston, M.V., & Lewis, F.D. (1991) Outcomes of community re-entry programmes for brain injury survivors. Part 1: Independent living and productive activities. *Brain Injury, 5,* 141–154.

Levin, H.S., Gary, H.E., Jr., Eisenberg, H.M., et al., and the Traumatic Coma Data Bank Research Group. (1990). Neurobehavioral outcome one year after severe head injury: Experience of the traumatic coma data bank. *Journal of Neurosurgery, 73,* 699–709.

Mackay, L.E., Bernstein, B.A., Chapman, P.E., Morgan, A.S., & Milazzo, L.S. (1992). Early intervention in severe head injury: Long-term benefits of a formalized program. *Archives of Physical Medicine and Rehabilitation, 73,* 635–641.

Mahoney, F.I., & Barthel, D.W. (1965). Functional evaluation: The Barthel Index. *Maryland State Medical Journal, 14,* 61–65.

Malec, J.F., & Basford, J.S. (1996). Postacute brain injury rehabilitation. *Archives of Physical Medicine and Rehabilitation, 77,* 198–207.

Malec, J.F., Smigielski, J.S., DePompolo, R.W., & Thompson, J.M. (1993). Outcome evaluation and prediction in a comprehensive-integrated post-acute outpatient brain injury rehabilitation programme. *Brain Injury, 7,* 15–29.

NIH Consensus Conference on Rehabilitation of Persons with Traumatic Brain Injury. (1999). Rehabilitation of persons with traumatic brain injury. *Journal of the American Medical Association, 282,* 974–983. Available on-line at http://consensus.nih.gov/109/109_intro.htm

Powell, J.M., Temkin, N.R., Machamer, J.E., & Dikmen, S. (2002). Nonrandomized studies of rehabilitation for traumatic brain injury: Can they determine effectiveness? *Archives of Physical Medicine and Rehabilitation, 83,* 1235–1244.

Prigatano, G.P., Fordyce, D.J., Zeiner, H.K., et al. (1984). Neuropsychological rehabilitation after closed head injury in young adults. *Journal of Neurology, Neurosurgery, and Psychiatry, 47,* 505–513.

Prigatano, G.P, Klonoff, P.S., O'Brien, K.P., et al. (1994). Productivity after neuropsychologically oriented milieu rehabilitation. *Journal of Head Trauma Rehabilitation, 9,* 91–102.

Putnam, S.H., & Adams, K.M. (1992). Regression-based prediction of long-term outcome following multidisciplinary rehabilitation for traumatic brain injury. *The Clinical Neuropsychologist, 6,* 383–405.

Rappaport, M., Hall, K.M., Hopkins, H.K., et al. (1982). Disability Rating Scale for severe head trauma: Coma to community. *Archives of Physical Medicine and Rehabilitation, 63*, 118–123.

Rappaport, M., Herrero-Backe, C., Rappaport, M.I., et al. (1989). Head injury outcome: Up to ten years later. *Archives of Physical Medicine and Rehabilitation, 70*, 885–892.

Rice-Oxley, M. (1999). Effectiveness of brain injury rehabilitation. *Clinical Rehabilitation, 13*, 7–24.

Rusk, H.A., Block, J.M., & Lowman, E.W. (1969a). Rehabilitation of the brain-injured patient: A report of 157 cases with long-term follow-up of 118. In A.E. Walher, W.F. Caveness, & M. Critchley (Eds.), *The late Effects of Head Injury* (pp. 327–332). Springfield, IL: C.C. Thomas.

Rusk, H.A., Lowman, E.W., & Block, J.M. (1969b). Rehabilitation of the patient with head injuries. *Clinical Neurosurgery, 12*, 312.

Sahgal, V., & Heinemann, A. (1989). Recovery of function during inpatient rehabilitation for moderate traumatic brain injury. *Scandinavian Journal of Rehabilitation Medicine, 21*, 71–79.

Salazar, A.M., Warden, D.L, Schwab, K., et al. (2000). Cognitive rehabilitation for traumatic brain injury: A randomized trial. *Journal of the American Medical Association, 283*, 3075–3081.

Sander, A.M., Roebuck, T.M., Struchen, M.A., Sherer, M., & High, W.M., Jr. (2001). Long-term maintenance of gains obtained in postacute rehabilitation by persons with traumatic brain injury. *Journal of Head Trauma Rehabilitation, 4*, 356–373.

Seale, G.S., Caroselli, J.S., High, W.M., Jr., et al. (2002). Use of the Community Integration Questionnaire (CIQ) to characterize changes in functioning for individuals with traumatic brain injury who participated in a post-acute rehabilitation programme. *Brain Injury, 16*, 955–967.

Semlyen, J.K., Summers, S.J., & Barnes, M.P. (1998). Traumatic brain injury: Efficacy of multidisciplinary rehabilitation. *Archives of Physical Medicine and Rehabilitation, 79*, 678–683.

Spettell, C.M., Ellis, D.W., Ross, S.E., et al. (1991). Time of rehabilitation admission and severity of trauma: Effect on brain injury outcome. *Archives of Physical Medicine and Rehabilitation, 72*, 320–325.

Spivack, G., Spettell, C.M, Ellis, D.W., & Ross, S.E. (1992). Effects of intensity of treatment and length of stay on rehabilitation outcomes. *Brain Injury, 6*, 419–434.

Teasdale, G., & Jennett, B. (1974). Assessment of coma and impaired consciousness: A practical scale. *Lancet, 2*, 81–84.

Tobis, J.S., Puri, K.B,, & Sheridan, J. (1982). Rehabilitation of the severely brain-injured patient. *Scandinavian Journal of Rehabilitation Medicine, 14*, 83–88.

Whitlock, J.A. (1992). Functional outcome of low-level traumatically brain-injured admitted to an acute rehabilitation programme. *Brain Injury, 6*, 447–459.

Whyte, J. (2002). Traumatic brain injury rehabilitation: Are there alternatives to randomized clinical trials? *Archives of Physical Medicine and Rehabilitation, 83*, 1320–1322.

Willer, B., Rosenthal, M., Kreutzer J.S., et al. (1993). Assessment of community integration following rehabilitation for traumatic brain injury. *Journal of Head Trauma Rehabilitation, 8*, 75–87.

II

REHABILITATION OF SPECIFIC COGNITIVE IMPAIRMENTS

3

Rehabilitation of Impaired Awareness

MARK SHERER

Self-awareness can be defined as "the capacity to perceive the 'self' in relatively 'objective' terms while maintaining a sense of subjectively" (Prigatano & Schacter, 1991, p. 13). Normal self-awareness represents a synthesis of an objective "third person point of view" of one's abilities and actions with the personal, emotional impact of these actions and self-perceptions. The appropriate balance of the objective and the subjective allows one to incorporate feedback from others and from one's own self-perceptions while maintaining a sense of personal identity and positive self-esteem. In patients with neurological disorders, impaired awareness may be manifested as failure to recognize a deficit caused by the disorder, failure to perceive problems in functioning as they are caused by the deficit, and/or failure to anticipate the future occurrence of problems due to the deficit (Crosson et al., 1989).

A variety of neurological disorders can impair the ability to have accurate self-awareness. Examples of such disorders include traumatic brain injury (TBI; Ben-Yishay et al., 1987; Prigatano et al., 1986; Sherer, Boake, et al., 1998), stroke (Appelros et al., 2002; Hartman-Maeir et al., 2003; Owens et al., 2002), brain tumor (Tucha et al., 2000), schizophrenia (Laroi et al., 2000; Lysaker et al., 2003), and various progressive neurological disorders including Alzheimer's disease (Koltai et al., 2001; Smith et al., 2000), Huntington's disease (Vitale et al., 2001), multiple sclerosis (Kolitz et al., 2003), and Parkinson's disease (Vitale et al., 2001).

Temporary impairment of self-awareness has been observed after intracarotid injections of barbiturates for Wada testing (Meador et al., 2000).

Various writers report that impairment of self-awareness is specifically associated with frontal lesions (Stuss et al., 2001) or with lesions in a variety of nonfrontal locations, depending on the specific impairments of which the patient is unaware (Heilman et al., 1998). Investigations of persons with TBI have produced inconclusive findings regarding lesion locations that may result in greater degrees of impairment of self-awareness (Sherer, Boake, et al., 1998). Investigations of persons with stroke generally find a greater incidence of one syndrome of unawareness, anosognosia for hemiparesis, in patients with right hemisphere stroke compared to left hemisphere stroke (Appleros et al., 2002). However, for other deficits, persons with right versus left hemisphere stroke do not differ in incidence of impaired awareness (Hartman-Maeir et al., 2002; Wagner & Cushman, 1994). Studies of normal subjects using functional magnetic resonance imaging have provided preliminary evidence that the mesial prefrontal areas and posterior cingulate gyri are involved in self-reflection (Johnson et al., 2002).

SIGNIFICANCE OF IMPAIRED AWARENESS FOR REHABILITATION

As shown in Table 3.1, impaired self-awareness is associated with poorer rehabilitation outcomes and with a number of problems that complicate rehabilitation efforts. Poorer self-awareness is associated with poorer compliance and participation in treatment, referral for more intense postacute rehabilitation services, longer length of stay in postacute rehabilitation services, greater caregiver distress, poorer functional status at discharge from inpatient rehabilitation, and poorer employment outcome after postacute rehabilitation. These associations with treatment process, caregiver distress, and treatment outcomes have increased rehabilitation clinicians' interest in developing treatment strategies to improve self-awareness.

MEASUREMENT OF SELF-AWARENESS

A variety of methodologies for measuring self-awareness have been developed for use in various investigations. Indices of self-awareness may be obtained by comparing patient self-ratings with independent evaluations of patient functioning. Patient self-ratings of abilities may be compared to ratings of patient abilities by family members or clinicians or to patient performance on neuropsychological tests. Degree of impairment of self-awareness may also be assessed by clinician rating (Fleming et al., 1996; Sherer, Boake, et al., 1998). Preliminary comparison of these

Table 3.1. Implications of Impaired Self-awareness for Rehabilitation

STUDIES	FINDINGS
Lam et al. (1998); Malec et al. (1991)	TBI patients in postacute rehabilitation with poorer self-awareness showed poorer compliance and participation in treatment.
Malec & Degiorgio (2002)	Acquired brain injury patients with poorer self-awareness were more likely to be referred for more intensive postacute rehabilitation services.
Malec et al. (2000)	Acquired brain injury patients with poorer self-awareness required longer lengths of stay in postacute rehabilitation before vocational placement.
Ergh et al. (2002)	When caregivers of persons with TBI had low social support, greater impairment of self-awareness was associated with greater caregiver distress.
Sherer, Hart, Nick, Whyte, et al. (2003)	Greater impaired self-awareness during acute inpatient rehabilitation following TBI is associated with poorer functional status at discharge.
Ezrachi et al. (1991); Sherer, Bergloff, Levin, et al. (1998); Trudel et al. (1998)	Poorer self-awareness for persons with TBI in postacute rehabilitation is associated with a poorer employment outcome.

TBI, traumatic brain injury

different methods of measuring self-awareness has shown that they result in differential, though overlapping, classifications of patients as having impaired self-awareness (Sherer, Bergloff, Levin, et al., 1998).

A number of measures have been developed for use in research on impaired self-awareness. The most commonly used of these are the Awareness Questionnaire (Sherer, Bergloff, Boake, et al., 1998), the Patient Competency Rating Scale (Prigatano et al., 1986), and the Self-Awareness of Deficits Interview (Fleming et al., 1996). There has been only limited investigation of the comparability of these scales. One study (Sherer, Hart, & Nick, 2003) found only modest correlations of scores from the Awareness Questionnaire and the Patient Competency Rating Scale, though both scales performed comparably in predicting functional status at discharge from inpatient rehabilitation.

CHARACTERISTICS OF IMPAIRED SELF-AWARENESS

Previous investigations have revealed a number of general characteristics of impaired self-awareness after TBI (see Sherer, Boake, et al., 1998, for a review). Persons with TBI are more likely to have impaired awareness of cognitive or behavioral deficits than of physical impairments. Impaired awareness is more likely to be exhibited in response to general questions about functioning than in response to specific questions about functioning in particular situations. Persons with unawareness in the postacute period are less likely to report symptoms of depression than those with more accurate awareness. Degree of self-awareness is modestly associated with severity of TBI, with patients with more severe injuries showing greater impairment of awareness.

ISSUES FOR ADDITIONAL INVESTIGATION

A number of basic issues regarding impaired self-awareness remain unresolved and require additional investigation. These issues include (1) the neuroanatomic basis of impaired self-awareness, (2) the measurement of impaired self-awareness, (3) the relationship of impairment in self-awareness to impairment of other executive functions, (4) the relationship of self–awareness to social perceptiveness and social skills, and (5) the degree of impairment of self-awareness needed to produce a decreased outcome.

As noted above, the neuroanatomic basis of impaired self-awareness after TBI remains unclear. Additional investigation using more sophisticated volumetric analysis of structural or functional brain images may clarify this issue. However, given the diffuse nature of brain injury after closed head trauma, it will be difficult to associate impairment of self-awareness in these patients with damage to any one brain area or system.

Also, as noted above, a wide range of methods and instruments have been used to measure impaired self-awareness in various studies. While some methods and instruments may be better suited to some investigations than others, the lack of a commonly agreed-upon method or instrument complicates the comparison between studies. Previous studies have shown that these various methods and instruments are only modestly associated with one another.

It is intuitively compelling that self-awareness should share a neurologic substrate with and be associated with other executive functions such as planning, initiation, and self-regulation. However, there has been only limited investigation of these relationships. Bogod and colleagues (2003) found only a modest association between degree of impairment of self-awareness and degree of executive dysfunction in a sample of 45 persons with TBI.

In addition to having impaired self-awareness, persons with TBI may exhibit impairment in social awareness and social interaction skills (Bohac et al., 1997). Some have hypothesized that these deficits are related (Mateer, 1999). In normal social interaction, subtle social cues may be an important source of information about the appropriateness of one's behavior and statements. Impaired ability to perceive or decode these cues may deprive the listener of information needed to form accurate self-perceptions. Preliminary investigation has found some association of impaired regulation of social behavior with impaired self-awareness (Ownsworth et al., 2002). Additional investigation in this area may have implications for alternative approaches to treatment of impaired self-awareness.

While investigators have reported that some degree of impaired self-awareness is common after TBI (Sherer, Bergloff, Levin, et al., 1998) and after stroke (Hartman-Maeir et al., 2002), there has been only limited investigation of the degrees of impaired awareness associated with poorer outcomes. Sherer, Hart, and Nick (2003) found that low levels of unawareness were not associated with decreased functional status at discharge from inpatient rehabilitation, while higher levels of unawareness were predictive of decreased functioning. Additional investigation is needed to identify more accurately which patients with impaired self-awareness are at risk for poor outcomes.

RECOMMENDED INTERVENTIONS FOR IMPAIRED AWARENESS

A number of writers have recommended a variety of possible interventions to improve self-awareness after acquired brain injury. These recommended interventions are summarized in Table 3.2. Educational approaches to improve self-awareness involve didactic training in the aftereffects of brain injury. While this training could address the general effects of brain injury, most writers recommend individualized education regarding the specific injury and deficits experienced by the client (Mateer, 1999). Such education may involve review of the client's medical record with the client to assist the client in linking the injury to the brain to changes in personal abilities (Sohlberg, 2000).

Various forms of feedback are the most frequently recommended interventions for improving self-awareness. Examples of modes of feedback include direct therapist to client feedback, videotape feedback, and peer feedback (Sherer, Oden, et al., 1998). Other forms of feedback may be indirect. Mateer (1999) recommended having the client monitor his or her own performance on tasks so that he or she can observe improvement over time. The occurrence of improvement confronts the client with the fact that the initial performance was impaired. The underlying concept of all feedback interventions is to direct the client's attention to aspects of his or her performance that he or she was not adequately perceiving or interpreting. Such

Table 3.2. Recommended Interventions for Impaired Self-Awareness

RECOMMENDATION	SOURCES
Education	Mateer (1999); Sohlberg (2000)
Feedback	Crosson et al. (1989); Mateer (1999); Sherer et al. (1998d)
Psychotherapy	Cicerone (1989); Langer & Padrone (1992); Prigatano (1999)
Therapeutic milieu	Ben-Yishay et al. (1985); Sherer, Oden et al. (1998)
Therapeutic alliance	Beiman-Copeland & Dywan (2000); Mateer (1999); Sherer, Oden et al. (1998)

direction is needed, as patients with impaired self-awareness show decreased ability to recognize mistakes or attempt to correct them (Hart et al., 1998).

Goals of psychotherapy after acquired brain injury include improving the client's understanding of the effects of the injury, reestablishing a sense of normality, and restoring a sense of purpose and meaning in life (Prigatano, 1999). Effective psychotherapy should increase the client's ability to behave in his or her best interest. This ability depends, at least in part, on having an accurate perception of one's abilities. Psychotherapy after acquired brain injury must strike a balance between confrontation and support so that the client can assimilate new information about the self without losing hope (Cicerone, 1989).

Ben-Yishay and colleagues (Ben-Yishay, 1996; Ben-Yishay et al., 1985, 1987) have developed an approach to postacute rehabilitation after acquired brain injury that involves immersion in a therapeutic milieu. In this model, the treatment program becomes a "community" that supports therapeutic activities for the community members. Therapists facilitate the client's progress through stages of recovery from brain injury. These stages include awareness and reestablishment of identity. Therapeutic activities may include individual and group psychotherapy as well as cognitive rehabilitation tasks. In the therapeutic milieu, use of compensatory strategies for cognitive impairment, frequent feedback on one's performance, and a shared sense of commitment to improving self-awareness are normal aspects of community life (Sherer, Oden, et al., 1998).

The term *therapeutic alliance* originated in the psychotherapy literature. In this context, a therapeutic alliance refers to an agreement of the client and the therapist on the tasks and goals of therapy, as well as the interpersonal bond between client and therapist (Bordin, 1979). The therapeutic alliance is thought to be the common underlying mechanism that facilitates progress in psychotherapy (Horvath & Greenberg, 1994). Many have suggested that the therapeutic alliance may serve a similar facilitative function in rehabilitation after acquired brain injury (Beiman-Copeland & Dywan, 2000; Mateer, 1999; Sherer, Oden, et al., 1998). Prigatano and colleagues (1994) found that stronger therapeutic alliances between the client and the treatment team, and between the client's family and the treatment team, were associated with improved outcomes after postacute rehabilitation. An enhanced therapeutic alliance may increase the effectiveness of any therapy activity, including activities designed to improve self-awareness. To date, there has been no investigation of the methods used to enhance the therapeutic alliance in rehabilitation settings.

INVESTIGATIONS OF INTERVENTIONS
FOR IMPAIRED AWARENESS

This review revealed 10 investigations of impaired awareness after acquired brain injury. These investigations are summarized in Table 3.3. Six of the studies were case reports involving a total of 17 participants. The remaining four studies reported group data involving a total of 81 participants. Most group studies reported pre-post comparisons, with only one study employing a control group. In this study, assignment to treatment versus control conditions was sequential rather than random. Patients with TBI were often placed in groups with patients with stroke or other neurologic disorders, with no report of findings by diagnostic group. In some cases, no specific diagnoses were given. Studies differed greatly in time from injury to intervention. Feedback of various types was used in six studies, psychotherapy was the intervention in two studies, and an educational game activity was the intervention in the remaining two studies. Findings of 8 of the 10 investigations were interpreted as indicating improvement in self-awareness following intervention. These results are encouraging though hardly definitive.

LIMITATIONS OF EXISTING STUDIES OF INTERVENTIONS
FOR IMPAIRED AWARENESS

While the 10 studies reviewed have many strengths and provide preliminary evidence that interventions to improve self-awareness could be successful, they reveal several limitations in the research in this area. These limitations may be categorized into three areas: (1) study sample, (2) study design, and (3) specification of interventions.

As noted above, existing studies report on a very small number of participants. In several studies, these participants were drawn from various clinical populations such as persons with TBI, occlusive stroke, hemorrhagic stroke, anoxia, schizophrenia, and so on. It is unclear at this point whether impaired self-awareness in these different disorders is similar in manifestation or in neurologic substrate. As a result, it is questionable whether findings from these distinct clinical populations should be combined. Study samples are drawn from several different clinical settings

Table 3.3. Investigations of Interventions for Impaired Awareness

STUDY	SUBJECTS	SETTING	INTERVENTION	FINDINGS	GENERALIZATION
Chittum et al. (1996)	3 adults with acquired brain injuries	Residential postacute rehabilitation facility	Educational game with rewards for correct responses	All 3 participants showed improvement in game performance	Knowledge gained generalized to related areas, but novel questions asked at follow-up
Katz et al. (2002)	1 patient with TBI, 1 patient with stroke, and 1 patient with schizophrenia	Inpatient hospitalization, outpatient rehabilitation	Direct therapist to client feedback, experiential feedback	Improved functional status in spite of minimal or no improvement in awareness	Not reported
Ownsworth et al. (2000)	16 adults with TBI, 3 with stroke, 2 with other injuries	Outpatient group program	Group educational and psychotherapy program	The majority of participants showed improvements in self-awareness and social behavior on pre-post assessment	Treatment gains were generally at 6-month follow-up
Ranseen et al. (1990)	32 adults with TBI	Inpatient rehabilitation program	Group psychotherapy	Trend ($p = .55$) for improvement in accuracy of self-awareness	Not reported
Rebman & Hannon (1995)	2 adults with TBI, 1 adult with subarachnoid hemorrhage	Outpatient individual treatment	Feedback on accuracy of estimations of memory performance	All 3 participants improved in accuracy of estimates	Not reported

Study	Participants	Setting	Intervention	Outcome	Generalization
Schlund (1999)	1 adult with TBI	Home-based rehabilitation program	Feedback on accuracy of prediction and recall of memory performance	Accuracy improved	Not reported
Tham et al. (2001)	4 adults with right stroke	Inpatient rehabilitation program	Therapist, experiential, and videotape feedback on left neglect	3 patients showed improved awareness of task performance	Improvements in self-awareness were associated with improved performance in activities of daily living
Tham & Tegner (1997)	14 adults with right stroke, 7 in treatment, 7 controls	Inpatient rehabilitation program	Videotape feedback was compared to standard verbal feedback	While no statistical test is reported, the authors state that those receiving videotape feedback had better awareness of left neglect	No generalization to other tasks
Youngjohn & Altman (1989)	19 adults with acquired brain injury	Day hospital rehabilitation program	Feedback on accuracy of estimates of performance on memory and math tasks	Group improvement on math task; trend toward improvement on memory task	No test of generalization, but investigators stated that subjective analysis indicated some generalization
Zhou et al. (1996)	3 adults with acquired brain injury	Residential postacute rehabilitation facility	Educational game with rewards for correct responses	All 3 participants showed improvement in game performance	Provide anecdotal accounts that suggest some generalization

including inpatient rehabilitation, outpatient postacute rehabilitation, and residential postacute rehabilitation. Patients seen in these different clinical settings may differ substantially in time from injury to assessment, severity of injury, availability of social support, and other factors that may influence the degree of impairment of self-awareness and the impact of impaired self-awareness on participation in rehabilitation and outcome. In addition, referral patterns at various clinical sites are likely to be idiosyncratic. In several of the studies reviewed, subjects were inadequately described, with such information as diagnosis, time from injury to assessment, injury severity, and so on being omitted. These factors greatly complicate comparison of findings among studies. The reader is largely unable to infer the extent to which findings from these studies may generalize to his or her clinical setting.

The majority of the studies reviewed were single or multiple case reports. Of the four investigations reporting group data, three were observational studies with no comparison group. The one study with a comparison group did not employ random assignment. These case reports and observational studies provide suggestive evidence that various interventions may be effective for improving self-awareness. However, alternative explanations for the findings, such as spontaneous recovery or some nonspecific effect due to therapist contact with the patients, cannot be ruled out. The one group study with a control group did not employ random assignment to the treatment condition; thus, these results, though encouraging, must be interpreted cautiously.

Finally, in several cases the interventions used in previous investigations were poorly described, making it difficult for later investigators to replicate the interventions. This is a general problem for studies using behavioral interventions, particularly when these interventions occur in the context of a larger treatment program. When interventions are incompletely described, contain multiple elements that are provided concurrently, and/or occur in the context of an overall treatment program, it may difficult or impossible to determine the true effectiveness of the intervention and which elements of the intervention are the "active ingredients."

RECOMMENDATIONS FOR FUTURE INVESTIGATIONS OF INTERVENTIONS FOR IMPAIRED AWARENESS

Based on this review of previous studies of interventions for impaired awareness, several recommendations are made for future research. These recommendations are intended to provide guidance to build on previous findings, correct methodologic weaknesses of previous investigations, and identify promising avenues for further investigation.

Previous investigations provide some preliminary evidence that interventions intended to improve self-awareness after acquired brain injury can be effective.

This evidence is seen for a variety of interventions, including interventions that are primarily educational, interventions that provide increased feedback to the client, and psychotherapeutic interventions. These findings provide encouragement to develop larger, more definitive studies to investigate the effectiveness of interventions for impaired self-awareness.

Future research on awareness interventions can be improved with regard to study samples. Study samples should be clearly defined so that consumers of research can determine the likely generalization of findings to various clinical populations. Descriptions of study samples should include number, diagnoses, injury severity, time from injury, appropriate demographic descriptors, and method of accrual (consecutive, convenience, etc.) at a minimum. Study samples should be restricted to one diagnostic group (e.g, TBI, stroke, Alzheimer's disease) or the study design should permit comparison of the different diagnostic groups. Study sample size should be adequate to ensure appropriate power for the primary outcome of the investigation. Qualified participants who decline to participate, as well as participants who drop out or are lost to follow-up, should be described.

Measures used in the investigation should have proven reliability and validity for the purposes of the study. Given the different findings obtained when different measures of self-awareness are used, it may be desirable to have multiple measures of self-awareness for comparison purposes. Selection of measures of impaired awareness should be guided by previous investigations.

Study designs should provide an appropriate control group or groups for comparison to the treatment condition(s). Assignment to treatment condition should be random, with stratification on appropriate factors that could be sources of bias. While blinding may be difficult or impossible for investigations of behavioral interventions, care should be taken to minimize possible bias in findings caused by participant or therapist awareness of key aspects of the study. Outcomes should be collected independently of the intervention by research assistants who are blind to the treatment condition assignments of participants. The primary outcome should be overall functional status or participation in the rehabilitation program, while degree of impaired self-awareness should be a secondary outcome.

Given the limited number and varied quality of investigations of interventions for impaired awareness to this point, there are many possible directions for future research. Based on the review of previous investigations, practical considerations, and clinical experience, three promising avenues for investigation are recommended. First, as noted above, various interventions to give persons with acquired brain injury additional feedback about their behavioral capabilities and their success on functional tasks have been recommended. Most previous investigations of treatments to improve self-awareness have used feedback interventions. The one investigation that employed a comparison group and had positive findings used a feedback intervention. These factors indicate that one direction for future research would be trials of various feedback interventions with appropriate control conditions for comparison. Elements of such trials should included careful description of the feedback intervention, random assignment to treatment versus control conditions, and appropriate numbers of participants to ensure adequate power. The issue of power will be of particular importance for trials that are conducted in the context of an overall treatment program. Since other elements of the treatment program may be expected to have some positive effect on self-awareness, the intervention will have to meet the demanding test of causing an even greater improvement.

Prigatano and colleagues (1994) found that the degree of the therapeutic alliance between the client and the treatment team predicted the outcome after postacute brain injury rehabilitation. A number of writers have argued that the quality of the relationship between the patient and the treatment team is an important factor in the effectiveness of rehabilitation interventions. However, to date, there has been no investigation of the relationship between therapeutic alliance and client self-awareness. A second avenue for future investigation would be the relationship between therapeutic alliance and self-awareness and the impact of an improved therapeutic alliance on the degree of self-awareness. Preliminary investigations should explore factors that contribute to an improved therapeutic alliance. Improved knowledge of these factors would form the basis of trials of interventions to improve the therapeutic alliance, with possible improvement in self-awareness and rehabilitation outcome.

Ownsworth and colleagues (2002) provided preliminary evidence of a relationship between regulation of social behavior and self-awareness. Clinical experience suggests that there may be a relationship between social perceptiveness and self-awareness. A third avenue of research on self-awareness would be exploration of the interrelationships of regulation of social behavior, social perceptiveness, and self-awareness. Improved understanding of these phenomena could lead to a variety of new interventions for persons with acquired brain injuries. Training to improve attention to social cues could be effective in improving self-awareness. Improving self-awareness may be an effective means to improve regulation of social behavior. Since there has been little investigation of these issues to this point, initial investigations should focus on developing reliable methodologies for measuring these phenomena. The next step would be exploration of the interrelationships and various factors that influence social regulation, social perceptiveness, and self-awareness.

The three avenues for future research mentioned here represent only a few of the possibilities. Investigations of psychotherapy or therapeutic milieu interventions are particularly intriguing, but may be difficult and expensive to conduct given the complexity of these modes of treatment. As a cautionary note, while several studies have found an association of impaired self-awareness with rehabilitation outcome, all these studies used correlational or predictive models. Thus, there is no evidence to this point that the relationship between self-awareness and outcome is causative. It is possible that the apparent relationship is due to confounding of self-awareness with executive functions, social abilities, or some other factor. Future investigations must clarify this issue to determine whether improvement of self-awareness should be a primary goal of brain injury rehabilitation. Katz and colleagues (2002) have argued that improvement in self-awareness is not necessary to improving rehabilitation outcomes.

ACKNOWLEDGMENTS

Preparation of this chapter was partially supported by National Institute on Disability and Rehabilitation Research Grant H133A020514, the TBI Model System of Mississippi.

REFERENCES

Appelros, P., Karlson, G.M., Seiger, A., & Nydevik, I. (2002). Neglect and anosognosia after first-ever stroke: Incidence and relationship to disability. *Journal of Rehabilitation, 34*, 215–220.

Beiman-Copeland, S., & Dywan, J. (2000). Achieving rehabilitative gains in anosognosia after TBI. *Brain and Cognition, 44*, 1–18.

Ben-Yishay, Y. (1996). Reflections on the evolution of the therapeutic milieu concept. *Neuropsychological Rehabilitation, 6*, 327–343.

Ben-Yishay, Y., Rattok, J., Lakin, P., Piasetsky, E.B., Ross, B., Silver, S., et al. (1985). Neuropsychologic rehabilitation: Quest for a holistic approach. *Seminars in Neurology, 5*, 252–259.

Ben-Yishay, Y., Silver, S.M., Piasetsky, E., & Rattok, J. (1987). Relationship between employability and vocational outcome after intensive holistic cognitive rehabilitation. *Journal of Head Trauma Rehabilitation, 2*(1), 35–48.

Bogod, N.M., Mateer, C.A., & Macdonald, S.W.S. (2003). Self-awareness after traumatic brain injury: A comparison of measures and their relationship to executive functions. *Journal of the International Neuropsychological Society, 9*, 450–458.

Bohac, D.L., Malec, J.F., & Moessner, A.M. (1997). Factor analysis of the Mayo-Portland Adaptability Inventory: Structure and validity. *Brain Injury, 11*, 469–482.

Bordin, E.S. (1979). The generalizability of the psychoanalytic concept of the working alliance. *Psychotherapy: Theory, Reseach and Practice, 16*, 252–260.

Chittum, W.R., Johnson, K., Chittum, J.M., Guercio, J.M., & McMorrow, M.J. (1996). Road to awareness: An individualized training package for increasing knowledge and comprehension of personal deficits in persons with acquired brain injury. *Brain Injury, 10*, 763–776.

Cicerone, K.D. (1989). Psychotherapy interventions with traumatically brain-injured patients. *Rehabilitation Psychology, 34*, 105–114.

Crosson, B., Barco, P.P., Velozo, C.A., Bolesta, M.M., Cooper, P.V., Werts, D., et al. (1989). Awareness and compensation in postacute head injury rehabilitation. *Journal of Head Trauma Rehabilitation, 4*(3), 46–54.

Ergh, T.C., Rapport, L.J., Coleman, R.D., & Hanks, R.A. (2002). Predictors of caregiver and family functioning following traumatic brain injury: Social support moderates caregiver distress. *Journal of Head Trauma Rehabilitation, 17*, 155–174.

Ezrachi, O., Ben-Yishay, Y., Kay, T., Diller, L., & Rattok, J. (1991). Predicting employment in traumatic brain injury following neuropsychological rehabilitation. *Journal
of Head Trauma Rehabilitation, 6*(3), 71–84.

Fleming, J.M., Strong, J., & Ashton, R. (1996). Self-awareness of deficits in adults with
traumatic brain injury: How best to measure? *Brain Injury, 10,* 1–15.

Hart, T., Giovannetti, T., Montgomery, M.W., & Schwartz, M.F. (1998). Awareness of
errors in naturalistic action after traumatic brain injury. *Journal of Head Trauma Rehabilitation, 13,* 16–28.

Hartman-Maeir, A., Soroker, N., Oman, S.D., & Katz, N. (2003). Awareness of disabilities in stroke rehabilitation—a clinical trial. *Disability and Rehabilitation, 25,* 35–44.

Hartman-Maeir, A., Soroker, N., Ring, H., & Katz, N. (2002). Awareness of deficits in
stroke rehabilitation. *Journal of Stroke Rehabilitation, 34,* 158–164.

Heilman, K.M., Barrett, A.M., & Adair, A.C. (1998). Possible mechanisms of anosognosia:
A deficit in self-awareness. *Philosophical Translations of the Royal Society of London, 353,* 1903–1909.

Horvath, A.O., & Greenberg, L.S. (1994). *The Working Alliance: Theory, Research, and
Practice.* New York: Wiley.

Johnson, S.C., Baxter, L.C., Wilder, L.S., Pipe, J.G., Heiserman, J.E., & Prigatano, G.P.
(2002). Neural correlates of self-reflection. *Brain, 125,* 1808–1814.

Katz, N., Fleming, J., Keren, N., Lightbody, S., & Hartman-Maeir, A. (2002). Unawareness and/or denial of disability: Implications for occupational therapy intervention.
Canadian Journal of Occupational Therapy, 69, 281–292.

Kolitz, B.P., Vanderploeg, R.D., & Curtiss, G. (2003). Development of the Key Behaviors Change Inventory: A traumatic brain injury outcome assessment instrument. *Archives of Physical Medicine and Rehabilitation, 84,* 277–284.

Koltai, D.C., Welsh-Bohmer, K.A., & Schmechel, D.E. (2001). Influence of anosognosia
on treatment outcome among dementia patients. *Neuropsychological Rehabilitation,
11,* 455–475.

Lam, C.S., McMahon, B.T., Priddy, D.A., & Gehred-Schultz, A. (1998). Deficit awareness and treatment performance among traumatic head injury adults. *Brain Injury, 2,*
235–242.

Langer, K.G., & Padrone, F.J. (1992). Psychotherapeutic treatment of awareness in acute
rehabilitation of traumatic brain injury. *Neuropsychological Rehabilitation, 2,* 59–70.

Laroi, F., Fannemel, M., Ronneberg, U., Flekkoy, K., Opjordsmoen, S., Dullerud, R.,
et al. (2000). Unawareness of illness in chronic schizophrenia and its relationship to structural brain measures and neuropsychological tests. *Psychiatry Research, 100,* 49–58.

Lysaker, P.H., Lancaster, R.S., Davis, L.W., & Clements, C.A. (2003). Patterns of
neurocognitive deficits and unawareness of illness in schizophrenia. *Journal of Nervous and Mental Disease, 191,* 38–44.

Malec, J.F., Buffington, A.L.H., Moessner, A.M., & Degiorgio, L. (2000). A medical/
vocational case coordination system for persons with brain injury: An evaluation of
employment outcomes. *Archives of Physical Medicine and Rehabilitation, 81,* 1007–
1015.

Malec, J.F., & Degiorgio, L. (2002). Characteristics of successful and unsuccessful completers of 3 postacute brain injury rehabilitation pathways. *Archives of Physical Medicine and Rehabilitation, 83,* 1759–1764.

Malec, J.F., Smigielski, J.S., & DePompolo, R.W. (1991). Goal attainment scaling and
outcome measurement in postacute brain injury rehabilitation. *Archives of Physical
Medicine and Rehabilitation, 72,* 138–143.

Mateer, C.A. (1999). Executive function disorders: Rehabilitation challenges and strategies. *Seminars in Clinical Neuropsychiatry, 4*, 50–59.

Meador, K.J., Loring, D.W., Feinberg, T.E., Lee, G.P., & Nichols, M.E. (2000).
Anosognosia and asomatognosia during intracarotid amobarbital inactivation. *Neurology, 55*, 816–820.

Owens, P.L., Bradley, E.H., Horwitz, S.M., Viscoli, C.M., Kernan, W.N., Brass, L.M.,
et al. (2002). Clinical assessment of function among women with a recent cerebrovas-
cular event: A self-reported versus performance-based measure. *Annals of Internal
Medicine, 136*, 802–811.

Ownsworth, T.L., McFarland, K., & Young, R.M. (2000). Self-awareness and psychosocial functioning following acquired brain injury: An evaluation of a group support
programme. *Neuropsychological Rehabilitation, 10*, 465–484.

Ownsworth, T.L., McFarland, K., & Young, R.M. (2002). The investigation of factors
underlying deficits in self-awareness and self-regulation. *Brain Injury, 16*, 291–309.

Prigatano, G.P. (1999). *Principles of Neuropsychological Rehabilitation*. New York:
Oxford University Press.

Prigatano, G.P., Fordyce, D.J., Zeiner, H.K., Roueche, J.R., Pepping, M., & Wood, B.C.
(1986). *Neuropsychological Rehabilitation After Brain Injury*. Baltimore: Johns
Hopkins University Press.

Prigatano, G.P., Klonoff, P.S., O'Brien, K.P., Altman, I., Amin, K., Chiapello, D.A.,
et al. (1994). Productivity after neuropsychologically oriented milieu rehabilitation.
Journal of Head Trauma Rehabilitation, 9(1), 91–102.

Prigatano, G.P., & Schacter, D.L. (1991). Introduction. In G.P. Prigatano & D.L. Schacter
(Eds.), *Awareness of Deficit After Brain Injury* (pp. 3–16). New York: Oxford University Press.

Ranseen, J.D., Bohaska, L.A., & Schmitt, F.A. (1990). An investigation of anosognosia
following traumatic head injury. *International Journal of Clinical Neuropsychology,
12*, 29–36.

Rebmann, M.J., & Hannon, R. (1995). Treatment of unawareness of memory deficits in adults
with brain injury: Three case studies. *Rehabilitation Psychology, 40*, 279–287.

Schlund, M.W. (1999). Self-awareness: Effects of feedback and review on verbal self-
reports and remembering following brain injury. *Brain Injury, 13*, 375–380.

Sherer, M., Bergloff, P., Boake, C., High, W., & Levin, E. (1998). The Awareness Questionnaire: Factor structure and internal consistency. *Brain Injury, 12*, 63–68.

Sherer, M., Bergloff, P., Levin, E., High, W.M., Oden, K.E., & Nick, T.G. (1998). Impaired awareness and employment outcome after traumatic brain injury. *Journal of
Head Trauma Rehabilitation, 13*(5), 52–61.

Sherer, M., Boake, C., Levin, E., Silver, B.V., Ringholz, G., & High, W.M., Jr. (1998).
Characteristics of impaired awareness after traumatic brain injury. *Journal of the International Neuropsychological Society, 4*, 380–387.

Sherer, M., Hart, T., & Nick, T.G. (2003). Measurement of impaired self-awareness after
traumatic brain injury: A comparison of the Patient Competency Rating Scale and the
Awareness Questionnaire. *Brain Injury, 17*, 25–37.

Sherer, M., Hart, T., Nick, T.G., Whyte, J., Thompson, R.N., & Yablon, S.A. (2003). Early
impaired self-awareness after traumatic brain injury. *Archives of Physical Medicine
and Rehabilitation, 84*, 168–176.

Sherer, M., Oden, K., Bergloff, P., Levin, E., High, W.M., Jr. (1998). Assessment and
treatment of impaired awareness after brain injury: Implications for community integration. *NeuroRehabilitation, 10*, 25–37.

Smith, C.A., Henderson, V.W., McCleary, C.A., & Murdock, G.A. (2000). Anosognosia and Alzheimer's disease: The role of depressive symptoms in mediating impaired insight. *Journal of Clinical and Experimental Neuropsychology*, *22*, 437–444.

Sohlberg, M.M. (2000). Assessing and managing unawareness of self. *Seminars in Speech and Language*, *21*, 135–151.

Stuss, D.T., Gallup, G.G., Jr., & Alexander, M.P. (2001). The frontal lobes are necessary for "theory of mind." *Brain*, *124*, 279–286.

Tham, K., Ginsburg, E., Fisher, A.G., & Tegner, R. (2001). Training to improve awareness of disabilities in clients with unilateral neglect. *American Journal of Occupational Therapy*, *55*, 46–54.

Tham, K., & Tegner, R. (1997). Video feedback in the rehabilitation of patients with unilateral neglect. *Archives of Physical Medicine and Rehabilitation*, *78*, 410–413.

Trudel, T.M., Tryon, W.W., & Purdum, C.M. (1998). Awareness of disability and long term outcome after traumatic brain injury. *Rehabilitation Psychology*, *43*, 267–281.

Tucha, O., Smely, C., Preier, M., & Lange, K.W. (2000). Cognitive deficits before treatment among patients with brain tumors. *Neurosurgery*, *47*, 324–334.

Vitale, C., Pellecchia, M.T., Grossi, D., Fragassi, N., Cuomo, T., DiMaio, L., et al. (2001). Unawareness of dyskinesias in Parkinson's and Huntington's diseases. *Neurological Science*, *22*, 105–106.

Wagner, M.T., & Cushman, L.A. (1994). Neuroanatomic and neuropsychological predictors of unawareness of cognitive deficits in the vascular population. *Archives of Clinical Neuropsychology*, *9*, 57–69.

Youngjohn, J.R., & Altman, I.M. (1989). A performance-based group approach to the treatment of anosognosia and denial. *Rehabilitation Psychology*, *34*, 217–222.

Zhou, J., Chittum, R., Johnson, K., Poppen, R., Guercio, J., & McMorrow, M.J. (1996). The utilization of a game format to increase knowledge of residuals among people with acquired brain injury. *Journal of Head Trauma Rehabilitation*, *11*(1), 51–61.

4

External Aids for Management
of Memory Impairment

McKAY MOORE SOHLBERG

The characteristic that most distinguishes the population of individuals who have acquired brain injury (ABI) is the heterogeneity of their symptoms. Neurogenic conditions such as traumatic brain injury (TBI), stroke, tumor, anoxic events (e.g., drowning or cardiac arrest), and infectious diseases comprise a vast array of complex and unique impairments in people's ability to learn and carry out everyday tasks (Coehlho et al., 1996; Sohlberg & Mateer, 2001). In spite of their heterogeneity, individuals with ABI share the disabilities of social isolation and diminished independence in home and community functioning (Dawson & Chipman, 1995; Ledorze & Brassard, 1995; Zicht, 1992).

The Big Picture. Cognitive impairments, particularly changes in memory, attention, and executive systems, are in part responsible for the reduced independence and lack of community integration in persons with ABI. Even mild changes in the ability to attend to, process, recall, and act upon information can have significant effects on the completion of basic everyday tasks (Sohlberg & Mateer, 2001). This chapter reviews literature relevant to managing difficulties specifically caused by memory impairments. However, we must recognize the interdependence of attention, memory, and executive functions and the somewhat artificial attempt to isolate the impairments and their associated interventions. It is difficult to evaluate the different cognitive operations independently, since completing activities that engage the mental circuitry for one process will necessarily activate other processes. Further, we recognize the influence of emotional functioning on cognitive processes. The primacy of emotion and personality variables in recovering from cognitive impairments is only beginning to be acknowledged in spite of its importance (Adams, 2003). Effective cognitive intervention requires that we remain mindful of the interactions between the different cognitive functions and the influence of emotional and contextual variables.

Types of Cognitive Intervention. Therapeutic methods designed to ameliorate the disabilities caused by cognitive impairments come in diverse packages. Regardless of the technique and the underlying treatment rationale, the ultimate goal of all interventions is to improve the day-to-day functioning of the individual seeking treatment.

The American Speech-Language Hearing Association published a technical report exploring the conceptual foundations of cognitive rehabilitation for individuals with brain injury (Ylvisaker, Hanks, & Jonson-Greene, 2003). They contrast two basic approaches: the *traditional* approach, with the primary goal of improving an individual's performance by eliminating or reducing underlying cognitive impairments, and the *contextualized* paradigm, with the broad goal of helping individuals achieve functional objectives and participate in chosen activities that are blocked by impairment. Many interventions, however, cannot easily be assigned to one camp or the other. For example, teaching the use of a metacognitive strategy for attentional disorders may be considered a process-oriented (i.e., traditional) treatment that boosts the client's actual executive function abilities. Alternatively, the same intervention may be viewed as a behavioral intervention aimed at training an individual to use a specific approach to task completion (i.e., a contexualized treatment) (Cicerone, 2002). A further complication in distinguishing intervention approaches stems from the fact that most clinicians combine treatments. For example, a common clinical regimen is to implement process-oriented therapy in conjunction with training the use of an external compensatory aid (Ylivsaker et al. 2003a).

Regardless of one's treatment philosophy or the underlying mechanism one perceives as responsible for observed changes, clinicians and researchers agree that the ultimate measure of efficacy must be functional improvement. Table 4.1 provides a taxonomy for cognitive interventions based on the treatment rationale and objective (Sohlberg, 2002). This classification reminds us of the myriad of options that have been reported to effectively address cognitive impairments.

The taxonomy described in Table 4.1 is part of the work undertaken by the Academy of Neurologic Communication Disorders and Sciences Evidence Based Practice Guidelines (ANCDS EBPG) Traumatic Brain Injury subcommittee (Ylvisaker, Coelho, et al., 2003). In an attempt to establish defensible, validated intervention practices, the field of cognitive rehabilitation has joined medicine's vigorous movement to develop evidence-based practice guidelines. The primary

Table 4.1. Types of Cognitive Treatment

TREATMENT APPROACH	RATIONALE
Direct training of cognitive processes	Repetitive stimulation of distinct components of damaged cognitive functions will lead to improved processing (e.g., Sohlberg et al., 2000)
Teaching task-specific routines	Teaching the steps that comprise a specific functional skill using a behavioral approach will result in learning (or relearning) the target skill (e.g., Martelli, 1999).
Metacognitive strategy training	Teaching self-monitoring or self-instructional strategies will regulate behavior and/or improve task execution ability (e.g., Levine et al., 2000)
Environmental modification/ task accommodation	Organizing the target setting or altering task variables will circumvent the cognitive impairment and promote successful task completion (e.g., Sohlberg & Mateer, 2001).
Collaboration-focused approaches	Forming partnerships and clinical alliances with people in the client's environment will result in successful goal selection and problem solving that alleviates the issues of concern (e.g., Ylvisaker & Feeney, 1998).
Training use of external aids	Identifying and training the use of devices that remind or cue individuals to initiate target behaviors will compensate for cognitive impairments and improve functional ability (e.g., Wilson et al., 1997).

Source: Modified from Sohlberg (2002).

goal of this burgeoning reform movement is to use empirical research evidence to develop treatment protocols that are causally linked to expected clinical outcomes (Robey, 2001). Current guidelines for the use of direct intervention for attention disorders have been completed (Sohlberg, Avery, et al., 2003) and are underway in the other areas.

Memory Treatments. In this chapter, we examine the evidence related to the treatment of memory disorders. We have acknowledged the somewhat artificial nature of isolating cognitive impairments; memory impairments most often occur in combination with other issues. This caveat notwithstanding, there are individuals for whom a severe impairment in memory is the predominant obstacle to performing everyday tasks.

Each of the interventions listed in Table 4.1 has been evaluated in the memory-disordered population. For example, early work described direct training of memory processes (e.g., list-learning techniques) as a way to boost memory (Glisky & Schacter, 1986). Unlike attention, however, there has been no empirical support of the efficacy of drill-oriented approaches for restoring memory. Published studies have repeatedly documented the failure of drill-oriented approaches in improving memory test scores or impacting functional memory (Godfrey & Knight, 1985; Schacter et al., 1985). One possible exception may be the use of prospective memory drills that require patients to remember and execute target tasks at increasingly long intervals (Sohlberg et al., 1992). Several authors have reported improved prospective memory functioning following the drills; however, there has been little systematic replication or evaluation of the extent of generalization (Raskin & Sohlberg, 1996), and the technique has not been widely adopted by clinicians.

In contrast to direct training of memory processes, the training of task-specific routines and environmental modification for people with memory impairments is a commonly used clinical technique that has been shown to have utility for those with significant memory impairments (Sohlberg & Mateer, 2001; Wilson & Moffat, 1992). People with severe memory impairments have been taught such functional skills as word processing (Evans et al., 2000; Glisky et al., 1986), driving (Kewman et al., 1985), swallowing techniques (Brush & Camp, 1998), and name–face associations (Carruth, 1997) using specific instructional techniques such as error-free learning (e.g., Evans et al., 2000) and spaced retrieval (e.g., Brush & Camp, 1998).

Historically, metacognitive strategy training has also been extensively studied and implemented with the memory-disordered population; currently, however, mnemonics plays a minor role in memory treatment and has received increasingly less scientific focus. A more recent study of imagery mnemonics calls for a reversal of this trend by demonstrating that simple imagery techniques can improve everyday memory performance and that positive effects are stable at the 3-month follow-up (Kaschel et al., 2002). Examples of predecessor studies with positive reports for metacognitive strategy training include Milders et al.'s (1995) description of a technique effective in increasing memory for names and Oberg and Turkstra's (1998) success in using an elaborative encoding technique to teach two adolescents with memory impairments specific vocabulary required for school.

Much less studied interventions to manage memory problems include environmental modification and collaboration approaches. Examples of using environmental modification include labeling cupboard contents or establishing a family message center on the refrigerator (Sohlberg & Mateer, 2001). Support for the efficacy of environmental modification is largely anecdotal and clinical word of mouth. A collaborative approach also prioritizes ecological and contextual factors (Adams, 2003; Ylvisaker & Feeney, 1998). This approach recognizes the clinical power inherent in collaborating and forming partnerships with families and care providers to set goals and develop plans to alleviate concerns caused by cognitive impairments (Sohlberg et al., 2001; Ylvisaker & Feeney, 1998). The experimental evidence supporting this approach is primarily indirect and comes from related fields or cross-population references evaluating the effectiveness of teaching knowledge and functional skills in meaningful contexts to individuals with learning problems due to developmental disorders (e.g. Koegel et al., 1997; Lucyshin et al., 1996).

External aids, the last treatment category, have been touted as the most effective and most widely used intervention for memory impairments (Sohlberg & Mateer, 2001; Wilson & Watson, 1996; Wilson et al., 2001; Zenicus et al., 1991). Given its popularity, this chapter seeks to explore the literature on the efficacy of teaching the use of compensatory aids in general and external aids in particular as a method to help individuals with significant memory impairments. We will review the evidence related to using external aids as a treatment method and the associated instructional practices for teaching new techniques or procedures to people with memory disorders.

EXTERNAL AIDS

External aids provide the user with a way of carrying out target tasks by compensating for existing impairments with the use of a tool or device that either limits the demands on the person's impaired ability or transforms the task or environment such that it matches the client's abilities. Other terms for external aids include *cognitive orthoses*, *cognitive prosthetics*, and *assistive technology* (Cole, 1999; Kirsch et al., 1987). In this chapter, the following attributes define external aids: (1) they directly assist individuals in performing some of their everyday activities and (2) they can be customized to the needs of an individual.

The development of external memory aids both designed for the general public and tailored for people with significant memory impairments is a fast-growing enterprise. Devices have been developed that can assist the latter population with organizing and carryiang out daily activities (e.g., Wilson et al., 2001), using e-mail (Sohlberg, Ehlhardt, et al., 2003), remembering a schedule (Tackett et al., 2001), and recalling conversation topics (Alm et al., 2003).

Types of External Aids

The literature describes a wide variety of aids ranging from highly technical assistive devices that compensate for memory impairments across environments and task domains to low-technology tools designed for single-task guidance. External aids can be divided loosely into low-tech and high-tech tools, depending upon the complexity of their design and the demands on the learner to master their use. A further classification dimension is whether the tool is domain specific, designed to guide the completion of a particular task or to prompt a discrete behavior, or a multipurpose device designed to compensate for memory problems in different settings and across tasks. Examples of low-tech devices that require no electronic technology and may either be domain specific or multifunctional include a broad range of paper-and-pencil systems such as checklists on note cards, planners or memory books, wall calendars, and alarm reminders. A myriad of low-tech, domain-specific tools to compensate for memory impairments are also available, including medication reminders, phone dialers, and key finders (Kapur, 1995). An interview study revealed that the most commonly used memory aids tend to be low-tech tools such as calendars, wall charts, and notebooks (Evans et al., 2003).

The development of high-tech tools to assist with memory and organization has expanded exponentially in the general population and is growing in the population of technology users with cognitive impairments (Sohlberg, Ehlhardt, et al., 2003). A recent review of the literature in assistive technology for cognition spanning the past 20 years concluded that technological solutions are available and can be effective in helping people with brain injury participate in many activities that would not otherwise be possible. The devices range from simple electronic tools developed for the nondisabled population such as the Voice Organizer, a dictaphone-type device designed to store the user's own messages (Van den Broek et al., 2000), to sophisticated personal digital assistants such as the Memory Aid Prompting system (LoPresti et al., 2004). The high-tech devices designed to assist more severely impaired individuals to manage daily activities tend to provide more prompting for using the device, activity guidance, and maintenance of daily information. Interestingly, the aforementioned survey study by Evans and colleagues (2003) found that in spite of their availability, many electronic aids may be too complex for people with significant memory impairments. They further suggest that such aids may not be routinely recommended by the rehabilitation staff. Table 4.2 provides a list of sample software and hardware tools that have been reported to assist people with memory impairments.

Efficacy of External Aids

A review of the literature confirms that external aids are effective in helping people with memory impairments compensate for forgetfulness. Unlike the literature on other cognitive rehabilitation techniques, the literature is unequivocal in reporting that the use of external aids and compensation devices is useful for increasing the independence and functionality of people with memory impairments; every article reviewed, including older and current evaluations, reported positive

Table 4.2. Examples of Assistive Devices Designed to Aid Individuals with
Impairments in Memory and Executive Functions

DEVICE/SOFTWARE	MANUFACTURER	DESCRIPTION
Planning and Executive Assistant and Trainer (PEAT)	Attention Control Systems, Inc., Mountain View, CA	Handheld reminding device with intelligent support for revising schedules.
ISAAC	Cogent Systems, Inc., Orlando, FL	Handheld reminding device to provide support for entering and following schedules by people with cognitive, physical, and sensory impairments.
CellMinder	Institute for Cognitive Prosthetics, Bala Cynwyd, PA	A system using a cell phone as a reminder. Software on the user's computer keeps track of a schedule and calls the user at designated times.
Neuropager	Oliver Zangwill Centre, Princess of Wales Hospital, Ely, Cambridgeshire, U.K.	Alphanumeric paging system to remind people to complete activities at designated times.
MemoJog	Department of Applied Computing, University of Dundee, Scotland	Paging system for use with a personal digital assistant (PDA) via a mobile phone network; enables communication with caregivers.
Memory Aid Prompting) System (MAPS)	Coleman Institute, the University of Colorado	A combination of a wireless interaction system between comprising a PDA, centralized clinician computer, and the caregiver's computer that allows the user or the system to contact a caregiver when problems arise that the system cannot automatically handle. There is a data logging feature that allows evaluation of system effectiveness.

outcomes with the implementation of external aids. While the basic question "Are external aids helpful?" can be answered affirmatively, the answers to such crucial questions as "Who is best helped?, "How best to train people with memory impairments?", and "What behaviors, processes, or skills are influenced by the introduction of external aids?" are far from clear. In this section, we review findings from research reports evaluating the general effectiveness of using external aids.

A literature search revealed studies evaluating the following types of external aids designed to increase independent initiation and follow-through of functional tasks:

- Voice recorders (e.g., Hart et al., 2002; Van den Broek et al., 2000; Yasuda et al., 2002)
- Pagers/mobile phones (e.g., Wade & Troy, 2001; Wilson et al., 2001)
- Electronic diaries or personal digit assistants (e.g., Kim et al., 2000; Wright et al., 2001)
- Written diaries or planners (e.g., Donaghy & Williams, 1998; Fluharty & Priddy, 1993; Ownsworth & MacFarland, 1999)

As noted, all of the studies reviewed reported positive outcomes. The majority of research reports concern Class II (well-designed observational clinical studies with concurrent controls including single-subject designs with multiple baselines across two or more subjects) and Class III (e.g., expert opinion, case series, case reports, and studies with historical controls) studies (Kennedy et al., 2002). Wilson and colleagues' (2001) study is the only true Class I experiment (i.e., randomized control trial) on the effectiveness of external aids.

Collectively, what has this work taught us about the effectiveness of external aids and what does future research need to address? A starting point for answering this question is to review the findings from experimental evaluations of using external aids with people who have memory impairments.

Class I and II Studies

Wilson et al. (2001) provided people displaying a wide range in severity of cognitive impairments of varying severity with paging systems that reminded them to carry out self-selected functional tasks. They conducted a randomized, controlled trial involving a crossover design with 143 people between the ages of 8 and 83 years, all of whom had memory, planning, attention, or organizational problems mostly due to TBI. They reported that more than 80% of the subjects who completed the 16-week trial were significantly more successful in carrying out everyday activities (e.g., self-care, self-medication, and keeping appointments) when using the pager in comparison with the baseline period. For most subjects, improvements were maintained when they were monitored 7 weeks after returning the pager. The authors concluded that the paging system significantly reduces everyday failures of memory and planning in people with brain injury. The study did not, however, investigate specific factors that contribute to continued use of the device (e.g., degree of caregiver support is not detailed) or measure the reliability of the daily recordings on whether the target had been achieved.

Schmitter-Edgcombe et al. (1995) conducted a group comparison of memory notebook training and supportive therapy for decreasing everyday memory failure (EMF). Eight individuals with memory impairments following severe closed head injury were randomly assigned to a group that received training in using a notebook or to a comparison group that received supportive therapy. In the treatment group, individuals participated in two 60-minute sessions per week for 8 weeks. Didactic lessons and homework sessions were used to teach them to record entries in their notebook and to use the notebook for such purposes as daily logs, calendar items, and remembering names. The supportive therapy group was given an opportunity to share frustrations and was taught some basic problem-solving techniques. At the end of the experiment, the participants and their family members assigned to the notebook training group reported significantly fewer EMFs using a daily checklist. Continued benefits of notebook use were reported at the 6-month follow-up. There were no differences on laboratory memory tests. The small sample size ($n = 8$) renders the results preliminary, but the study provides important information about the utility of a daily checklist for measuring memory performance. Like the Wilson et al. (2001) study, this study supports the use of an external aid in compensating for everyday memory problems, as well as providing additional information about training and measurement.

Wright and colleagues (2001) compared two different styles of pocket computer memory aids for people with brain injury. They loaned 12 adult volunteers two different computers with little training beyond an initial demonstration, and found that all participants could operate the aids and most found them useful. One predictor of usage was whether the participant had employed reminding systems before joining the project; another was speed in calculator addition. It should be noted that the majority of the participants scored in the average or slightly impaired range on all cognitive indices. The authors concluded that devices for this population should rely on participants' problem-solving skills rather than expecting them to remember procedures.

Another experimental comparison looked at differences in training as opposed to evaluating differences in types of devices. Ownsworth and McFarland (1999) used a baseline across groups' design to evaluate the relative effectiveness of two different approaches for teaching the use of a memory notebook. One treatment group was taught a behavioral sequence for using a book that contained personal information/address pages as well as a calendar section. The other group was taught a metacognitive self-instructional technique to help them mediate the use of their memory notebook. The training was completed via telephone. Results suggested that the group provided with self-instructional training made more entries, reported fewer memory problems, and rated treatment efficacy more highly. The authors encourage the use of self-instruction when training people to use external aids.

Within-subject experimental designs have been used to show the efficacy of voice organizers for assisting individuals with memory impairments to carry out intended actions (Hart et al., 2002; van den Broek et al., 2000; Yasuda et al., 2002). For example, Hart et al. (2002) demonstrated that a portable voice organizer (Parrot Voice Mate III) can promote the retention and use of behaviors (e.g., using relaxation techniques when episodes of anxiety occur) as well as performance of simple prospective memory tasks (e.g., remembering to get the mail).

Class III Studies

There are a number of case reports describing improved independence in people with acquired cognitive impairment who have been provided with specially designed low- and high-tech assistive devices or devices for the general public. For example, several researchers describe the benefits of memory notebooks for increasing independence in everyday memory performance in selected clients with brain injury (e.g., Burke et al., 1994; Donaghy & Williams, 1998; Fluharty & Priddy, 1993; Ownsworth & McFarland, 1999; Sohlberg & Mateer, 1989; Squires et al., 1997).

Similarly, there are a wide variety of case reports on the successful use of aids to facilitate the completion of specific tasks. For example, Kirsch and colleagues (1992) have discussed the benefits of a task guidance system in helping four individuals with brain injury perform janitorial tasks. Other authors have demonstrated the effectiveness of task guidance devices in helping subjects follow a recipe (Steele et al., 1989) and complete the steps for shaving (Napper & Narayan, 1994). A study by Wade and Troy (2001) reported on five individuals with memory impairments who had been given mobile phones that were programmed to ring and remind them to complete predetermined target tasks. The results of diary observations and qualitative feedback suggested that the phones were successful in increasing initiation of the target tasks.

While reports on the utility of different devices and/or training techniques are uniformly positive, methods of measuring the effectiveness of training or the utility of specific devices vary greatly. A review of the literature reveals five distinct types of measurement parameters:

- Laboratory-based memory measures (e.g., Schmittter-Edgcombe et al., 1995; Wilson et al., 2001; Wright et al., 2001)
- Observed performance on structured tasks designed to capture the demands of everyday memory (van den Broek et al., 2000)

- Retrospective questionnaires or diary reports assessing everyday memory performance (Ownsworth & McFarland, 1999; Schmitter-Edgecombe et al., 1995; Wade & Troy, 2001; Wilson et al., 2001)
- Observed performance on everyday memory tasks or use of external aids (Fluharty & Priddy, 1993; Schmitter-Edgecombe et al., 1995; Wilson et al., 2001; Wright et al., 2001; Yasuda et al., 2001)
- Participant preference, satisfaction, or symptom ratings (e.g., Schmitter-Edgecombe et al., 1995; Wilson et al., 2001; Wright et al., 2001)

Most studies combine several indices to gain a picture of effectiveness and client satisfaction.

THE RESEARCH GAPS

Potential Pitfalls

Despite their utility and availability, the use of compensatory aids for people with memory impairments is a bit of a double-edged sword. The employment of aids is itself a memory task, and the people who would gain the most benefit experience the greatest difficulty using them (Wilson et al., 2001). A similar problem exists for training the use of mnemonic strategies. In their review, Kaschel et al. (2002) suggest that such factors as the complexity of the strategy, the context for transferring strategy use, and the nature of the training affect the treatment outcome. These same factors have been reported as potential obstacles to teaching people with memory impairments to use external aids (Parente & DiCesare, 1991; Schmitter-Edgecombe et al., 1995; van den Broek et al., 2000).

The complexity of the external aid is an obvious factor that influences successful adoption (Evans et al., 2003). For example, several of the tools listed in Table 4.2 require sophisticated programming and support. Some clients may need to be independent in their use of a system in order for it to be effective (Van den Broek et al., 2000).

A factor that has received some research attention is the user characteristics that affect the adoption of an external aid. A number of researchers have noted that a person's level of self-awareness and insight is a critical factor (e.g., Fleming & Strong, 1995; Prigatano & Schacter, 1991). Client beliefs and attitudes also appear to influence treatment outcomes; clients may abandon the use of systems if they believe that such systems draw attention to their problems (e.g., Fluharty & Priddy, 1993) or perceive that their use will slow recovery and make them less reliant on their own abilities (Wilson & Watson, 1996). Severity of memory impairment and concomitant cognitive issues have also been reported to influence external aid treatment outcomes (Kaschel et al., 2002; Wilson, 1995).

Interestingly, there is little research on the effectiveness of or requirements for successfully evaluating and training an individual to use an external aid. Although it is widely acknowledged that training people with memory impairments to follow new procedures is challenging, very few reports delineate specific training or instructional procedures. Even nondisabled users of devices, particularly technology users, recognize the critical import of training and support. There are even fewer reports on evaluation practices for selecting appropriate external aids. Successful long-term adoption of external aids requires that an appropriate aid is selected for the client and that he or she is effectively trained to use it in a manner that accommodates cognitive impairments. The next sections review the research related to evaluation, training, and instruction in the use of external aids.

Evaluation

No formal evaluation protocols have been validated for use with individuals who require external aids. Instead the field offers informal descriptions of needs assessments (e.g., Sohlberg & Mateer, 2001). There is almost no information on the relationship between the clinical characteristics of persons with cognitive impairments and the specific tools or aids most suitable for their needs (LoPresti et al., 2004). We can look to other fields, however, for models that can guide our work in evaluating client needs for adopting external aids.

Evaluation protocols have been designed for a variety of people with cognitive difficulties to assess their needs for using assistive technology, including individuals with learning disabilities (e.g., Bryant & Bryant, 1998), autism (Ager, 2001), and the elderly (Fozard et al., 2000). They all offer methods for matching an individual to a specific technology. Applied research fields such as alternative augmentative communication (AAC) and rehabilitation technology also describe evaluation models that emphasize a *user-centered* approach to selcting devices and assessing outcomes. For example, both the Participation Model widely adopted within the AAC literature (Beukelman & Mirenda, 1998) and the Assistive Technology Outcomes Model (ATOM) (Weiss-Lambrou, 2002) used in rehabilitation technology stress the importance of striving for a careful match among the person, the technology, and the environment in which the technology will be used.

The lack of ecological validity when relying on standardized cognitive measures is clearly articulated across fields. Evaluating a potential external aid user within his or her personal ecology, and assessing individual characteristics in conjunction with environmental supports and barriers, is a core assessment principle in all the models reviewed.

Training and Instruction

There are no large-scale studies evaluating effective methods for teaching the use of external aids. Several of the experimental reports indicating positive outcomes do not emphasize or even explain the training or instruction that was provided (e.g., Wade & Troy, 2001; Yasuda et al., 2002). For example, in their evaluation of the Voice Organizer, Van den Broek et al. (2000) indicated that patients were trained to use the device at the beginning of the experiment, but the authors did not provide specific details on training. Similarly, in their randomized, controlled trial, Wilson et al. (2001) reported that many of the participants needed only minimal training with the pager before they could benefit from it, whereas those who were more impaired needed help from a carer for a longer period of time. The type of training, however, was not specified, only that it was carried out by natural caregivers.

In their evaluation of electronic memory aids, Wright et al. (2001) reported that training consisted of an office visit at which the researcher demonstrated how to use the device, with a follow up check-in visit 1 week later. In contrast, Ownsworth and MacFarland (1999) acknowledged the importance of systematic training for successful use of a memory notebook, but as in the Wilson et al. (2001) study, the training was carried out in the natural environment and was not monitored by the researchers. They provided instructions by mail and by phone.

There are several reports specifying procedures and principles important for teaching the use of aids. One of the first reports that specified an explicit protocol for teaching people with severe memory impairments presented a training sequence based on the direct instruction literature (Engelmann & Carnine, 1991)—an instructional methodology that promotes systematic, explicit training. Sohlberg and Mateer (1989) reported success with the following training sequence: (1) acquisition (how to use it), (2) application (where and when to use it) and (3) adaptation (how to update it). This sequence was implemented to teach an individual with a severe memory impairment to use a multisection memory notebook. Several subsequent reports described modifications of this sequence but maintained the principles of direct instruction. For example, Schmitter-Edgecombe et al. (1995) incorporated both behavioral learning principles and educational strategies in an individualized training program for each client receiving memory notebook training. They augmented Sohlberg and Mateer's (1989) behavioral training sequence and described four training stages: Anticipation, Acquisition, Application, and Adaptation. Within each stage, didactic lessons and homework assignments were presented by the therapists and incorporated into a Learning Activities Packet to reinforce learning.

Donaghy and Williams (1998) also reported utility with explicit training procedures that provided error-free learning during an acquisition phase and gave the learner adequate practice with each of the notebook procedures. They further improved Sohlberg and Mateer's (1989) model by simplifying the structure of the notebook that was trained.

The reason that some reports do not emphasize or even acknowledge training, while others describe it as the primary part of the rehabilitation process, may be related to the level of memory impairment in the subject population. For example, the cognitive impairment of the participants in the Wright et al., (2001) study was relatively mild; thus, training may not have been as critical. When training was carried out in the natural setting, it is not possible to know from the reports how much and what type of support was given by the care providers. It may be that the carers offered explicit instruction. Another explanation for some of the reports of successful use of devices with seemingly little training may focus on the nature of the task targeted by the external aid. For example, the Neuropager (Wilson et al., 1997) and mobile phones (Wade & Troy, 2001) are used to cue discrete target behaviors (e.g., taking medication). By contrast, memory books and electronic devices designed to assist with organizing, initiating, and planning multiple prospective tasks during a day are multidimensional and place a greater demand on the learner.

All of the reports specifying the benefits of training described systematic, theoretically grounded instruction. The next section examines the relevant instructional literature, including cross-population references in order to determine effective instructional procedures that can be used to train the use of external aids.

Direct Instruction Methodology

Direct instruction is a well-established *explicit* instructional methodology shown to be effective in teaching a wide range of material (e.g., reading, math, social skills) across many different populations, particularly individuals with learning challenges such as those experienced by individuals with brain injury. The key features of direct instruction practices are listed in Table 4.3.

Recent meta-analyses of intervention studies involving learners with cognitive disabilities show that direct instruction that includes strategy-based instruction is superior to other instructional methods (Swanson, 1999; Swanson & Hoskyn, 1998). A component analysis of instructional features showed that explicit practice (i.e., distributed review and practice, repeated practice; sequenced reviews, daily feedback; weekly reviews) was the single most important instructional component contributing to effect sizes (Swanson & Hoskyn, 2001). Design and implementation of a direct instruction curriculum has also been shown to be efficacious in teaching academic skills and behavioral self-management, as well as the use of external aids with students who have cognitive impairments from brain injury (Glang et al., 1992; Kerns & Thomson, 1998).

The field of cognitive rehabilitation has evaluated the efficacy of isolated aspects of direct instruction with individuals with brain injury. Researchers have shown that

Table 4.3. Instructional Features Effective in Teaching Individuals with Acquired Cognitive Impairment

INSTRUCTIONAL FEATURE	RATIONALE	SUPPORTING REFERENCES
Errorless learning (facilitated by features listed below)	Optimal for learners with severe anterograde memory impairment, who have difficulty with trial-and-error approaches	Brush & Camp (1998); Evans et al. (2000); Kalla et al. (2001); Komastu et al. (2000); Wilson et al. (1994)
Task analysis	Facilitates step-by-step instruction	Stein et al. (1998)
Chaining	Facilitates learning of initial step	Smith (1999); Spooner & Spooner (1984)
Focus on one task in depth	Facilitates skill mastery	Stein et al. (1998)
Cumulative review	Increases practice time	Madigan et al. (1997); Stein et al. (1998)
Preexposure stimulus	Enhances effects of errorless learning	Kalla et al. (2001)
Prediction-reflection (meta-cognitive) strategy with screenshots	Increases awareness of performance and task demands; checklist helps decrease memory load	Cicerone & Giacino (1992)
Instructor model/guided practice	Facilitates errorless learning	Stein et al. (1998); Swanson (1999)
Multiple opportunities to practice	Consolidates learning	Stein et al., (1998)
Spaced retrieval	Expanded retrieval intervals enhance consolidation of information	Brush & Camp (1998)
Carefully faded prompts	Facilitates errorless learning	Hunkin et al. (1998); Madigan et al. (1997)
Varied training examples	Facilitates generalization	Horner et al. (1986)
Training to criterion	Ensures task mastery	Stein et al. (1998); Swanson (1999)

errorless learning during the acquisition of new procedures is superior to "guess and correct" learning for teaching the use of external memory aids when individuals have severe memory impairments (Evans et al., 2000; Wilson et al., 1994).

Another instructional element that has been shown to be effective in the field of cognitive rehabilitation is metacognitive strategy training. Key features of successful metacognitive strategy use identified across studies are (1) use of strategies that promote the deliberate evaluation of one's own performance; (2) verbal self-regulation; (3) application of the strategy to multistep processes; (4) use of external aids to support strategy use; and (5) comparison of before/after performance to raise awareness of task demands (e.g., Cicerone & Giacino, 1992; Levine et al., 2000; von Cramon & von Cramon, 1994). As previously described, Ownsworth and McFarland (1999) showed the effectiveness of adding a metacognitive component when training the use of memory notebooks.

Although there is a solid literature ow effective instructional techniques for memory-impaired learners, there are few studies of participants with brain injury and no experimental evaluations on employment of these techniques for teaching the use of external aids. Further research is needed to determine which direct instruction features are most important for this population and how different profiles (e.g., a memory-impaired client with impulsivity versus a client with poor initiation) may benefit from certain instructional techniques.

Training for Clinicians

It is not enough to identify effective instructional methods for teaching clients with cognitive impairments to use assistive technology; clinicians must be able to implement techniques in the settings in which they work with clients. Several studies have shown that rehabilitation therapists working in medical settings can be taught to implement direct instruction techniques and that when they do so, the patient's independence increases (e.g., Ducharme & Spencer, 2001; Glang et al., 1990; Mozzoni & Bailey, 1996). For example, Ducharme and Spencer (2001) showed that when therapists were taught teaching strategies such as how to provide systematic practice, errorless learning, and faded cueing, they implemented the techniques with clients. Glang et al. (1990) demonstrated improved performance with clients with traumatic brain injury on functional memory tasks (e.g., remembering their home phone number) when rehabilitation therapists were taught explicit teaching techniques. Mozzoni and Baily (1996) demonstrated that when therapists were taught direct instruction techniques, their patients' independence in a rehabilitation setting increased.

The development of effective instructional guidelines does not ensure their adoption. Clinicians must be explicitly trained in effective instructional methodology if they are to adopt these practices. Currently, instructional methodology is not strongly emphasized in clinical training programs or in the actual practice of cognitive rehabilitation.

Summary

Scrutinzing the literature and comparing findings across studies is critical in carrying out informed clinical practice. Recommended key questions that should be applied to clinical research in order to develop practice guidelines include the following:

(1) Who is the subject population? (2) What was the treatment and how was it administered? (3) What were the outcomes? and (4) What research methodology was used to evaluate the treatment? (Sohlberg, Avery, et al., 2003). We recognize that the studies examining the efficacy of external aids differ vastly on each of these dimensions, making it difficult to compare types of aids, methods of introducing them, and their associated outcomes. Currently, the Academy of Neurologic Communication Disorders and Sciences Evidence Based Practice Guidelines (ANCDS EBPG) Traumatic Brain Injury subcommittee is working on an in-depth analysis of the research, including evaluating expert opinions in order to develop specific practice guidelines for the use of external aids with cognitively impaired individuals (Kennedy et al., in progress). Albeit preliminary, analysis of the collective research related to the use of external aids as a treatment for managing memory impairments reveals the following:

- External aids can be effective for a variety of people with memory impairment.
- A multitude of devices and tools are available.
- External aids are most effective when they are customized for individuals, particularly when there are significant cognitive impairments.
- Evaluation of a potential user of external aids should take place within his or her own ecology.
- Evaluation of the efficacy of external aids should include a daily checklist or direct observation of everyday memory tasks and/or use of the aid, as well as a subjective measurement of the preferences and satisfaction of the users of the devices.
- There are validated instructional practices effective in teaching new procedures to individuals with severe learning difficulties.
- Clinicians can be trained to implement effective instructional techniques.

In the last section, we suggest directions for future research that will build on what we have learned and increase the effectiveness of external aids for people with memory impairments.

FUTURE RESEARCH

The research to date underscores the potential of a wide variety of external aids for improving the lives of people with memory impairments. It further provides preliminary information on the potential obstacles to successfully introducing external aids and systematically training people with learning problems to implement them. However, the field is at risk for piecemeal development and delivery of isolated aids that are usable by only a small number of individuals and that are easily abandoned as needs or ecology change. There is virtually no research on the factors critical to *long-term* adoption of external aids. We must conduct research that addresses each link in the chain of services necessary for successful use of external aids: design, evaluation, instruction, and ongoing monitoring. Examples of specific outstanding research questions include:

1. What are the individual and environmental factors that affect the long-term, continuous use of a broad range of external aids by persons with memory impairments?
2. What are the evaluation components that lead to the selection (and development) of the most appropriate aids or devices for an individual consumer with memory impairment?
3. What are the instructional design and "help" features most likely to lead to efficient, long-term use of an external aid?
4. Can effective instructional features be integrated into a curriculum and teaching methods easily adopted by clinicians and paraprofessionals?
5. What factors are important to monitor in order to determine when an aid is at risk of abandonment or that there have been changes within a client or the environment that warrant support or action?
6. When individuals successfully use external aids, what are the impacts on their independence and social integration?
7. What are the most effective mechanisms to encourage rehabilitation clinicians to adopt evaluation and training techniques?
8. What are the most effective mechanisms to provide information to developers about useful device features and to encourage incorporation of these features into the design of external aids?

The following four-pronged research agenda is suggested to respond to these research questions.

1. *Retrospective Studies*: A series of retrospective studies establish a strong knowledge base to guide the design of experimental evaluations. The following studies are recommended: (*a*) systematic review of existing research relevant to external aids (including assistive technology) in people with memory impairments due to acquired brain injury; (*b*) survey studies to learn the perspectives of potential users of the aids, their support providers, clinicians, and developers; and (*c*) focus groups with clients to learn in depth about specific issues that have led to device adoption or abandonment.
2. *Controlled Experiments*: It is necessary to systematically compare and evaluate the utility of different features of external aids and their

suitability for particular population characteristics. It is also necessary to investigate evaluation and training methods, as well as the specific impact of external aids on the day-to-day functioning of individuals with memory impairment.

3. *Longitudinal Field Studies*: Investigation of clients and their care providers in natural contexts over time is critical in considering issues related to long-term adoption.

4. *Randomized, Controlled Trials*: Work in the aforementioned three research areas would reveal the best questions to evaluate using randomized, controlled trials.

It is clear that external aids can have a positive impact on the lives of persons with memory impairment. Current research is sorely lacking, however, in providing information about how best to select and implement the use of these aids. Much of the information available is from conference proceedings showcasing specialized devices that are not widely available or from case studies describing specific applications (e.g., LoPresti et al., 2004). The isolated reports of people with cognitive impairments successfully using assistive devices do not begin to address the complex factors related to adoption and long-term use of these aids. It is hoped that the proposed research agenda will encourage a systematic inquiry within the field.

REFERENCES

Adams, K.M. (2003). Realizing the potential of cognitive rehabilitation for the brain-injured: Next steps. *Brain Impairment, 4*(1), 1–11.

Ager, A. (2001). Microcomputers—Europe: Cognition disorders. *British Journal of Educational Technology, 32*(3), 373.

Alm, N., Ellis, M, Astell, A., Dye, R., Gowans, G., & Campbell, J. (2003). A cognitive prosthesis and communication support for people with dementia. *Neuropsychological Rehabilitation*, In-press.

Beukelman, D., & Mirenda, P. (1998). *Augmentative and Alternative Communication: Management of Severe Communication Disorders in Children and Adults*. Baltimore: Paul H. Brookes.

Brush, J.A., & Camp, C.J. (1998). Spaced retrieval during dysphagia therapy: A case study. *The Clinical Gerontologist, 19*(2), 96–99.

Bryant, D.P., & Bryant, B.R. (1998). Using assistive technology adaptations to include students with learning disabilities in cooperative learning activities. *Journal of Learning Disabilities, 31*(1), 41–54.

Burke, J.M., Danick, J.A., Bernis, B., & Durgin, C.J. (1994). A process approach to memory book training for neurological patients. *Brain Injury, 8*(1), 71–81.

Carruth, E.K. (1997). The effects of singing and the spaced retrieval technique on improving face-name recognition in nursing home residents with memory loss. *Journal of Music Therapy, 34*(3), 165–186.

Cicerone, K.D. (2002). Remediation of "working attention" in mild traumatic brain injury. *Brain Injury*, *16*(3), 185–195.

Cicerone, K.D., & Giacino, J.T. (1992). Remediation of executive function deficits after traumatic brain injury. *Neuropsychological Rehabilitation*, *2*(3), 12–22.

Coelho, C.A., De Ruyter, F., & Stein, M. (1996). Treatment efficacy: Cognitive-communicative disorders resulting from traumatic brain injury in adults. *Journal of Speech and Hearing Research*, *39*, S5–S17.

Cole, E. (1999). Cognitive prosthetics: An overview to a method of treatment. *Neuro-Rehabilitation*, *12*, 39–51.

Cole, E., Dehdashti, P., Petti, L., & Angert, M. (1994). Design and outcomes of computer-based cognitive prosthetics for brain injury: A field study of three subjects. *Neuro-Rehabilitation*, *4*(3), 174–186.

Dawson, D., & Chipman, M. (1995). The disablement experienced by traumatically brain-injured adults living in the community. *Brain Injury*, *9*, 339–353.

Donaghy, S., & Williams, W. (1998). A new protocol for training severely impaired patients in the usage of memory journals. *Brain Injury*, *12*(12), 1061–1070.

Ducharme, J.M., & Spencer, T. (2001). Training brain injury rehabilitation therapists to use generalized teaching and interaction skills. *Brain Injury*, *15*(4), 333–347.

Engelmann, S.E., & Carnine, D.W. (1991). *Theory of Instruction*. Eugene, OR: Association for Direct Instruction.

Evans, J., Wilson, B.A., Needham, P., & Brentnall, S. (2003). Who makes good use of memory aids? Results of a survey of people with acquired brain injury. *Journal of the International Neuropsychological Society*, *9*, 925–935.

Evans, J.J., Wilson, B.A., Schuri, U., Andrade, J., Baddelely, A.D., Bruna, O., Canavan, T., Della Salla, S., Green, R., Laaksonen, R., Lorenzi, L., & Taussik, I. (2000). A comparison of "errorless" and "trial and error" learning methods for teaching individuals with acquired memory deficits. *Neuropsychological Rehabilitation*, *19*(1), 67–101.

Fleming, J., & Strong, J. (1995). Self-awareness of deficits following acquired brain injury: Considerations for rehabilitation. *British Journal of Occupational Therapy*, *58*, 55–60.

Fluharty, G., & Priddy, D. (1993). Methods of increasing client acceptance of a memory book. *Brain Injury*, *7*(1), 85–88.

Fozard, J.L., Rietsema, J., & Bouma, H. (2000). Gerontechnology: Creating enabling environments for the challenges and opportunities of aging. *Educational Gerontology*, *26*(4), 331–344.

Glang, A., Gersten, R., & Singer, G. (1990). Computer-assisted video instruction in training paraprofessionals to teach brain-damaged clients. *Journal of Special Education Technology*, *10*(3), 137–146.

Glang, A., Singer, G., Cooley, E., & Tish, N. (1992). Tailoring Direct Instruction techniques for use with elementary students with brain injury. *Journal of Head Trauma Rehabilitation*, *7*(4), 93–108.

Glisky, E.L., & Schacter, D.L. (1986). Remediation of organic memory disorders: Current status and future prospects. *Journal of Head Trauma Rehabilitation*, *19*, 54–63.

Glisky, E.L., Schacter, D.L., & Tulving, E. (1986). Learning and retention of computer-related vocabulary in amnesic patients: Method of vanishing cues. *Journal of Clinical and Experimental Neuropsychology*, *8*, 292–312.

Godfrey, H., & Knight, R. (1985). Cognitive rehabilitation of memory functioning in amnesic alcoholics. *Journal of Consulting and Clinical Psychology*, *43*, 555–557.

Hart, T., Hawkey, K., & Whyte, J. (2002). Use of a portable voice organizer to remember therapy goals in traumatic brain injury rehabilitation: A within-subjects trial. *Journal of Head Trauma Rehabilitation, 17*(6), 556–570.

Horner, R., McDonnell, J., & Bellamy, G. (1986). Teaching generalized skills: General case instruction in simulation and community settings. In R. Horner, L. Meyer, & H. Fredericks (Eds.), *Education of Learners with Severe Handicaps* (pp. 289–314). Baltimore: Paul H. Brookes.

Hunkin, N.M., Squires, E.J., Aldrich, F.K., & Parkin, A.J. (1998). Errorless learning and the acquisition of word processing skills. *Neuropsychological Rehabilitation, 8*(4), 433–449.

Hunkin, N.M., Squires, E.J., Parkin, A.J., & Tidy, J.A. (1998). Are the benefits of errorless learning dependent upon implicit memory? *Neuropsychologia, 36*(1), 25–26.

Kalla, T., Downes, J.J., & Van den Broek, M. (2001). The pre-exposure technique: Enhancing the effects of errorless learning in the acquisition of face–name associations. *Neuropsychological Rehabilitation, 11*(1), 1–16.

Kapur, N. (1995). Memory aids in the rehabilitation of memory disordered patients. In A.D. Baddelely, B.A. Wilson, & F.N. Watts (Eds.), *Handbook of Memory Disorders* (pp.   ). Chichester, England: Wiley.

Kaschel, R., Della Sala, S., Cantagallo, A., Fahbock, A., Laaksonen, R., & Kazen, M. (2002). Imagery mnemonics for the rehabilitation of memory: A randomized group controlled trial. *Neuropsychological Rehabilitation, 12*(2), 127–153.

Kennedy, M.R.T., Avery, J., Coelho, C., Sohlberg, M.M., Turkstra, L., Ylvisaker, M., et al. (2002). Evidence-based practice guidelines for cognitive-communication disorders after traumatic brain injury: Initial committee report. *Journal of Medical Speech-Language Pathology, 10*, ix–xiii.

Kennedy, M.R.T., Sohlberg, M.M., & Avery, J. (in progress). *Evidence-Based Guidelines for Memory Rehabilitation in Clients with Traumatic Brain Injury.* Project supported by ASHA Division 2 and ANCDS Evidence Based Practice Guidelines Project.

Kerns, K.A., & Thomson, J. (1998). Implementation of a compensatory memory system in a school age child with severe memory impairment. *Pediatric Rehabilitation, 2*(2), 77–87.

Kewman, D.G., Seigerman, C., Kinter, H., Chu, S., Henson, D., & Redder, C. (1985). Simulation training of psychomotor skills: Teaching the brain injured to drive. *Rehabilitation Psychology, 30*, 11–27.

Kim, H., Burke, D.T., Dowds, M., Boone, K.A., & Parks, G.J. (2000). Electronic memory aids for outpatient brain injury: Follow-up findings. *Brain Injury, 14*(2), 187–196.

Kim, H., Burke, D., Dowds, M., & George, J. (1999). Utility of a microcomputer as an external memory aid for a memory-impaired head injury patient during inpatient rehabilitation. *Brain Injury, 13*, 147–150.

Kime, S., Lamb, D., & Wilson, B. (1995). Use of a comprehensive program of external cueing to enhance procedural memory in a patient with dense amnesia. *Brain Injury, 10*, 17–25.

Kirsch, N.L., Levine, S.P., Fallon-Kreuger, M., & Jaros, L. (1987). The microcomputer as an "orthotic" device for patients with cognitive deficits. *Journal of Head Trauma Rehabilitation, 2*(4), 77–86.

Kirsch, N.L., Levine, S.P., Lajiness-O'Neill, R., & Schneider, M. (1992). Computer-assisted interactive task guidance: Facilitating the performance of a simulated vocational task. *Journal of Head Trauma Rehabilitation, 7*(3), 13–25.

Koegel, L.K., Koegel, R.L., & Dunlap, G. (1997). *Positive Behavioral Support: Including People with Difficult Behavior in the Community.* Baltimore: Paul H. Brookes.

Komatsu, S., Mimura, M., Kato, M., Wakamatsu, N., & Kashima, H. (2000). Errorless and effortful processes involved in the learning of face-name associations by patients with alcoholic Korsakoff's syndrome. *Neuropsychological Rehabilitation, 10*(2), 113–132.

Ledorze, G., & Brassard, C. (1995). A description of the consequences of aphasia on aphasic persons and their relatives and friends, based on the WHO model of chronic diseases. *Aphasiology, 9,* 239–255.

Levine, B., Roberston, I.H., Clare, K., Carter, G., Hong, J., Wilson, B.A., Duncan, J., & Stuss, D.T. (2000). Rehabilitation of executive functioning: An experimental-clinical validation of Goal Management Training. *Journal of the International Neuropsychological Society, 6,* 299–312.

LoPresti, E.F., Mihailidis, A., & Kirsch, N. (2004). Assistive technology for cognitive rehabilitation: State of the art. *Neuropsychological Rehabilitation, 14*(1/2), 5–39.

Lucyshyn, J.M., Nixon, C., Glang, A., & Cooley, E. (1996). Comprehensive family support for behavior change in children with ABI. In G.H.S. Singer, A. Glang, & J.M. Williams (Eds.), *Children with Acquired Brain Injury: Educating and Supporting Families.* Baltimore: Paul H. Brookes.

Lynch, W. (2002). Historical review of computer-assisted cognitive retraining. *Journal of Head Trauma Rehabilitation, 17*(5), 446–457.

Madigan, K., Hall, T., & Glang, A. (1997). Effective assessment and instructional practices for students with ABI. In A. Glang, G.H. Singer, & B. Todis (Eds.), *Students with Acquired Brain Injury* (pp. 123–160). Baltimore: Paul H. Brookes.

Milders, M.V., Berg, I.J., & Deelman, B.G. (1995). Four year follow up of a controlled memory training study in closed head injured patients. *Neuropsychological Rehabilitation, 5,* 223–238.

Mozzoni, M., & Bailey, J. (1996). Improving training methods in brain injury rehabilitation. *Journal of Head Trauma Rehabilitation, 11*(1), 1–17.

Napper, S.A., & Narayan, S. (1994). Cognitive orthotic shell. *Proceedings of the Rehabilitation Engineering Society of North America (RESNA)* (pp. 423–425). Arlington, VA.

Oberg, L., & Turkstra, L.S. (1998). Use of elaborative encoding to facilitate verbal learning after adolescent traumatic brain injury. *Journal of Head Trauma Rehabiltation, 13*(3), 44–62.

Ownsworth, T.L., & McFarland, K. (1999). Memory remediation in long-term acquired brain injury: Two approaches in diary training. *Brain Injury, 13*(8), 605–626.

Parente, R., & DiCesare, A. (1991). Retraining memory: Theory, evaluation and practice. In J.S. Kreutzer & P.E. Wehman (Eds.), *Cognitive Rehabilitation for Persons with Traumatic Brain Injury.* Baltimore: Paul H. Brookes

Prigatano, G., & Schacter, D. (1991). *Awareness of Deficit after Brain Injury: Theoretical and Clinical Implications.* New York: Oxford University Press.

Raskin, S.A., & Sohlberg, M.M. (1996). The efficacy of prospective memory training in two adults with brain injury. *Journal of Head Trauma Rehabilitation, 11*(3), 32–51.

Robey, R. (2001). CEU part III: Evidence-based practice. *ASHA Special Interest Division 2 Newsletter, 11*(1), 10–15.

Schacter, D., Rich, S., & Stampp, A. (1985). Remediation of memory disorders: Experimental evaluation of the spaced-retrieval technique. *Journal of Clinical and Experimental Neuropsychology, 7,* 79–96.

Scherer, M.J. (Ed.). (2002). *Assistive Technology: Matching Device and Consumer for Succesful Rehabilitation.* Washington, DC: American Psychological Association.

Schmitter-Edgecombe, M., Fahy, J., Whelan, J., & Long, C. (1995). Memory remediation after severe closed head injury. Notebook training versus supportive therapy. *Journal of Consulting Clinical Psychology, 63*, 484–489.

Smith, G. (1999). Teaching a long sequence of behavior using whole task training, forward chaining, and backward chaining. *Perceptual and Motor Skills, 89*, 951–965.

Sohlberg, M.M. (2002). An overview of approaches for managing attention impairments. In M.R.T. Kennedy (Issue Ed.), *Perspectives on Neurophysiology and Neurogenic Speech and Language Disorders, 12*(3), 4–8.

Sohlberg, M.M., Avery, J., Kennedy, M., Ylvisaker, M., Coelho, C., Turkstra, L., & Yorkston, K. (2003). Practice guidelines for direct attention training. *Journal of Medical Speech Language Pathology, 11*(3), xix–xxxix.

Sohlberg, M.M., Ehlhardt, E., Fickas, S., & Sutcliff, A. (2003). A pilot study exploring electronic mail in users with acquired cognitive-linguistic impairments. *Brain Injury, 17*(7), 609–629.

Sohlberg, M.M., & Mateer, C.A. (1989). Training the use of compensatory memory books: A three stage behavioral approach. *Journal of Clinical and Experimental Neuropsychology, 11*, 871–891.

Sohlberg, M.M., & Mateer, C.A. (2001). *Cognitive Rehabilitation: A Neuropsychological Perspective*. New York: Guildford Press.

Sohlberg, M.M., McLaughlin, K.A., Todis, B., Larsen, J., & Glang, A. (2001). What does it take to collaborate with families affected by brain injury: A preliminary model. *Journal of Head Trauma Rehabilitation, 16*(5), 498–511.

Sohlberg, M.M., White, O., Evans, E., & Mateer, C.A. (1992). An investigation into the effects of prospective memory training. *Brain Injury, 6*(2), 139–154.

Spooner, F., & Spooner, D. (1984). A review of chaining techniques: Implications for future research and practice. *Education and training of the mentally retarded, 19*, 114–124.

Squires, E.J., Hunkin, N.M., & Parkin, A.J. (1997). Erroless learning of novel associations in amnesia. *Neuropsychologia, 1*, 117–134.

Steele, R.D., Weinrich, M., & Carlson, G.S. (1989). Recipe preparation by a severely impaired aphasic using the VIC 2.0 interface. *Proceedings of the Rehabilitation Engineering Society of North America (RESNA)* (pp. 218–219). Arlington, VA.

Stein, M.S., Carnine, D., & Dixon, R. (1998). Direct instruction: Integrating curriculum design and effective teaching practice. *Intervention in School and Clinic, 33*(4), 227–234.

Swanson, H.L. (1999). Instructional components that predict treatment outcomes for students with learning disabilities: Support for the combined strategy and Direct Instruction Model. *Learning Disabilities Research and Practice, 14*(3), 129–140.

Swanson, H.L., & Hoskyn, M. (1998). A synthesis of experimental intervention literature for students with learning disabilities: A meta-analysis of treatment outcomes. *Review of Educational Research, 68*, 277–321.

Swanson, H.L., & Hoskyn, M. (2001). Instructing adolescents with learning disabilities: A component and composite analysis. *Learning Disabilities Research and Practice, 16*(2), 109–119.

Tackett, S.L., Rice, D.A., Rice, J.C., & Butterbaugh, G.J. (2001). Using a palmtop PDA for reminding in prospective memory deficit. *Proceedings of the Rehabilitation Engineering Society of North America (RESNA)* (pp. 23–25). Arlington, VA:

van den Broek, M.D., Downes, J., Johnson, Z., Dayus, B., & Hilton, N. (2000). Evaluation of an electronic memory aid in the neuropsychological rehabilitation of prospective memory deficits. *Brain Injury, 14*(5), 455–462.

von Cramon, D.Y., & Matthes-von Cramon, G. (1994). Back to work with a chronic dysexecutive syndrome: A case report. *Neuropsychological Rehabilitation*, *4*, 399–417.

Wade, T., & Troy, J. (2001). Mobile phones as a new memory aid: A preliminary investigation using case studies. *Brain Injury*, *15*(4), 305–320.

Weiss-Lambrou, R. (2002). Satisfaction and comfort. In M.J. Scherer (Ed.), *Assistive Technology: Matching Device and Consumer for Successful Rehabilitation* (pp. 77–94). Washington, DC: American Psychological Association.

Wilson, B.A. (1995). Management and remediation of memory problems in brain injured adults. In A.D. Baddeley, B.A. Wilson, & F.N. Watts (Eds.), *Handbook of Memory Disorders* (pp. 451–480). Chichester, England: Wiley.

Wilson, B.A., Baddeley, A.B., Evans, J., & Shiel, A. (1994). Errorless learning in the rehabilitation of memory impaired people. *Neuropsychological Rehabilitation*, *4*(3), 307–326.

Wilson, B.A., Emslie, H.C., Quirk, K., & Evans, J.J. (2001). Reducing everyday memory and planning problems by means of a paging system: A randomised control crossover study. *Journal of Neurology, Neurosurgery, and Psychiatry, 70*(4), 477–482.

Wilson, B.A., Evans, J.J., Emslie, H., & Malinek, V. (1997). Evaluation of NeuroPage: A new memory aid. *Journal of Neurology, Neurosurgery, and Psychiatry, 63*, 113–115.

Wilson, B.A., & Moffat, N. (Eds.) (1992). *Clinical Management of Memory Problems.* San Diego, CA: Singular.

Wilson, B.A., & Watson, P.C. (1996). A practical framework for understanding compensatory behavior in people with organic memory impairment. *Memory*, *4*, 465–486.

Wright, P., Rogers, N., Hall, C., Wilson, B., Evans, J., Emslie, H., & Bartram, C. (2001). Comparison of pocket-computer memory aids for people with brain injury. *Brain Injury*, *15*(9), 787–800.

Yasuda, K., Misu, T., Beckman, B., Watanabe, O., Ozawa, Y., & Nakamura, T. (2002). Use of an IC recorder as voice output memory aid for patients with prospective memory impairment. *Neuropsychological Rehabilitation*, *12*(2), 155–166.

Ylvisaker, M., Coelho, C., Kennedy, M., Sohlberg, M.M., Turkstra, L., Avery, J., & Yorkston, K. (2003). Reflections on evidence-based practice and rational clinical decision making. *Journal of Medical Speech-Language Pathology*, *10*(3), xxv–xxxiii.

Ylvisaker, M., & Feeney, T. (1998). *Collaborative Brain Injury Intervention: Positive Everyday Routines.* San Diego, CA: Singular.

Ylvisaker, M., Hanks, R., & Johnson-Greene, D. (2003). Rehabilitation of children and adults with cognitive-communication disorders after brain injury. *ASHA Supplement*, *23*, 59–72.

Zenicus, A., Wesolowski, M.D., & Burke, W.H. (1991). Memory notebook training with traumatically brain-injured clients. *Brain Injury*, *5*, 321–325.

Zicht, M.S. (1992). The community integration of individuals with severe traumatic brain injury. *Dissertation Abstracts International.*

5

Rehabilitation of Executive Function Impairments

KEITH D. CICERONE

Disturbances of executive functioning (e.g., planning, self-monitoring, behavioral and emotional self-regulation) are common after traumatic brain injury (TBI) and represent significant obstacles to resuming social participation and productivity. Executive dysfunction also represents a challenge to the rehabilitation process. In many cases, remedial interventions for acquired cognitive impairments often emphasize the acquisition of specific compensations in controlled situations. Responsibility for the selection and application of compensatory strategies may initially rest with the therapist, with the assumption that the patient will be capable of implementing these compensations independently with adequate practice. In contrast, disturbances of executive functioning are most likely to be evident when the patient is required to assume responsibility for the application of compensatory strategies (Shallice & Burgess, 1991) or to cope with novel situations (Godefrey & Rousseaux, 1997). Disturbances of executive functioning often coexist with impaired self-awareness, representing an additional challenge to rehabilitation. The prevalence of executive function disturbance after TBI is probably associated with the frequency of frontal lobe involvement after TBI. The concepts of frontal lobe function and executive functioning have been intimately related, and discussion of the nature of executive function impairments relies on the analysis of frontal lobe function and dysfunction. (It should also be noted that disturbances of executive functioning can be seen without observable frontal lobe damage, and with various forms of focal or diffuse damage throughout the cerebral axis.) An adequate conceptualization of the nature of executive abilities, and their dissolution, is critical to the development of effective therapeutic interventions.

THE NATURE OF EXECUTIVE FUNCTION IMPAIRMENTS

The modern concept of *executive function* can be traced to Teuber (1964), who noted that neurologic concepts of cerebral functioning had typically relied on descriptions of the afferent organization of the nervous system, with an emphasis on the sensory to motor connections. In contrast, Teuber proposed that the critical function of the frontal lobes was maintained through a process of "corollary discharge—i.e., a discharge from motor to sensory structures—that prepares the sensory structures for an anticipated change." In this view, all voluntary behavior involved two neural correlates, the activation of impulses to the effector organs and a simultaneous corollary discharge to central neural receptors that preset these receptors for the detection of changes occurring as a result of the particular behavior. According to Teuber, then, "it is not in the reaction to incoming stimuli, *but in the prediction of them . . .* that the significance of frontal structures lies" (emphasis added). The corollary discharge therefore establishes an internal representation of behavior independent of the external response, and also establishes a feedback mechanism and allows for the monitoring of discrepancies among intentions, actions, and behavioral outcomes (Fink et al., 1999). While most prior concepts of frontal lobe function invoked *sensationalist* constructs, such as *will*, Teuber's description of corollary discharge provided a neurophysiologic mechanism that could serve as the basis for intentional behavior, and for the disturbances of volitional behavior that appeared to characterize lesions of the frontal lobes.

Luria (1966) viewed the effects of frontal lobe injury as a disturbance in the conscious and volitional self-regulation of behavior. Disruption of the capacity for self-regulation after neurologic injury is likely to result in two basic symptoms: loss of intentionality, manifested by decreased spontaneity or initiative, and loss of a critical attitude toward one's own behavior, manifested as a deficiency in matching one's actions with the original intention. According to Luria, the formulation of an internalized plan of action and subsequent self-regulation of behavior are accomplished through the verbal mediation of purposeful activity. This *inner speech*, while distinct from the communicative function of speech, acquires its directive function through the act of progressive speech internalization. Through normal development, the initially overt, expanded form of speech becomes abbreviated, evolving into self-directed *whispered speech*. Gradually, this speech becomes covert and internalized and takes on a planning and self-regulatory role "between the general intention to solve a problem and its concrete solution" (Luria, 1981). In describing the effects of frontal lobe lesions, Luria (1966) also noted that the more primitive or reflexive forms of behavior were left intact or even enhanced. Lhermitte (1986) also provided extensive descriptions of the release of automatic behaviors after the development of frontal lobe lesions, particularly with lesion of the orbitofrontal region.

The supervisory role of the frontal lobes, as well as the potential for release of automatic or habitual behaviors after development of frontal lobe lesions, are central to the influential model of executive functioning developed by Shallice (1981). In this model, there are two levels of neuropsychological control over behavioral schemata. *Routine* control can be accomplished through contention scheduling, based on the habitual activation of schemata in response to invariant or overlearned environmental contingencies. The supervisory-executive system represents a second level of voluntary, *strategic* control that is necessary when planning is required, when the correction of unexpected errors is required, when the appropriate responses are novel or not well learned, or when habitual responses and schemata need to be inhibited. Impairments of the supervisory system result in heightened expression of lower-level habitual schemata while reducing the ability to initiate more highly adaptive responses. An improvement in executive functioning due to facilitation of the supervisory-executive control process would be expected to result in two types of change. First, patients should show enhanced performance on tasks requiring novel problem solving and error correction. Second, there should be an improved ability to inhibit the release of inappropriate responses.

Duncan (1986) noted that a fundamental aspect of executive dysfunction was the loss of "control of action by its desired results." He suggested that most behavior is under the control of a particular set of goals, and that these goals elicit the relevant actions from a large potential store of (covert and overt) actions. Through a process of means–end analysis, the result of each action is evaluated in order to detect differences between the current state and the goal state, and this process continues to elicit actions until the mismatch between the current and goal states is reduced to zero. As a consequence of frontal lobe damage, this typical structure of goal-directed behavior is disrupted and behavior therefore loses its purposeful character. This formulation relied explicitly on the work of Luria (1966; Luria et al., 1964) and Shallice (1982). Duncan and colleagues (1996) also noted that patients with frontal lobe damage may exhibit relative preservation of verbal knowledge but the failure of this knowledge to guide behavior through the activation of the appropriate goals and actions (Luria, 1966; Milner, 1963). This tendency to disregard the requirements of a given task, even when these are verbally appreciated, represented a fundamental aspect of executive dysfunction, referred to as *goal neglect.*

REMEDIATION OF EXECUTIVE FUNCTION IMPAIRMENTS

For this review, I identified 17 peer-reviewed journal articles addressing the remediation of disturbances of executive functioning, involving a total of 84 clinical participants. These studies included primarily participants with TBI, although several studies included persons with executive function deficits due to other neurologic conditions. I did not include articles that were primarily clinical case descriptions, those that were primarily experimental manipulations, or those addressing primarily behavioral disturbance (e.g., verbal outbursts) rather than cognitive impairments after TBI. There are three prospective, randomized, controlled (Class I) studies of the rehabilitation of executive function deficits involving a total of 62 participants receiving the treatment under study and 54 participants who received an alternative form of intervention. There have been two additional small (Class II) studies that either used an untreated comparison group or used the treatment subjects as their own control, involving a total of nine participants. Nine additional studies evaluated interventions for executive functioning deficits of 13 participants using single-subject methodologies and one group study of 21 patients without a control group (Class III designs).

Class I Studies

The three randomized, controlled trials of executive function remediation all used training in a formal problem-solving algorithm. Von Cramon et al. (1991) used a problem-solving intervention intended to facilitate patients' ability to reduce the complexity of a multistage problem by breaking it down into manageable subgoals. Training was provided to 37 subjects with brain damage of various etiologies, who were identified as poor problem solvers on formal tests of planning and response regulation. Twenty participants received an intervention directed at remediation of executive function deficits, and 17 participants received an alternative intervention consisting of memory retraining. The experimental intervention was based on five aspects of problem solving (D'Zurilla & Goldfried, 1971) and included training in problem orientation, problem definition and formulation, generation of alternatives, decision making, and solution verification. Compared with participants who received the alternative treatment directed at memory training, those who received the problem-solving training demonstrated significant gains on measures of planning ability, as well as improvement on behavioral ratings of executive dysfunction, such as awareness of cognitive deficits, goal-directed ideas, and problem-solving ability.

   Levine, Robertson, and colleagues (2000) developed a formalized intervention for executive dysfunction, referred to as *goal management training* (GMT), based on Duncan's (1986, 1996) theory of goal neglect. The process of GMT involves five discrete stages of what is essentially a general purpose problem-solving algorithm similar to that employed by von Cramen et al. (1991). In stage one, participants are trained to evaluate the current state of affairs and relevant goals ("What am I doing?"). The relevant goals are selected in stage two (the *main task*) and further partitioned into subgoals in the third stage (the *steps*). In stage four, participants are assisted with the learning and retention of goals and subgoals ("Do I know the steps?"). In the fifth stage, participants are taught to self-monitor the results of their actions in regard to the intended goal state ("Am I doing what I planned to do?"), and in the event of a mismatch the entire process is repeated.

Thirty patients with mild to severe TBI were randomly assigned to receive either a brief trial of GMT or an alternative treatment of motor skills training. The GMT consisted of a single session in which participants were instructed to apply the problem-solving algorithm to two functional tasks (proofreading and room layout) that involved keeping goals in mind, analyzing subgoals, and monitoring outcomes. Patients in the motor skills training condition practiced reading and tracing mirror-reversed text and designs; a trainer provided general instruction and encouragement, but the treatment procedure did not include any processes related to GMT. Treatment effectiveness was assessed on several paper-and-pencil tasks that resembled the training tasks and were intended to simulate the kinds of unstructured everyday situations that might elicit goal management deficits. Participants who received the GMT demonstrated significant reduction in errors and prolonged time to task completion (presumably reflecting increased care and attention to the tasks) on two of the three outcome measures following the intervention.

The entire treatment in this study consisted of 1 hour of intervention, which may be adequate to suggest the putative efficacy of GMT but provides little evidence of its clinical effectiveness. Levine, Robertson, et al. (2000) did describe the use of GMT with a single postencephalitic patient seeking to improve her meal preparation abilities. The treatment consisted of two sessions of GMT, supplemented by exercises involving recipes, real-life cooking exercises in her home, homework assignments, and use of a checklist during meal preparation over 13 sessions. Naturalistic observation and self-report suggested that the patient experience fewer difficulties during meal preparations following the training.

Rath and his colleagues (2003) evaluated the effectiveness of an *innovative* group treatment focused on the treatment of problems-solving deficits ($n = 27$) compared with a *conventional* neuropsychological group treatment ($n = 19$) for patients with TBI. The participants were selected from a large outpatient neuropsychological rehabilitation program as being "higher functioning" but with documented, persistent impairments in social/vocational functioning (e.g., job loss, marital difficulties) an average of 4 years postinjury. Both groups received 2 to

3 hours of small-group intervention per week for 24 weeks. The conventional treatment consisted of group exercises intended to improve cognitive skills and support for coping with emotional reactions and changes after injury. The innovative problem-solving intervention focused on the development of emotional self-regulation strategies as the basis for maintaining an effective problem orientation, along with a *clear thinking* component that included cognitive-behavioral training in problem-solving skills (similar to the D'Zurrila and Goldfried approach), a systematic process for analyzing real-life problems, and role play of real-life examples of problem situations. Both groups showed significant improvement of their memory functioning after treatment. Only the problem-solving group treatment resulted in significant beneficial effects on measures of executive functioning, self-appraisal of clear thinking, self-appraisal of emotional self-regulation, and objective observer ratings of interpersonal problem-solving behaviors in naturalistic simulations. These gains were maintained at 6 months after treatment but did not translate into significant improvements on a measure of community integration.

The study by Rath et al. (2003) is particularly noteworthy in two regards. First, the inclusion of a treatment component directed specifically at patients' developing improved emotional self-regulation in the context of the cognitive intervention is innovative, and is particularly relevant to the clinical treatment of patients with executive function deficits after TBI. Second, the study included observations of participants' actual interpersonal behaviors in naturalistic situations. Given the lack of an established relationship between psychometric measures of executive functioning and everyday behaviors, and the well-known potential for dissociation between verbal and behavioral responses after frontal lobe damage, the use of real-life behavioral observations to assess treatment outcomes is well advised.

Class II Studies

Fox et al. (1989) conducted a small observational study of remediation for impaired "real-life" problem-solving skills. The treatment consisted of cuing and feedback to develop effective problem solutions, using verbal analogs of problem situations in four general areas of everyday life relevant to community placement and adjustment (e.g., community awareness and transportation, using medications, and responding to emergency situations). Training was provided to three participants with TBI in a residential rehabilitation facility; three subjects in the same facility served as untreated controls. Throughout the course of training, appropriate verbal responses to analogous problem situations showed significant increases. The participants who received the treatment also demonstrated generalization to simulated interactions conducted in the natural environment, while the performance of the untreated subjects was essentially unchanged. The use of ecologically relevant problems and situational simulations in this area of cognitive remediation appears promising.

Several studies have attempted to remediate executive function impairments through the development and internalization of strategies for effective self-regulation. Luria and Homskaya (1964) noted that simply having the patient repeat the task instruction is insufficient to reestablish self-regulation. Cicerone and Giacino (1992) used a modification of Meichenbaum and Goodman's (1971) self-instructional training procedure to encourage planning and self-monitoring while inhibiting inappropriate behaviors. The training procedure included three stages of self-verbalization, progressing from overt verbalization, through faded verbal self-instruction, to covert verbal mediation of appropriate responses. This study replicated an earlier single case study (Cicerone & Wood, 1987) and described the results of treatment with six patients in a multiple baseline across-subjects design. All of the participants had documented frontal lobe damage, five due to TBI and one due to a falx meningioma. The participants were all at least 1 year since the onset of their injury or illness, and all had evidence of damage to the frontal lobes (although this anatomic information was not a criterion for inclusion in the treatment study). The patients were selected for the intervention because they exhibited impaired planning and self-monitoring on the basis of family observations and therapist reports, as well as evidence of impaired performance on at least one of three neuropsychological measures of executive functioning. Treatment was again delivered in three stages to promote the progressive internalization of verbal self-regulation, as described above. Five of the six patients showed marked reduction in task-related errors and perseverative responses, suggesting that the effectiveness of training was related to their improved ability to inhibit inappropriate responses.

Class III Studies

Ownsworth and coworkers (2000a) evaluated a group intervention directed at improving participants' self-regulation abilities and self-awareness. Participants receiving the treatment consisted of 21 patients with acquired brain injury (16 with TBI). Sixteen patients had documented frontal lobe damage, and all exhibited severe cognitive impairments and poor self-awareness an average of 8.6 years after injury. The intervention incorporated elements of problem-solving training, role plays, and training in compensatory strategies over a 16-week period. Following treatment, participants exhibited reliable clinical improvement on measures reflecting their knowledge and use of self-regulatory strategies, and the self-rated effectiveness of strategies in their daily functioning, and these gains were maintained after 6 months.

Several interventions directed at improving patients' ability to self-monitor their behavior have been described. A number of these have relied explicitly on training participants in the use of verbal self-regulation strategies. As mentioned above, Cicerone and Wood (1987) used a self-instructional training procedure with a patient with traumatic frontal lobe damage who exhibited executive dysfunction (*planning disorder*) 4 years postinjury. The initial period of self-instructional treatment was provided in three stages over an 8-week period, followed by 12 weeks of treatment to promote the application of self-regulation strategies in the patient's everyday functioning. Over the initial course of self-instructional training, there was a dramatic reduction in task-related errors, as well as more gradual reduction and eventual cessation of off-task behaviors. Generalization to the patient's functional real-life behaviors was observed only with additional instruction and practice in the application and self-monitoring of the verbal mediation strategy to his everyday behaviors. Sohlberg et al. (1988) treated a patient with traumatic frontal lobe damage who exhibited decreased initiation and range of affect. The therapist provided the patient with intermittent external cues (such as placing an index card in front of the subject with an instruction to initiate conversation), which placed little demand on internal self-monitoring, to increase verbal initiation and response acknowledgments. Both behaviors increased during application of the external cueing procedure; the patient's verbal initiation decreased when cueing was withdrawn, although the level remained above baseline.

Alderman and colleagues (1995) used a program of prompts and rewards to enable a patient to exert control over inappropriate behaviors through increased self-monitoring. This was effective in reducing the frequency of inappropriate behaviors in both the treatment and community environments. Of interest, the greatest effect of treatment occurred when external prompts and rewards were withdrawn and the patient was responsible for independent self-monitoring. There have been several attempts to remediate executive function deficits through the combined prediction and self-monitoring of behaviors, with the implicit objective of establishing an expectation that enables patients to compare the predicted and actual results of their behavior.

Cicerone and Giacino (1992) described the use of a prediction paradigm in two patients with TBI, both of whom exhibited chronic difficulties in social functioning over a year after their injuries. Both patients performed well on formal neuropsychological measures of executive functioning and were capable of functioning independently in performing fundamental activities of daily living, but exhibited poor judgment and difficulties in social functioning due to their apparent inability to anticipate the detrimental effects of their behavior. The training procedure consisted of having the patients predict the steps required for different versions of a problem-solving task, varying randomly in their complexity. Verbal feedback was provided for incorrect predictions, and the subject again predicted the steps required for a solution. There was a significant overall increase in response latencies when the patients were required to predict their results, with the increased response latencies most apparent for the more complex trials. In addition, response latencies were correlated with response complexity, a relationship that was not evident prior to treatment, suggesting that the amount of cognitive processing was now proportionate to problem difficulty. Two additional studies of patients with TBI suggest that having subjects predict their task performance and providing them with tangible feedback may reduce discrepancies between their predicted and actual performance (Rebmann & Hannon, 1995; Youngjohn & Altman, 1989). In both of these latter studies, the primary effect of the intervention was related to modification of patients' predictions rather than a change in actual task performance, suggesting an impact on their self-monitoring and appraisal.

These interventions all emphasized the need for patients to anticipate and monitor the outcomes of their behavior. In most cases, the goal of remediation was not the training of task-specific performance, but the training and internalization of regulatory cognitive processes. In contrast, Evans et al. (1998) evaluated the use of an external cueing-monitoring system (NeuroPage) and a paper-and-pencil checklist in the rehabilitation of executive problems following anterior stroke. The subject had difficulty with timely initiation of intended actions despite having relatively preserved memory functioning. External cueing and monitoring were useful in increasing the probability that she would successfully initiate and complete specific tasks as part of her daily routine, with no attempt to remediate her executive functioning per se. Burke and colleagues (1991) have also described the effective use of external compensatory strategies to support patients' performance of relevant functional tasks (e.g., checklists for cueing and monitoring completion of job steps).

FUNDAMENTAL QUESTIONS FOR FUTURE RESEARCH

Future research in this area will need to address three fundamental issues involving (1) specification of the interventions used; (2) specification of the patient samples, including more precise identification of the executive function components targeted for intervention; and (3) specification of outcomes that are congruent with the intended effects of the interventions and reflect patient-centered results of treatment.

Specification of Interventions

Much of the literature regarding cognitive rehabilitation after TBI has failed to provide adequate descriptions of the interventions under investigation. This is a significant barrier to evaluating the effectiveness of treatment, replicating interventions across studies, and translating research into clinically effective practice. In this regard, the published studies on rehabilitation of executive functioning have been relatively strong. The three randomized, controlled studies in this area have all used problem-solving interventions. While there are differences among the specific interventions used in these studies, the interventions are similar enough to allow replication in future research as well as the clinical application of these treatment protocols. One difference among the protocols that does merit further study concerns the extent to which the problem-solving tasks used in treatment are veridical with real-life problem situations, particularly as this might relate to generalization of treatment. Attempts to restore effective executive functioning must address not only the cognitive aspects of behavior, but the emotional and social aspects as well. The incorporation of an additional treatment component directed at emotional self-regulation (Rath et al., 2003) merits further investigation.

Interventions intended to remediate executive function impairments through the development and internalization of strategies for effective self-regulation have been addressed primarily in single-subject studies. Further validation of these interventions will require evaluation of their efficacy using more rigorous research designs. The potential utility of internal compensations, compared with reliance on external cueing and environmental compensations, also needs to be addressed in future research. It is likely that the relative effectiveness of internal versus external compensations will be related to differences in patient characteristics. Ultimately, the evaluation of effectiveness of specific interventions must address the question of which interventions work for which patients.

Specifications of Participants and Impairments

Future studies should provide greater specification regarding the patient samples and the nature of the impairments being addressed. Relevant patient characteristics might include the presence and location of focal cerebral injuries, the nature and severity of executive dysfunction, and the presence of comorbid cognitive impairments. For example, two case descriptions suggest that patients with orbitofrontal damage may be both less likely to exhibit impairments on standard testing and more refractory to treatment. Von Cramon and Matthes-von Cramon (1994) described the treatment of a physician with bilateral orbitofrontal trauma resulting in decreased social behavior. The patient's difficulties were attributed to an inability to use subtle social signals and monitor the effect of his behavior on others, as well as an inability to use his preserved knowledge to organize his behavior. The treatment consisted of training on a formal problem-solving algorithm, as described in these authors' group study. This algorithm was applied to the patient's ability to make accurate histopathologic diagnoses. Initially, the therapist, who provided the patient with an invariant set of questions to guide his behavior, guided these rules externally. External guidance was gradually replaced by overt self-instruction and internal guidance until the patient could work alone. Following treatment, the authors noted that the patient was able to use a routinized external structure to improve *specific behaviors in the situations in which they had been trained*, but this improvement was not apparent in novel situations and he continued to generally overestimate his level of intellectual competence.

Cicerone and Tanenbaum (1997) reported a case of impaired social cognition following traumatic orbitofrontal injury, which included efforts to rehabilitate the patent's neuropsychological functioning. The patient exhibited pathologic laughter and crying, rigidity, and "obsessive" behaviors during the course of her daily homemaking activities, as well as increased sensitivity to feedback or criticism, which had resulted in increasingly frequent arguments and interpersonal conflicts with her family. Although many standard tests of executive function were within normal limits, she demonstrated significant impairments in her ability to interpret nonverbal interpersonal interactions, to understand the meaning of social exchanges in different contexts, and to predict the most likely consequences of social situations. During the course of her treatment, she exhibited an inability to inhibit socially inappropriate behaviors or to appreciate an alternative perspective. She was able to acknowledge these behaviors when viewed on videotape, and was able to modify her behavior when external cues were present. However, she remained unable to internalize these constraints in order to guide her behavior. She had particular difficulty using subtle cues arising from social interactions, and she remained largely unable to monitor her behavior in real-life interactions. Although she benefited from tangible cues to signal her behavior (such as direct instruction or prompting from the therapist), she was unable to use her own emotional states or feelings of cognitive dissonance to guide her behavior. Her attempts to control her behavior, such as her pathologic laughing and her verbal tangentiality, often involved the suppression of almost all spontaneous behavior. Following nearly 9 months of treatment, she exhibited persistent functional impairments in monitoring and controlling her emotional responses, and she continued to exhibit a profound impairment in her social functioning. Evaluation of this patient's treatment suggests that she was able to benefit from explicit feedback concerning her social and emotional behavior in specific situations, and this enabled her to correct her mistakes and produce the appropriate response in those situations. However, in novel real-life situations, she remained unable to appreciate the subtle social cues required to guide her behavior effectively, and she appeared unable to monitor her own emotional responses or to acknowledge the socially inappropriate aspects of her behavior.

These latter two cases suggest that patients with disturbances of social cognition after the development of orbitofrontal lesions may improve their functioning through the establishment of specific competencies, but there is little evidence for the effectiveness of treatments designed to allow them to regain the ability to integrate and respond fully to the subtle complexities and nuances of the social environment. In these cases, the training of relatively stable and invariant behavioral routines may allow patients to function in specific situations in the absence of higher-order executive functioning. Lengfelder and Gollwitzer (2001) noted that the automatic control of habitual behavior remains relatively intact after frontal lobe damage. They argued that patients with frontal lobe dysfunction might therefore benefit from linking situational cues to goal-directed behavior through the use of *implementation intentions* (e.g., "if situation y arises, I will perform the goal-directed behavior z") that do not require conscious deliberation. Among 34 patients with frontal or nonfrontal brain injuries, implementation intentions were found to improve the efficiency of reactions on a dual task. Several additional studies have suggested that patients who are unable to develop compensations that allow them to regulate their own behavior might benefit from modifications to their environment such as external cuing and stimulus control (Burke et al., 1991; Evans et al., 1998; Manly et al., 2002).

While it is commonly assumed that executive function deficits are common in certain types of neurologic illness, such as TBI, our ability to demonstrate the effectiveness of interventions will undoubtedly be diluted if interventions are conducted without adequate specification of samples. For example, participants were selected for the study "because of the prevalence of goal management deficits in patients with TBI" (Levine, Robertson, et al., 2000). While this may be clinically true, as a research criterion, it is somewhat akin to assessing the effectiveness of an aphasia intervention for all patients with left hemisphere stroke "because of the prevalence of aphasia" following lateralized stroke. Levine, Robertson, et al. did indicate that their sample, as a group, was impaired on a measure of executive functioning relative to normal controls; however, they did not indicate the degree of variability of impairment in their sample on this measure. This may be a critical element in assessing the effectiveness of an intervention. For example, Lengfelder and Gollwitzer (2001) did not find differences in the effect of treatment based on whether patients had frontal or nonfrontal lesions, but they did detect a marked difference in treatment effects according to whether or not the patients had impaired performances on measures of planning and self-regulation.

Continued refinements to the concept of executive functioning will clearly impact on clinical and methodological issues in rehabilitation. Efforts to *fractionate* the functioning of the frontal lobes, at both the neurophysiologic and neuropsychological levels, are likely to result in more precise formulations of the nature and subtypes of executive dysfunction (e.g., Burgess et al., 1998). Even with our present knowledge, it is critical to tailor the intervention to the nature of the deficit. For example, at a basic level, disturbances of executive function can be char-

acterized as both negative behaviors (e.g., apathy, adynamia, loss of abstract attitude) and behaviors of excess (e.g., disinhibition, lability, perseveration), and there
is little evidence to indicate which interventions are more appropriate for which
deficit areas. The need to target interventions to specific problem behaviors will
increase as we become better able to define the nature of executive impairments,
and is likely to be a critical factor in determining the efficacy of different interventions. It is worth investing in well-controlled studies of single subjects or small
series of patients to identify specific interventions effective for specific impairments prior to conducting larger-scale investigations.

While impairments of executive functioning might be considered as a fundamental, profound loss of self-regulation and autonomy, the development of interventions for subtler high-level impairments of executive functioning merits further
consideration and investigation. In clinical practice, patients with mild TBI are
sometimes believed to exhibit such higher-level executive impairments. This belief appears to be based primarily on their subjective complaints of difficulty with
attention regulation and organization of multiple task demands. Certainly, caution is advised with regard to accepting popular notions that "underachievers may
suffer from neurologic abnormalities affecting the brain's executive functions"
(Saltus, 2003). However, there is some empirical evidence to suggest that relatively subtle impairments in the *central executive* component of working memory,
identified through impaired functioning with dual-task demands, are related to
behavioral indices of executive dysfunction (Baddeley et al., 1997; Cicerone,
1996). There is also evidence that interventions derived from, and directed at, the
central executive component of working memory can be effective in remediating
the subjective and objective attention difficulties in patients with mild TBI (Cicerone, 2002).

Specification of Outcomes

There is a need for continued development of appropriate outcome measures and
efforts to ensure that interventions translate into meaningful changes in real-world
functioning. While this is true for all aspects of brain injury rehabilitation, it may
be particularly salient in the area of executive functioning given the potential discrepancy between performance on laboratory measures and indices of real-life
performance. Fortunately, there appears to be continuing development of both
laboratory (e.g., Levine, Dawson, et al., 2000) and clinical (e.g., Bamdad et al.,
2003; Ownsworth et al., 2000b) assessment procedures.

At a more basic level, impairments of executive functioning represent a distinct challenge to effective rehabilitation. Most current studies of cognitive rehabilitation rely on the teaching and reinforcement of compensatory strategies for
underlying deficits. This appears to be true whether the deficits are defined in the

domain of attention, memory, perception, language, or social functioning. Disturbances of executive functioning, however, impact on the very ability to select and apply strategies in the shifting contexts of everyday functioning. Among patients being treated for memory deficits, the presence of comorbid executive function impairments has been shown to reduce the use (Wilson & Watson, 1996) and effectiveness (Evans et al., 2003) of compensatory memory strategies. Thus, executive function impairments are likely to impact the success of rehabilitation across a wide range of functional abilities. Attempts to evaluate the effectiveness of interventions using naturalistic observations and/or simulations of participants' behavior in real-life situations (e.g., Fox et al., 1989; Rath et al., 2003) should be considered in future research.

A number of studies have suggested that the benefits of treatment for executive dysfunction can be maintained for 6 months after treatment (Ownsworth et al., 2000a; Rath et al., 2003). There is limited evidence regarding the generalization of treatment to functional settings, although there is some suggestion that generalization is enhanced when the relationship between the intervention and its application in functional situations is made explicit (Cicerone & Wood, 1987; Fox et al., 1989). Disturbances of executive functioning after TBI represent a significant obstacle to social integration and productivity (Hanks et al., 1999; Simpson & Schmitter-Edgecombe, 2002). However, none of the treatment studies conducted so far have demonstrated that our interventions in this area of functioning are translated into improvements at this level of outcome. Future research will need to formally assess the effects of interventions on community integration and social participation, and this may require us to develop additional patient-centered outcome measures. Efforts to demonstrate the effectiveness of interventions for executive dysfunction should be accompanied by efforts to ensure that treatment-related changes reflect meaningful improvements in patients' lives.

REFERENCES

Alderman, N., Fry, R.K., Youngson, H.A. (1995). Improvement of self-monitoring skills, reduction of behavior disturbance and the dysexecutive syndrome. *Neuropsychological Rehabilitation 5*, 193–222.

Baddeley, A., Della Sala, S., Papagno C., Spinnler, H. (1997). Dual-task performance in dysexecutive and nondysexecutive patients with a frontal lesion. *Neuropsychology, 11*, 187–194.

Bamdad, M.J., Ryan, L.M., & Warden, D.L. (2003). Functional assessment of executive abilities following traumatic brain injury. *Brain Injury, 17*, 1011–1020.

Burgess, P.W., Alderman, N., Evans, J., Emslie, H., & Wilson, B.A. (1998). The ecological validity of tests of executive function. *Journal of the International Neuropsychological Society, 4*, 547–558.

Burke, W.H., Zencius, A.H., Weslowski, M.D., et al. (1991). Improving executive function disorders in brain injured clients. *Brain Injury*, *5*, 241–252.

Cicerone, K.D. (1996). Attention deficits and dual task demands after mild traumatic brain injury. *Brain Injury*, *10*, 79–89.

Cicerone, K.D. (2002). Remediation of "working attention" in mild traumatic brain injury. *Brain Injury*, *16*, 185–195.

Cicerone, K.D., & Giacino, .J.T. (1992). Remediation of executive function deficits after traumatic brain injury. *NeuroRehabiliation*, *2*(3): 12–22.

Cicerone, K.D., & Tanenbaum L.N. (1997). Disturbance of social cognition after traumatic orbitofrontal brain injury. *Archives of Clinical Neuropsychology*, *12*, 173–188.

Cicerone, K.D., & Wood, J.C. (1987). Planning disorder after closed head injury: A case study. *Archives of Physical Medicine and Rehabilitation*, *68*, 111–115.

Cramon D.Y. von, & Matthes-von Cramon, G. (1994). Back to work with a chronic dysexecutive syndrome? (a case report). *Neuropsychological Rehabilitation*, *4*, 399–417.

Cramon, D.Y. von, Mathes-von Cramon, & Mai, N. (1991). Problem solving deficits in brain injured patients: A therapeutic approach. *Neuropsychological Rehabilitation*, *1*, 45–64.

Duncan, J. (1986). Disorganization of behaviour after frontal lobe damage. *Cognitive Neuropsychology*, *3*, 271–290.

Duncan, J., Emslie, H., Williams, P., Johnson, R., & Freer, C. (1996). Intelligence and the frontal lobe: The organisation of goal-directed behaviour. *Cognitive Psychology*, *30*, 2257–2303.

D'Zurilla, T.J., & Goldfried, M.R. (1971). Problem solving and behavior modification. *Journal of Abnormal Psychology*, *78*, 107–126.

Evans, J.J., Emslie, H., & Wilson, B.A. (1998). External cueing systems in the rehabilitation of executive impairments of action. *Journal of the International Neuropsychological Society*, *4*, 399–408.

Evans, J.J., Wilson, B., Needhan, P., & Brentnall, S. (2003). Who makes good use of memory aids? Results of a survey of people with acquired brain injury. *Journal of the International Neuropsychological Society*, *9*, 925–935.

Fink, G.R., Marshall, J.C., Halligan, P.W., Frith, C.D., Driver, J., Frackowiak, R.S.J., & Dolan, R.J. (1999). The neural consequences of conflict between intention and the senses. *Brain*, *122*, 497–512.

Fox, R.M., Martella, R.C., & Marchand-Martella, N.E. (1989). The acquisition, maintenance and generalization of problem-solving skills by closed head injured adults. *Behavior Therapy*, *20*, 61–76.

Godefrey, O., & Rousseaux, M. (1997). Novel decision making in patients with prefrontal or posterior brain damage. *Neurology*, *49*, 695–701.

Hanks, R.A., Rapport, L.J., Millis, S.R., & Deshpande, S.A. (1999). Measures of executive functioning as predictors of functional ability and social integration in a rehabilitation sample. *Archives of Physical Medicine and Rehabilitation*, *80*, 1030–1037.

Lengfelder, A., & Gollwitzer, P.M. (2000). Reflective and reflexive action control in patients with frontal brain lesions. *Neuropsychology*, *15*, 80–100.

Levine, B., Dawson, D., Boutet, I., Schwartz, M., & Stuss, D.T. (2000). Assessment of strategic self-regulation in traumatic brain injury: Its relationship to injury severity and psychosocial outcome. *Neuropsychology*, *14*, 491–500.

Levine, B., Robertson, I.A., Clare, L., Carter, G., Hong, J., Wilson, B.A., Duncan J., & Stuss, D.T. (2000). Rehabilitation of executive functioning: An experimental-clinical validation of goal management training. *Journal of the International Neuropsychological Society, 6,* 299–312.

Lhermitte, F. (1986). Human autonomy and the frontal lobes. Part II: Patient behavior in complex and social situations: The "environmental dependency syndrome." *Annals of Neurology, 19,* 335–343.

Luria, A.R. (1966). *Higher Cortical Functions in Man.* New York: Basic Books.

Luria, A.R. (1981). *Language and Cognition.* Washington, DC: Winston.

Luria, A.R., & Homskaya, E.D. (1964). Disturbance in the regulative role of speech with frontal lobe lesions. In J.M. Warren & K. Akert (Eds.), *The Frontal Granular Cortex and Behavior.* New York: McGraw Hill.

Luria, A.R., Pribram, K.H., & Homskaya, E.D. (1964). An experimental analysis of the behavioral disturbance produced by a left frontal arachnoidal endothelioma. *Neuropsychologia, 2,* 257–280.

Manly, T., Hawkins, K., Evans, J., Woldt, K., & Roberson, I.H. (2002). Rehabilitation of executive function: Facilitation of effective goal management on complex tasks using periodic auditory alerts. *Neuropsychologia, 40,* 271–281.

Meichenbaum, D., & Goodman, J. (1971). Training impulsive children to talk to themselves: A means of developing self-control. *Journal of Abnormal Psychology, 77,* 115–126.

Milner, B. (1963). Effects of different brain lesions on card sorting. *Archives of Neurology, 9,* 100–110.

Ownsworth, T.L., McFarland, K., & Young, R.M. (2000a). Self-awareness and psychosocial functioning following acquired brain injury: An evaluation of a group support programme. *Neuropsychological Rehabiltation, 10,* 465–484.

Ownsworth, T.L., McFarland, K., & Young, R.M. (2000b). Development and standardization of the Self-Regulation Skills Interview (SRSI): A new clinical assessment tool for acquired brain injury. *The Clinical Neuropsychologist, 14,* 76–92.

Rath, J.F., Simon, D., Langenbahn, D.M., Sherr, R.L., & Diller, L. (2003). Group treatment of problem-solving deficits in outpatients with traumatic brain injury: A randomized outcome study. *Neuropsychological Rehabilitation, 13,* 461–488.

Rebmann, M.J., & Hannon, R. (1995). Treatment of unawareness deficits in adults with brain injury: Three case studies. *Rehabilitation Psychology, 40,* 279–287.

Saltus, R.C. (2003, August 26). Lack direction? Evaluate your brain's C.E.O. *The New York Times.*

Shallice, T. (1981). Neurologic impairment of cognitive processes. *British Medical Bulletin, 37,* 187–192.

Shallice, T. (1982). Specific impairments of planning. *Philosophic Transactions of the Royal Society of London [Biology]* 298, 199–209.

Shallice, T., & Burgess P. (1991). Deficits in strategy application following frontal lobe damage in man. *Brain, 114,* 727–741.

Simpson, A., & Schmitter-Edgecombe, M. (2002). Prediction of employment status following traumatic brain injury using a behavioral measure of frontal lobe functioning. *Brain Injury, 16,* 1075–1091.

Sohlberg, M.M., Sprunk, H., & Metzelaar, K. (1988). Efficacy of an external cuing system in an individual with severe frontal lobe damage. *Cognitive Rehabilitation, 6,* 36–41.

Teuber, H.-L. (1964). The riddle of frontal lobe function in man. In J.M. Warren &

K. Akert (Eds.), *The Frontal Granular Cortex and Behavior* (pp. 410–444). New York: McGraw Hill.

Wilson, B.A., & Watson, P.C. (1996). A practical framework for understanding compensatory behaviours in people with organic memory impairment. *Memory, 4,* 465–486.

Youngjohn, J.F., & Altman, I.M. (1989). A performance-based group approach to the treatment of anosognosia and denial. *Rehabilitation Psychology, 34,* 217–222.

6

Social Communication Interventions

MARGARET A. STRUCHEN

Interventions targeting social communication abilities have been a subject of great interest in the field of traumatic brain injury (TBI) rehabilitation (e.g., Ben-Yishay et al., 1980; Boake, 1991; Hartley, 1995; Marsh, 1999; Snow & Douglas, 1999; Sohlberg et al., 1992). This strong interest among rehabilitationists has likely been due to consistent findings that social isolation is a major consequence following injury, at least among individuals with moderate to severe TBI (Klonoff et al., 1986; Marsh & Knight, 1991; Morton & Wehman, 1995; Rappaport et al., 1989; Seibert et al., 2002; Thomsen, 1974, 1984; Weddell et al., 1980). Several studies have demonstrated a decrease in social network size, and preinjury friendships are lost over time (Bergland & Thomas, 1991; Hoofien et al., 2001; Jacobs, 1988; Kersel et al., 2001; Kozloff, 1987; Thomsen, 1974; Weddell et al., 1980), with loneliness often reported as the greatest difficulty for persons with TBI (Harrick et al., 1994; Karpman et al, 1985; Lezak, 1988; Oddy et al., 1985; Thomsen, 1984). The role of social competence has been acknowledged as one of the most significant factors in successful reintegration into home, work, and school following TBI, and is particularly important in establishing new friendships and maintaining previous social networks following injury (Brooks et al., 1987; Hartley, 1995; Marsh, 1999; Morton & Wehman, 1995).

Social communication abilities are at the core of socially skilled behavior (Hartley, 1995; Marsh, 1999; Ylvisaker et al., 1992). Changes in social communication abilities following TBI are common (Bergland & Thomas, 1991; Brooks & Aughton, 1979; Marsh et al., 1998; Morton & Wehman, 1995; Oddy, 1984; Weddell et al., 1980). Cognitive and personality changes resulting from brain injury are thought to be major contributors to impairments in social communication skills following TBI (Godfrey & Shum, 2000: Mooney, 1988; Oddy & Humphrey, 1980; Oddy et al., 1978; Prigatano, 1999). However, it is acknowledged that premorbid ability, emotional reactions to disability, and environmental factors also play significant roles in shaping social outcomes after injury (Gomez-Hernandez et al., 1997; Jorge et al., 1993; Prigatano, 1999).

Cognitive, behavioral, and social communication changes following TBI can be the direct result of the primary pathologic mechanisms of injury. Focal injuries, such as contusions and hematomas, occur primarily on the orbital and lateral surfaces of the frontal and temporal lobes of the brain, which are particularly vulnerable to injury due to trauma because of their proximity to the bony protuberances of the skull (Adams et al., 1980; Holbourn, 1943; Ommaya & Corrao, 1971). Diffuse axonal injury is caused by shearing strains due to angular acceleration forces that occur during incidents like motor vehicle accidents or falls (Ommaya & Gennarelli, 1974; Strich, 1956). These injury mechanisms contribute to the most common cognitive impairments experienced following TBI, namely, problems with slowed processing, attention and memory functioning, and executive dysfunction. A complete discussion of the disruptions of cognitive and behavioral processes that occur secondary to TBI is beyond the scope of this chapter; however, an illustration of the potential impact of such impairments on social competence is presented in Table 6.1.

SOCIAL COMMUNICATION INTERVENTION APPROACHES IN TRAUMATIC BRAIN INJURY

Social communication interventions that have been employed for use with persons with TBI have been adapted largely from the extensive body of work on social skills training (SST) that has been conducted in other clinical populations, such as persons with schizophrenia (e.g., Bellack et al., 1989; Benton & Schroeder, 1990; Liberman et al., 2001; Wallace & Liberman, 1985), social anxiety disorders (e.g., Hambrick et al., 2003; Twentyman & McFall, 1975; van Dam-Baggen & Kraaimaat, 2000), and developmental disabilities (e.g., Foxx et al. 1983; Frea & Hughes, 1997; Kennedy, 2001). Primary components of such treatment approaches are based on behavioral principles and include modeling; shaping, cueing, and fading; behavioral rehearsal and role playing; feedback; coaching; positive reinforcement; and homework (e.g., Hersen & Bellack, 1976; Wallace & Liberman, 1985).

While the results from this extensive literature in other disability populations can inform rehabilitationists about the types of intervention approaches that might

Table 6.1. Examples of Common Cognitive/Behavioral Changes Seen After Brain Injury and the Possible Impact of Such Changes on Social Communication Functioning

COGNITIVE/BEHAVIORAL CHANGES DUE TO TRAUMATIC BRAIN INJURY	POSSIBLE IMPACT ON SOCIAL COMMUNICATION ABILITIES
Attention/Concentration	
Poor concentration	Difficulty maintaining a topic, difficulty keeping track of conversation in presence of distractions
Difficulty shifting attention	Difficulty switching topics, problems in shifting between speaker and listener roles
Slowed processing speed	Long pauses in speaking, slowed speaking rate, difficulty comprehending others when speaking at a normal rate
Learning and Memory	
Poor immediate memory	Repeats self, loses track of conversation topic
Intrusions, susceptibility to interference	Mixes up instructions or messages, has difficulty staying on- topic
Poor organization of learning/recall	Disorganized speech, rambling
Executive Functioning	
Difficulty with integration	Difficulty reconciling conflicting verbal/nonverbal information
Reduced initiation	Reduced initiation of conversation, apparent lack of interest in others.
Poor self-monitoring	Poor use of feedback, poor recognition of errors
Poor planning/organization	Poor sequencing in giving directions, poorly organized speech
Egocentricity	Interruptions, excessive talking, difficulty taking others' perspectives
Perseveration	Difficulty changing topics, stereotyped responses
Poor regulation of emotion/behavior	Unpredictable social behavior, inappropriate laughter, excessive expression of anger
Poor self-awareness	Described unrealistic goals or life situations, lack of credibility, poor use of compensatory strategies

be beneficial for persons with TBI, it is necessary to conduct empirical investigations that examine the extent to which extrapolation of these approaches to persons with TBI is appropriate and effective. Certain characteristics commonly found in persons with TBI may be unique to this population. For example, it is likely that, for the majority of adults with TBI who sustained their injuries as adults, social cognitive skills were well developed prior to injury. That is, for example, unlike persons with developmental disabilities or for many persons with chronic mental illness, many individuals with TBI had adequate knowledge of how to handle social situations (e.g., giving compliments, asking for assistance in a store) prior to their injuries. Therefore, some aspects of typical social skills training programs may be less applicable to persons with TBI. Certain patterns of cognitive impairment that may be seen with TBI might also affect the efficacy of a given treatment approach.

EFFECTIVENESS OF SOCIAL COMMUNICATION INTERVENTIONS FOR PERSONS WITH TRAUMATIC BRAIN INJURY

Despite the substantial amount of research conducted since the late 1970s reporting both that social integration decreases following TBI and that social communication is commonly affected, the number of empirical studies on the efficacy of social communication interventions in this population is surprisingly limited. In identifying articles for this review, the PubMed and PsycInfo databases were searched using combinations of the following key terms: *social skills*, *treatment*, *communication*, *intervention*, and *traumatic brain injury*. Additional materials were identified through review of the reference sections for each article revealed by the database search, as well as through materials known to the author. This process yielded numerous published materials. The following types of articles were eliminated from review: (1) non-peer-reviewed articles or book chapters, (2) conceptual or theoretical papers describing a treatment approach, (3) articles not addressing intervention, and (4) articles in languages other than English or Spanish.

Using this methodology, a total of 19 peer-reviewed studies were identified that evaluated the effectiveness of social communication interventions for individuals with acquired brain injury (ABI). Thirteen of these studies were either case studies or case series involving a total of 19 persons with TBI. Two additional case studies involved one individual with anoxic brain injury. Six group studies were identified involving a total of 56 persons with ABI, with three of these studies involving a mixed case sample. The studies identified employed a variety of treatment approaches; feedback, self-monitoring, modeling, behavioral rehearsal, role play, and social reinforcement were commonly used components.

Studies were reviewed and classified using a modification of the American Academy of Neurology (AAN) (2004) approach for classification of evidence. For this review, Class I studies are those where evidence was provided by a prospective, randomized, controlled clinical trial with masked outcome assessment in a representative population. Additional criteria included clearly defined primary outcomes, clearly stated inclusion and exclusion criteria, adequate accounting of dropouts and crossovers, and relevant baseline characteristics that are substantially equivalent among treatment groups. Class II studies include evidence provided by a prospective matched group cohort study in a representative population with masked outcome assessment that meets the additional criteria of Class I studies or a randomized, controlled clinical trial that meets all but one of the additional criteria stipulations for Class I studies. Class III studies include all other controlled trials and clinical series without concurrent controls where outcome assessment is independent of treatment or studies of one or more single cases where appropriate single-subject methodologies and independence of outcome assessment has been used. Class IV studies include all group studies where outcome assessment is not independent of treatment, case series or case reports without appropriate single-subject design or independent outcome measurement, or expert opinion. Inclusion of rigorous case studies as Class III level evidence is a modification of the AAN (2004) guidelines. Studies meeting Class I, II, or III levels of evidence criteria using this system will be described in detail. A brief summary of all studies is provided in Table 6.2.

REVIEW OF STUDIES

In the only Class I study conducted to date, Helffenstein and Wechsler (1982) randomized 16 persons with nonprogressive brain injury to either 20 hours of interpersonal process recall (IPR) treatment or 20 hours of nontherapeutic attention. Treatment sessions for the IPR group consisted of participation in a videotaped interaction; structured review of the taped interaction with feedback provided by the participant, conversational partner, and therapist; development of an alternative skill; modeling; and rehearsal. At post-treatment assessment, persons receiving the IPR treatment reported significantly reduced anxiety and improved self-concept. More interestingly, these persons were rated to have significantly greater improvement in specific interpersonal skills by both professional staff and independent observer raters, both of whom were unaware of group placement. Changes seen were maintained at 1-month follow-up. This study had several strengths, including its randomized, controlled design, use of independent outcome ratings, reliance on multiple measures to assess effectiveness of the intervention, and multiple methods to assess generalization of skills to outside treatment settings. However, characterization of the small study sample was limited, with injury etiology and severity undefined and a clear description of the process of selection to participate in the trial (e.g., consecutive series, convenience sample) lacking.

In a Class II study, Thomas-Stonell et al. (1994) conducted a randomized, controlled clinical trial examining the effectiveness of a computer-based program, TEACHware, for remediating several areas of higher-level cognitive-communicative functioning. Sessions were facilitated by a therapist or teacher. Twelve persons with TBI, ranging in age from 12 to 21 years, with a wide range of injury severity as measured by length of loss of consciousness, were randomly assigned to receive the computer-based intervention or the "standard of care" for

Table 6.2. Studies of Interventions for Social Communication Abilities in Traumatic Brain Injury

STUDY	PARTICIPANTS	DESIGN	TREATMENT	OUTCOME MEASURES	FINDINGS	GENERALIZATION
Class I Studies						
Helffenstein & Wechsler (1982)	16 adults with nonprogressive brain injury.	Randomized, controlled clinical trial with masked outcome ratings.	20 hours of interpersonal process recall treatment (see text) vs. non-therapeutic attention.	State-Trait Anxiety Scale; Tennessee Self-Concept Scale; Interpersonal Communication Inventory; Interpersonal Relationship Rating Scale; Independent Observer Report Scale; videotape analysis.	Reduced anxiety and improved self-concept; improved interpersonal and communication skills. Greater frequency of specific communication skills. No significant changes seen on videotape analysis.	Improved interpersonal and communication skills in non-treatment settings. Limited follow-up.
Class II Studies						
Thomas-Stonell et al. (1994)	12 adolescents and young adults (aged 12–21) with mixed-severity TBI.	Randomized, controlled clinical trial. A-A'-B design	Computer-based program targeting cognitive-communicative functions vs. standard of care.	Multiple language and neuropsychological test measures.	Found statistically significant improvements on 8 of 28 measures, yet no correction for number of tests made.	Not reported. No follow-up.

(continued)

Table 6.2. Continued

STUDY	PARTICIPANTS	DESIGN	TREATMENT	OUTCOME MEASURES	FINDINGS	GENERALIZATION
Class III Studies						
Gajar et al., (1984)	2 adult men with TBI of unknown severity (2 others without TBI also in group). Social comparison group.	Case series: multiple baseline across treatments: A_1-B_1-C_1-A_2-B_2-C_2.	Group treatment: feedback for negative or positive communication behaviors (B) and self-monitoring of such behaviors (C).	Frequency of positive conversational behaviors as rated by independent observers.	Conversational behaviors improved to within the range of the comparison group for both participants during treatment conditions; however, at second baseline, fell to pre-treatment levels.	Treatment effect seen across different settings (clinic room vs. lounge) and different contexts (structured vs. unstructured). No follow-up.
Schloss et al. (1985)	2 adult men with severe TBI. Social comparison group.	Case series: multiple baseline across behaviors.	Individual treatment: focus on self-monitoring by counting target behaviors. No instruction to increase or decrease behaviors.	Frequency of target behaviors as rated by independent observers. Ratings of social competence on several skills made by independent raters.	Both showed an increase in giving compliments and asking others, which was within the normal range of the comparison group. Variable performance on self-disclosure target and below that of the comparison group.	Improvements in compliments and asking others generalized to method of counting, setting, and instructional set. No follow-up.

Study	Participants	Design	Treatment	Measures	Results	Generalization/Maintenance
Burke & Lewis (1986)	1 adult man with anoxic brain injury.	Case study: modified multiple baseline across behaviors design.	Individual treatment: used behavioral point system targeting three communication behaviors.	Frequency of target negative communication behaviors made by observer. Independent observer made random checks for reliability.	All three negative behaviors reduced in response to treatment, although increased with withdrawal of point system. Changes in nonsensical talk variable.	Generalized to alternative setting, but little maintenance. No follow-up.
Johnson & Newton (1987)	10 adults with severe TBI: 8 men, 2 women.	Prospective pre-post design with comparison cohort of psychiatric patients and nonclinical controls.	Group treatment: review, discussion, practice role play, and feedback (peer and therapist) for 90 minutes/week for 1 year.	Katz Adjustment Scale, Social Performance rating, Questionnaire of Social and Evaluative Anxiety, Rosenberg Self-esteem Scale, Neurophysical Scale.	Group changes on these measures were not significant. However, before treatment, only 1 person was in normal range of comparison groups; after treatment, 6 were in this range.	Limited generalization attempts and not tested. No follow-up.
Brotherton et al. (1988)	4 adults with severe TBI: 3 men, 1 woman.	Case series: multiple baseline across behaviors design.	Individual treatment: role play, instruction, modeling, behavioral rehearsal, video feedback, social reinforcement.	Ratings of social behavior using a scale developed by Kolko and Milan. Ratings made by independent raters.	2 with clear improvements and maintenance of gain over 1 year. The other 2 more variable, with no evidence in performance at 1 year. Greater gains for motoric vs. complex verbal.	Generalization attempted to "free" interaction. Also homework and family education, but no data. One-year follow-up.

(continued)

Table 6.2. Continued

STUDY	PARTICIPANTS	DESIGN	TREATMENT	OUTCOME MEASURES	FINDINGS	GENERALIZATION
Giles et al. (1988)	1 adult man with severe TBI.	Case study: pre-test, post-test, follow-up.	Individual treatment: verbal instruction, positive reinforcement, TOOTS. Target is concise speech.	Numbers of words per minute.	3 × 3 two-factor (question type and time period) ANOVA showed significant main effects, both factors. Structured questions best. Follow-up > pre-treatment.	TOOTS used across all treatment settings. Generalization data not presented.
Lewis et al. (1988)	1 adult man with anoxic brain injury (same case as Burke & Lewis, 1986).	Case study: alternating treatment design, counterbalanced across therapists.	Individual treatment: use of alternate feedback types: attention, ignoring, correction.	Frequency of socially inappropriate remarks.	Irrespective of therapist, correction feedback best; ignoring only slightly above baseline, attention led to more inappropriate remarks	Treatment design allowed for use across settings and contexts. Follow-up anecdotal.
Zencius et al. (1990)	1 adult man with TBI of unknown severity.	Case study: multiple baseline across settings.	Individual treatment: feedback with visual cue to reduce profanity.	Frequency of profanity in treatment settings. Counted by therapists and by independent raters.	Decrease of profanity to virtually none.	Decrease across treatment settings. Outside treatment unknown.

Study	Design	Treatment	Outcome measures	Results	Comments
Wiseman-Hakes et al. (1998)	Prospective, uncontrolled, pre-post design.	Group treatment: modified group approach to Sohlberg's pragmatics program.	RIC Rating Scale of Pragmatic Communication Skills (RSPCS), Communication Performance Scale, Vineland Adaptive Behavior Scale. Independent ratings made.	Significant improvements on RIC RSPCS for nonverbal communication, use of linguistic context, conversational skills, and organization of narrative.	Ratings made in nontreatment context. Gains maintained at 6-months follow-up.
Class IV Studies					
Ehrlich & Sipes (1985)	6 adolescents: 5 with severe TBI, 1 unknown brain injury.	Prospective, uncontrolled, pre-post design.	Group treatment: 4 modules focused on communication areas using video feedback, modeling, and social reinforcement.	Communication Performance Scale. Outcome ratings not independent of treatment.	Improvements reported, but statistical analyses unclear.	Not reported. No follow-up.
Braunling-McMorrow et al. (1986)	6 adults with TBI of unknown severity: 5 men, 1 woman.	Case series: pre-post design.	Group treatment: Used "Stacking the Deck" revised game. Used faded feedback and social reinforcement.	Use of rating scale developed for "Stacking the Deck" game.	All 3 were reported to improve with role play across treatment.	Improvements noted to occur in other settings; however, blinded house staff ratings showed no change.
Godfrey & Knight (1988)	3 adults with severe TBI.	Case study: pre-test. 1-year follow-up	Individual treatment: unclear individualized approach using social reinforcement.	Adaptive Behavior Scale.	Significant improvement in independent functioning, physical development, and socialization subscales.	Anecdotal only.
	1 adult man with severe TBI.				

(continued)

Table 6.2. Continued

STUDY	PARTICIPANTS	DESIGN	TREATMENT	OUTCOME MEASURES	FINDINGS	GENERALIZATION
Sladyk (1992)	1 adult woman with severe TBI, less than 2 months postinjury.	Case study: pre-post design.	Group treatment: assertiveness training and projective art techniques.	Descriptive report of changes.	Reported decreases in demanding behavior. No data or analysis. Outcome not independent	Reported general improvements, but acute injury. Not data.
Uomoto & Brockway (1992)	2 adult men, 1 with severe TBI, 1 with neoplasm.	Case series: pre-post, follow-up.	Individual and family treatment: self-talk method to decrease tension, family training to learn behavior modification.	Frequency of anger outbursts.	Decrease in anger outbursts seen for both men, as rated by family members. Increased social interaction for man with TBI.	Anecdotal only. Gains maintained at 1- and 3-month follow-ups.
Yuen (1997)	1 adult man with severe TBI.	Case study: pre-post design.	Individual treatment: daily 5-minute focus on "positive" talk, modeling, role play.	Frequency of positive statements.	Reported improvements, although no data presented.	Reported improvements in other settings. No data.
Ojeda del Pozo et al. (2000)	6 adults with acquired brain injury, 4 with TBI.	Uncontrolled, prospective, pre-post design.	Individual/group treatment: stated use of errorless learning, but poorly described treatment.	Profile of Functional Impairment in Communication.	"Improved functioning" reported, but no data presented.	Not reported.
O'Reilly et al. (2000)	2 adult men with severe TBI, both in supported employment.	Case series: multiple baseline across-behavior design.	Individual treatment: problem solving for work-related social skills. Modeling, role play, feedback, social reinforcement.	Rating of work-related skills developed by the authors. Ratings made by co-workers and job coaches, not independent.	Improvement in targeted skills noted during intervention compared to baseline.	Generalized to work setting by job coach rating. Maintained at follow-up 6 weeks post-treatment.

TBI, traumatic brain injury; TOOTS, timed out on the spot.

cognitive communication issues. The study reported statistically significant improvements on 8 of 28 standardized test measures (primarily measures of language functioning); however, given the number of tests conducted, a more conservative significance level should have been adopted. Strengths of this study included its design as a randomized, controlled trial; however, several methodological problems were present. In addition to the lack of correction for multiple comparisons in statistical analyses, the data presented suggested that although random assignment was used, the two groups appeared to differ with respect to injury severity and chronicity of injury. The control group appeared to have more severely and chronically injured persons than did the treatment group, which may be supported by the data presented on the slope of test score results between baseline and repeat baseline assessment, which were much flatter than those for the treatment group. Thus, it is unclear whether apparent changes seen on test performance for the treatment group are attributable to treatment effects or to spontaneous recovery. In addition, no data on functional outcomes were presented, so the relevance of this treatment for functional goals is unknown.

Several Class III studies have also provided supporting evidence for the benefits of social communication interventions for persons with TBI. In an early study, Gajar et al. (1984) conducted a social skills training program with two 22-year-old men who had each sustained TBI due to motor vehicle accidents that had occurred at least 18 months prior to the intervention. Interventions consisted of either feedback or self-monitoring procedures and were provided in a group setting. The design included 12 treatment sessions provided in a multiple baseline across-treatment design. Nontreatment baseline sessions were conducted prior to beginning the intervention. For the feedback condition, trained observers provided feedback using a light signal (red light for "negative" and green light for "positive" conversational behaviors). Self-monitoring used the same light apparatus; however, group members initiated use of the red or green light signal regarding communication performance. Conversational behaviors, as rated by independent observers, improved to within the range of a comparison group of noninjured individuals for both patients during implementation of both treatment conditions, suggesting that at least some clients can benefit from feedback and/or learn to self-monitor their social behavior. However, at the time of the second baseline measurement, both patients returned to pretreatment baseline performance. The inability of this study to demonstrate generalization to nontreatment conditions may have been due to the limited number of treatment sessions that were provided and the lack of further follow-up to assess maintenance of treatment effects after the second set of treatment sessions.

Schloss and colleagues (1985) focused on self-monitoring to learn conversational skills with female peers for two adult men with severe TBI who were both at least 1 year postinjury at the time of the intervention. The men were trained to count the number of specific target behaviors (compliments, asking others, and self-disclosure) that they performed when interacting with female peers; however, no specific instructions to increase or decrease these behaviors were provided. The study was conducted in a multiple baseline across-behaviors design, with each conversational behavior addressed in a different stage to training. Self-monitoring was initially done with a mechanical counter and later transferred to covert monitoring. Both participants in the program showed an increase in the number of compliments and "asking other" communication behaviors that fell within the range of communication behaviors exhibited by a noninjured comparison group. Decreases in self-disclosure were also noted for these participants; however, there was greater variability in performance and more self-disclosing statements than found in a social comparison group. Results were maintained over a 1-month follow-up period for the participants on whom such data were available.

Burke and Lewis (1986) reported on the use of a behavioral point system to modify three target communication behaviors (loud verbal outbursts, interrupting, nonsensical talk) for a man with anoxic brain injury. Behaviors were addressed in a modified multiple baseline across-behaviors design. The intervention consisted of using a reinforcement menu, tracking behaviors on a point card, and delivering reinforcements plus verbal feedback. All three behaviors were reduced in frequency in response to treatment, and results generalized to an alternative nontreatment setting. However, when the point system was withdrawn and only verbal feedback was provided, negative behaviors increased; these were reduced with reintroduction of the point system. Thus, although the intervention was demonstrated to be effective, it is unclear how well it will lead to generalization of reduced negative behaviors outside of the treatment setting. In addition, results were more variable for nonsensical talk, which was little affected by the intervention. This was thought to be due to its being a less easily defined construct and its susceptibility to variations by others in communication contexts.

Johnson and Newton (1987) conducted a prospective study of a group of 10 individuals who participated in a group that met for 90 minutes each week over a 1-year period. Group sessions were divided into two parts: the first half involved the group meeting as a whole to consider a specific communication issue (e.g., starting a conversation, listening), and the second half consisted of smaller breakout groups to allow for more detailed individual work. A list of group themes and issues was generated for the group based on a theory of interpersonal development. Sessions consisted of a review of the previous meeting, introduction of a specific topic, discussion of the main issues, practice on specific issues, role play, and feedback from peers and therapists. Finally, generalization was encouraged by developing social opportunities so that group members would have a chance to work on these skills in social settings. Group changes on measures of social adjustment, social performance, social anxiety, and self-esteem were not found to be significantly different following treatment. However, categorical analysis revealed that while only one participant performed within the range of a normal social comparison group at pre-treatment, six individuals performed within this range at post-treatment assessment. This study had several methodological problems, including multiple statistical tests with small samples, size, limited generalization attempts, and an intervention that would likely be impractical for clinical use given its year-long involvement.

Brotherton and coworkers (1988) conducted individual interventions for a series of four individuals with TBI who were all more than 2 years postinjury. Three to four target behaviors were identified during baseline assessment for each participant, and a multiple baseline across-behaviors methodology was used. The skills training program contained the following components: role play, increasing understanding of the rationale for changing the target behaviors, modeling the correct behaviors, behavioral rehearsal, videotape feedback on performance, and social reinforcement of correct behaviors. One-hour training sessions were conducted twice per week, consisting of a period of free interaction followed by role-play scenarios and then 30 minutes of training. Two of the four participants demonstrated clear improvements and maintenance of improvements over a 1-year follow-up period for motoric communication behaviors (e.g., posture, self-manipulation) and some improvements during training for verbal behaviors, although maintenance of such improvements was limited. The other two participants had variable findings, with no evidence of improvement in performance on the target behaviors at 1-year follow-up. This intervention was more effective for motoric communication behaviors than for more complex verbal behaviors; however, it appeared that fewer treatment sessions focused on these more complex verbal behaviors overall. In addition, since the treatment included a combination of various social skill interventions, the role of any one technique is unclear.

Giles et al. (1988) used a conversational skills training program to reduce verbosity and circumstantial speech in a 27-year-old man with severe TBI who was more than 2 years postinjury at the time of treatment. The training program consisted of verbal instruction regarding the rationale for behavior change, with an emphasis on the phrase "short answers" to prompt concise responses. Half-hour sessions were provided 5 days per week for 1 month, with cues for "short answers" and "permission to think before responding" given at least twice per session. Three tasks were conducted at each session: (1) asking questions to which the patient was to respond with one-word answers, (2) asking questions with specific content that would require brief answers, and (3) unstructured conversation. Successfully completing each task resulted in social reinforcement (verbal praise). Failure resulted in the participant's being *timed out on the spot* (TOOTS). After a 20-second delay, the patient was cued with the phrase "short answers" and a new question was asked. A 3×3 two-factor [question type and treatment period (baseline, post-treatment, follow-up)] ANOVA for a single-subject design revealed significant main effects for both factors but no significant interaction. Greatest improvements were seen with structured questions with one-word responses, which were significantly better than semistructured questions with a brief response requirement. Furthermore, performance at follow-up was significantly better than at baseline assessment.

Lewis and colleagues (1988) utilized various forms of feedback to attempt to reduce the number of "socially inappropriate comments" in a 21-year-old man with anoxic brain injury (interestingly, the same individual described above in the study by Burke and Lewis, 1986). Using an alternating treatment design, three forms of feedback were applied contingent upon the client's engaging in inappropriate social talk. Feedback conditions included attention and interest, systematic ignoring, or correction and were counterbalanced across therapists so that each administered all three forms of feedback over a 3-week training period, and the client received all three types of feedback concurrently on any given treatment week. Irrespective of the therapist, the correction feedback condition resulted in the greatest reduction in socially inappropriate remarks, while systematic ignoring resulted in only slight improvements from baseline and attention increased the inappropriate behaviors. The naturalistic design of the study allowed the intervention to be used across many settings and contexts.

Zencius and coworkers (1990) administered a simple *visual cue* intervention to attempt to reduce profanity in a 24-year-old man who sustained a severe TBI 8 years prior to treatment. A multiple baseline across-settings (different therapy rooms) design was used. Therapists recorded the frequency of profanity used in each of the three target sessions per day, and an independent observer also recorded this information for 30% of all sessions. After a baseline period, each incident of profanity resulted in the therapist's holding up a sheet of paper with the word *swearing* on it but did nothing else. Implementation of the visual cue decreased the use of profanity from about five or six times per session at treatment outset to less than one per session after an approximately 3- to 4-week training period.

Wiseman-Hakes et al. (1998) conducted a group intervention for six adolescents with ABI, four of whom were less than 8 months post-TBI, one of whom was 8 years post-TBI, and one of whom had acquired brain injury of unspecified etiology. These six participants participated in an intervention of Sohlberg and colleagues (1992), "Improving Pragmatic Skills in Persons with Head Injury," modified for use with a group. Four modules were taught: initiation, topic maintenance, turn taking, and active listening, and each module consisted of an awareness phase, a practice phase, and a generalization phase. The intervention emphasized repetition, consistency, and feedback. Peers provided feedback and cueing, and conversational exchanges were practiced among the participants. At completion of the treatment program, significant improvements were found for ratings of pragmatic communication skills made by independent observers in nontreatment contexts, and these improvements were maintained at 6-month follow-up. Given that the majority of participants were less than 8 months postinjury and no control group was used for the study, it is unclear to what extent changes reflect the effects of intervention versus spontaneous recovery.

Summary

The existing studies provide evidence that supports the use of interventions to address social communication abilities. Evidence from the Class I randomized trial (Helffenstein & Wechsler, 1982) is particularly compelling and is supported by several well-designed Class III case studies. In particular, the use of structured feedback, videotaped interactions, modeling, rehearsal, and training of self-monitoring have been shown to be useful strategies for improving social communication skills. In the evidence-based review of cognitive rehabilitation conducted by the Brain Injury Interdisciplinary Special Interest Group (BI-ISIG) of the American Congress of Rehabilitation Medicine, the committee recommended that interventions directed at improving interpersonal communication skills be considered a Practice Standard for the field of cognitive rehabilitation (Cicerone et al., 2000).

METHODOLOGICAL LIMITATIONS OF EXISTING RESEARCH

While the evidence supporting the use of interventions for social communication abilities for persons with TBI is encouraging, relatively little empirical research in this area has been conducted to date. This current review revealed only two randomized, controlled clinical trials of interventions involving functional or social communication abilities and eight case studies or series with strong research designs. The remaining studies were either uncontrolled prospective group trials or case series with pre-post assessment, and several studies presented only descriptive results of the treatment.

While randomized, controlled clinical trials are often considered the gold standard for evidence-based practice, usefulness of the results of such trials for clinical decision making depends to a large extent on how similar participants in the clinical trial are to the individuals or groups to whom the treatment is to be applied, and how similar the actual treatment and treatment delivery are to those in the clinical trial. Case studies and series present limitations due to the inherent problems with selection bias. However, a well-conducted case or case series can certainly provide useful evidence that may be valuable for clinical practice, particularly if the individual for whom clinical decisions are to be made is similar in relevant characteristics to the case presented.

While the type of study (randomized, controlled trial, case study, etc.) conducted has implications for the generalizability of study results, there are several other methodological issues that greatly impact the utility of research findings. Researchers may be limited to conducting a certain type of study due to setting, circumstance, or funding issues; however, all clinicians and researchers can improve the quality of evidence regarding social communication interventions by attending to the following methodological issues: characterization of the study sample, specification of the intervention, independence of outcome ratings, assessment and enhancement of generalization and generality, and statistical analyses.

Regardless of the type of study conducted, it is imperative that careful characterization of the study participants be presented. In order to know reasonably whether a given treatment would be applicable for a given individual, group, or setting, one must be able to determine how similar the studied sample is to the sample or setting to which the treatment might be applied. Unfortunately, in several of the studies identified in this review, participants were inadequately described, leaving the reader essentially unable to infer the degree to which the results might generalize to a different setting or population.

Clarification of etiology is essential, and while there may be relevant similarities among various forms of ABI, it is unclear at this time whether social communication problems might present differently among persons with disorders of different etiologies. Therefore, the cause of injury should be specified, and when a study includes persons with "acquired brain injury," which implies individuals of mixed etiology, results for various etiologies should be presented separately, along with any overall group results.

Characteristics of study participants that should be clearly identified in research articles include the following:

- Data on injury severity (including method of determining severity)
- Chronicity of injury (length of time postinjury at the time of intervention)
- Etiology of the injury
- Demographic information (e.g., age, gender, ethnicity)
- Psychosocial information (e.g., education, occupation)
- Social communication strengths/weaknesses (including method of assessing social communication abilities)
- Coexisting areas of cognitive impairment (optional, but especially relevant for case studies)

In addition to a careful description of study participants, an equally important but often overlooked aspect of the sample description is information about selection of the case or group. Details regarding the setting from which participants were selected (e.g., comprehensive inpatient rehabilitation program, post-ABI rehabilitation program, a community support group members) and the method of selection (consecutive admissions, convenience sample referred to a group, self-identified participants, etc.) constitutes valuable information for evaluating the applicability of a study to another setting or group. In addition to this information, data comparing those persons chosen for the study to those who were eligible but did not participate provide further clarification of the degree to which the case(s) or group(s) studied are representative.

For many studies of social communication intervention, the absence of sufficient detail regarding the specific intervention or approach that is being evaluated limits the usefulness of research. While many studies do an excellent job of describing the intervention approach used (e.g., Gajar et al., 1984; Helffenstein & Wechsler, 1982), a number of studies fail to provide information that would allow study replication or application of the intervention in a clinical setting.

Measurement issues pose another methodological limitation in social skill intervention following TBI. There is no accepted standard method of assessing the social communication skills of persons with brain injury. While many of the studies reviewed for this chapter presented some data or behavioral description of selected social communication abilities, such information was largely limited to informal observations or unpublished, "home-grown" rating scales. Notable exceptions include studies by Helffenstein and Wechsler (1982), Ehrlich and Sipes (1985), Johnson and Newton (1987), Godfrey and Knight (1988), and Wiseman-Hakes et al. (1998), which used measures such as the Interpersonal Communication Inventory (Bienvenue, 1971), the Interpersonal Relationship Rating Scale (Hipple, 1972; Pfeiffer et al., 1976), the Adaptive Behavior Scale (Nihira et al., 1974), the Communication Performance Scale (Ehrlich & Sipes, 1985), and the Rehabilitation Institute of Chicago Rating Scale of Pragmatic Communication Skills (Burns et al., 1985). The use of published assessment measures can increase our understanding of the impact of interventions by facilitating comparisons across studies, populations, and settings.

Over half of the studies that used ratings of communication skill as outcome measures for the interventions used raters who did not provide treatment and were unaware of the treatment approach employed. However, a sizable number of studies used ratings made by therapists involved in the treatments themselves, which raises the possibility of rating bias. Finally, across the studies reviewed, information on generalization of results to nontreatment situations or settings and posttreatment follow-up data were limited, so relatively little is known about the generalization and maintenance of gains from social communication interventions.

GAPS IN CURRENT KNOWLEDGE AND FUTURE DIRECTIONS FOR RESEARCH

Although the literature supports the use of interventions targeting social interaction skills for persons with TBI, there are several unanswered questions that need to be addressed. Issues that would benefit from attention include the limited availability of quality measurement tools, the lack of information about what types of interventions are most appropriate for specific communication issues, and limited empirical data about the extent to which interventions generalize to impact functional and sustained change outside of the treatment setting.

How Do We Measure Social Communication Abilities?
How Do We Demonstrate Treatment Outcome?

Despite awareness of the importance of social communication changes following TBI and the impact of such changes on social outcomes, the use of standardized assessment instruments that measure relevant aspects of social communication has been limited (Boake, 1991; Douglas et al., 2000; Flanagan et al., 1995; Linscott et al., 1996; McDonald et al., 2003). Development of new instruments and approaches to the measurement of social skills, adaptation of measures used for other clinical populations, and refinement of existing measures and approaches should be emphasized among TBI rehabilitation researchers and clinicians. In order for us to demonstrate the impact of a given intervention approach, we must have adequate tools. Social communication instruments should address receptive, processing, and expressive aspects of communication. Measurement tools should allow for a broad approach to assessment of communication behaviors, including the use of self-report, other-report, and behavioral measures.

Instruments that have been used in the TBI intervention literature have focused primarily on evaluating the expressive or *performance* aspects of social interaction. Relatively little attention has been paid to the measurement of receptive components of social communication skill in intervention studies. However, failure to evaluate receptive communication factors, such as the ability to perceive facial expressions, prosody, and nonverbal aspects of communication, as well as the ability to identify social problem situations, may mean that important targets for intervention are left unidentified (Blair & Cipolotti, 2000; Braun et al., 1989; Jackson & Moffat, 1987; Prigatano & Pribram, 1982). Use of existing instruments to measure perception of facial affect and prosody, such as the Florida Affect Battery (FAB; Bowers et al., 1991), the Iowa Emotion Recognition Battery (IERB; Kubu, 1992, 1999), or newer measures that incorporate dynamic emotional stimuli, such as The Awareness of Social Inference Test (TASIT; McDonald et al., 2003), may help identify intervention targets and allow investigation of the impact of intervention on social perception and skill. More complex receptive communication skills, such as interpretation of conflicting verbal and nonverbal cues, interpretation of sarcasm, and identification of social problems may be assessed in part with the FAB, IERB, and TASIT, as well as through the use of a number of measures of social problem solving that have been developed in other disability populations [e.g., Assessment of Interpersonal Problem Solving Skills (AIPSS; Donahoe et al., 1990)].

Similarly, limited attention to the assessment of processing aspects of social communication, such as the ability to generate alternative possible communication responses, may limit identification of important treatment targets. Use of existing social problem solving measures, such as the AIPSS or other such measures (e.g., the Social Problem-Solving Inventory; D'Zurilla & Nezu, 1990; Kendall et al., 1997) would provide one means of assessing the processing of communication skills. Adaptation of script generation and script execution tasks (Chevignard et al., 2000; Grafman, 1989; Sirigu et al., 1995) for social situations might also provide important information about social communication processing skills.

Use of published behavioral rating scales to measure social communication expression would facilitate comparison between studies. A focus on intermediate-level measures that provide sufficient depth of information while being reasonable for clinical use may be most fruitful for clinical research applications. Global measures provide limited data on which to base intervention goals, while molecular analyses (such as discourse analysis approaches; Coelho et al., 1991; Erlich, 1988; Snow et al., 1998) are rich in information but of limited practicality in clinical settings. While several of the reviewed studies employed intermediate-level scales (e.g., Brotherton et al., 1988; Ehrlich & Sipes, 1985; Helffenstein & Wechsler, 1982; Ojeda del Pozo et al., 2000; Wiseman et al., 1998), many studies used home-grown measures with limited psychometric information. Several rating scales are available for use in social communication intervention studies. Some of these scales were developed specifically for use with persons with brain injury, such as the Profile of Functional Impairment in Communication (Linscott et al., 1996) and the Communication Performance Scale (Ehrlich & Sipes, 1985). Others were developed for other populations, such as the Interpersonal Relationship Rating Scale (Kolko & Milan, 1985; Pfeiffer et al., 1976) and the Behavioral Referenced Rating System of Intermediate Social Skills (Wallander et al., 1985).

Defining relevant outcome measures is another area of need. While pre-post behavioral measures of social communication abilities are certainly one outcome of importance, there are a number of other potential outcomes that would be relevant to assess. Once such outcome is the perception of communication abilities from the perspective of the person with injury, close family or friends, and/or rehabilitation professionals. Perceptions of social communication abilities in TBI have received fairly superficial attention in most studies that have identified social skill deficits. For example, many studies have examined "psychosocial status," "communication skills," or "behavioral/emotional functioning" via either a single item or a group of items on self- or other-report measures of symptoms following TBI (Brooks et al., 1987; Kreutzer et al., 1994; Levin et al., 1987). Only more recently have self- or other-report instruments that focus solely on communication or interpersonal skills following TBI been developed. The LaTrobe Communication Questionnaire (Douglas et al., 2000) enables the collection of data from various sources and allows the determination of perceived changes in communication from preinjury status.

Other relevant outcomes to consider include secondary effects of the intervention on quality of life and community integration. While changes in social communication skill are one measure of success for a given intervention, the impact on secondary outcomes is likely of more interest to persons with injury and their families. Are changes in social communication skill associated with improved emotional functioning, such as decreased symptoms of depression, decreased loneliness, or decreased symptoms of anxiety? Are changes in social communication abilities associated with improved community integration, such as facilitating successful interactions at work, increasing social activities, and improving the individual's ability to form and maintain satisfying relationships? To that end, identification and/or development of relevant measures of social integration that are sufficiently sensitive to change would be useful. Measures such as the Community Integration Questionnaire (Willer et al., 1994; Sander et al., 1999) and the Craig Handicap Assessment and Reporting Technique (Whiteneck et al., 1992) provide useful information on social integration; however, they are limited in the depth and scope of information obtained regarding relationships and social activities, and thus may be somewhat less sensitive to changes.

Which Interventions? Which Individuals?

There is an obvious need for well-conducted empirical studies of social communication interventions for persons with TBI. Only 19 such studies have been published; of these, 11 were conducted in the 1970s and 1980s. Unfortunately, despite some promising initial findings, none of these studies were followed up with replication or refinement of a tested treatment approach. Design and implementation of randomized, controlled trials, carefully conducted cohort studies, and well-designed case series and case studies will increase our understanding of which interventions appear to be useful for persons with TBI. Future studies could address several questions, such as:

- Who benefits from what type of treatment?
- What interventions work best for what clinical issues?
- When and in what setting should interventions be provided?
- How long and how intensively should interventions be used?
- Should the person with TBI be the target of intervention, or should the person's support system be the target, or both?

Understanding to what extent the effectiveness of various interventions is affected by individual characteristics, such as injury severity, chronicity of injury, or patterns of cognitive ability, would be useful. Evaluating whether treatments targeted to specific patterns of receptive, processing, or expressive skill impairments are more effective than a more general approach to treatment would also be important. Descriptions in the literature support the notion that there may be subtypes of social communicative ability among persons with brain injury (Hartley & Jensen, 1992). Identification of subtypes or patterns of cognitive-communicative performance may lead to more efficient communication interventions. For some subgroups of individuals with social communication problems, an emphasis on addressing perceptual difficulty might be needed (e.g., teaching through direct instruction to monitor facial affect), while for others, addressing problems with generation of responses (e.g., developing a set repertoire of responses for a given situation or setting) might be useful.

While the majority of empirical studies have relied on this behavioral social skills training approach, a metacognitive/social cognition framework for social communication interventions has also been described (e.g., Ylvisaker et al., 1992). Increasing understanding of the relationship between cognitive functions and social communication abilities through empirical studies, rather than simply through conceptual frameworks, would also be useful. It would be interesting to compare the metacognitive/social cognition approach to the traditional behavioral social skills training approach to determine if there are relative differences in efficacy for either approach or whether specific individuals might benefit from one approach versus another. Examination of the relative effectiveness of interventions that focus on communication strengths versus deficit-focused interventions might also be useful.

The limited number of studies of social communication intervention for persons with TBI may be due, in part, to both perceived and real obstacles to conducting such research. Referral patterns to rehabilitation settings have changed over time, and limitations in funding for treatment have contributed to increasingly shortened lengths of stay in inpatient and outpatient settings. Therefore, conducting thorough assessment and standardized treatment protocols is increasingly difficult in clinical settings unless research funding is available. Despite these potential barriers, careful case studies and clinical trials can be conducted. At the very least, carefully conducted case studies or series (with adequate descriptions of participants and sampling issues) will continue to provide some evidence of support for interventions. Clinical trials can be conducted, and while a no-treatment control is not possible in most clinical settings, treatments can be tested against each other. Multicenter studies might also increase the size of samples for evaluating various treatment approaches, although such studies have other methodological problems.

To What Extent Do Changes Generalize? How Can We Promote Generalization and Maintenance?

In most of the studies reviewed for this chapter, information about generalization or maintenance of treatment gains is limited. Some studies used a less structured interaction (e.g., free discussion vs. structured topic, lounge setting vs. clinic) to examine generalization of skills to a different context. While such attempts are one step in looking at generalization, such attempts typically involved fairly minor variations and may provide only limited information about the real-world impact of the intervention. In addition, few studies conducted follow-up evaluations, so our knowledge about how well treatment gains have been maintained over time is virtually nonexistent.

Demonstrating generalization of treatment gains to nontreatment settings and situations has long been difficult in social skills training across populations, and there has been extensive development of methodologies to assess the generalization and social validity of such treatments (Fox & McEvoy, 1993). When designing a clinical trial, group comparison study, or case series, TBI clinicians and researchers would benefit from review of the extensive cross-disability social skills training literature so that methodological problems can be avoided and generalization can be enhanced.

To facilitate generalization, some recent articles in the TBI literature have described the targeting of social communication skills in the setting in which such skills would be used (e.g., work), with the hope of increasing the transfer of training (Carlson & Buckwald, 1993; O'Reilly et al., 2000). Context-specific social communication interventions may be one avenue of research for future studies. Another approach that is receiving increasing cross-disability attention is the use of supported relationships or in vivo amplified skills training to bridge the gap between the clinic and community settings (Johnson & Davis, 1998; Liberman et al., 2002; Uomoto & Brockway, 1992). Liberman and colleagues (2002) used specialist case managers to provide individualized community-based teaching of behavioral techniques in order to improve the social skills of clients with schizophrenia. Uomoto and Brockway (1992) trained family members in the use of behavioral techniques to help improve communication skills for two clients with brain injury. Finally, Johnson and Davis (1998) used nondisabled community peers to increase integrated social contacts for three individuals with TBI. These studies all had promising results. Such approaches may help impact the secondary outcomes of interest, such as changes in community integration and socialization.

CONCLUSION

Social communication abilities continue to be a major focus of rehabilitation efforts for persons with TBI. Although the extant empirical studies provide tentative support for such interventions, there are many questions that need to be addressed. Social competence is acknowledged as one of the most significant factors in successful community integration. Given these facts, efforts to increase the base of evidence for social communication interventions, as well as to test context-specific and community-based approaches, are of great importance.

ACKNOWLEDGMENTS

Preparation of this chapter was supported, in part, by Grants H133B990014 and H133G010152 from the National Institute on Disability and Rehabilitation Research, U.S. Department of Education. Special thanks also go to Laura Rosas, MA, for her assistance with the review of Spanish language manuscripts.

REFERENCES

Adams, J.H., Graham, D.I, Scott, G., Parker, L.S., & Doyle, D. (1980). Brain damage in fatal non-missile head injury. *Journal of Clinical Pathology, 33*, 1132–1145.

American Academy of Neurology. (2004). *Clinical Practice Guideline Process Manual.* St. Paul, MN: Author.

Bellack, A.S., Morrison, R.L., & Mueser, K.T. (1989). Social problem solving in schizophrenia. *Schizophrenia Bulletin, 15*, 101–116.

Benton, M.K., & Schroeder, H.E. (1990). Social skills training with schizophrenics: A meta-analytic evaluation. *Journal of Consulting and Clinical Psychology, 58*, 741–747.

Ben-Yishay, Y., Lakin, P., Ross, B., Rattok, J., Cohen, J., & Diller, L. (1980). Developing a core "curriculum" for group exercises designed for head trauma patients who are undergoing rehabilitation. In Y. Ben-Yishay (Ed.), *Working Approaches to Remediation of Cognitive Deficits in Brain Damaged Persons* (Rehabilitation Monograph No. 61). New York: New York University Medical Center, Institute of Rehabilitation Medicine.

Bergland, M.M., & Thomas, K.R. (1991). Psychosocial issues following severe head injury in adolescence: Individual and family perceptions. *Rehabilitation Counseling Bulletin, 35*, 5–22.

Bienvenue, M.J. (1971). An interpersonal communication inventory. *Journal of Communication, 21*, 381–388.

Blair, R.J.R., & Cipolotti, L. (2000). Impaired social response reversal: A case of "acquired sociopathy." *Brain, 123*(Pt. 6), 1122–1141.

Boake, C. (1991). Social skills training following head injury. In J.S. Kreutzer & P.H. Wehman (Eds.), *Cognitive Rehabilitation for Persons with Traumatic Brain Injury.* Baltimore: Paul H. Brookes.

Bowers, D., Blonder, L.X., & Heilman, K.M. (1991). *The Florida Affect Battery.* Gainesville, FL: Center for Neuropsychological Studies, University of Florida.

Braun, C., Baribeau, J., Ethier, M., Daigneault, S., & Proulix, R. (1989). Processing of pragmatic and facial affective information by patients with closed head injuries. *Brain Injury, 3*, 5–17.

Braunling-McMorrow, D., Lloyd, K., & Fralish, K. (1986). Teaching social skills to head injured adults. *Journal of Rehabilitation, 52*, 39–44.

Brooks, D.N., & Aughton, M.E. (1979). Psychological consequences of blunt head trauma. *International Rehabilitation Medicine, 1*, 160–165.

Brooks, D.N., McKinlay, A., Symington, C., et al. (1987). Return to work within the first seven years of severe head injury. *Brain Injury, 1*, 5–19.

Brotherton, F.A., Thomas, L.L., Wisotzek, I.E., & Milan, M.A. (1988). Social skills training in the rehabilitation of patients with traumatic closed head injury. *Archives of Physical Medicine & Rehabilitation, 69,* 827–832.

Burke, W.H., & Lewis, F.D. (1986). Management of maladaptive social behavior of a brain injured adult. *International Journal of Rehabilitation Research, 9(4),* 335–342.

Burns, M., Halper, A.S., & Mogil, S.I. (1985). *Clinical Management of Right Hemisphere Dysfunction.* Rockville, MD: Aspen.

Carlson, H.B., & Buckwald, M.W. (1993). Vocational communication group treatment in an outpatient head injury facility. *Brain Injury, 7,* 183–187.

Chevignard, M., Pillon, B., Pradat-Diehl, P., Taillefer, C., Rousseau, S., Le Bras, C., & Dubois, B. (2000). An ecological approach to planning dysfunction: Script execution. *Cortex, 36,* 649–669.

Cicerone, K.D., Dahlberg, C., Kalmar, K., Langenbahn, D.M., Malec, J.F., Bergquist, T.F., Felicetti, T., Giacino, J.T., Preston Harley, J., Harrington, D.E., Herzog, J., Kneipp, S., Laatsch, L., & Morse, P.A. (2000). Evidence-based cognitive rehabilitation: Recommendations for clinical practice. *Archives of Physical Medicine and Rehabilitation, 81,* 1596–1615.

Coelho, C.A., Liles, B.Z., & Duffy, R.J. (1991). Analysis of conversational discourse in head injured adults. *Journal of Head Trauma Rehabilitation, 6,* 92–99.

Donahoe, C.P., Carter, M.J., Bloem, W.D., Hirsch, G.L., Laasi, N., & Wallace, C.J. (1990). Assessment of interpersonal problem-solving skills. *Psychiatry, 53,* 329–339.

Douglas, J.M., O'Flaherty, C.A., & Snow, P.C. (2000). Measuring perception of communicative ability: The development and evaluation of the La Trobe Communication Questionnaire. *Aphasiology, 14,* 251–268.

D'Zurilla, T.J., & Nezu, A.M. (1990). Development and preliminary evaluation of the Social Problem-Solving Inventory. *Psychological Assessment, 2,* 156–163.

Ehrlich, J.S. (1988). Selective characteristics of narrative discourse in head injured and normal adults. *Journal of Communication Disorders, 21,* 1–9.

Ehrlich, J.S., & Sipes, A.L. (1985). Group treatment of communication skills for head trauma patients. *Cognitive Rehabilitation, 3,* 32–37.

Flanagan, S., McDonald, S., & Togher, L. (1995). Evaluating social skills following traumatic brain injury: The BRISS as a clinical tool. *Brain Injury, 9,* 321–338.

Fox, J.J., & McEvoy, M.A. (1993). Assessing and enhancing generalization and social validity of social-skills interventions with children and adolescents. *Behavior Modification, 17,* 339–366.

Foxx, R.M., McMorrow, M.J., & Schloss, C.N. (1983). Stacking the deck: Teaching social skills to retarded adults with a modified table game. *Journal of Applied Behavior Analysis, 6,* 157–170.

Frea, W.D., & Hughes, C. (1997). Functional analysis and treatment of social-communicative behavior or adolescents with developmental disabilities. *Journal of Applied Behavior Analysis, 30,* 701–704.

Gajar, A., Schloss, P.J., Schloss, C.N., & Thompson, C.K. (1984). Effects of feedback and self-monitoring on head trauma youths' conversation skills. *Journal of Applied Behavior Analysis, 17,* 353–358.

Giles, G.M., Fussey, I., & Burgess, P. (1988). The behavioral treatment of verbal interaction skills following severe head injury: A single case study. *Brain Injury, 2,* 75–79.

Godfrey, H.P.D., & Knight, R.G. (1988). Memory training and behavioral rehabilitation of a severely head-injured adult. *Archives of Physical Medicine and Rehabilitation, 69,* 458–460.

Godfrey, H.P.D., & Shum, D. (2000). Executive functioning and the application of social skills following traumatic brain injury. *Aphasiology*, *14*(4), 433–444.

Gomez-Hernandez, R., Max, J.E., Kosier, T., Paradiso, S., & Robinson, R.G. (1997). Social impairment and depression after traumatic brain injury. *Archives of Physical Medicine and Rehabilitation*, *78*, 1321–1326.

Grafman, J. (1989). Plans, actions, and mental sets: Managerial knowledge units in the frontal lobes. In E. Perecman (Ed.), *Integrating Theory and Practice in Clinical Neuropsychology* (pp. 93–138). Hilldale, NJ: Erlbaum.

Hambrick, J.P., Weeks, J.W., Harb, G.C., & Heimberg, R.G. (2003). Cognitive-behavioral therapy for social anxiety disorder: Supporting evidence and future directions. *CNS Spectrums*, *8*, 373–381.

Harrick, L., Krefting, L., Johnston, J., Carlson, P., & Minnes, P. (1994). Stability of functional outcomes following transitional living programme participation: 3-year follow-up. *Brain Injury*, *8*, 439–447.

Hartley, L.L. (1995). *Cognitive-Communicative Abilities following Brain Injury.* San Diego, CA: Singular.

Hartley, L.L., & Jensen, P.J. (1992). Three discourse profiles of closed-head-injury speakers: Theoretical and clinical implications. *Brain Injury*, *6*, 271–281.

Helffenstein, D.A., & Wechsler, F.S. (1982). The use of Interpersonal Process Recall (IPR) in the remediation of interpersonal and communication skill deficits in the newly brain-injured. *Clinical Neuropsychology*, *4*, 139–143.

Hersen, M., & Bellack, A.S. (1976). A multiple-baseline analysis of social skills training in chronic schizophrenics. *Journal of Applied Behavior Analysis*, *9*, 239–245.

Holbourn, A.H.S. (1943). Mechanics of head injuries. *Lancet*, *2*, 438–441.

Hoofien, D., Gilboa, A., Vakil, E., & Donvick, P.J. (2001). Traumatic brain injury (TBI) 10–20 years later: A comprehensive outcome study of psychiatric symptomatology, cognitive abilities, and psychosocial functioning. *Brain Injury*, *15*, 189–209.

Jackson, H.F., & Moffat, N.J. (1987). Impaired emotional recognition following severe head injury. *Cortex*, *23*, 293–300.

Jacobs, H.E. (1988). The Los Angeles head injury survey: Procedures and initial findings. *Archives of Physical Medicine and Rehabilitation*, *69*, 425–431.

Johnson, D. A., & Newton, A. (1987). Social adjustment and interaction after severe head injury: II. Rationale and basis for intervention. *British Journal of Clinical Psychology*, *26*, 289–298.

Johnson, K., & Davis, P.K. (1998). A supported relationships intervention to increase the social integration of persons with traumatic brain injuries. *Behavior Modification*, *22*, 502–528.

Jorge, R.E., Robinson, R.G., Arndt, S.V., Starkstein, S.E., Forrester, A.W., & Geisler, F. (1993). Depression following traumatic brain injury: A 1 year longitudinal study. *Journal of Affective Disorders*, *27*, 233–243.

Karpman, T., Wolfe, S., & Vargo, J.W. (1985). The psychological adjustment of adult clients and their parents following closed head injury. *Journal of Rehabilitation Counseling*, *17*, 28–33.

Kendall, E., Shum, D., Halson, D., Bunning, S., & Teh, M. (1997). The assessment of social-problem solving ability following traumatic brain injury. *Journal of Head Trauma Rehabilitation*, *12*, 68–78.

Kennedy, C.H. (2001). Social interaction interventions for youth with severe disabilities should emphasize interdependence. *Mental Retardation and Developmental Disabilities Review*, *7*, 122–127.

Kersel, D.A., Marsh, N.V., Havill, J.H., & Sleigh, J.W. (2001). Psychosocial functioning during the year following severe traumatic brain injury. *Brain Injury, 15*, 683–
   696.
Klonoff, P.S., Snow, W.G., & Costa, L.D. (1986). Quality of life in patients 2 to 4 years
   after closed head injury. *Neurosurgery, 19*, 735–743.
Kolko, D.J., & Milan, M.A. (1985). Women's heterosocial skills observational rating
   system: Behavior-analytic development and validation. *Behavior Modification, 9*, 165–
   192.
Kozloff, R. (1987). Networks of social support and the outcome from severe head injury.
   Journal of Head Trauma Rehabilitation, 2, 14–23.
Kreutzer, J.S., Gervasio, A.H., & Camplair, P.S. (1994). Patient correlates of caregivers'
   distress and family functioning after traumatic brain injury. *Brain Injury, 8*(3), 211–
   230.
Kubu, C.S. (1992). *An Investigation of Emotion Recognition in Individuals with Closed
   Head Injury.* Dissertation thesis, University of Iowa, Iowa City.
Kubu, C.S. (1999). Emotion recognition and psychosocial behavior in closed head injury.
   In N.R. Varney & R.J. Roberts (Eds.), *The Evaluation and Treatment of Mild Trau-
   matic Brain Injury.* Mahweh, NJ: Erlbaum.
Levin, H.S., High, W.M., Goeth, K.E., Sisson, R.E., Overall, J.E., Rhoades, H.M.,
   Eisenberg, H.M., Kalisky, Z., & Gary, H.E. (1987). The Neurobehavioral Rating Scale:
   Assessment of the behavioral sequelae of head injury by the clinician. *Journal of Neu-
   rology, Neurosurgery, and Psychiatry, 50*, 183–193.
Lewis, F.D., Nelson, J., Nelson, C., & Reusink, P. (1988). Effects of three feedback contingencies on the socially inappropriate talk of a brain-injured adult. *Behavior Therapy,
   19*, 203–211.
Lezak, M.D. (1988). Brain damage is a family affair. *Journal of Clinical and Experimental Neuropsychology, 10*, 111–123.
Liberman, R.P., Eckman, T.A., & Marder, S.R. (2001). Training in social problem solving among persons with schizophrenia. *Psychiatric Services, 52*, 31–33.
Liberman, R.P., Glynn, S., Blair, K.E., Ross, D., & Marder, S.R. (2002). In vivo amplified skills training: Promoting generalization of independent living skills for clients
   with schizophrenia. *Psychiatry, 65*, 137–155.
Linscott, R.J., Knight, R.G., & Godfrey, H.P.D. (1996). The Profile of Functional Impairment in Communication (PRIC): A measure of communication impairment for
   clinical use. *Brain Injury, 10*, 397–412.
Marsh, N.V. (1999). Social skill deficits following traumatic brain injury: Assessment and
   treatment. In S. McDonald, L. Togher, & C. Code (Eds.), *Communication Disorders
   Following Traumatic Brain Injury* (pp. 175–210). East Sussex, England: Psychology
   Press.
Marsh, N.V., Kersel, D.A., Havill, J.H., & Sleigh, J.W. (1998). Caregiver burden at 1 year
   following sever traumatic brain injury. *Brain Injury, 12*(12), 1045–1079.
Marsh, N.V., & Knight, R.G. (1991). Behavioral assessment of social competence fol-
   lowing severe head injury. *Journal of Clinical and Experimental Neuropsychology,
   13*(5), 729–740.
McDonald, S., Flanagan, S., Rollins, J., & Kinch, J. (2003). TASIT: A new clinical tool
   for assessing social perception after traumatic brain injury. *Journal of Head Trauma
   Rehabilitation, 18*, 219–238.
Meghiji, C. (2002). An innovative self-monitoring treatment approach for use with the
   brain injured population. *The Journal of Cognitive Rehabilitation, 20*, 6–9.

Mooney, G.P. (1988). Relative contributions of neurophysical, cognitive, and personality changes to disability after brain injury. *Cognitive Rehabilitation, Sept/Oct.*, 14–20.

Morton, M.V., & Wehman, P. (1995). Psychosocial and emotional sequelae of individuals with traumatic brain injury: A literature review and recommendations. *Brain Injury, 9*, 81–92.

Nihira, K., Foster, R., Shellaas, M., & Leland, H. (1974). *AAMD Adaptive Behavior Scale.* Washington, DC: American Association on Mental Deficiency.

Oddy, M. (1984). Head injury and social adjustment. In N. Brooks (Ed.) *Closed Head Injury: Psychological, Social, and Family Consequences.* Oxford, England: Oxford University Press.

Oddy, M., Coughlan, T., Tyerman, A., & Jenkins, D. (1985). Social adjustment after closed head injury: A further follow-up seven years later. *Journal of Neurology, Neurosurgery, and Psychiatry, 48*, 564–568.

Oddy, M.J., & Humphrey, M.E. (1980). Social recovery during the year following severe head injury. *Journal of Neurology, Neurosurgery, and Psychiatry, 43*, 798–802.

Oddy, M.J., Humphrey, M., & Uttley, D. (1978). Stresses upon the relatives of head-injured patients. *British Journal of Psychiatry, 133*, 507–513.

Ojeda del Pozo, N., Ezquerra-Iribarren, J.A., Urrutiocoechea-Sarriegui, I., Quemada-Ubis, J.I., & Muñoz-Cespedes, J.M. (2000). Entrenamiento en habiladades sociales en pacientes con daño cerebral adquirido. *Review of Neurology, 30*, 783–787.

Ommaya, A.K., & Corrao, P. (1971). Pathologic biomechanics of central nervous system injury in head impact and whiplash injury. In K.M. Bringhaus (Ed.), *Accident Pathology* (pp. 160–181). Washington, DC: U.S. Government Printing Office.

Ommaya, A.K., & Gennarelli, T.A. (1974). Cerebral concussion and traumatic unconsciousness: Correlation of experimental and clinical observations on blunt head injuries. *Brain, 97*, 633–654.

O'Reilly, M. F., Lancioni, G. E., & O'Kane, N. (2000). Using a problem-solving approach to teach social skills to workers with brain injuries in supported employment settings. *Journal of Vocational Rehabilitation, 14*, 187–193.

Pfeiffer, W., Helsine R., & James, J. (1976). *Instrumentation in Human Relations Training.* La Jolla, CA: University Associates.

Prigatano, G.P. (1999). *Principles of Neuropsychological Rehabilitation* (pp. 117–147). New York: Oxford University Press.

Prigatano, G.P., & Pribram, K.H. (1982). Perception and memory of facial affect following brain injury. *Perceptual and Motor Skills, 54*, 859–869.

Rappaport, M., Herrero-Backe, C., Rappaport, M.L., & Winterfield, K.M. (1989). Head injury outcome up to ten years later. *Archives of Physical Medicine and Rehabilitation, 70*, 885–892.

Sander, A.M., Fuchs, K.L., High, W.M., Jr., Hall, K.M., Kreutzer, J.S., & Rosenthal, M. (1999). The Community Integration Questionnaire revisitd: An assessment of factor structure and validity. *Archives of Physical Medicine and Rehabilitation, 80*, 1303–1308.

Schloss, P.J., Thompson, C.K., Gajar, A.H., & Schloss, C.K. (1985). Influence of self-monitoring on heterosexual conversational behaviors of head trauma youth. *Applied Research in Mental Retardation, 6*, 269–282.

Seibert, P.S., Reedy, D.P., Hash, J., Webb, A., Stridh-Igo, P., Basom, J., & Zimmerman, C.G. (2002). Brain injury: Quality of life's greatest challenge. *Brain Injury, 10*, 837–848.

Sirigu, A., Zalla, T., Pillon, B., Grafman, J., Dubois, B., & Agrid, Y. (1995). Planning and script analysis following prefrontal lobe lesions. *Annals of the New York Academy of Science, 769,* 277–288.

Sladyk, K. (1992). Traumatic brain injury, behavioral disorder, and group treatment. *The American Journal of Occupational Therapy, 46,* 267–270.

Snow, P., & Douglas, J. (1999). Discourse rehabilitation following traumatic brain injury. In S. McDonald, L. Togher, & C. Code (Eds.), *Communication Disorders Following Traumatic Brain Injury* (pp. 271–320). East Sussex, England: Psychology Press.

Snow, P., Douglas, J., & Ponsford, J. (1998). Conversational discourse abilities following severe traumatic brain injury. *Brain Injury, 12,* 911–935.

Sohlberg, M.M., Perlewitz, P.G., Johansen, A., Schultz, J., Johnson, L., & Hartry, A. (1992). *Improving Pragmatic Skills in Persons with Head Injury.* Tucson, AZ: Communication Skill Builders.

Strich, S.J. (1956). Diffuse degeneration of the cerebral white mater in severe dementia following head injury. *Journal of Neurology, Neurosurgery, and Psychiatry, 19,* 163–185.

Thomas-Stonell, N., Johnson, P., Schuller, R., & Jutai, J. (1994). Evaluation of a computer-based program for remediation of cognitive-communication skills. *Journal of Head Trauma Rehabilitation, 9,* 25–37.

Thomsen, I.V. (1974). The patient with severe head injury and his family. *Scandinavian Journal of Rehabilitation Medicine, 6,* 180–183.

Thomsen, I.V. (1984). Late outcome of very severe blunt head trauma: A 10–15 year second follow-up. *Journal of Neurology, Neurosurgery, and Psychiatry, 47,* 260–268.

Twentyman, C.T., & McFall, R.M. (1975). Behavioral training of social skills in shy males. *Journal of Consulting and Clinical Psychology, 43,* 384–395.

Uomoto, J.M., & Brockway, J.A. (1992). Anger management training for brain injured patients and their family members. *Archives of Physical Medicine and Rehabilitation, 73,* 674–679.

van Dam-Baggen, R., & Kraaimaat, F. (2000). Group social skills training or cognitive group therapy as the clinical treatment of choice for generalized social phobia? *Journal of Anxiety Disorders, 14,* 437–451.

Wallace, C.J., & Liberman, R.P. (1985). Social skills training for patients with schizophrenia: A controlled clinical trial. *Psychiatry Research, 15,* 239–247.

Wallander, J.L., Conger, A.J., & Conger, J.C. (1985). Development and evaluation of a behaviorally referenced rating system for heterosocial skills. *Behavioral Assessment, 7,* 137–153.

Weddell, R., Oddy, M., & Jenkins, D. (1980). Social adjusment after rehabilitation: A two-year follow-up of patients with severe head injury. *Psychological Medicine, 10,* 257–263.

Whiteneck, G., Chralifue, S., Gerhart, K., Overholser, J., & Richardson, G. (1992). Quantifying handicap: A new measure of long-term rehabilitation outcomes. *Archives of Physical Medicine and Rehabilitation, 73,* 519–526.

Willer, B., Ottenbacher, K.J., & Coad, M.L. (1994). The Community Integration Questionnaire: A comparative examination. *American Journal of Physical Medicine and Rehabilitation, 73,* 103–111.

Wiseman-Hakes, C., Stewart, M.L., Wasserman, R., & Schuller, R. (1998). Peer group training of pragmatic skills in adolescents with acquired brain injury. *Journal of Head Trauma Rehabilitation, 13,* 23–38.

Ylvisaker, M., Urbanczyk, B., & Feeney, T.J. (1992). Social skills following traumatic brain injury. *Seminars in Speech and Language, 13*(4), 308–322.

Yuen, H.K. (1997). Positive talk training in an adult with traumatic brain injury. *The American Journal of Occupational Therapy, 51*, 780–783.

Zencius, A.H., Wesolowski, M.D., & Burke, W.H. (1990). The use of a visual cue to reduce profanity in a brain injured adult. *Behavioral Residential Treatment, 5*, 143–147.

7

Therapy for Emotional
and Motivational Disorders

GEORGE P. PRIGATANO

The nature of higher integrative or cerebral functions is not purely cognitive. These functions reflect a natural integration of both thinking and feeling to maximize adaptive problem solving (Chapman & Wolff, 1959; Prigatano, 1999). Disturbances in affect are as common after traumatic brain injury (TBI) as cognitive deficits (Borgaro & Prigatano, 2002; Newcombe, 2001; Prigatano & Wong, 1999; Oddy et al., 1985). This outcome is to be expected given the neuropathologic lesions common among this patient group (Gentry, 2002).

Growing experimental and clinical evidence indicates that improvement in affective functioning is as important to rehabilitation outcomes as improvement in cognitive function (Ben-Yishay & Prigatano, 1990; Prigatano, 1999; Prigatano & Wong, 1999; Prigatano et al., 1986). Finally, persistent difficulties in the personalities of TBI patients create a considerable burden for caregivers (Brooks & McKinlay, 1983) as well as rehabilitation staff (Prigatano, 1999).

Two major challenges for our field are to improve methods for assessing personality disturbances after TBI (Prigatano, 1999) and to find cost-effective methods for treating them (Pepping & Prigatano, 2003). Given the interest of the neuroscientific community in *affective neuroscience* (Davidson et al., 2003) and efforts to describe the *neurocircuitry of emotion*, the time may be ripe for such renewed efforts. As contemporary neuroimaging studies are applied to the study of affect, there is a reawakening of awareness of the intimate connection between thinking and feeling and the need to study this intimate interaction of cognitive and personality disturbances in rehabilitation (Principle 5, Prigatano, 1999). For example, when considering "some general lessons from research on the neuroscience of emotion" (p. 5), Davidson et al. (2003) recently remarked:

> The notion that emotions are somehow limbic and subcortical and cognitions cortical is giving way to a much more refined and complex view. . . . It is simply not possible to identify regions of the brain devoted exclusively to affect or exclusively to cognition." (p. 5)

Although not cited by the authors, Chapman and Wolff (1959) made this same point years ago.

The effective treatment of emotional and motivational disorders after TBI begins by clarifying the definition of the terms and by providing a framework for conceptualizing personality disorders associated with TBI.

BACKGROUND INFORMATION AND A FRAME OF REFERENCE

The following three definitions are used in this discussion.

Emotions are complex feeling states that serve an interrupt function during goal-seeking behavior. *Motivation* reflects complex feeling states that serve a maintaining and hierarchical arrangement function during goal-seeking behavior. Both contribute an arousal component to behavior and subjective experience. *Personality* is long-standing individual patterns of emotion and motivational responding, whose expression is modified by environmental contingencies, the biological and psychological needs of the organism, and cognitive processes (see Prigatano et al., 1986).

A Conceptual Model for Understanding Personality Disorders after Brain Injury

Clinically, patients' reports of disturbances in emotion and motivation seem to fall within three broad categories: reactionary, neuropsychological, and characterological, as the following cases illustrate.

A 60-year-old right-handed man reported the following about 4 years after surgical resection of a cavernous malformation in the left temporal lobe: "I don't like who I am. I am not fit to live with anyone. I am irritable all the time, I want to live alone." This patient suffered from language and memory disturbances that resulted in his early retirement. He appeared to be demonstrating a reaction to his residual neuropsychological impairments and the consequences they had on his life. His emotional and motivational difficulties could be considered *reactionary*.

After surgical resection of the left anterior tip of the temporal lobe to control partial complex seizures, a 19-year-old right-handed woman reported the following: "My seizures are under control now. I am really happy and happy that I can drive a car again. I am frustrated, however, that I can't comprehend what I am reading in school as well as I used to. Despite several hours of studying each day, my grades have dropped. I also noticed that right after my surgery I experienced severe panic attacks. They have diminished in frequency, but I still have them about once a month." This patient was reporting changes in emotion (i.e., panic attacks) that may well reflect a direct disturbance of brain function (i.e., related to amygdaloid dysfunction). This type of difficulty can be classified as a *neuropsychological* disturbance in emotion (personality).

The third patient, a 48-year-old physician, had suffered a severe TBI. He made an excellent neuropsychological recovery but still struggled with what he would do in the future. As he stated, "I just want to go back to work. I don't like talking about my feelings; I never have." After several months of psychotherapy, in which a therapeutic alliance was slowly established, he made the following comment: "You asked me about what has been making me sad or angry. It has taken me a long time to think about it. What really upsets me is that my wife and children did not seem to show for me the kind of care that I would have shown for them after such an injury. I don't know how to handle this." This patient reported he was one of eight children, and throughout his life and childhood felt that he never received adequate support from his parents. It appears that his problem represents a previous difficulty in psychological adjustment that was restimulated as a consequence of the brain injury. It may, therefore, be referred to as a *characterological* feature of personality (i.e., a premorbid factor).

All three types of personality disorders or disturbances can be seen in persons with a TBI. Typically, the first two types (i.e., the reactionary and neuropsychological problems) have been the focus of studies involving this patient population. The third type, however, should not be forgotten because it may influence the expression of the first two disturbances.

Understanding the Symptom Picture Improves Treatment

The neuropsychologically based problems have been described as *direct* symptoms of brain injury. Goldstein (1942, 1952) noted, as John Hughlings Jackson did before him, that both direct and indirect symptoms follow brain injury. In Goldstein's terminology, a *direct symptom* refers to a change in function that is clearly related to brain damage. That is, a cause–effect relationship is demonstrated or assumed. The change in function is related to a neurologic variable such as the severity of brain injury [like the Glasgow Coma Scale (GCS) score] or the location of brain injury. When a direct effect is present, there is often some form of a *dose–response relationship* between the neuropsychological variable and the measure of brain damage or dysfunction. For example, Dikmen et al. (1995) demonstrated that the Halstead Impairment Index score was directly related to the severity of TBI 1 year after injury. Patients who took longer to follow commands after TBI had significantly worse Halstead Impairment Index scores than patients who were able to follow commands soon after injury. Borgaro and colleagues (2002) recently demonstrated that performance on various measures of affect expression and perception was worse for persons with a mild TBI and a complication (i.e., a space-occupying lesion) compared to those who had TBI alone. This relationship was observed within the first 10 to 15 days after trauma.

Empirical and clinical evidence suggests that the following changes in emotion and motivation may reflect direct symptoms:

- Apathy (and diminished drive or motivation) associated with bifrontal lesions (Lishman, 1968; Luria, 1948/1963; Ota, 1969).
- Agitation/restlessness (Reyes et al., 1981).
- Emotional lability, aggression, and disinhibition (often associated with cognitive impairment in children with TBI; Max et al., 2000).
- Depression (in the acute phase) associated with left anterior brain lesions (Robinson and Szetela, 1981). Damage to the left anterior rather than the right anterior regions of the brain may produce differences in approach versus avoidance behavior (Davidson, 1992).
- Paranoid reactions (and suspicious ideation) may be associated with temporal and frontal lesions (Prigatano, 1999).
- Disturbance of *somatic markers* necessary for subjective representation of feeling states may lead to disturbed social behavior and disturbances in consciousness (Craig, 2002; Damasio et al., 2000).
- Diminished impulse control with associated "child-like" behaviors in adults with TBI (Thompson et al., 1984) often occurs with significant right hemisphere dysfunction with associated frontal lobe involvement.
- Reduced tolerance of frustration (clinical observation).
- Diminished self-awareness (which is partially a change of personality) related to damage of the heteromodal cortex (Prigatano, 1999).

Emotional and motivational changes, which are direct symptoms, are frequently observed in the presence of various cognitive impairments (Lishman, 1968).

Indirect symptoms (reactionary problems) often reflect the struggle to adapt or the tendency to avoid the struggle (Goldstein, 1942). Typical studies find little or no correlation between this class of symptoms and a *neurological marker* of severity of brain injury (like the GCS score) or the location of brain injury.

Empirical and clinical evidence suggests that the following changes in emotion and motivation may be indirect symptoms:

- Depression associated with angry reactions (especially postacutely) in patients facing the problem of lost normality (Prigatano, 1999: Prigatano et al., 1986).
- Anxiety reactions, panic attacks, and somatic complaints during a catastrophic reaction (Prigatano, 1999; Prigatano et al., 1986).
- Social withdrawal and diminished seeking of the nonadaptive state (challenge, adventure, or exploration) (Kiev et al., 1962; Kozloff, 1987).
- Irritability, possibly related to sleep disturbance and depression (van Zomeren and van den Burg, 1985), report a correlation between posttraumatic amnesia [PTA] and memory which is significant [$r = +.54$], but the correlation between PTA and ratings of irritability [$r = +.11$] is nonsignificant.
- Denial of disability (with associated poor choices related to families, friends, work, and rehabilitation). This behavior can be distinguished from the problem of impaired awareness (Prigatano, 1999).

Finally, as noted above, TBI patients had a personality before their brain injury. Premorbid methods of coping, interest patterns, values, interpersonal relationships, and so on may interact with direct (neuropsychologically based) and indirect (reactionary) disturbances to produce a complex symptom picture. Prigatano (1999) provided case examples of how injury at different stages of life can produce different patterns of reactionary, neuropsychologically based, and characterological problems associated with TBI.

Treatments

Broadly speaking, there are three classes of treatments for TBI: pharmacologic, nonpharmacologic, and possibly neurosurgical. Pharmacologic and surgical interventions are not discussed. This chapter considers how nonpharmacologic or psychiatric/psychological treatments may help patients with TBI.

Prigatano and colleagues (2003) have outlined four major ingredients in the nonpharmacologic treatment of patients with brain dysfunction. These components include providing *information*, applying appropriate *contingencies* on behavior with associated reinforcers, helping the patient attain greater *awareness* of residual difficulties, and establishing a therapeutic alliance or *relationship* that helps guide the patient to make appropriate choices. A discussion of how these components of treatment can be applied is beyond the scope of this chapter. To some degree, however, most nonpharmacologic methods use these four components to influence behavior.

The Important Role of Psychotherapy in Brain Injury Rehabilitation

While there have been no comprehensive reviews on the effectiveness of various forms of psychotherapy following TBI, several authors have summarized clinical observations emanating from this work (Langer and Laatsch, 1999; Pepping and Prigatano, 2003; Prigatano et al., 1984, 2003). There is a recognition that various techniques, ranging from behavioral modification (Howard, 1988) to formal family therapy (Larøi, 2003), may be helpful in certain circumstances. Many forms of psychotherapy focus on helping the patient with the "personal" side of brain injury. A broad psychotherapeutic model is necessary and must consider the individual's learning history, as well as potential psychodynamic and cultural factors, in understanding what each patient must face after brain injury. Detailed clinical descriptions of how psychotherapeutic interventions might be applied to some TBI patients have been presented elsewhere (Freed, 2003; Prigatano, 1999; Prigatano et al., 1984).

Briefly, however, three scenarios highlight the potential role of psychotherapeutic interventions. These interventions can help patients cope with their residual impairments. A young woman shot in the left temporal lobe suffered the associated difficulties with language impairment and memory. She was angry and ashamed about what had happened to her. However, she was able to express her feelings artistically. Her drawing highlighted what many brain dysfunctional patients experience. She spontaneously asked, "You mean I can have a brain injury and still be creative?" (Prigatano, 1999, p. 41). The answer was obvious. As she came to understand this reality, she experienced considerable emotional relief and became progressively less angry.

Psychotherapeutic interventions can also help at the level of disability. Some brain dysfunctional patients know that they have permanent disabilities with which they must always contend. One young man had persistent hemiparesis and aphasia after a severe TBI to the left hemisphere. Ultimately, he was able to accept his difficulties as he recognized that meaning in life derived from many factors other than having normal cognitive or motor functions. As he was able to give to others, he established a sense of purpose that transcended his TBI (see the drawing on p. 85 in Prigatano et al., 1986).

Psychotherapy also can help TBI patients confront their personal suffering at the phenomenological level. Prigatano (1995) described the role of psychotherapy in helping patients deal broadly with the problem of lost normality. That paper recounts a story about a man from South Vietnam who had to come to grips with his brain injury. His philosophical approach to life allowed him to recognize that the meaning of a brain injury could not be known until later in life (see the story "The Man Named Thong" in Prigatano, 1995).

Evidence

What is the evidence that working with the emotional and motivational disturbances of brain dysfunctional patients substantially improves their rehabilitation outcome? A number of studies address this problem directly and indirectly.

Prigatano et al. (1984) provided the first empirical support that patients who had undergone an intensive neuropsychologically oriented rehabilitation program (which included psychotherapy) were more often employed than patients who did not receive such treatment. Interestingly, the treated patients showed only mild improvement in their cognitive functioning but substantial reduction in emotional and motivational disturbances, as judged by their relatives. Ben-Yishay et al. (1985), using 100 TBI patients (but unfortunately no control group), arrived at similar conclusions. Scherzer (1986) reported rates of return to work comparable to those of untreated control groups (approximately one-third). His form of rehabilitation did not include psychotherapeutic interventions.

Prigatano et al. (1994) extended their earlier research findings on an independent sample of 38 TBI patients with a historical control group. They demonstrated that the working alliance, or the therapeutic relationship between the patient and therapist, was related to positive rehabilitation outcomes. Klonoff et al. (2000) extended these observations with a larger sample and replicated the original finding.

Prigatano (1999) reported on a man who showed continued cognitive recovery after rehabilitation but whose ability to control his anger deteriorated several years after injury. This patient had been brought into rehabilitation "too early." This case highlights the point that if a patient's emotional and motivational problems are not treated at the appropriate time, they can worsen as time passes.

Salazar et al. (2000) reportedly provided a neuropsychological rehabilitation program for patients with TBI during the early stages after brain injury. The program, however, was developed for postacute TBI patients. The authors' failure to find significant treatment effects may be related to the fact that patients were treated too early using such methods. To study the efficacy of neuropsychological rehabilitation, of which psychotherapeutic interventions are one major ingredient, treatment programs have to be provided at a time when patients can benefit maximally from them. Clinically, patients often deteriorate from a psychiatric point of view if treatment is given at inappropriate times (see Prigatano, 1999). Prigatano (2000) has discussed the limits of the Salazar et al. (2000) study.

GAPS IN KNOWLEDGE AND METHODOLOGICAL DIFFICULTIES WHEN STUDYING AND TREATING DISORDERS OF EMOTION AND MOTIVATION

There are many gaps in our knowledge concerning emotional and motivational disturbances after brain injury. There are also considerable limitations in terms of how to study these difficulties. Consequently, the field has not progressed substantially in the past 50 years. Many potential areas for study can be identified. The following discussion presents my own clinical impression about where the biggest gaps exist.

First, premorbid personality characteristics (or patterns of emotional and motivational responding) have never been measured adequately. More effort should be exerted to characterize core patterns of emotional and motivational responding *before injury* to determine how various brain injuries interact with these premorbid patterns to produce the complex symptom picture that emerges after injury (Prigatano, 1999).

Second, emotion and motivation are not measured directly in a clinical neuropsychological examination. Clinicians rely on self-reports from the patient or ratings from family members. This situation must be corrected. The BNI Screen for Higher Cerebral Functions provides four items that approach this problem (Borgaro & Prigatano, 2002). Patients are asked to read a sentence in a happy and then in an angry tone of voice. They are asked to identify facial affect. Finally, their ability to show spontaneous affect is determined. Other such tests that directly sample impulsivity, angry outbursts, depression, and anxiety are needed. Using innovative methods such as psychophysiologic recordings in conjunction with subjective reports may be especially helpful in this regard.

A third major gap is knowledge about how emotions and motivations change over time. What happens with and without various forms of treatment? Do the patterns differ for direct and indirect symptoms?

A fourth major gap is the limited information on how cognitive deficits interact with emotional and motivational disturbances. Lishman's (1968) early work documented that patients with significant psychiatric sequelae often exhibit changes in intellectual functioning. This basic finding needs to be expanded. Exactly how do different cognitive deficits produce different emotional and motivational disturbances? Conversely, how do different emotional and motivational disturbances affect the cognitive process?

A fifth gap is the failure to distinguish direct from indirect symptoms when studying emotional and motivational disturbances after brain injury. This failure can lead to less effective ideas for future research.

A sixth gap is the failure to identify the types of strategies and experiences that might be most helpful for treating the emotional and motivational disturbances that follow mild, moderate, and severe TBI.

THE MOST PRESSING UNANSWERED RESEARCH QUESTIONS

Research advances when clear hypotheses and a methodology/technology for testing those hypotheses exist. The question posed should have both clinical and theoretical relevance. Many unanswered research questions could be formulated about emotional and motivational disturbances after TBI and how best to treat them. The following questions, however, appear most relevant from a clinical perspective:

- How does one control angry, aggressive outbursts in severely injured TBI patients?
- How does one help TBI patients to improve their impulse control in social interactions? Are any compensatory techniques really helpful?
- How does one specifically help TBI patients with orbitofrontal injuries, who frequently have major difficulties controlling emotional lability and who have associated problems with interpersonal judgment?
- How does one improve the energy level of TBI patients to decrease their fatigue and, potentially, their related problem of irritability?
- How does one teach patients the concept of *catastrophic reaction* and help them anticipate such reactions in every day life? (This issue has been a major thrust of neuropsychologically oriented rehabilitation; Prigatano et al., 1984.)
- How does one help persons adjust to the losses imposed by brain injury and reconstruct a life worth living?
- How does one overcome or reduce the problem of impaired awareness, which partially reflects a disturbance in personality?
- How does one avoid and treat the development of psychotic reactions, particularly paranoid ideation after TBI? This problem is underreported in this patient group.

RECOMMENDATIONS FOR FUTURE RESEARCH PRIORITIES

The following areas of research would seem to be especially pertinent to clinicians involved in the treatment of the emotional and motivational disturbances of TBI patients:

1. Develop brief, direct measures of affective responding that can be monitored over time, similar to memory disturbances and speed of information processing deficits after TBI.
2. Relate these measures of affective functioning systematically to cognitive disturbances and determine their interaction. For example, how does decreased speed of information processing result in the misinterpretation of comments, lower tolerance for frustration, and contribute to angry or depressive reactions?
3. Conduct quantitative and funtional magnetic resonance imaging studies relating structural and dynamic changes in the brain to both cognitive and affective disturbances simultaneously. The research design should

always include how affective disturbances are or are not present when cognitive disturbances are measured. Studying the role of the amygdala and the orbitofrontal cortex as mediators of different affective states after TBI would likely be fruitful. Davidson et al. (2003) recently summarized research on the *circuitry of emotion*, and their ideas are relevant to the study of TBI patients. They noted that the prefrontal cortex plays an important role in the representation of goals. Damage to this region may therefore affect motivation as well as emotion. Citing the work of Damasio (see Damasio et al., 2000), they noted that the ventromedial prefrontal cortex seems to help guide decision making from an emotional perspective. This observation should be pursued in TBI patients. The work of Thayer and Lane (2002) suggests that the anterior cingulate cortex may be the bridge between attention and emotion. Given the overall thrust of this chapter (i.e., to study the interaction of cognition and disturbances of emotion and motivation simultaneously), this would be an excellent area to study.

4. Study how damage to the frontal and temporal lobes may be particularly important in the production of visual and auditory perceptual disturbances that may be the basis of suspicious ideation or paranoid reactions.

5. Study how people adjust emotionally to losses after brain injury and how to teach therapists working with brain dysfunctional patients to attend to this dimension of care.

6. Establish a database for TBI children and study them prospectively for 20–25 years. Assess specifically how cognitive and affective disturbances change over time, how they are related, and their implications for psychosocial adjustment.

CONCLUSIONS

Research on understanding and treating emotional and motivational disturbances after TBI involves a wide variety of options. Studying the neurocircuitry of emotion and motivation may lead to better treatment of direct symptoms or neuropsychologically based personality disorders. To date, no effective treatments have emerged in this area. Longitudinal studies of patients' reactions to limitations imposed by TBI may improve insights into the treatment of indirect symptoms. Holistic approaches (which include psychotherapeutic as well as pharmacologic interventions) have been helpful in dealing with this type of symptom.

Our understanding of how premorbid features of the personality interact with direct and indirect symptoms imposed by TBI is inadequate. This area would seem to be extremely fruitful to pursue. In clinical practice, the clinician's assumptions concerning premorbid personality characteristics greatly influence the approach to patients.

At this time, helping patients reduce their personal suffering over lost normality is the most important component of treating emotional and motivational disturbances after TBI.

ACKNOWLEDGMENTS

Financial support from the Newsome Chair in Clinical Neuropsychology at the Barrow Neurological Institute provided the resources to prepare this manuscript.

REFERENCES

Ben-Yishay, Y., & Prigatano, G.P. (1990). Cognitive remediation. In E. Griffin, M. Rosenthal, M.R. Bond, & J.D. Miller (Eds.), *Rehabilitation of the Adult and Child with Traumatic Brain Injury* (pp. 393–409). Philadelphia: F.A. Davis.

Ben-Yishay, Y., Rattok, J., Lakin, P., Piasetsky, E.D., Ross, B., Silver, S., Zide, E., & Ezrachi, O. (1985). Neuropsychological rehabilitation: Quest for a holistic approach. *Seminars in Neurology*, 5, 252–258.

Borgaro, S.R., & Prigatano, G.P. (2002). Early cognitive and affective sequelae of traumatic brain injury: A study using the BNI Screen for Higher Cerebral Functions. *Journal of Head Trauma Rehabilitation*, 17(6), 526–534.

Borgaro, S.R., Prigatano, G.P., Kwasnica, C., & Rexer, J. (2002). Cognitive and affective sequelae in complicated and uncomplicated mild traumatic brain injury. *Brain Injury*, 17(3), 189–198.

Brooks, D.N., & McKinlay, W. (1983). Personality and behavioral change after severe blunt head injury—a relative's view. *Journal of Neurology, Neurosurgery, and Psychiatry*, 46, 336–344.

Chapman, L.F., & Wolff, H.G. (1959). The cerebral hemispheres and the highest integrative functions of man. *Archives of Neurology*, 1, 357–424.

Craig, A.D. (2002). How do you feel? Interoception: the sense of the physiological condition of the body. *Nature Reviews. Neuroscience*, 3(8), 655–666.

Damasio, A.R., Grabowski, T.J., Bechara A., et al. (2000). Subcortical and cortical brain activity during the feeling of self-generated emotions. *Nature Neuroscience*, 3(10), 1049–1056.

Davidson, J.R. (1992). Anterior cerebral asymmetry and the nature of emotion. *Brain and Cognition*, 20, 125–151.

Davidson, R.J., Scherer, K.R., & Goldsmith, H.H. (2003). *Handbook of Affective Sciences*. New York: Oxford University Press.

Dikmen, S., Machamer, J., Winn, H., et al. (1995). Neuropsychological outcome at 1-year post head injury. *Neuropsychology*, 9, 80–90.

Freed, P. (2002). Meeting of the minds: Ego reintegration after traumatic brain injury. *Bulletin of the Menninger Clinic*, 66(1), 61–76.

Gentry, L.R. (2002). Head trauma. In S.W. Atlas (Ed.), *Magnetic Resonance Imaging of the Brain and Spine* (pp. 1059–1098).

Goldstein, K. (1942). Aftereffects of Brain Injury in War. New York: Grune and Stratton.

Goldstein, K. (1952). The effect of brain damage on the personality. *Psychiatry*, 15, 245–260.

Howard, M. (1988). Behavior management in the acute care rehabilitation setting. *Journal of Head Trauma Rehabilitation*, 3, 14–22.

Kiev, A., Chapman, L.F., Guthrie, T.C., & Wolff, H.G. (1962). The highest integrative functions and diffuse cerebral atrophy. *Neurology, 12*, 385–393.

Klonoff, P.S., Lamb, D.G., & Henderson, S.W. (2000). Milieu-based neuro-rehabilitation in patients with traumatic brain injury: Outcome at up to 11 years post-discharge. *Archives of Physical Medicine and Rehabilitation, 81*(11), 1535–1537.

Kozloff, R. (1987). Network of social support and the outcome from severe head injury. *Journal of Head Trauma Rehabilitation, 2*, 14–23.

Langer, K.G., & Laatsch, L. (Eds.). (1999). Psychotherapeutic Interventions for Adults with Brain Injury or Stroke: A Clinician's Treatment Resource (pp. 131–148). Madison, CT: Psychosocial Press.

Larøi, F. (2003). The family systems approach to treating families of persons with brain injury: A potential collaboration between family therapist and brain injury professional. *Brain Injury, 17*(2), 175–187.

Lishman, W.A. (1968). Brain damage in relation to psychiatric disability after head injury. *British Journal of Psychiatry, 114*, 373–410.

Luria, A.R. (1948/1963). Restoration of Function After Brain Trauma (in Russian). Moscow: Academy of Medical Science; London: Pergamon.

Max, J.E., Koele, S.L., Castillo, S.D., Lindgren, S.A., Bokura, H., Robin, D.A., Smith, W.L., & Sato, Y. (2000). Personality change disorder in children and adolescents following traumatic brain injury. *Journal of the International Neuropsychological Society, 6*, 279–289.

Newcombe, F. (2002). An overview of neuropsychological rehabilitation: A forgotten past and a challenging future. In Brouwer, van Zomeren, Berg, Bouma & de Haan (Eds.), *Cognitive Rehabilitation: A Clinical Neuropsychological Approach* (pp. 23–52).

Oddy, M., Coughlan, T., Tyerman, A., & Jenkins, D. (1985). Social adjustment after closed head injury: A further follow-up 7 years after injury. *Journal of Neurology, Neurosurgery, and Psychiatry, 48*, 564–568.

Ota, Y. (1969). Psychiatric studies on civilian head injuries. In A.E. Walker, W.F. Caveness, & M. Critchley (Eds). *The Late Effects of Head Injury* (pp. 110–119). Springfield, IL: C.C. Thomas,.

Pepping, M., & Prigatano, G.P. (2003). Psychotherapy after brain injury: Costs and benefits. In G.P. Prigatano & Pliskin (Eds.), *Clinical Neuropsychology and Cost Outcome Research* (pp. 313–328). New York: Psychology Press.

Prigatano, G.P. (1995). 1994 Sheldon Barrol, M.D., Senior Lectureship: The problem of lost normality after brain injury. *Journal of Head Trauma Rehabilitation, 10*(3), 53–62.

Prigatano, G.P. (1999). *Principles of Neuropsychological Rehabilitation.* New York: Oxford University Press.

Prigatano, G.P. (2000). Rehabilitation for traumatic brain injury (letter). *Journal of the American Medical Association, 284*(14), 1783.

Prigatano, G.P., Borgaro, S.R., & Caples, H.S. (2003). Nonpharmacological management of psychiatric disturbances after traumatic brain injury. *International Review of Psychiatry, 15*, 371–379.

Prigatano, G.P., Fordyce, D.J., Zeiner, H.K., Roueche, J.R., Pepping, M., & Wood, B. (1984). Neuropsychological rehabilitation after closed head injury in young adults. *Journal of Neurology, Neurosurgery and Psychiatry 47*:505–513.

Prigatano, G.P., Fordyce, D.J., Zeiner, H.K., Roueche, J.R., Pepping, M., & Wood, B.C. (1986). *Neuropsychological Rehabilitation after Brain Injury.* Baltimore: Johns Hopkins University Press.

Prigatano, G.P., Klonoff, P.S., O'Brien, K.P., Altman, I., Amin, K., Chiapello, D.A., Shep-
    herd, J., Cunningham, M., & Mora, M. (1994). Productivity after neuropsychologically
    oriented milieu rehabilitation. *Journal of Head Trauma Rehabilitation, 9*(1), 91–102.
Prigatano, G.P., & Wong, J.L. (1999). Cognitive and affective improvement in brain dys-
    functional patients who achieve inpatient rehabilitation goals. *Archives of Physical
    Medicine and Rehabilitation, 80*(1), 77–84.
Reyes, R.L, Bhattacharyya, A.K., & Heller, D. (1981). Traumatic head injury: Restless-
    ness and agitation as prognosticators of physical and psychologic improvement in
    patients. *Archives of Physical Medicine and Rehabilitation, 62*, 20–23.
Robinson, R.G., & Szetela, B. (1981). Mood change following left hemispheric brain in-
    jury. *Annals of Neurology, 9*, 447–453.
Salazar, A.M., Warden, D.L., Schwab, K., et al. (2000). Cognitive rehabilitation for trau-
    matic brain injury: A randomized trial. *Journal of the American Medical Association,
    283*, 3075–301.
Scherzer, B.P. (1986) Rehabilitation following severe head trauma: Results of a three-
    year program. *Archives of Physical Medicine and Rehabilitation, 67*, 366–374.
Thayer, J.F., & Lane, R.D. (2000). A model of neurovisceral integration in emotion regu-
    lation and dysregulation. *Journal of Affective Disorders, 61*, 201–216.
Thomsen, I.V. (1984). Late outcome of very severe blunt head trauma: A 10–15 year sec-
    ond follow-up. *Journal of Neurology, Neurosurgery and Psychiatry, 47*, 260–268.
van Zomeren, A.H., & van den Burg, W. (1985). Residual complaints of patients two
    years after severe head injury. *Journal of Neurology, Neurosurgery and Psychiatry,
    48*, 21–28.

III

FACTORS AFFECTING OUTCOME

8

Substance Abuse

JOHN D. CORRIGAN

This chapter provides a review of current research on traumatic brain injury (TBI) and problems associated with the use of alcohol and other drugs. While these problems are primarily substance use disorders [abuse and dependence as described in the *DSM-IV* (American Psychiatric Association, 1994)], intoxication at time of injury and potentially harmful patterns of consumption after injury (that may not rise to the definition of abuse) are also discussed. Unfortunately, there is far more information on the problem and its scope than there is on treatment approaches to ameliorate use-related disorders. This imbalance will be reflected in this chapter as well. The topics covered will elucidate the scope of the problem, including intoxication at the time of injury, a preinjury history of substance use disorder, use following the injury, the combined effect of TBI and substance abuse on brain structure and function, and negative psychosocial outcomes. Interventions and treatment approaches that have specifically addressed substance use following TBI are reviewed as well. This chapter concludes with a proposed research agenda to address substance use and TBI.

INTOXICATION AT THE TIME OF INJURY

The relationship between intoxication and TBI is well known (Corrigan, 1995; Jernigan, 1991). The only population-based estimate of the occurrence of intoxication at the time of TBI comes from the Colorado TBI Surveillance Follow-up System (C. Harrison-Felix, personal communication, 2003). For persons 16 years of age and older admitted to hospitals in Colorado with a diagnosis of TBI, 20.8% had a blood alcohol content above 80 mg/dL, the legal limit for intoxication in that state. As Corrigan (1995) has observed, persons with TBI treated in rehabilitation tend to have more severe markers of substance use disorders, including intoxication at the time of injury. Based on 3893 acute rehabilitation admissions included in the TBI Model Systems National Dataset, 37% had a blood alcohol level greater than or equal to 100 mg/dL, the legal limit in most states during the time these data were being collected (Traumatic Brain Injury Model Systems National Dataset, Annual Report for 2002). In a consecutive sample of 356 patients admitted for acute rehabilitation to the Brain Injury Unit at the Ohio State University (OSU) Medical Center, 25% were found to have a blood alcohol content above 100 mg/dL. Those with positive toxicology screens for other drugs comprised 12% of the cohort. Because there is extensive overlap between those intoxicated due to alcohol and those intoxicated due to other drugs, the percentage of patients intoxicated due to either was 32%. Estimating the rate of intoxication among persons with TBI from these few studies, for all patients hospitalized it would be reasonable to project that 20% to 30% will be high at the time of the injury. Among patients admitted for rehabilitation after TBI, the rate appears to be between 30% and 40%.

Corrigan (1995) summarized reports from the research literature indicating that those acutely intoxicated were more likely to have more severe injuries, require intubation, develop pneumonia and have other forms of respiratory distress, manifest greater neurologic impairment at discharge, have longer-term agitation and lower cognitive function at acute hospital discharge, and require greater time from admission to rehabilitation. However, other studies that examined the effect of intoxication found no relationship to mortality and morbidity, and in some cases an inverse relationship. Even highly reliable indices of outcome such as neuropsychological effects have been found by some investigators but not others. For instance, Kaplan and Corrigan (1994) found that there was no difference in neuropsychological performance among those with and without acute intoxication. However, Tate et al. (1999) concluded that after controlling for a preinjury history of alcohol abuse, alcohol intoxication at admission was predictive of poor delayed verbal memory, a greater decrement in verbal memory over time, and poor visuospatial functioning. Tate et al.'s methodology controlled for a prior history of abuse, which may account for this discrepancy in findings. The ambiguous findings regarding the consequences of intoxication also have been mirrored in results of animal models. Some studies have shown both the deleterious effect of intoxication at the time of injury (Zink, Stern, et al., 1998; Zink, Sheinberg, et al., 1998) and a neuroprotective effect posited by Kelly and colleagues (Kelly et al., 1997, 2000). Whether there is a neuroprotective effect in humans for the presence of ethanol at the time of injury is an issue beyond the scope of this chapter.

However, the question cannot be easily extracted from determination of the effects of a prior history of substance use, which, based on clinical studies, appears to exert a greater impact on initial acuity and longer-term outcomes.

PRIOR HISTORY OF SUBSTANCE USE DISORDER

There is growing recognition that the more important risk factor related to substance abuse is a prior history of substance use disorders, whether or not the person was intoxicated at the time of injury. Corrigan (1995) found that studies of the effect of a prior history of substance abuse were far less equivocal in finding immediate consequences than the studies of intoxication. A prior history was found to be associated with mortality, the likelihood of mass lesions, a poor Glasgow Outcome Score at discharge, and poorer neuropsychological performance at both 1 month and 1 year postinjury. Only one study found no differences between persons with and without a history of substance use disorders (Drubach et al., 1993). In the only study that compared the relationship to the outcome of both a history of substance abuse disorder and intoxication (Ruff et al., 1990), significant effects on mortality and morbidity were found for a history but not intoxication. This greater likelihood of morbidity may have accounted in part for the observation that a greater proportion of persons with prior histories of substance use disorders are found in rehabilitation populations of persons treated for TBI compared to those treated in trauma centers only (Corrigan, 1995).

The Colorado TBI Registry and Follow-up System reported that 10% of persons age 16 and older hospitalized in Colorado had been treated previously for substance abuse, and 17% had used an illicit drug in the 12 months preceding their injury (Whiteneck et al., 2001). In both cases, males, younger persons, and those with lower initial Glasgow Coma Scale scores were more likely to manifest these conditions. Two epidemiologic studies have examined TBI or substance abuse as a risk factor for the other (Fann et al., 2002; Timonen et al., 2002). Fann et al. (2002) conducted a case control study in a large staff model health maintenance organization and found that persons diagnosed with a substance abuse disorder in a given 12-month period had a 60% greater chance of incurring a TBI requiring hospitalization or treatment in an emergency department or a physician's office. Timonen et al. (2002) examined the birth cohort of northern Finland for indications of childhood TBI as a risk factor for the development of psychiatric disorders, substance use disorders, or criminality. While TBI in childhood was found to be associated with certain psychiatric diagnoses and criminality, childhood injury did not appear to predict the occurrence of substance use disorders. Thus, one epidemiologic study found evidence that substance abuse was a risk factor for later TBI; the other did *not* find TBI to be a risk factor for later substance abuse, at least for TBI incurred in childhood.

From studies that used a prospective method of detection to evaluate rehabilitation populations, Corrigan (1995) concluded that almost two-thirds of adolescents and adults treated in rehabilitation for TBI have prior histories of substance use disorders. Since that time, at least three studies have provided additional data about the frequency of a prior history of abuse and dependence among rehabilitation patients. Corrigan, Bogner, et al. (2003) analyzed the TBI Model Systems National Database for the rate of prior histories of problem use. Problem use was defined as either at-risk consumption of alcohol or use of an illicit drug. The author found that 43% of subjects in the TBI Model Systems National Database had prior histories of at-risk alcohol use, 29% reported preinjury use of illicit drugs, and 48% had either condition before injury. A prospective study of 356 consecutive admissions to acute rehabilitation at the OSU Medical Center (Bogner et al., 2001) reported that 54% were diagnosed as having preinjury alcohol dependence or alcohol abuse, and 34% were diagnosed as having preinjury abuse of or dependence on other drugs. Given the high rate of co-occurrence of alcohol and other drug use disorders, 58% of the sample showed one or the other or both. Bombardier, Rimmele and Zintel (2003) reported very similar results for 142 consecutive admissions to acute rehabilitation at the University of Washington. In this sample, 58% had active alcohol use problems (or worse), 39% had recently used illicit drugs, and 61% had either or both histories. As shown in Figure 8.1, the rates from these three sources suggest relatively consistent results in terms of the frequency of a prior history of substance use disorder in persons receiving rehabilitation for TBI. Because the OSU and University of Washington studies used more thorough methods of detection, it would appear reasonable that they also found higher rates than those in the TBI Model Systems Database. It would appear reasonable to estimate that as many as 60% of adolescents and adults treated in acute rehabilitation for TBI are problem drinkers or have diagnosable substance use disorders.

SUBSTANCE USE FOLLOWING TRAUMATIC BRAIN INJURY

Definitive studies of the rates of substance use disorders following TBI have not been reported; however, the Colorado Follow Survey reported that 10% of persons hospitalized with a TBI used an illicit drug in the first year after injury (Whiteneck et al., 2001). Selassie and coworkers (2003) reported that 20% of persons hospitalized with a TBI in South Carolina exhibited problem alcohol use in the first year after injury. Silver et al. (2001) found that approximately 25% of a population-based sample of persons with TBI also had alcohol use disorders (versus 10% of those without TBI), and 11% had other drug use disorders (versus 5% of those without TBI). Like other patients hospitalized due to injury, persons with TBI consume less alcohol or other drugs in the immediate postinjury period

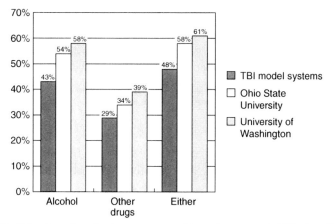

Figure 8.1. Prior histories of substance use problems in acute rehabilitation. TBI, traumatic brain injury.

(Bombardier, Temkin, et al., 2003; Corrigan, Lamb-Hart, & Rust, 1995; Kreuzer et al., 1990, 1996b). However, there are also indications that a significant proportion return to preinjury levels of use relatively quickly (Corrigan, Rust, & Lamb, 1995; Corrigan, Smith-Knapp, et al., 1998; Kreutzer, Witol, & Marwitz, 1996; Kreutzer, Witol, Sando, et al., 1996.)

Kreutzer et al. (1990) first reported that persons with TBI consumed significantly more alcohol before their injuries than same-age peers; but after injury, their consumption was reduced to comparable levels. These authors questioned whether drinking as much as other young adults was appropriate for persons who had sustained significant TBI. Later data from the TBI Model Systems National Database indicated that significant individual changes occur in drinking patterns over the first 4 years after injury (Kreutzer, Witol, Sander, et al., 1996). Of particular interest was the number of subjects who were abstinent and infrequent drinkers at 1 year postinjury who had increased their consumption by the second year; almost 25% of this longitudinal sample increased their alcohol use between the first and second years. Other drug use was not examined. Kreutzer, Witol and Marwitz (1996) studied 87 16- to 20-year-olds at an average of 8 months and 28 months postinjury. Before their injuries, 51% were moderate or heavy alcohol users. At 8 months postinjury this proportion was halved, with 25% reporting moderate and heavy drinking; however, by the second follow-up year, this proportion had increased to 35%. Illicit drug used appeared to follow a different pattern, with 29% reporting any use before injury, dropping to 6% and 8% at the first and second follow-ups, respectively. Corrigan et al. (1998) found that substance abuse problems increased dramatically between the second and third years postinjury in a cross-sectional study of rehabilitation patients with TBI. Bombardier, Rimmele, et al. (2003) studied 197 adults hospitalized with TBI and found that

65% were moderate to heavy drinkers preinjury, declining to 41% 1 year after injury. When only (1) heavy drinking and (2) whether the subject experienced functional problems as a result of alcohol use were included in a composite index, the preinjury rate was 51%, while that for 1 year postinjury was 26%. These study findings may have been confounded by the sample composition (a disproportionate number of subjects with a known risk for seizures) and the failure to include other drug use.

Finally, there is evidence that some proportion of persons with no preinjury substance use problems develop them afterward. For instance, among clients with TBI admitted for substance abuse treatment after injury, approximately 20% of those who had abstained from alcohol or were infrequent drinkers before injury became heavy users afterward (Corrigan, Rust, Lamb-Hart, 1995). This rate may have been inflated by including clients whose TBI occurred in childhood. However, Bombardier, Temkin, et al. (2003) found that 15% of preinjury abstinent and light drinkers were moderate or heavy drinkers 1 year postinjury. Neither study considered other drug abuse onset; however, clinical experience suggests that some proportion of patients with TBI initiate other drug use to alleviate pain, depression, or anxiety. More research on the onset of other drug use would clearly be useful.

AN ADDITIVE EFFECT ON BRAIN STRUCTURE AND FUNCTION

There is accumulating evidence that substance use disorders and TBI have a negative additive effect on brain structure and function. Bigler and colleagues (1996) reported results of quantitative magnetic resonance imaging (QMRI) for 99 adults with TBI and 197 without it. Of the TBI subjects, 18 were identified as having a history of substance use disorder. All TBI subjects differed significantly from noninjured controls on various indices of structural brain damage reflecting atrophy, including the ventricle-to-brain ratio (VBR). The TBI subjects with a history of substance use disorder showed even greater atrophy compared to TBI subjects without such a history. However, a subgroup of the TBI patients with no substance use history matched for initial Glasgow Coma Scale score did not show significantly different measures of cerebral atrophy from those with substance use disorders. While this may indicate that the effect was not additive, it is also possible that the Glasgow Coma Scale scores for those with substance use disorders were artificially lowered by intoxication at the time of injury. Despite this trend toward the abusing group's having potentially less severe injury than the group matched on the Glasgow Coma Scale, the abusing group still had a higher VBR, though it was not statistically significant. A follow-up study by Barker et al. (1999) that examined polysubstance abusers with and without TBI concluded that when the effects of TBI severity were controlled, the effects of substance abuse in combination with TBI resulted in greater brain atrophy than that observed with either substance abuse or TBI alone. In this study, neuropsychological test performance did not show a similar additive effect. The authors concluded that the neuropathologic changes detected by QMRI may be more sensitive than the neuropsychological performance.

Baguley et al. (1997) examined the interaction of alcohol abuse and TBI using event-related evoked potentials. Forty male subjects were divided into four equal groups based on the presence or absence of TBI and a history of heavy social drinking. Subjects with TBI had experienced a severe TBI 1 year or more before being evaluated. Heavy social drinking was determined by the Alcohol Use Disorders Identification Test (AUDIT; Babor et al., 1992) and is often considered equivalent to a diagnosis of alcohol abuse. Neuropsychological testing was also performed. No significant differences in average age or neuropsychological performance were observed among the four groups defined by TBI and alcohol abuse, TBI or alcohol abuse, or neither. Both the N200 latency and P300 amplitude were impaired in persons with alcohol abuse and in nondrinking subjects with TBI compared to the control subjects. Significant impairment was observed in subjects with both TBI and alcohol abuse. A similar relationship was not observed for neuroprocesses resulting from less complex cognitive tasks. These authors concluded that heavy social drinking after TBI has a measurable impact on electrophysiologic correlates of cognition. While two of these studies of brain structure and function did not find differences in neuropsychological performance among subjects, other studies showed more definitive findings. Dikmen and colleagues (1993) found that individuals with chronic alcohol use disorders had greater neuropsychological impairment immediately following injury and 2 years later.

SUBSTANCE ABUSE AND NEGATIVE OUTCOMES

Persons with TBI and substance abuse problems appear to have significantly worse outcomes than persons with TBI alone. Persons with TBI and substance abuse problems are less likely to be working (Corrigan et al., 1997; MacMillan et al., 2002; Sherer et al., 1999), have lower subjective well-being (Bogner et al., 2001; Corrigan, Bogner, Mysiw, et al., 2001), have an increased likelihood of committing suicide (Teasdale & Engberg, 2001), and are at greater risk for seizure (Verma et al., 1992). There is also evidence that the increased risk of aggressive behavior after TBI is further exacerbated by substance abuse. Indirect support for this hypothesis includes the apparently high proportion of prison inmates with TBI who have co-occurring substance use disorders.

Numerous studies have observed that substance use problems preceding injury are often a significant predictor of postinjury employment. For instance, MacMillan and coworkers (2002) studied 45 adults 2 years after moderate or severe TBI. They hypothesized that severe premorbid psychiatric and substance abuse problems, as well as less social support following injury, would be associated with poorer postinjury employment, poorer independent living, and greater neurobehavioral symptom manifestation. They found that both preinjury psychiatric and substance abuse histories predicted a lower likelihood of employment and that preinjury substance abuse also was associated with less independence in living situation. Sherer et al. (1999) studied 76 persons with moderate or severe TBI who received services through a specialized day treatment program. Their employment status 3 months following discharge from this program was assessed, on average, 2 years postinjury. Predictors of employment status included severity of injury, premorbid education, preinjury substance abuse, and need for physical, cognitive, and behavioral supervision at discharge from acute rehabilitation. Multiple logistic regressions revealed that only level of preinjury substance use was predictive of later productivity. Subjects with no history of preinjury substance abuse were more than eight times as likely as those with such a history to be employed at follow-up. Bogner et al. (2001) investigated the relative contribution of substance abuse and violent injury etiology in a sample of 351 consecutive admissions for acute brain injury rehabilitation. One year following injury, a prior history of substance use disorder was a significant predictor of postinjury employment, as were age, preinjury employment, and cognitive function at rehabilitation discharge. Despite the consistent finding that preinjury substance abuse is associated with postinjury unemployment, the relationship with postinjury use may be more complex. Sander, Kreutzer, and Fernandez (1997) found that employed persons who had incurred moderate or severe TBI and were on average 16 months postinjury reported consuming more alcohol than similar subjects who were unemployed. This finding may be consistent with clinical observations that return to work can be a trigger for substance use because it provides money to purchase alcohol or other drugs, as well as increased stressors arising from the work environment.

Bogner and colleagues (2001) also considered whether life satisfaction was more affected by a substance abuse history or by violent injury etiology. As with employment, they found that a substance abuse history was the more important predictor, along with preinjury employment and motor function at discharge. Corrigan and coworkers (2001) reported that a prior history of substance use disorder was highly associated with life satisfaction both 1 and 2 years after injury. At year 1, prior substance abuse was the strongest independent predictor of life satisfaction, and it continued to be a significant predictor 2 years after injury, even after the effects of depressed mood, social integration, and employment had been accounted for. In the general population there is a well-documented relationship between depression and substance abuse (Silver et al., 2001), and given the high rate of depression following TBI, the co-occurrence of depression and substance abuse would be expected in this population as well. Indeed, there has been some indication of an independent relationship between substance abuse and the likelihood of suicide following TBI. Teasdale and Engberg (2001) examined suicide after TBI using the Danish population register for hospital admissions between 1979 and 1993. Standardized mortality ratios stratified by sex and age indicated that the incidence of suicide relative to the general population was increased by 2.7 for concussions, 3.0 for cranial fractures, and 4.1 for intracranial hemorrhage. When substance use diagnosis × TBI diagnosis was examined, standardized mortality ratios increased significantly. Silver et al. (2001) reported the relative risks of psychiatric problems for a randomly selected subgroup of the New Haven, Connecticut, portion of the National Institute of Mental Health (NIMH) Epidemiologic Catchment Area study. Traumatic brain injury alone significantly increased the risk of suicide by an odds ratio of 5.7. After controlling for alcohol abuse and dependence, the likelihood of a suicide attempt declined by 4.5, suggesting that alcohol use accounted for approximately 20% of the risk of suicide after TBI.

Verma and coworkers (1992) studied the relationship between chronic abusers' withdrawal from alcohol and the occurrence of a seizure episode. They separated a sample of 54 adult male alcoholics who had experienced seizures into three groups—those for whom there was always a clear relationship between withdrawal and the seizure episode (the last drink occurring 6 to 96 hours prior to seizure), those for whom some but not all seizure episodes were associated with withdrawal, and those for whom none of the seizure episodes were associated with withdrawal. They found that a history of severe TBI preceding the onset of seizure disorder was present for none of the patients in the first group, approximately 40% of those in the second group, and more than 75% of those in the third group. They concluded that the lack of a constant relationship between alcohol withdrawal and seizures for the second and third groups appears to be a result of the higher incidence of prior TBI in those subjects, and that this relationship may account for the previously observed heterogeneity in the relationship between alcohol withdrawal and seizure episodes.

A final relationship between substance abuse and poor outcomes following TBI is the high association that has been observed with aggression and criminal activity (Kreutzer et al., 1995). Increased aggression following TBI has been reported in multiple studies (Brooks et al., 1986; Hall et al., 1994; Mauss-Clum and Ryan, 1981). Persons with TBI are more likely to be involved with the criminal justice system (Kreutzer et al., 1991, 1995), and there is evidence of a high prevalence among of TBI prisoners. A sample of 1000 consecutively admitted offenders to the Illinois state prison system found that 25% had had at least one TBI (Morrell et al., 1998). Of those reporting a TBI, approximately 20% indicated that they experienced residual symptoms—most often problems with memory and learning, followed by changes in mood or behavior, seizures, and difficulties with balance and coordination. In a follow-up study, Merbitz et al. (1995) found that those inmates with TBI had 50% more disciplinary tickets accrued per day of stay than a comparison group of inmates without TBI. In some studies of the prevalence of TBI and criminal activity and/or incarceration, there is additional evidence of a three-way co-occurrence of involvement with the criminal justice system, TBI, and substance abuse. A study of medical center patients with TBI found that those who had preinjury histories of arrest were more likely to be men, with lower education, who were injured in assaults and had a history of substance abuse (Kolakowsky-Hayner & Kreutzer, 2001). Barnfield and Leathem (1998a, 1998b) reported two studies of persons with TBI and substance abuse problems in the New Zealand prison population. Their sample was considerably smaller than that of Morrell and colleagues, consisting of 118 prisoners who both were allowed to participate and agreed to do so. Subjects were asked to "estimate how many head injuries they had sustained, how each had occurred, and the duration of any loss of consciousness associated with each injury." Barnfield and Leathem used a combination of reported loss of consciousness and frequency of injuries to derive a categorization system for severity that classified each subject as having none, light, mild, moderate, or severe TBI. Half of their sample had incurred a TBI that was mild or worse, with 17% reporting moderate or severe injuries. Inmates with mild or worse TBI were approximately 17% more likely to have severe substance use disorders.

INTERVENTION AND TREATMENT OF SUBSTANCE USE FOLLOWING TRAUMATIC BRAIN INJURY

Clinicians and researchers have repeatedly observed that cognitive and emotional impairments caused by brain injury present unique problems when addressing coexisting substance use disorders (Center for Substance Abuse Treatment, 1998; Corrigan et al., 1999; Langley, 1991). While several models of how substance abuse treatment can be adapted to TBI rehabilitation were proposed in the past (Blackerby & Baumgartnen, 1990; Langley, 1991), most presumed protracted inpatient or residential treatment that is no longer available to most persons with TBI. Bombardier and colleagues (1997, 1999) have promoted brief interventions based on motivational interviewing techniques for use during acute rehabilitation. Cox et al. (2003) found some support for the efficacy of Structured Motivational Counseling based on a quasi-experimental design using a nonrandom comparison group. In contrast, Corrigan, Bogner, et al. (in press) found that a brief motivational intervention did no better than an attention control condition in terms of engaging clients with TBI and substance use disorders in substance abuse treatment. In contrast, a financial incentive condition and a condition in which logistical barriers were systematically addressed both resulted in significantly better engagement than the motivational interviewing and attention control conditions.

However, the very brief duration of the intervention, delivered via telephone, may have undermined the effectiveness of the motivational interviewing.

The only community-based model other than Cox et al.'s (2003) Structured Motivational Counseling is the model proposed by Corrigan and colleagues (Bogner et al., 1997; Corrigan, Lamb-Hart, & Rust, 1995; Heinemann et al., 2004). This model uses consumer and professional education, intensive case management, and interprofessional consultation to address substance use disorders in adults with TBI. Program evaluation data suggest significant differences in outcomes, depending on whether discharge occurred before an eligible client could be engaged in treatment (eligible but untreated), after initiation of treatment but before treatment goals were met (premature termination), or upon mutual agreement with the staff that goals had been met (treated). The network's three programmatic outcomes (abstinence, return to work or school, and subjective well-being) assessed 3 months postdischarge are shown in Figure 8.2. The median length of stay for those discharged successfully is 2 years. As might be expected, dropout is a significant problem in this model. Retrospective analysis of 1000 consecutive referrals indicated that 66% of those eligible for treatment either were not engaged or dropped out prematurely. Heinemann et al. (2004) used a quasi-experimental design to study initial progress in two programs using the model and a nonrandom comparison group of persons with TBI and substance use disorders who were not receiving treatment. Nine months after admission to treatment, actual use did not change for either the treatment or the comparison group; however, life and family satisfaction were significantly better for the treated group. Program referral early after injury was associated with larger gains in physical

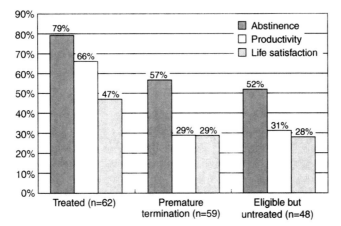

Figure 8.2. Outcomes at 3 months postdischarge for randomly selected treated and untreated clients.

well-being, employment, and community integration. The authors concluded that change in substance use requires a longer duration of treatment and also noted the challenge of premature termination. If a case management model is found to be a useful treatment approach for this population, its effectiveness would be improved by determining better methods to engage and retain clients in treatment.

There is also substantial evidence of the co-occurrence of TBI and substance use disorders in the caseloads of substance abuse treatment providers. Alterman and Tarter (1985) found that 53% of a sample of 76 male alcoholics had a history of TBI. Hillbom and Holm (1986) observed that 38% of a sample of 157 alcoholics had a history of TBI with loss of consciousness or hospitalization. Malloy et al. (1990) found that 58% of a sample of 60 alcoholics had TBI marked by loss of consciousness, hospitalization, or major neurologic change. In a more recent study, Gordon et al. (2002) reported finding that 63% of 243 consecutive admissions to 13 publicly funded programs in upstate New York had suffered a TBI, as had 48% of 404 clients screened in 12 facilities in New York City. Researchers at Ohio State University studied a sample of 119 clients receiving residential treatment, intensive outpatient treatment, or ambulatory detoxification in a publicly funded substance abuse facility (Corrigan, Lamb-Hart, & Bogner, in review). They found that 68% had had at least one TBI with loss of consciousness for at least 5 minutes or requiring emergency department care or hospitalization. Perhaps more remarkably, 35% of the entire sample had had at least one TBI with loss of consciousness of at least 1 hour or requiring hospitalization. Furthermore, 53% of the sample had had at least one TBI from which symptoms persisted at the time of screening. This study also found that clients with substance dependence and TBI

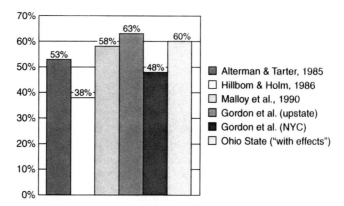

Figure 8.3. Percentage of clients in substance abuse treatment with a history of traumatic brain injury.

showed selected differences on tests of cognitive functioning and emotional control compared to clients with substance dependence only.

When these findings are viewed together (see Fig. 8.3), it appears justified to expect as many as half of the clients in substance abuse treatment to have a history of TBI. Cognitive impairments arising from TBI may affect a person's learning style, making participation in didactic training and group interventions more difficult. Misinterpretation of attention or memory problems as resistance to treatment can undermine a treatment relationship. Damage to the frontal lobes affects executive thinking skills and promotes socially inappropriate behavior. It is easy to interpret these behaviors as intentionally disruptive, particularly when the individual with TBI shows no visible signs of disability (Center for Substance Abuse Treatment, 1998).

GAPS IN RESEARCH

While descriptive information is beginning to accumulate about the scope and nature of substance use and TBI, research on interventions for this problem is almost nonexistent. The only randomized, controlled trial was a test of methods for improving engagement in treatment (Corrigan, Bogner, et al., in press). Quasi-experimental studies have provided modest support for the efficacy of motivational interviewing and case management. There is ample reason to suspect that persons with TBI present for treatment with characteristics unique enough that the effectiveness of proven substance abuse treatment approaches should be evaluated specifically in this population. The greater the cognitive and emotional sequelae of the TBI, the more necessary this research becomes. The effectiveness of both pharmacologic and behavioral interventions is required.

Additionally, treatment approaches are being developed for special populations within the substance abuse treatment field that merit further consideration for persons with TBI. For instance, several treatment models have been developed for persons with co-occurring substance abuse and mental illness (Substance Abuse and Mental Health Services Administration, 2002). There are many parallels between these dually diagnosed clients and persons with TBI and substance use disorders. Both populations have cognitive and emotional sequelae arising from their disorders; members of both groups report using drugs for regulation of emotional symptoms; and both groups often have multiple other psychosocial needs (e.g., housing, finances, transportation) that arise from or are interdependent with their treatment needs. Techniques developed and lessons learned in the treatment of persons with substance abuse and mental illness may be fruitful sources of ideas for addressing the needs of persons with substance abuse and TBI.

CHALLENGES IN CONDUCTING RESEARCH ON TRAUMATIC
BRAIN INJURY AND SUBSTANCE ABUSE

Discussion of the multiple challenges in conducting research on substance abuse interventions is beyond the scope of this chapter. However, there are several twists to methodological issues unique to research on TBI and substance abuse treatment that warrant mention. Often, the first question confronted by researchers new to substance abuse treatment studies is the validity of self-reports of use. While multiple studies have supported the validity of instruments using self-report to assess the extent of lifetime or recent substance use (Del Boca & Noll, 2000; Neale & Robertson, 2003; Tournier et al., 2003), skepticism reemerges in studies of TBI due to concerns that subjects may lack sufficient memory or awareness to report their use accurately. Two studies have reported comparisons between self-reported and proxy-reported alcohol consumption among persons with TBI (Corrigan, Rust, & Lamb-Hart, 1995; Sander, Witol, & Kreutzer, 1997). Both studies found high rates of concordance between self-reports and proxy reports, and no consistent directionality (over- or underreporting) when inaccuracies occurred. These studies support the use of self-report in studies of persons with TBI (and proxy report when needed as well). As in the general population, techniques should ground the individual in the information wanted (e.g., what beverages are alcoholic and how much constitutes a drink, specific drugs that are considered illicit, interest in prescription medications used to excess) and specific time frames in which substances were used. Most important is that the interviewer elicit this information in a comfortable manner, free of judgment (or awe), in an environment conducive to confidentiality.

Depending on the specific nature or target of the intervention, there is considerable potential for confounding variables. For instance, a propensity for violent behavior can be both the cause and the effect of both substance abuse and TBI. Similarly, a tendency to behave impulsively is associated with both substance abuse and TBI, and can contribute to and/or emerge as a consequence of both conditions. Many other traits and behaviors are intricately intertwined with substance abuse and TBI (e.g., sociopathy, cognitive impairment, affective disorders). This complexity makes randomized, controlled trials the most useful design for intervention studies, as quasi-experimental research is susceptible to confounding. Multivariate analyses will be more robust if they are based on theory or guided by a logic model to reduce their susceptibility to confounding effects. In studies of clients in treatment, we have found psychiatric symptomatology to be associated with several process variables (e.g., missed appointments, dropout, therapeutic relationship, length of stay), which suggests that randomized designs consider this characteristic for stratification. In studies of educational or other brief interventions, current beliefs and attitudes (e.g., readiness to change, expectancies regarding use, extent to which the individual feels that substance use contributed to the TBI) should be controlled for in either design or statistical analyses. Finally, again in our own work, we have found a prior history of TBI to be an important covariate in substance-abusing populations.

In our research, there has been a somewhat higher than normal refusal rate when recruiting subjects for substance abuse research from populations of persons with TBI. While stigma appears to be part of this increased rate, participation is also hampered by concerns that information about a person's substance use could affect criminal or legal proceedings. Thus, the possibility that sampling bias could affect generalizability must be given special attention. The potential for sampling bias also occurs in longitudinal research on TBI when subjects are lost to follow-up. Two studies have found that a prior history of substance abuse is a risk factor for loss to follow-up in longitudinal studies (Corrigan et al., 1997; Corrigan, Harrison-Felix, et al., 2003). In epidemiologic studies and multivariate analyses, sampling bias can affect estimates of incidence or prevalence rates, as well as the strength of a relationship. In randomized clinical trials, sampling bias can affect sample size and can be a factor in translation to clinical use. However, while there are some unique issues to consider in studies of substance abuse treatment for persons with TBI, they are not insurmountable and may not be any more challenging than design issues encountered in other areas of TBI research.

A RESEARCH AGENDA FOR SUBSTANCE ABUSE AND TRAUMATIC BRAIN INJURY

There are a number of questions requiring further research that go beyond treatment intervention. To help establish a context for a comprehensive research agenda, we have developed a schema for considering variations in individual presentation and the association with treatment venues and approaches. The starting point for the schema was borrowed from the literature on persons with co-occurring substance abuse and mental illness (Substance Abuse and Mental Health Services Administration, 2002). As shown in Figure 8.4, persons with substance abuse and TBI are assumed to vary according to the severity of each condition. When they are mapped orthogonally, four quadrants are defined by high or low severity of each condition. While dichotomizing severity is relatively arbitrary, it proves useful in considering the service delivery systems where individuals are likely to be found. For instance, persons with low-severity substance use disorders (e.g., high-risk use or substance abuse) and low-severity TBI are not found in treatment systems dedicated to substance abuse or TBI as often as they are found in primary care settings and treatment systems for injury (e.g., emergency departments or trauma centers). Only with more severe substance abuse or TBI is a person likely to receive treatment in programs dedicated to chemical dependency or TBI, respectively. In our schema, the co-occurrence of severe presentations of both conditions requires specialized treatment programs; however, given the essential absence of such services, this quadrant of the model is hypothetical.

Differences in the service delivery systems where individuals are most likely to be identified, in turn, dictate different treatment approaches. For instance, in Quadrant I, the most effective interventions will need to be compact in order to accommodate the more pressing agenda of primary care or treatment of an injury. Thus, screening and brief intervention are the most likely services to be provided. Indeed, there is a significant body of literature on screening and brief interventions for both primary and emergent care (Hungerford & Pollock, 2002). Similarly, Quadrants II–IV dictate different service delivery opportunities, though in contrast to Quadrant I, there is very little research to guide clinical practice. While more detailed research questions can be generated specific to each of Quadrants II–IV, in Table 8.1 we have suggested a series of initial questions, the results of which would guide both clinical practice and the configuration of health-care delivery systems.

CONCLUSIONS

Several general conclusions can be drawn from this review of research on substance abuse and TBI. While more research is needed to fully understand the causes, effects, and consequences, it would appear safe to conclude that substance abuse

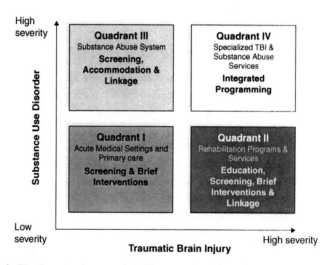

Figure 8.4. The four-quadrant model of interventions for substance abuse and traumatic brain injury (TBI).

Table 8.1. Proposed Agenda for Research on Substance Abuse and Traumatic Brain Injury (TBI)

Clinical Research
- Who ceases substance use, who starts or resumes it, and why?
- To what extent does use after TBI impede recovery? Limit the outcome?
- How effective are existing treatments for substance use disorders among persons with TBI?
- Do existing substance use disorder treatments need to be adapted to be more effective for persons with TBI?
- How does neurobehavioral impairment due to TBI differ from that due to chronic use, and does it make a difference?

Health Services Research
- What is the most effective method of screening for substance use disorders among persons with TBI?
- What brief interventions are effective with persons who have neurobehavioral impairments due to TBI?
- What are the most effective methods of screening for TBI among persons with substance use disorders?
- What are the essential effective ingredients of parallel treatment? Of integrated treatment?
- How can integrated treatment be made available widely?

is a ubiquitous negative influence on the quality of life of persons with TBI. (It also may be true that TBI is a ubiquitous negative influence on the quality of life of persons with substance use disorders.) For adolescents and adults treated in rehabilitation settings for TBI, we can expect approximately 75% to be at risk for recurrence or development of a substance use disorder. The majority of those at risk are persons who had preinjury abuse or dependence. While all have some period of abstinence during hospitalization and many cease use for a period of time after discharge, so far the data suggest that there is a steady return to preinjury use for a substantial portion of these individuals. Added to those at risk because of preinjury substance use disorders are the estimated 10% to 20% who develop problems for the first time after their TBI. Much more research is needed to confirm this rate and understand which persons with TBI develop these problems. With as many as 75% of rehabilitation patients at risk, the need to address substance use is obvious. We would take this need a step further and suggest that 100% of persons treated in rehabilitation for TBI need to understand the potential negative consequences of both substance use and abuse after injury. The additive effect of substance use and TBI on brain structure and function needs far more research, but there appear to be sufficient data in hand to caution our patients. And of course, knowing what educational approaches are effective is still another area in which research is needed.

The greatest research need concerns the interventions for persons with TBI who develop a substance use disorder. The most obvious starting place is with interventions that have proven effective for the general population. One area of study that would appear to hold promise for persons with TBI is brief interventions. These techniques have proven effective in primary care and trauma programs. In the latter settings, there are many individuals with TBI, though persons with more severe injuries may have been excluded from research samples. Still, knowing how to effectively screen, intervene, and refer patients with TBI in acute settings, as well as clients receiving outpatient rehabilitation services, would appear to be a discrete research objective focusing on techniques that, if found effective as practiced in other settings, would be affordable for use in rehabilitation. Pharmacologic treatments found effective in the general population could also have an immediate impact on interventions by rehabilitation professionals. While the research required may be more expensive than that for brief interventions, pharmacologic agents such as naltrexone that help sustain abstinence gained through hospitalization or behavioral interventions would appear to share the advantage of ease of adoption. Persons with TBI also deserve to benefit from new drugs under development, as well as medications used for other purposes that are being investigated for their utility in substance abuse treatment.

The substance abuse service delivery system needs to be capable of treating persons with TBI. Substance abuse service providers tend to overlook individual differences that mediate important behaviors for many persons who have experienced TBI. These differences include communication capabilities, problems in learning and memory, executive functioning, and interpersonal skills. For instance, in clinical experience we repeatedly identify instances when poor memory is mistaken for lack of interest, missed appointments for resistance, or disinhibition for intentional disruption. While persons with substance use disorders and TBI are certainly capable of the full range of behaviors, it is countertherapeutic to assume that behaviors arise from emotional or motivational attributes without considering cognitive and neurobehavioral possibilities first. There is a significant need for research on the incidence and consequences of TBI in substance abuse service delivery systems, as well as methods for making basic accommodations for common cognitive and behavioral sequelae of TBI. The brain injury rehabilitation field will benefit from greater exposure to research on substance abuse treatment; concomitantly, the substance abuse field will benefit from accumulated knowledge on brain injury rehabilitation.

REFERENCES

Alterman, A.I., & Tarter, R.E. (1985). Relationship between familial alcoholism and head injury. *Journal of Studies on Alcohol, 45,* 256–258.

American Psychiatric Association. (1994). *Diagnostic and Statistical Manual of Mental Disorders* (4th ed.). Washington, DC: Author.

Babor, T.F., de la Fuente, J.R., Saunders, J., & Grant, M. (1992). *The Alcohol Use Disorders Identification Test: Guidelines for Use in Primary Health Care.* Geneva: World Health Organization.

Baguley, I.J., Felmingham, K.L., Lahz, S., Gordan, E., Lazzaro, I., & Schotte, D.E. (1997). Alcohol abuse and traumatic brain injury: Effect on event-related potentials. *Archives of Physical Medicine and Rehabilitation, 78*(11), 1248–1253.

Barker, L.H., Bigler, E.D., Sterling, C., Johnson, C.V., Russo, A.A., Boineau, B., & Blatter, D.D. (1999). Polysubstance abuse and traumatic brain injury: Quantitative magnetic resonance imaging and neuropsychological outcome in older adolescents and young adults. *Journal of the International Neurospychological Society, 5*, 593–608.

Barnfield, T.V., & Leathem, J.M. (1998a). Incidence and outcomes of traumatic brain injury and substance abuse in a New Zealand prison population. *Brain Injury, 12*(6), 455–466.

Barnfield, T.V., & Leathem, J.M. (1998b). Neuropsychological outcomes of traumatic brain injury and substance abuse in a New Zealand prison population. *Brain Injury, 12*(11), 951–962.

Bigler, E.D., Blatter, D.D., Johnson, S.C., Anderson, C.V., Russo, A.A., Gale, S.D., Ryser, D.K., MacNamara, S.E., & Bailey, B.J. (1996). Traumatic brain injury, alcohol and quantitative neuroimaging: Preliminary findings. *Brain Injury, 10*(3), 197–206.

Blackerby, W.F., & Baumgarten, A. (1990). A model treatment program for the head-injured substance abuser: Preliminary findings. *Journal of Head Trauma Rehabilitation, 5*(3), 47–59.

Bogner, J.A., Corrigan, J.D., Mysiw, W.J., Clinchot, D., & Fugate, L.P. (2001). A comparison of substance abuse and violence in the prediction of long-term rehabilitation outcomes following traumatic brain injury. *Archives of Physical Medicine and Rehabilitation, 82*(5), 571–577.

Bogner, J.A., Corrigan, J.D., Spafford, D.E., & Lamb-Hart, G.L. (1997). Integrating substance abuse treatment and vocational rehabilitation following traumatic brain injury. *Journal of Head Trauma Rehabilitation, 12*(5), 57–71.

Bombardier, C.H., Ehde, D., & Kilmer, J. (1997). Readiness to change alcohol and drinking habits after traumatic brain injury. *Archives of Physical Medicine and Rehabilitation, 78*, 592–596.

Bombardier, C.H., & Rimmele, C.T. (1999). Motivational interviewing to prevent alcohol abuse after traumatic brain injury: A case series. *Rehabilitation Psychology, 44*(1), 52–67.

Bombardier, C.H., Rimmele, C.T., & Zintel, H. (2003). The magnitude and correlates of alcohol and drug use before traumatic brain injury. *Archives of Physical Medicine and Rehabilitation, 83*, 1765–1773.

Bombardier, C.H., Temkin, N.R., Machamer, J., & Dikmen, S.S. (2003). The natural history of drinking and alcohol-related problems after traumatic brain injury. *Archives of Physical Medicine and Rehabilitation, 84*, 185–191.

Brooks, N., Campsie, L., Symington, C., et al. (1986). The five year outcome of severe blunt head injury: A relative's view. *Journal of Neurology, Neurosurgery and Psychiatry, 46*, 764–770.

Cahalan, D., & Cisin, I.H. (1968). American drinking practices: Summary of findings from a national probability sample: I. Extent of drinking by population subgroup. *Quarterly Journal of Studies on Alcohol, 29*, 130–151.

Center for Substance Abuse Treatment. (1998). *Substance Use Disorder Treatment for People with Physical and Cognitive Disabilities.* Treatment Improvement Protocol (TIP) Series Number 29. Washington, DC: U.S. Government Printing Office.

Centers for Disease Control and Prevention. (1998). *Behavioral Risk Factor Surveillance System User's Guide.* Atlanta: Author.

Corrigan, J.D. (1995). Substance abuse as a mediating factor in outcome from traumatic brain injury. *Archives of Physical Medicine and Rehabilitation, 76*(4), 302–309.

Corrigan, J.D., Bogner, J.A., & Lamb-Hart, G.L. (1999). Substance abuse and brain injury. In M. Rosenthal, E. R. Griffith, J.D. Miller, & J. Kreutzer (Eds.), *Rehabilitation of the Adult and Child with Traumatic Brain Injury* (3rd ed.). Philadelphia: F.A. Davis.

Corrigan, J.D., Bogner, J.A., Lamb-Hart, G.L., Heinemann, A.W., & Moore, D. (in press). Increasing substance abuse treatment compliance for persons with traumatic brain injury.

Corrigan, J.D., Bogner, J.A., Lamb-Hart, G.L., & Sivak-Sears, N. (2003). *Problematic Substance Use Identified in the TBI Model Systems National Dataset.* Retrieved November 1, 2003 from the Center for Outcome Measurement in Brain Injury (COMBI) Web site: http://tbims.org/combi/subst/index.html

Corrigan, J.D., Bogner, J.A., Mysiw, W.J., Clinchot, D., & Fugate, L. (1997). Systematic bias in outcome studies of persons with traumatic brain injury. *Archives of Physical Medicine and Rehabilitation, 78*(2), 132–137.

Corrigan, J.D., Bogner, J.A., Mysiw, W.J., Clinchot, D., & Fugate, L. (2001). Life satisfaction following traumatic brain injury. *Journal of Head Trauma Rehabilitation, 16*(6), 543–555.

Corrigan, J.D., Harrison-Felix, C., Bogner, J., Dijkers, M., Terrill, M.S., & Whiteneck, G. (2003). Systematic bias in traumatic brain injury outcome studies due to loss to follow-up. *Archives of Physical Medicine and Rehabilitation, 84,* 153–160.

Corrigan, J.D., Lamb-Hart, G.L., & Bogner, J.A. (in review). Detecting traumatic brain injury in clients receiving substance abuse treatment services.

Corrigan, J.D., Lamb-Hart, G.L., & Rust, E. (1995). A program of intervention for substance abuse following traumatic brain injury. *Brain Injury, 9,* 221–236.

Corrigan, J.D., Rust, E., & Lamb-Hart, G.L. (1995). The nature and extent of substance abuse problems among persons with traumatic brain injuries. *Journal of Head Trauma Rehabilitation, 10*(3), 29–45.

Corrigan, J.D., Smith-Knapp, K., & Granger, C.V. (1998). Outcomes in the first 5 years after traumatic brain injury. *Archives of Physical Medicine and Rehabilitation, 79*(3), 298–305.

Cox, W.M., Heinemann, A.W., Miranti, S.V., Schmidt, M., Klinger, E., & Blount, J. (2003). *Journal of Addictive Diseases, 22*(1), 93–110.

Del Boca, F.K., & Noll, J.A. (2000). Truth or consequences: The validity of self-report data in health services research on addictions. *Addiction, 95*(Suppl 3), S347–S360.

Dikmen, S.S., Donovan, D.M., Loberg, T., Machamer, J.E., et al. (1993). Alcohol use and its effects on neuropsychological outcome in head injury. *Neuropsychology, 7*(3), 296–305.

Dikmen, S., Machamer, J.E., Donovan, D.M., Winn, H.R., & Temkin, N.R. (1995). Alcohol use before and after traumatic head injury. *Annals of Emergency Medicine, 26,* 167–176.

Drubach, D.A., Kelly, M.P., Winslow, B.A., & Flynn, J.P.G. (1993). Substance abuse as a factor in the causality, severity, and recurrence rate of traumatic brain injury. *Maryland Medial Journal, 42*(10), 989–993.

Ewing, J.A. (1984). Detecting alcoholism: The CAGE questionnaire. *Journal of the American Medical Association, 252,* 1905–1907.

Fann, J.R., Katon, W.J., Uomoto, J.M., & Esselman, P.C. (1995). Psychiatric disorders and functional disability in outpatients with traumatic brain injuries. *American Journal of Psyciatry, 152*(10), 1493–1499.

Fann, J.R., Leonetti, A., Jaffe, K., Katon, W.J., Cummings, P., & Thompson, R.S. (2002). Psychiatric illness and subsequent traumatic brain injury: A case control study. *Journal of Neurology, Neurosurgery & Psychiatry, 72*(5), 615–620.

Gordon, W.A., Hough, C., Perez, K., Hibbard, M., & Brandau, S. (2002, October 4). *Co-Morbidity of Traumatic Brain Injury in a Substance Abuse Population.* Poster presentation, American Congress of Rehabilitation Medicine, Philadelphia.

Hall, K., Karzmark, P., Stevens, M., et al., (1994). Family stressors in traumatic brain injury: A two-year follow-up. *Archives of Physical Medicine and Rehabilitation, 75,* 876–874.

Heinemann, A.W., Corrigan, J.D., & Moore, D. (2004). Case management for tbi survivors with alcohol problems. *Rehabilitation Psychology, 49,* 156–166.

Hillbom, M., & Holm, L. (1986). Contribution of traumatic head injury to neuropsychological deficits in alcoholics. *Journal of Neurology, Neurosurgery and Psychiatry, 49,* 1348–1353.

Hungerford, D.W., & Pollock, D.A. (Eds.). (2002). *Alcohol Problems among Emergency Department Patients: Proceedings of a Research Conference on Identification and Intervention.* Atlanta: National Center for Injury Prevention and Control, Centers for Disease Control and Prevention.

Jernigan, D.H. (1991). Alcohol and head trauma: Strategies for prevention. *Journal of Head Trauma Rehabilitation, 6*(2), 48–59.

Kaplan, C.P., & Corrigan, J.D. (1994). The relationship between cognition and functional independence in adults with traumatic brain injury. *Archives of Physical Medicine and Rehabilitation, 75,* 643–647.

Kelly, D.F., Kozlowski, D.A., Haddad, E., Echiverri, A., Hovda, D.A., & Lee, S.M. (2000). Ethanol reduces metabolic uncoupling following experimental head injury. *Journal of Neurotrauma, 17*(4), 261–272.

Kelly, D.F., Lee, S.M., Pinanong, P.A., & Hovda, D.A. (1997). *Journal of Neurosurgery, 86,* 876–882.

Kolakowsky-Hayner, S., & Kreutzer, J.S. (2001). Pre-injury crime, substance abuse, and neurobehavioral functioning after traumatic brain injury. *Brain Injury, 15*(1), 53–63.

Kreutzer, J.S., Doherty, K.R., Harris, J.A., & Zasler, N.D. (1990). Alcohol use among persons with traumatic brain injury. *Journal of Head Trauma Rehabilitation, 5*(3), 9–20.

Kreutzer, J.S., Marwitz, J.H., & Witol, A.D. (1995). Interrelationships between crime, substance abuse, and aggressive behaviours among persons with traumatic brain injury. *Brain Injury, 9*(8), 757–768.

Kreutzer, J.S., Wehman, P.H., Harris, J.A., Burns, C.T., & Young, H.F. (1991). Substance abuse and crime patterns among persons with traumatic brain injury referred for supported employment. *Brain Injury, 5*(2), 177–187.

Kreutzer, J.S., Witol, A.D., & Marwitz, J.H. (1996). Alcohol and drug use among young persons with traumatic brain injury. *Journal of Learning Disabilities, 29*(6), 643–651.

Kreutzer, J.S., Witol, A.D., Sander, A.M., Cifu, D.X., Marwitz, J.H., & Delmonico, R. (1996). A prospective longitudinal multicenter analysis of alcohol use patterns among persons with traumatic brain injury. *Journal of Head Trauma Rehabilitation, 11*(5), 58–69.

Langley, M.J. (1991). Preventing post-injury alcohol-related problems: A behavioral approach. In B.T. McMahon & L.R. Shaw (Eds.), *Work Worth Doing: Advances in Brain Injury Rehabilitation*. Orlando, FL: Paul M. Deutsch Press.

MacMillan, P.J., Hart, R.P., Martelli, M.M., & Zasler, N.D. (2002). Pre-injury status and adaptation following traumatic brain injury. *Brain Injury, 16*(1), 41–49.

Malloy, P., Noel, M., Longabaugh, R., & Beattie, M. (1990). Determinants of neuropsychological impairment in antisocial substance abusers. *Addictive Behaviors, 15*, 431–438.

Mauss-Clum, N., & Ryan, M. (1981). Brain injury and the family. *Journal of Neurosurgical Nursing, 13*, 165–169.

Merbitz, C.T., Jain, S., Good, G.L., & Jain, A. (1995). Reported head injury and disciplinary rule infractions in prison. *Journal of Offender Rehabilitation, 22*(3/4), 11–19.

Morrell, R.F., Merbitz, C.T., Jain, S., & Jain, S. (1998). Traumatic brain injury in prisoners. *Journal of Offender Rehabilitation, 27*(3/4), 1–8.

National Association on Alcohol, Drugs and Disability. (1998). *Access Limited—Substance Abuse Services for People with Disabilities: A National Perspective*. San Mateo, CA: Author.

Neale, J., & Robertson, M. (2003). Comparisons of self-report data and oral fluid testing in detecting drug use amongst new treatment clients. *Drug and Alcohol Dependence, 71*(1), 57–64.

Ruff, R.M., Marshall, L.F., Klauber, M.R., Blunt, B.A., Grant, I., Foulkes, M.A., Eisenberg, H., Jane, J., & Marmarou, A. (1990). Alcohol abuse and neurological outcome of the severely head injured. *Journal of Head Trauma Rehabilitation, 5*(3), 21–31.

Sander, A.M., Kreutzer, J.S., & Fernandez, C.C. (1997). Neurobehavioral functioning substance abuse, and employment after brain injury: Implications for vocational rehabilitation. *Journal of Head Trauma Rehabilitation, 12*(5), 28–41.

Sander, A.M., Witol, A.D., & Kreutzer, J.S. (1997). Alcohol use after traumatic brain injury: Concordance of patients' and relatives' reports. *Archives of Physical Medicine and Rehabilitation, 75*, 138–142.

Selassie, A.W., Pickelsimer, E.E., Tyrell, M.L., Gu, J.G., & Turner, R.P. (2003). The conundrum of mild TBI: The evidence against the misnomer. *Brain Injury, 17*(Suppl. 1), 128.

Sherer, M., Bergloff, P., High, W., & Nick, T.G. (1999). Contribution of functional ratings to prediction of long-term employment outcome after traumatic brain injury. *Brain Injury, 13*(12), 973–987.

Silver, J.M., Kramer, R., Greenwald, S., & Weissman, M. (2001). The association between head injuries and psychiatric disorders: Findings from the New Haven Epidemiologic Catchment Area Study. *Brain Injury, 15*(11), 935–945.

Substance Abuse and Mental Health Services Administration. (1998). *National Household Survey on Drug Abuse: Population Estimates 1998*. Rockville, MD: U.S. Department of Health and Human Services, Substance Abuse and Mental Health Services Administration, Office of Applied Studies.

Substance Abuse and Mental Health Services Administration. (2002). *Report to Congress on the Prevention and Treatment of Co-Occurring Substance Abuse Disorders and Mental Disorders*. Rockville, MD: U.S. Department of Health and Human Services, Substance Abuse and Mental Health Services Administration.

Tate, P.S., Freed, D.M., Bombardier, C.H., Harter, S.L., & Brinkman, S. (1999). Traumatic brain injury: Influence of blood alcohol level on postacute cognitive function. *Brain Injury, 13*, 767–784.

Teasdale, T.W., & Engberg, A.W. (2001). Suicide after traumatic brain injury: A population study. *Journal of Neurology, Neurosurgery and Psychiatry, 71*, 436–440.

Timonen, M., Miettunen, J., Hakko, H., Zitting, P., Veijola, J., von Wendt, L., & Rasaned, P. (2002). The association of preceding traumatic brain injury with mental disorder, alcoholism and criminality: The Northern Finland 1966 Birth Cohort Study. *Psychiatry Research, 113*(3), 217–226.

Tournier, M., Molimard, M., Abouelfath, A., Cougnard, A., Fourrier, A., Haramburu, F., Begaud, B., & Verdoux, H. (2003). Accuracy of self-report and toxicological assays to detect substance misuse disorders in parasuicide patients. *Acta Psychiatrica Scandinavica, 8*(6), 410–418.

Traumatic Brain Injury Model Systems National Dataset, Annual Report 2002. West Orange, NJ: Kessler Medical Rehabilitation and Research Center. http://www.tbindc.org.

U.S. Department of Health and Human Services. (1990). *Nutrition and Your Health: Dietary Guidelines for Americans* (3rd ed.). Washington, DC: U.S. Government Printing Office.

Verma, N.P., Policherla, H., & Buber, B.A. (1992). Prior head injury accounts for the heterogeneity of the alcohol–epilepsy relationship. *Clinical Electroencephalography, 23*(3), 147–151.

Whiteneck, G., Mellick, D., Brooks, C., Harrison-Felix, C., Noble, K., & Sendroy Terrill, M. (2001). *Colorado Traumatic Brain Injury and Follow-up System Databook.* Englewood: Craig Hospital.

World Health Organization. (1992). The *ICD-10 Classification of Mental and Behavioural Disorders: Clinical Descriptions and Diagnostic Guidelines* (10th rev.). Geneva: Author.

Zink, B.J., Sheinberg, M.A., Wang, X., Mertz, M., Stern, S.A., & Betz, A.L. (1998). Acute ethanol intoxication in a model of traumatic brain injury with hemorrhagic shock: Effects on early physiological response. *Journal of Neurosurgery, 89*, 983–990.

Zink, B.J., Stern, S.A., Wang, X., & Chudnofsky, C.C. (1998). Effects of ethanol in an experimental model of combined traumatic brain injury and hemorrhagic shock. *Academy of Emergency Medicine, 5*, 9–17.

9

Interventions for Caregivers

ANGELLE M. SANDER

In recent years, researchers and policy makers have emphasized the substantial contribution of the environment to the ability of persons with physical, cognitive, or emotional impairments to achieve full participation in their communities (Tate & Pledger, 2003; Whiteneck et al., 1987). The family is an aspect of the person's immediate environment that has the potential to significantly aid or impede resumption of community activities. The role of the family or other caregivers may be especially important for persons with traumatic brain injury (TBI). There is evidence that persons with TBI are frequently dependent upon caregivers in a variety of areas, including transportation, finances, leisure, and emotional support (Jacob, 1988). This dependence is attributable to high rates of unemployment (Dikmen et al., 1994; Kreutzer et al., 2003; Sander et al., 1996) and poor social integration (Kozloff, 1987; Oddy & Humphrey, 1980; Oddy et al., 1985) for many persons with TBI. Given their potential importance for increasing the participation of persons with TBI in community activities, understanding the impact of TBI on caregivers and the family and implementing appropriate interventions is crucial.

IMPACT OF TRAUMATIC BRAIN INJURY ON CAREGIVERS

Unfortunately, a wealth of evidence gathered in the past three decades indicates that caregivers of persons with TBI experience substantial emotional distress

(Brooks, 1991; Florian & Katz, 1989; Kreutzer et al., 1992; Lezak, 1978). This distress includes high levels of perceived stress or *burden*, depression, and anxiety, beginning as early as 3 months after injury and persisting at intervals ranging from 5 to 15 years (Brooks et al., 1986, 1987; Rappaport et al., 1989; Thomsen, 1984). Relationships among family members are negatively impacted by injury, as evidenced by decreased marital satisfaction and longevity, disruption of family roles, and decreased communication among family members (Kreutzer, Gervasio, & Camplair, 1994; Peters et al., 1990, 1992). Caregivers of persons with TBI report increased use of alcohol and other tranquilizing medications (Hall et al., 1994; Panting & Merry, 1972), and they more frequently seek services for mental health problems (Hall et al., 1994). A recent three-center study indicated that the preinjury family environments of many persons with TBI were characterized by emotional distress and unhealthy family interactions (Sander et al., 2003).

A potential contributor to caregivers' distress is their difficulty in getting injury-related needs met. In a series of studies conducted in Virginia, Kreutzer and colleagues have shown that the need to receive honest information regarding the injury and its expected consequences was rated as most important by caregivers (Kreutzer, Serio, & Bergquist, 1994; Serio et al., 1995; Witol et al., 1996). This need for information was perceived by most caregivers as being met. In contrast, the need for emotional and practical support (e.g., help with housekeeping) was perceived as unmet by the majority of caregivers. This perception of unmet needs persists as long as 2 years following injury (Witol et al., 1996). These unmet needs have the potential to further exacerbate injury-related distress and to reduce the ability of caregivers to assist persons with injury in achieving maximal community participation.

TYPES OF INTERVENTIONS

Following the research regarding caregivers' emotional distress and perception of unmet needs, three main types of interventions have been proposed for caregivers (Kreutzer et al., 1990; Rosenthal & Young, 1988). The first type of intervention is the provision of information and education to caregivers. The goal is to increase caregivers' understanding of brain injury and its associated problems, and to prepare them to deal with the physical, cognitive, and/or emotional problems that the person with injury may exhibit. Educational interventions can consist of either written or videotaped information or verbal one-on-one instruction with family members.

The second type of intervention is support. Two types of support have generally been offered. The first type is peer support, which is often provided by a traditional support group. These groups involve caregivers of persons with TBI coming together to share experiences and feelings and to learn from each other's efforts to cope with injury-related changes. Support groups are sometimes mediated by a professional, such as a social worker or psychologist, but often involve just the caregivers. Another form of peer support that has recently emerged in the literature is formal peer mentorship. This involves the pairing of family members by a professional or by persons in an organization such as a brain injury association. Family members are typically matched on similar characteristics, such as gender, race, relationship to the injured person, and geographic proximity. Once matched up, family members are usually left on their own to determine the amount of contact they have with each other and how they spend their time together. In addition to peer support, another type of support is that offered by professionals following discharge from a rehabilitation facility. This form of support usually follows a case management model, whereby a professional initiates regular contact with family members to answer questions, provide emotional support, and make referrals when needed.

The third type of intervention that has been proposed for family members after TBI is formal therapy. The content and structure of this therapy vary greatly, depending on the setting and the therapist. Treatments have included family systems therapy involving the entire family, or individual therapy for the primary caregiver or any other family member who is experiencing distress. Interventions described in the literature have included both psychodynamic and cognitive-behavioral approaches and have been conducted in a group and individually. The therapies focus on assisting individual family members or the entire family to adjust to injury-related changes and their emotional impact.

PURPOSE OF THIS CHAPTER

The purpose of this chapter is to review the existing evidence for the effectiveness of interventions with family members of persons with TBI. Studies were chosen for review if they used formal assessment of the outcome, even if the measures used were qualitative. Case studies were not included for review unless they employed controls, such as a multiple baseline design. All studies involving persons with TBI were included, even if the sample also contained persons with brain injury of mixed etiology. The evidence is organized according to the three types of interventions described above: education, support, and formal therapy. The evidence for each type of intervention is classified according to the American Academy of Neurology's (2004) scheme for evidence classification. The criteria for various levels of classification are described in Table 9.1.

Each of the studies discussed below is shown in Table 9.2, along with the type of intervention delivered, the sample size and recruitment procedure, the design, the time postinjury, outcome measures, and the evidence classification. The review of evidence for the various family interventions is followed by a discussion

Table 9.1. Criteria for Classification of Evidence

Class I: prospective, randomized, controlled trial with masked outcome assessment, in a representative population, that includes the following:

1. Primary outcomes are clearly defined.
2. Exclusion and inclusion criteria are clearly defined.
3. There is adequate accounting for dropouts and crossovers, and the number of these is low enough to avoid bias.
4. Relevant baseline characteristics are described and are equivalent among groups or there is statistical adjustment for differences.

Class II: prospective matched-group cohort study in a representative population, with masked outcome assessment that meets criteria 1–4 above *or* a randomized, controlled trial in a representative population that lacks one of criteria 1–4

Class III: all other controlled trials (including well-defined natural history controls or patients serving as their own controls, such as in multiple baseline designs) conducted in representative populations where outcomes are assessed independently or assessment of outcomes is objective

Class IV: evidence from uncontrolled studies, case series, case reports, or expert opinion

---

of methodological issues limiting conclusions based on these intervention studies. The chapter concludes with suggestions for future research on interventions for family members.

A REVIEW OF THE EVIDENCE FOR FAMILY INTERVENTIONS

Educational Interventions

Only one study to date has directly investigated the effectiveness of education for family members. Morris (2001) provided written educational information to 34 primary caregiver of persons with mild, moderate, or severe TBI. Participants fell into two groups with respect to time since injury: an early group (2–9 months postinjury) and a late group (≥1 year postinjury). Participants were involved in two sessions. During the first session, they completed baseline questionnaires and were given a written informational booklet. The booklet contained general information about TBI; a description of common cognitive, emotional, and behavioral impairments and what the caregiver could do about them; and a description of ways that caregivers could cope with their own emotional reactions to the injury. While the research staff did not review the educational materials with the caregiver, 26 of the 27 participants reported that they had read the materials. Caregivers received a phone call 1 week later to ask if they had any questions about the

Table 9.2. Evidence for Effectiveness of Interventions for Caregivers

STUDY	TYPE OF INTERVENTION	SAMPLE	RECRUITMENT PROCEDURE	DESIGN	TIME POST-INJURY	OUTCOME MEASURES	EVIDENCE CLASSIFICATION
Morris (2001)	Written information	34 caregivers of persons with mild to severe TBI	Referrals to psychology services and discharges from neurosurgery and rehabilitation units	Pre-test, post-test	Early group (2–9 months) and late group (≥1 year)	Symptom Checklist of neurobehavioral problems in person with injury; General Health Questionnaire; Hospital Anxiety and Depression Scale	IV
Man (1999)	Structured support group (empowerment program)	60 family members of persons with brain injury of mixed etiology	Volunteer sample recruited through advertisement	Pre-test, post-test	Not described	Empowerment questionnaire developed by authors; Chinese version of General Health Questionnaire; rating scale of family members' ability to cope with neurobehavioral problems	IV
Brown et al. (1999)	Support group (on-site versus telephone)	91 caregivers of persons with brain injury of mixed etiology	Invitation to caregivers of current and former patients at a rehabilitation hospital	Nonrandomized group comparison	3 months to 28 years	Family Assessment Device; Caregiver Burden Inventory; Profile of Mood States	IV

Hibbard et al. (2002)	Peer support in the form of peer mentors	9 caregivers of persons with TBI	Volunteer sample recruited through advertisement	Post-test only	Not described	Structured interview using questions from existing measures, including the Questionnaire on Resources and Stress–short form; Frequency of Family Coping Behaviors; Social Support Questionnaire–short form; and Empowerment Scale; qualitative interview questions	IV
Albert et al. (2002)	Professional support: social work liaison	27 caregivers of persons with brain injury of mixed etiology	Consecutive discharges from a brain injury unit during a 15-month period; study reports on 27 persons with 6-month follow-up	Cohort study with historical comparison group	Not described; 6 months postdischarge for treatment group; 12 months postdischarge for comparison group	Caregiver Appraisal Scale	III
Hauber & Jones (2002)	Professional support via telehealth communication	10 caregivers of persons with brain injury of unspecified etiology	Consecutive discharges from a specialized brain injury rehabilitation unit who met criteria for reduced state of consciousness	Treatment versus control (not clear if randomized)	Range of 21 to 165 days (not equivalent between groups)	Modified Family Needs Questionnaire (27 items applicable to postdischarge period)	III

(continued)

Table 9.2. Continued

STUDY	TYPE OF INTERVENTION	SAMPLE	RECRUITMENT PROCEDURE	DESIGN	TIME POST-INJURY	OUTCOME MEASURES	EVIDENCE CLASSIFICATION
Perlesz & O'Loughlan (1998)	Family systems therapy	15 families (32 family members) of persons with severe TBI	Self-referrals who sought counseling at a family therapy center in Australia over a 6-month period	Pre-test, post-test	Average of 39 months	General Health Questionnaire; Profile of Mood States (Anger); Subjective Burden Scale; Social Adjustment Scale (marital functioning and functioning of the family unit); Family Environment Scale (Cohesion and Conflict scales)	IV
Singer et al. (1994)	Combined psychoeducational and cognitive-behavioral stress management training	15 parents of 9 children with acquired brain injury of mixed etiology	Volunteers from a rehabilitation program	Randomized group comparison: information only versus information plus stress management	Average of 23 months	Beck Depression Inventory; State-Trait Anxiety Inventory	III

Study	Intervention	Sample	Selection	Design	Timing	Measures	Level
Smith & Godfrey (1995)	Home-based cognitive-behavioral program addressing training in stress management and in management of neurobehavioral problems in persons with injury	28 persons with TBI and their family members	Consecutive discharges from a rehabilitation unit during a 14-month period	Nonrandomized cohort study comparing control group (n = 14) group (n = 14); with treatment assessment was conducted independently of treatment	Baseline at 6 months postinjury; follow-up at 2 years postinjury	Symptom Distress Scale; Zung Self-Rating Depression Scale; Rosenberg Self-Esteem Inventory	II
Carnevale et al. (2002)	Education and training in behavior management	27 caregivers of persons with brain injury of mixed etiology	Partially volunteer and partially referred; preselected for high levels of stress	Randomized, controlled trial: education only; education plus behavior management; control; outcome not assessed independently of treatment	Average of 6 to 12 months	Questionnaire on Resources and Family Stress; Maslach Burnout Inventory	III

TBI, traumatic brain injury.

materials. They were then visited 4 weeks later and asked to complete follow-up questionnaires. The results showed no statistically significant change from pre- to post-test for either the early or late groups with regard to neurobehavioral symptoms in the person with injury or caregiver emotional distress. While a majority of caregivers in the early group showed some reduction in scores on the General Health Questionnaire and the Hospital Anxiety and Depression Scale, the improvement was not considered to be clinically meaningful, since they still scored above the recommended cutoffs for emotional distress.

Support Interventions

Peer Support

Three studies have focused on the effectiveness of peer supports for caregivers. Man (1999) investigated the effectiveness of an empowerment group for caregivers. The study was conducted in Hong Kong. Participants were 60 family members of persons with brain injuries of mixed etiology (22% with TBI). The group met for 8 weeks, with one 2-hour session per week. The meeting consisted of providing information, teaching skills to build self-efficacy with regard to management of injury-related problems, teaching coping and stress reduction strategies, increasing social support, increasing awareness of resources, and developing plans for the future. Participants completed a series of questionnaires before the group met and again at a 3-month follow-up. A total of six groups met over a 15-month period. The results showed significant pre- to post-test change in participants' sense of empowerment, injury-related burden, emotional distress, perception of social support, and efficacy in coping with physical and cognitive problems. The gains in sense of empowerment and in ability to deal with cognitive problems were maintained at the 3-month follow-up.

Brown et al. (1999) compared on-site to telephone information and support groups in 91 caregivers of persons with brain injury of mixed etiology (51% with TBI) who were discharged from a rehabilitation hospital. Those who lived within 40 kilometers of the hospital were invited to participate in the on-site group, while those residing farther away were invited to join the telephone group. The groups were led by a social worker, psychologist, or neuropsychologist. Twenty groups were conducted over a 2-year period, 10 on-site and 10 by telephone. Halfway through the study, an educational videotape was made and was sent to participants prior to the group meeting. This tape was sent to an equal number of on-site and telephone groups, but no adjustment in analyses were made for its receipt. Assessment measures were completed on the day of the first group meeting, on the day of the last meeting, and 6 months later. The results showed a significant decrease in emotional distress over time for both groups but no difference for caregiver burden or family functioning. The on-site group showed greater distress and burden compared to the telephone group in all time periods. However, this difference might have been due to group differences in regard to the number of persons with TBI versus other etiologies, time postinjury, gender of caregivers, and duration of post-traumatic amnesia. These differences were not accounted for in analyses.

A formal peer mentor program was described by Hibbard and colleagues (2002). While 52 family members participated in the program, only 9 who completed follow-up questionnaires were included in the published study. Mentors were trained by the investigators with regard to knowledge of TBI and community re-sources, communication skills, and advocacy. Mentors included persons with TBI as well as family members. Mentors were matched to mentees on the basis of simi-larities in demographic and injury-related characteristics, as well as similar inter-ests and the ability of the mentor to meet the needs of the mentee. The frequency of contact, duration of the relationship, and how the time together was spent were left up to the mentors. No participants reported a major impact on their life in any of the areas assessed. Over half of the participants reported that participation had some impact on their ability to cope with TBI, general outlook on life, ability to cope with emotional distress, and knowledge of TBI and community resources. Surprisingly, less than one-fourth of participants reported feeling an increase in social support. Eleven percent reported dissatisfaction with the mentor match, which may have been due to the fact that family members were often matched to a mentor with TBI. One-third of participants were dissatisfied with the frequency of contact they had with their mentor. One of the most beneficial aspects of the program mentioned by participants was learning ways to navigate the system to obtain needed resources for their injured family member.

Professional Support

Two studies have investigated the impact of professional support on caregivers. Albert et al. (2002) implemented a liaison program in which social workers pro-vided support to caregivers via telephone. Participants in the study were caregivers of 72 persons with stroke, TBI, or other brain injury who were consecutively dis-charged from a brain injury unit over a 15-month period. The treatment consisted of caregiver education at discharge, assignment of a social work liaison to each caregiver during the rehabilitation stay, and regular phone calls from the liaison to the caregiver for 6 months following discharge. Caregivers were also encour-aged to phone their liaison with questions and concerns or simply for emotional support. Persons in the social work liaison program were compared to a histori-cal control group consisting of caregivers of persons discharged from the unit during the year prior to implementation of the program. The groups were equiva-lent with regard to age, gender, education, relationship to the person with in-jury, and neurobehavioral status. However, there was a greater number of white persons in the treatment group, and they had less financial need than the control group. Participants in the treatment group were assessed on measures of caregiver burden, mastery, and satisfaction at admission, discharge, 2-month follow-up, and 6-month follow-up. The assessment with the control group was conducted an average of 12 months postdischarge. The study reported only on participants who had completed a 6-month follow-up ($n = 27$). Relative to the historical comparison group, the treatment group showed less burden on 9 of 14 indicators, greater satisfaction on 3 of 4 indicators, greater mastery on 4 of 6 indicators, greater perception of support, and a better overall quality of life. No differences were noted with regard to physical health or ability to cope with daily issues.

The other study (Hauber & Jones, 2002) investigated professional support delivered via videoconferencing to caregivers of 10 persons who were discharged from a specialized brain injury unit in a reduced state of consciousness. Caregivers in the videoconferencing group ($n = 5$) were compared with those in a comparison group ($n = 5$), but the authors did not specify how group assignments were made. The videoconferencing group received weekly sessions of 20 to 40 minutes each for 10 to 12 weeks. The sessions consisted of review by a certified neuroscience nurse on care activities taught to caregivers during the hospital stay, as well as provision of emotional support and monitoring of neurologic status in the injured person. Caregivers in the videoconferencing group reported that more needs were met and fewer needs were unmet. However, the differences noted were not large, and no statistical analyses were performed, limiting the conclusions that can be drawn. It was also noted that the videoconferencing group had a higher number of persons who received subsequent rehabilitation. The authors attributed this to the fact that the closer monitoring of patients' neurologic status after discharge led to more appropriate referrals when progress was noted.

Formal Therapy

The majority of the literature on family systems therapy has involved case descriptions aimed at illustrating a model of therapy (Laroi, 2003; Maitz & Satz, 1995; Soderstrom et al., 1992). Since these studies have not formally assessed the outcomes or presented their results as research studies, they will not be reviewed here. One study employed a pre-test, post-test design to study the impact of family systems therapy on 32 family members of persons with severe TBI who referred themselves for therapy over a 6-month period in Australia (Perlesz & O'Loughlan, 1998). The average number of therapy sessions per family was 8.4, and the average length of time in therapy was 9.4 months. Family members completed outcome measures prior to treatment and at 12- and 24-month follow-up intervals. Using paired t-tests, the authors found a reduction in family conflict, emotional distress, and subjective burden and an improvement in overall family adjustment from pre-treatment to 12-month follow-up. These changes were maintained at the 24-month follow-up. However, the authors also found an increase in anger and a decrease in marital adjustment at the 24-month follow-up. They noted that these occurred in families where the injured member was a spouse rather than a child.

Three studies have investigated the effectiveness of cognitive-behavioral therapy for family members. One study was conducted in a group setting, and the other two were home-based therapies. Singer and colleagues (1994) conducted a randomized, controlled trial comparing a group treatment combining information and training in stress management with an information-only group. Participants included 15 parents of nine children with brain injuries of mixed etiology (couples were assigned to groups in pairs). Time postinjury ranged from 3 to 66 months. Both treatment and control groups involved nine 2-hour sessions. Using baseline scores as covariates, the results showed a reduction in depression and anxiety for the stress management group.

Smith and Godfrey (1995) implemented a home-based cognitive-behavioral therapy program that included training in management of neurobehavioral problems and in stress management. The treatment was given once per week for 4 weeks, with follow-up visits conducted once every 12 weeks for 2 years. The average number of contact hours per family was 28. Participants were 14 persons with moderate to severe TBI and their family members who were recruited from two hospitals in New Zealand over a 15-month period. The treatment group was compared to a control group of persons recruited from a prior study at the same facility. They underwent assessment at the same time periods as the treatment group but received no treatment following rehabilitation discharge. The control group was matched to the treatment group with regard to demographics, injury severity, and baseline neuropsychological performance. No persons in the comparison group had received rehabilitation services following hospital discharge. This study is unique in that the assessment of outcome was conducted by persons who were uninvolved in the treatment portion of the study and did not know whether participans were in the treatment or control group. At 2 years postinjury, the treatment group showed a decrease in symptom-related distress, a reduction in depression, and an increase in self-esteem and fewer physician visits. Family members in the comparison group showed an increase in symptom-related distress. There was also some evidence of impact on the person with injury, as persons in the treatment group were noted to become aware of deficits more quickly. The authors noted that family members expressed a preference for receiving home-based rather than facility-based services.

A second home-based therapy study was conducted by Carnevale and colleagues (2002). Participants were 27 caregivers who reported high levels of stress related to caregiving. Caregivers were randomly assigned to one of three groups: no treatment, education only, or education plus intervention. Both treatment groups participated in a baseline phase involving naturalistic observation and time sampling of problem behaviors. Both groups then received education that involved four sessions of general training by a clinical psychologist in management of problem behaviors. The education phase was followed by a measurement phase for both groups. The education plus intervention group subsequently received 8 weeks (2 hours per week) of training focused on direct implementation of behavioral management techniques to reduce specific target behaviors in the person with injury. All groups underwent reassessment at 14 weeks. Using baseline scores as covariates, no between-group differences were noted in caregiver burden or burnout. No change across time was noted for any group.

SUMMARY OF EVIDENCE FOR CAREGIVER INTERVENTIONS

The research to date shows that evidence for the effectiveness of interventions for caregivers after TBI is minimal. There have been no Class I studies. There is only one Class II study, and this study supports home-based cognitive-behavioral interventions for family members. The majority of studies meet only the criteria for Class III or IV evidence. Based upon the existing evidence, the only recommendation that can be made is that education of family members regarding TBI, combined with specific training in how to manage neurobehavioral problems, is possibly effective (Level C recommendation). This recommendation is supported by one Class II study. There are also two Class III studies lending credence to this recommendation, but both included persons with brain injuries other than TBI, making the conclusions less valid for persons with TBI. The Class II study, as well as one of the Class III studies, combined education in TBI and management of neurobehavioral problems with training in stress management for family members. This equal emphasis on compensating for problems of the person with injury and attending to the emotional needs of family members would seem to hold promise, but it requires further research. While two Level III studies investigated the effectiveness of professional supports, they differed widely with respect to population and type of support. Thus, no formal recommendation can be made regarding the effectiveness of professional support programs.

METHODOLOGICAL LIMITATIONS OF EXISTING STUDIES

The studies to date have been limited by small sample size. In the studies reviewed above, sample sizes ranged from 9 to 91, with an average of 36. In spite of small sample sizes, the studies typically included multiple outcome measures, with no control for Type I error. Interpretation of the results of many of these studies was made more difficult by the inclusion of persons with various etiologies, including TBI, stroke, tumors, and encephalopathy. While all of these groups experience cognitive impairment, the course of recovery and the complications of coexisting medical problems differ in each. For example, stroke occurs more often in older females, while TBI occurs primarily in younger males. Persons with stroke often have preexisting medical problems, including hypertension, diabetes, and/or prior stroke. These may result in differential caregiver responses and different intervention needs. Due to the small sample size in most studies, it was not possible to divide the sample by etiology. The resulting inability to determine the specific impact of interventions on caregivers of persons with TBI is a limitation in guiding future interventions.

The recruitment and characterization of samples is a further limitation of the majority of studies reviewed. The only study to recruit consecutive admissions or discharges was the Albert et al. (2002) study. The remainder of the studies included samples that were drawn primarily from treatment referrals or volunteer samples, such as those recruited via advertisement. Samples were often poorly characterized with regard to injury severity and the functional abilities and neurobehavioral problems of the person with injury. Prior literature has indicated that differences in the cognitive, emotional, and behavioral functioning of the person with injury can impact caregivers' emotional distress and perceived burden, and should thus be accounted for in studies addressing caregiver intervention. None of the studies described the characteristics of persons who refused to participate or who dropped out of treatment. Thus, it is difficult to determine whether caregivers participating in the intervention were representative of other caregivers. The result is limited generalizability of findings.

The lack of control for other variables that could impact the outcome is a serious methodologic limitation of most of the studies reviewed. While two of the studies used a historical control group, no study used a concurrent no-treatment control group. Thus, attribution of improvements to the intervention in contrast to other variables cannot be determined with certainty. Most of the samples were also poorly described with respect to time since injury. The studies that did report time since injury often included a wide range, with no statistical control for the amount of time. Since caregivers' stress and needs change over time, the generalizability of results to caregivers at different points in the recovery process is not clear. A few of the studies found between-group differences in factors other than the intervention that could impact the outcome, but they did not control statistically for these differences. For example, Albert and colleagues (2002) found that their treatment group included a greater number of white caregivers and that their historical control group contained more persons with higher financial needs. However, there was no statistical control for race or socioeconomic status. Brown et al. (1999) assigned caregivers to on-site versus telephone support groups on the basis of proximity to the rehabilitation facility. This may have resulted in a difference between the groups with respect to socioeconomic status and urban and rural settings. This difference could have impacted caregivers' coping styles, available support networks, and access to other services. None of these issues were accounted for by the authors.

The choice of assessment measures was a further limitation of many studies. The majority of studies included no theoretical model to guide the choice of outcome measures. The measures were often not matched to the type of intervention provided. Many studies provided interventions aimed at educating family members regarding the consequences of injury and how to manage cognitive and behavioral problems in the person with injury. Many of these studies used global outcome measures assessing caregiver emotional distress, although few studies included specific interventions addressing stress management and coping with negative emotions. While education may impact caregivers' feeling of efficacy and their perceived burden, a change in overall emotional distress and coping may require more specific interventions. Five of the studies reviewed used home-made questionnaires or checklists as outcome measures, with no description of reliability or validity.

IMPLICATIONS FOR METHODOLOGY OF FUTURE STUDIES

There is an obvious need for well-designed prospective cohort studies or randomized trials. While use of a no-treatment control group may be difficult in rehabilitation samples, a comparison of specific caregiver interventions with the standard of care at the facility is warranted. Given the current short lengths of stay in rehabilitation programs, studies involving caregivers at long-term postrehabilitation periods are important. Use of a no-treatment control group or a wait-list control group in these populations would carry no ethical concerns, since caregivers are typically receiving no other services. Prospective studies recruiting consecutive admissions or discharges are recommended, with comparison of persons who participate with those who do not. This type of design can still apply to studies conducted after the rehabilitation process has ended. For example, past discharge lists can be used as a basis to contact and recruit consecutive discharges. The use of volunteer samples and referred samples is discouraged, since the generalizability of results is uncertain. Persons with brain injuries other than TBI should be excluded to enable appropriate conclusions to be drawn. Studies should be designed so that they recruit a sample size that has adequate power for the number of statistical analyses planned and the number of variables included. Matching of treatment and control groups with respect to demographic variables, injury severity, and neurobehavioral functioning of the person with injury is also a priority. When matching is not possible, the studies should include statistical control of those variables that may impact the outcome.

Prior research on caregivers' response to injury and changes in their response over time provides valuable information that could be used to design intervention studies. Interventions should take into account different stages of recovery. For example, education may be most effective at earlier points in the recovery process, while family therapy may be more effective later on. Interventions should be developed to address the needs that family members have reported as most unmet over time, including needs for emotional and instrumental support (Kreutzer, Serio, & Bergquist, 1994; Serio et al., 1995; Witol et al., 1996). Interventions should also address issues that have been shown in the literature to predict caregivers' emotional functioning, including use of coping strategies, cognitive appraisals, and social support (Douglas & Spellacy, 1996; Minnes et al., 2000; Sander et al., 1997). The use of valid and reliable measures that address outcomes targeted by the intervention is also important.

Finally, the fact that caregivers vary in regard to adjustment to injury and need for services should be taken into account when designing intervention studies. Inclusion of caregivers who are not experiencing emotional or coping difficulties has the potential to mask the effect of an intervention. Screening of family members for emotional distress or maladaptive coping would be beneficial in addressing this problem. Alternatively, baseline scores on outcome measures should be used as a covariate when investigating the impact of interventions.

CONCLUSIONS AND DIRECTIONS FOR FUTURE RESEARCH

The research to date can serve as a basis for future studies on the effectiveness of interventions for caregivers. Direct comparison of different intervention strategies, such as education, support groups, and therapy, would be beneficial. Studies should include the differential impact of these different types of interventions on the outcome. An investigation of the relative cost efficacy of these interventions is also warranted. The relative efficacy of different interventions at different time points in the recovery process is recommended.

Future research should account for the fact that one type of intervention may not be effective for all caregivers. Provision of educational materials may be adequate for many caregivers, while others may require more intensive services. When designing studies, investigators could benefit from the research on predictors of emotional distress in caregivers. Early identification of caregivers who are at risk for greater adjustment difficulties is helpful in targeting interventions appropriately. For example, previous research has shown that a substantial proportion of family members of persons with TBI have a preinjury history of emotional distress and unhealthy family functioning (Sander et al., 2003). Early screening of caregivers may indicate the need for more intensive intervention services. Future studies should also focus on investigating predictors of the response to treatment. For example, persons with different educational, racial/ethnic, or socioeconomic backgrounds may respond differentially to certain interventions. Use of family systems theory would be beneficial in determining different subtypes of families who may respond differentially to treatment.

The importance of community-based rehabilitation services for persons with disability has recently been emphasized (Frieden, 2002). The home is one setting where community-based services can be delivered. Providing services in the home is often more convenient and comfortable for clients and can increase the generalizability of strategies and skills learned. The home setting may be especially conducive to caregiver interventions since this is the daily setting in which caregivers interact with the injured person. Preliminary studies of home-based interventions for caregivers of persons with TBI (Carnevale et al., 2002; Smith & Godfrey, 1995) have indicated promise for this technique. Future randomized, controlled trials investigating the effectiveness of home-based therapies and comparing them to standard facility-based rehabilitation services for caregivers are warranted.

The impact of greater involvement of family members in the rehabilitation process is also a topic for future investigation. Family involvement in setting rehabilitation goals and developing treatment plans can have benefits in terms of transfer of skills to the home setting. Sohlberg and colleagues (2001) described a program in which family members were trained to systematically observe the environment and the person with injury, develop strategies, and monitor the success of strategies and progress toward goals. Training of caregivers in this process has the potential to carry over into everyday situations and to improve their ability to assist the person with injury in integrating into the community.

Research on effective interventions for caregivers of persons with TBI is still in its infancy. Many may question the need for devoting resources to studying interventions for caregivers when there is still much to be learned about rehabilitating persons with injury. However, given the current environment of short rehabilitation stays, the family is most likely to be the primary vehicle for ensuring that persons with injury continue to make progress following rehabilitation. Training family members to carry on the strategies taught in rehabilitation, as well as to advocate for needed services and accommodations in the community, may be the best way to maximize community integration for the person with injury. Assisting caregivers to manage stress and to improve emotional health can only benefit the person with injury.

ACKNOWLEDGMENTS
This work was supported by Grants H133A980058 and H133A70015 from the National Institute on Disability.

REFERENCES

Albert, S.M., Im, A., Brenner, L., Smith, M., & Waxman, R. (2002). Effect of a social work liaison program on family caregivers to people with brain injury. *Journal of Head Trauma Rehabilitation*, *17*, 175–189.

American Academy of Neurology. (2004). *Clinical Practice Guideline Process Manual.* St. Paul, MN: American Academy of Neurology.

Brooks, D. (1991). The head-injured family. *Journal of Clinical and Experimental Neuropsychology, 13,* 155–188.

Brooks, N., Campsie, L., Symington, C., Beattie, A., & McKinlay, W. (1986). The five year outcome of severe blunt head injury: A relative's view. *Journal of Neurology, Neurosurgery and Psychiatry, 49,* 764–770.

Brooks, N., Campsie, L., Symington, C., Beattie, A., & McKinlay, W. (1987). The effects of severe head injury on patient and relatives within seven years of injury. *Journal of Head Trauma Rehabilitation, 2,* 1–13.

Brown, R., Pain, K., Berwald, C., Hirschi, P., Delehanty, R., & Miller, H. (1999). *Journal of Head Trauma Rehabilitation, 14,* 257–268.

Carnevale, G.J., Anselmi, V., Busichio, K., & Millis, S.R. (2002). Changes in ratings of caregiver burden following a community-based behavior management program for persons with traumatic brain injury. *Journal of Head Trauma Rehabilitation, 17,* 83–95.

Dikmen, S.S., Temkin, N.R., Machamer, J.E., Holubkov, A.L., Fraser, R.T., & Winn, H.R. (1994). Employment following traumatic head injuries. *Archives of Neurology, 51,* 177–186.

Douglas, J.M., & Spellacy, F.J. (1996). Indicators of long-term family functioning following severe traumatic brain injury in adults. *Brain Injury, 10,* 819–839.

Florian, V., & Katz, S.L.V. (1989). Impact of brain damage on family dynamics and functioning: A review. *Brain Injury, 3,* 219–233.

Frieden, L. (2002). The John Stanley Coulter Memorial Lecture: Listening for footsteps. *Archives of Physical Medicine and Rehabilitation, 83,* 150–153.

Hall, K.M., Karzmark, P., Stevens, M., Englander, J., O'Hare, P., & Wright, J. (1994). Family stressors in traumatic brain injury: A two-year follow-up. *Archives of Physical Medicine and Rehabilitation, 75,* 876–884.

Hauber, R.P., & Jones, M.L. (2002). Telerehabilitation support for families at home caring for individuals in prolonged states of consciousness. *Journal of Head Trauma Rehabilitation, 17,* 535–541.

Hibbard, M.R., Cantor, J., Charatz, H., Rosenthal, R., Ashman, T., Gunderson, N., Ireland-Knight, L., Gordon, W., Avner, J., & Gartner, A. (2002). Peer support in the community: Initial findings of a mentoring program for individuals with traumatic brain injury and their families. *Journal of Head Trauma Rehabilitation, 17,* 112–131.

Jacob, H.E. (1988). The Los Angeles Head Injury Survey: Procedures and initial findings. *Archives of Physical Medicine and Rehabilitation, 69,* 425–431.

Kozlof, R. (1987). Networks of social support and the outcome from severe head injury. *Journal of Head Trauma Rehabilitation, 2,* 14–23.

Kreutzer, J.S., Gervasio, A.H., & Camplair, P.S. (1994). Primary caregivers' psychological status and family functioning after traumatic brain injury. *Brain Injury, 8,* 197–210.

Kreutzer, J.S., Marwitz, J.H., & Kepler, K. (1992). Traumatic brain injury: Family response and outcome. *Archives of Physical Medicine and Rehabilitation, 73,* 771–778.

Kreutzer, J.S., Marwitz, J.H., Walker, W., Sander, A., Sherer, M., Bogner, J., Fraser, R., & Bushnik, T. (2003). Moderating factors in return to work and job stability after traumatic brain injury. *Journal of Head Trauma Rehabilitation, 18,* 123–138.

Kreutzer, J.S., Serio, C.D., & Bergquist, S. (1994). Family needs after brain injury: A quantitative analysis. *Journal of Head Trauma Rehabilitation, 9,* 104–115.

Kreutzer, J.S., Zasler, N.D., Camplair, P.S., & Leininger B.E. (1990). A practical guide to family intervention following adult traumatic brain injury. In J.S. Kreutzer &

P. Wehman (Eds.), *Community Integration Following Traumatic Brain Injury* (pp. 249–284). Baltimore: Paul H. Brookes.

Laroi, F. (2003). The family systems approach to treating families of persons with brain injury: A potential collaboration between family therapist and brain injury professional. *Brain Injury, 17,* 175–187.

Lezak, M. (1978). Living with the characterologically altered brain injured patient. *Journal of Clinical Psychiatry, 39,* 592–598.

Maitz, E.A., & Sachs, P.R. (1995). Treating families of individuals with traumatic brain injury from a family systems perspective. *Journal of Head Trauma Rehabilitation, 10,* 1–11.

Man, D. (1999). Community-based empowerment programme for families with a brain injured survivor: An outcome study. *Brain Injury, 13,* 433–445.

Minnes, P., Graffi, S., Nolte, M.L., Carlson, P., & Harrick, L. (2000). Coping and stress in Canadian family caregivers of persons with traumatic brain injuries. *Brain Injury, 14,* 737–748.

Morris, K.C. (2001). Psychological distress in carers of head injured individuals: The provision of written information. *Brain Injury, 15,* 239–254.

Oddy, M., Coughlan, T., Tyerman, A, & Jenkins, D. (1985). Social adjustment after closed head injury: A further follow-up seven years later. *Journal of Neurology, Neurosurgery, and Psychiatry, 48,* 564–568.

Oddy, M., & Humphrey, M. (1980). Social recovery during the year following severe head injury. *Journal of Neurology, Neurosuregry, and Psychiatry, 43,* 798–802.

Panting, A., & Merry, P. (1972). The long-term rehabilitation of severe head injuries with particular reference to the need for social and medical support for the patient and family. *Rehabilitation, 38,* 33–37.

Perlesz, A., & O'Loughlin, M. (1998). Changes in stress and burden in families seeking therapy following traumatic brain injury: A follow-up study. *International Journal of Rehabilitation Research, 21,* 339–354.

Peters, L.C., Stambrook, M., & Moore, A.D. (1990). Psychosocial sequelae of closed head injury: Effects on the marital relationship. *Brain Injury, 4,* 39–47.

Peters, L.C., Stambrook, M., Moore, A.D., Zubek, E., Dubo, H., & Blumenschein, S. (1992). Differential effects of spinal cord injury and head injury on marital adjustment. *Brain Injury, 6,* 461–467.

Rappaport, M., Herrero-Backe, C., & Winterfield K.M. (1989). Head injury outcome up to ten years later. *Archives of Physical Medicine and Rehabilitation, 70,* 885–892.

Rosenthal, M., & Young, T. (1988). Effective family intervention after traumatic brain injury. *Journal of Head Trauma Rehabilitation, 3,* 42.

Sander, A.M., High, W., Hannay, H.J., & Sherer, M. (1997). Predictors of psychological health in caregivers of patients with closed head injury. *Brain Injury, 11,* 235–249.

Sander, A.M., Kreutzer, J.S., Rosenthal, M., Delmonico, R., & Young, M.E. (1996). A multicenter longitudinal investigation of return to work and community integration following traumatic brain injury. *Journal of Head Trauma Rehabilitation, 11,* 70–84.

Sander, A.M., Sherer, M., Malec, J.F., High, W.M., Jr., Thompson, R.N., Moessner, A.M., & Josey, J. (2003). Preinjury emotional and family functioning in caregivers of persons with traumatic brain injury. *Archives of Physical Medicine and Rehabilitation, 84,* 197–203.

Serio, C.D., Kreutzer, J.S., & Gervasio, A.H. (1995). Predicting family needs after brain injury: Implications for intervention. *Journal of Head Trauma Rehabilitation, 10,* 32–45.

Singer, G., Glang, A., Nixon, C., Cooley, E., Kerns, K., Williams, D., & Powers, L. (1994). A comparison of two psychosocial interventions for parents of children with acquired brain injury: An exploratory study. *Journal Head Trauma Rehabilitation, 9*, 38–49.

Smith, L., & Godfrey, H. (1995). *Family Support Programs and Rehabilitation: A Cognitive Behavioral Approach to Traumatic Brain Injury.* New York: Plenum Press.

Soderstrom, S., Fogelsjoo, A., Fugl-Meyer, K.S., & Stenson, S. (1992). Traumatic brain injury crisis intervention and family therapy—management and outcome. *Scandinavian Journal of Rehabilitation Medicine, 26*, 132–141.

Sohlberg, M.M., McLaughlin, K.A., Todis, B., Larsen, J., & Glang, A. (2001). What does it take to collaborate with families affected by brain injury? A preliminary model. *Journal of Head Trauma Rehabilitation, 16*, 498–511.

Tate, D.G., & Pledger, C. (2003). An integrative conceptual framework of disability. *American Psychologist, 58*, 289–295.

Thomsen, I.V. (1984). Late outcome of very severe blunt head trauma: a 10–15 year second follow-up. *Journal of Neurology, Neurosurgery, and Psychiatry, 47*, 260–268.

Whiteneck, G.G., Fougeyrollas, P., & Gerhart, K.A. (1987). Elaborating the model of disablement. In M.J. Fuhrer (Ed.), *Assessing Medical Rehabilitation Practices: The Promise of Outcomes Research* (pp. 91–102). Baltimore: Paul H. Brookes.

Witol, A.D., Sander, A.M., & Kreutzer, J. (1996). A longitudinal analysis of family needs following traumatic brain injury. *NeuroRehabilitation, 7*, 175–187.

10

Vocational Rehabilitation

JAMES F. MALEC

STATE OF THE SCIENCE

Regional surveys of people with traumatic brain injury (TBI), family/significant others (Kolakowsky-Hayner et al., 2001; "A vision for the future: TBI town meetings 1994," 1994) and the professional literature (Malec & Basford, 1996) identify employment services, along with service coordination and public awareness, as primary needs after significant TBI. Nonetheless, almost 20 years of data on vocational outcomes after TBI indicate that no more than 40% (and possibly less than 30%) of people with moderate to severe TBI obtain and maintain community-based employment (CBE) after their injuries. In contrast, reports on specialized programs and demonstration projects have reported marked improvement (over 70% of people served in CBE) over the historical benchmark of less than 40% in CBE.

Initial review through the National Institute on Disability and Rehabilitation Research (NIDRR)-funded Research and Training Center at the University of Wisconsin–Stout (Corthell, 1990; Corthell & Tooman, 1985) of studies and reports in the 1980s of vocational outcomes after TBI estimated that less than 30% of people with moderate to severe TBI were able to maintain CBE after injury. The situation has not clearly improved almost 20 years later. Follow-up data collected (as of year end 2002) through the NIDRR-funded TBI Model Systems

1 year after injury on 720 people records only 27% competitively employed, 5% in other employment (not necessarily community-based), and 10% as full- or part-time students. People with TBI served through the TBI Model Systems have the benefit of the highest-quality inpatient medical rehabilitation services available in the United States. Despite such excellent initial rehabilitative care, CBE after significant TBI appears to remain below 40%. (Without such services, employment after TBI is likely to be even lower and may remain below the 30% CBE rate reported 20 years ago.) This disturbing benchmark of less than 40% in CBE after moderate to severe TBI is substantiated by numerous other studies that will be reviewed subsequently in greater detail. However, there are also a number of examples of intensive postacute rehabilitation programs and specialized vocational demonstration projects that have markedly improved upon these baseline CBE rates.

REVIEW OF THE LITERATURE

Vocational Outcomes *without* Specific Vocational Intervention

In their reviews of the literature, Ben-Yishay et al. (1987), Wehman, West, et al. (1993), and Yasuda et al., (2001) concluded that TBI frequently results in impairments that interfere with return to work. Wehman, West and colleagues (1993) report that estimates of the rate of unemployment after TBI are greater than 60%, with some estimates as high as 70% to 80%. Overall prior studies show a larger range for rate of unemployment following TBI (Bruckner & Randle, 1972; Denny-Brown, 1945; Drudge et al., 1984; Fahy et al., 1967; Gilchrist & Wilkinson, 1979; Gjone et al., 1972; Heiskanen & Sipponen, 1970; Hpay, 1971; Lewin, 1959, 1967, 1976; London, 1967; MacIver et al., 1958; Matheson, 1982; McKinlay et al., 1983; McLean et al., 1984; Miller & Stern, 1965; Oddy & Humphrey, 1980; Oddy et al., 1978, 1985; O'Shaughnessy et al., 1984; Reyes et al., 1981; Richardson, 1971; Rimel et al., 1981, 1982; Rowbotham et al., 1954; Rusk et al., 1966, 1969; Steadman & Graham, 1970; Stuss et al., 1985; Thomsen, 1974, 1984; VanZomeren & Van den Berg, 1985; Weddel et al., 1980; Wrightson & Gronwall, 1981). In reviewing this literature, however, Ben-Yishay and associates (1987) concluded that lower rates of unemployment are more typical following mild TBI and that unemployment following moderate to severe TBI may be greater than 90%.

Participants in most studies reviewed by Ben-Yishay's group did not receive formal medical rehabilitation. However, two studies did involve follow-up of patients who participated in rehabilitation. More recent studies yield similar results. These studies suggest that inpatient medical rehabilitation alone does not increase the probability of return to work and that employment rates diminish with greater initial injury severity and increased associated neuropsychological impairment (Brooks et al., 1987; Dacey et al., 1991; Dikmen et al., 1994; Godfrey et al., 1993; McMordie et al., 1990; Rao & Kilgore, 1992; Ruff et al., 1993; Stambrook et al., 1990; Wehman, Kregel et al., 1993.) Two of the most recent studies provide no evidence that vocational outcomes for people with moderate to severe TBI have improved over the past 20 years or that medical rehabilitation alone significantly enhances vocational outcomes. Gollaher and colleagues (1998) described vocational outcomes for 99 people followed up 1 to 3 years after brain injury. Eighty-three percent of the sample were severely injured, and 88% were competitively employed prior to injury. Of these, only 31% were employed at follow-up. Education, preinjury employment, and severity of initial postinjury disability predicted the long-term vocational outcome. Kreutzer and colleagues (2003) reviewed vocational outcomes for a sample of 186 adults with TBI from six NIDRR TBI Model Systems followed up at 1, 2, and 3 years postinjury. At one year postinjury, only 34% were competitively employed; this rate increased to 37% at 2-year and 42% at 3-year follow-ups. Only 34% were employed at all three follow-ups. Age, education, severity of injury, and severity of disability contributed significantly to the prediction of the vocational outcome. Other factors that contributed to the vocational outcome prediction were minority status, marital status, and ability to drive.

A study of Vietnam veterans presents a somewhat more optimistic estimate of return to work following significant TBI, with only 44% unemployed (Kraft et al., 1993). This study, however, is not representative of shorter-term outcomes for the general population since (1) the veterans studied were screened for physical or mental impairments prior to admission to the armed services, (2) outcomes were studied 15 years after injury, and (3) the veterans studied had the benefit of educational services and other supports provided through the Veterans Administration; most (82%) took advantage of educational benefits.

Taken together, the literature supports Wehman and colleagues' proposal of greater than 60% unemployment as an optimistic benchmark following moderate to severe TBI.

Vocational Outcomes *with* Specific Vocational Intervention

A greater impact on vocational outcome has been documented for intensive postacute rehabilitation efforts that include a specialized vocational component. Following acute medical interventions and inpatient rehabilitation, outpatient postacute rehabilitative interventions following TBI typically follow one of two general models. Ben-Yishay and Prigatano developed the first model, which may be called *Comprehensive Day Treatment* (CDT) (Ben-Yishay & Prigatano, 1990; Prigatano et al., 1986). These programs provide intensive multimodal outpatient treatment and may be most applicable to patients with severely impaired self-awareness, interpersonal functioning, and cognition following TBI (Malec et al, 1992). The second model is a *Community Reintegration* (CR) approach that may be most appropriate for individuals with less impaired self-awareness. The CR programs focus on developing functional skills and community supports that are necessary for independent living and work (Cope et al., 1991a, 1991b; Evans & Jones, 1991; Mills et al., 1992). Either of these models for outpatient treatment may include *supported employment* (Wehman, West et al., 1993) as a method for enhancing vocational outcomes. Supported employment involves on-site supports, frequently with the direct assistance of a *job coach* who assists the client with TBI to maintain satisfactory job performance (Kreutzer et al., 1991). Job supports may be provided either temporarily or long term, depending on the level of the client's disabilities. Supported employment has been found to significantly enhance vocational outcomes (Wehman et al., 1989, 1990; Wehman, Sherron et al., 1993; Wehman, West et al., 1993)

An early report of vocational outcomes following one CDT program indicated a 50% unemployment rate following program participation (Prigatano et al., 1984). However, more recent CDT outcome studies have reported an overall unemployment rate of only 15% to 25% following treatment (Malec, 2001; Malec et al., 1993; Prigatano et al., 1994). Typically these studies have reported that approximately 50% of program participants are in independent CBE following program participation; another 25%–35% are in community-based educational programs or supported employment. Malec and colleagues (Malec, 2001) and Ben-Yishay and associates (1987) have shown that low unemployment levels are generally maintained 1 year following program completion, with a very slight (less than 5%) increase in unemployment.

Vocational outcomes for CR programs have been similar (Cope et al., 1991a, 1991b; Ellerd & Moore, 1992; Evans & Jones, 1991; Fryer, 1987; Lyons & Morse, 1988; Mills et al., 1992; Wall et al., 1998; Wehman, West et al., 1993). Wehman, West and associates (1993) reported unemployment to be only 29% for individuals with severe TBI using supported employment. Ellerd and Moore (1992) reported that 71% of 24 participants with TBI were employed 12 months after placement using a supported employment model, with a significant decline in employment at 30-month follow-up underscoring the importance of long-term follow-up for employment maintenance. Wall et al. (1998) tested a vocational intervention that used a *Clubhouse* CR approach with a very challenging group of individuals with acquired brain injury (over 60% unemployed at the time of injury/onset, average 8.91 years postinjury/onset, 90% with moderate to severe injuries). Although maintaining participant engagement in the program was problematic (a 42% dropout rate), 68% of those who completed the program were placed and remained employed for at least 60 days; 59% maintained employment at long-term follow-up conducted an average ot 18.7 months postplacement. Future research with such difficult-to-engage participants might profitably focus on methods to enhance program involvement and completion, since outcomes appear good for those who fully participated in the intervention.

Our own studies through the Mayo Clinic TBI Model System have produced similar results. As a result of participation in the Mayo Clinic CDT program, 67% were employed in the community 1 year after program completion (39% with no support, 10% with temporary support or in training, 18% with permanent support) (Malec, 2001). Research over the past 8 years at the Mayo Clinic to develop methods that enhance vocational reintegration after moderate to severe TBI has contributed to the development of the Traumatic Brain Injury Vocational Case Coordinator (TBI–VCC) Model. This model may involve the participant in CDT, CR, or very minimal outpatient rehabilitation, depending on the participant's needs and goals.

THE TRAUMATIC BRAIN INJURY VOCATIONAL CASE COORDINATOR (TBI-VCC) MODEL

The linchpin of the TBI-VCC Model is a Vocational Case Coordinator (VCC) who provides case coordination and has specialized knowledge of vocational rehabilitation after TBI (Fig. 10.1). The TBI-VCC Model is based on seminal work in the vocational rehabilitation of people with TBI synthesized through the University of Wisconsin–Stout (Corthell, 1990; Corthell & Tooman, 1985; Thomas et al., 1993) and in supported employment by Paul Wehman, Jeffrey Kreutzer, and their associates (Kreutzer et al., 1991; Wehman et al., 1989, 1990, Wehman, Sherron et al., 1993 1989) The TBI-VCC Model includes key elements of successful vocational interventions after TBI previously reported in the literature. These key elements are described in Table 10.1. Key differences between this model and traditional vocational rehabilitation services are described in Table 10.2.

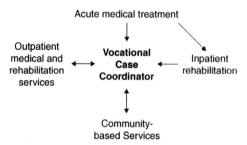

Figure 10.1. The Traumatic Brain Injury Vocational Case Coordinator Model.

Table 10.1. Key Elements of the Traumatic Brain Injury Vocational Case Coordinator (TBI-VCC) Model

- Focus on early vocational intervention
- Identify residual impairments that may interfere with vocational reintegration and refer for appropriate medical rehabilitation services
- Integrate vocational goals with rehabilitation therapy goals
- Develop comprehensive return-to-work plans that address issues ranging from number of hours worked to the work environment to compensation techniques
- Improve community agency linkages to develop a team approach
- Provide a smooth transition from medical to community-based services
- Use on-the-job evaluations to gather the best information about a person's work skills
- Provide appropriate support during work evaluations and after placement, including job coaching and work trials
- Provide reasonable work accommodations before the client starts the job
- Provide TBI education to employers, coworkers, and community service providers
- Clearly identify a TBI resource person for the client and employer
- Provide regular, frequent follow-up after placement

In a published study of the TBI-VCC approach (Malec et al., 2000), we demonstrated a marked improvement in sustained CBE rates for 114 people with TBI 1 year after participation in the project. At 1-year follow-up, 81% were employed in the community (53% independently with no support). Although longer time since injury was associated with more services required for vocational placement, almost half of those served entered the project more than 1 year postinjury, and most of these also maintained CBE for at least 1 year after placement.

In a further refinement of the TBI-VCC model (Malec & Degiorgio, 2002), we found that the level of postacute rehabilitation required to obtain and sustain CBE for 1 year varied with severity of disability (as measured by the Mayo-Portland Adaptability Inventory; (Malec & Lezak, 2003; Malec et al., 2003) and time since injury. Those with mild to moderate disability, particularly if they entered postacute rehabilitation within 1 year after injury/onset, generally were able to secure and maintain CBE with relatively limited intervention (that is, specialized vocational services and a few hours each week of outpatient rehabilitation). Those who had lived with severe disabilities and unemployment for many years after brain injury usually required more intensive outpatient rehabilitation, that is, CDT, in addition to specialized vocational services to successfully join the world of work. The probability of maintaining CBE for at least 1 year after initial placement based on time since injury, level of disability, and intensity of intervention is presented in Table 10.3.

Table 10.2. Key Differences between the Traumatic Brain Injury Vocational Case Coordinator (TBI-VCC) Model and Traditional Vocational Rehabilitation

TBI-VCC MODEL	TRADITIONAL VOCATIONAL REHABILITATION
• Provides early intervention	• Waits for person to apply
• Bridges gap between hospital and community	• No involvement in medical rehabilitation
• On-the-job evaluations	• Interest and aptitude testing, work samples
• Integrates vocational and rehabilitation goals	• Focuses only on vocational goals
• Places and trains	• Trains and places
• Employer and coworker education	• No educational outreach
• Addresses psychosocial and functional issues before job placement	• Addresses psychosocial and functional issues after they arise
• Team approach	• One counselor per client
• Sequence of short-term goals	• One long-term vocational goal
• Supported risk taking	• High risk for failure

METHODOLOGICAL ISSUES

A lack of clear characterization of samples studied constitutes a weakness in prior vocational outcomes research after TBI both with and without intervention. Typically these studies have not described the array of participant characteristics that may affect the vocational outcome after TBI, such as injury severity, severity of persistent disability and impairment including impaired self-awareness, time since injury, preinjury unemployment, history of substance abuse, age, and education. In addition to making it difficult to compare studies, this absence of participant information creates controversies about how best to describe people with TBI that pervade TBI research more generally. For instance, Novack, Bush, and colleagues (Bush et al., 2003; Novack et al., 2001) have provided evidence that measures of early impairment and disability may be a better predictor of long-term outcome than traditional measures of injury severity. Their observation is consistent with clinical experience. A person with a severe TBI, as defined by the initial Glasgow Coma Scale (GCS), may make a strong initial recovery and be more employable than a person with a less severe initial injury who demonstrates more persistent impairment and disability following acute care and rehabilitation. However, there is no general agreement about how best to measure initial disability. As will be reviewed in a later section of this chapter, controversy has also arisen even about the use of traditional measures of injury severity such as the GCS.

Of particular concern is whether samples in interventional studies are comparable to those in natural history studies. Conceivably interventional studies may show superior vocational outcomes because they have selected those participants

Table 10.3A. Probability of Community-Based Employment (CBE) at 1 Year with Limited Intervention Predicted by Months Since Injury and Staff Mayo-Portland Adaptability Inventory (MPAI) Standard Score (Mean = 500; SD = 100)*

MONTHS SINCE INJURY	STAFF MPAI STANDARD SCORE								
	300	350	400	450	500	550	600	650	700
6	.98	.97	.94	.90	.82	.70	.56	.40	.26
12	.98	.97	.94	.89	.81	.69	.53	.38	.24
24	.98	.96	.93	.87	.78	.65	.49	.33	.21
36	.97	.95	.91	.85	.74	.60	.44	.29	.18
60	.96	.93	.88	.79	.67	.51	.36	.23	.13
96	.94	.89	.81	.69	.54	.38	.24	.14	.08
120	.91	.85	.75	.61	.45	.30	.18	.11	.06
180	.81	.69	.54	.39	.25	.15	.08	.05	.02

Table 10.3B. Probability of CBE at 1 Year with Comprehensive Day Treatment (CDT) Predicted by Staff MPAI Standard Score†

CDT	.98	.96	.92	.86	.77	.63	.47	.32	.20

Source: Malec and Degiorgio (2002).
†*Source*: Malec (2001).

who have the strongest potential for employment. It is difficult to evaluate this concern because of the lack of comparable participant descriptions across studies. Our own interventional research has demonstrated superior vocational outcomes for largely unselected samples with generally moderate to severe initial injuries and significant persistent disabilities who present for outpatient rehabilitation services. A significant minority had preinjury histories of substance abuse or psychiatric disturbance. Wall et al. (1998) reported a high level of employment for participants who completed their program despite having 60% unemployment prior to injury in their sample. These studies suggest that methods included in the TBI-VCC Model can be effective even with participants whose histories include factors that represent significant barriers to employment.

The definition of employment has also been variable. Various researchers have included full-time, part-time, homemaking, education and training, and volunteer work in this definition. A number of definitional questions can be raised that are difficult to answer. For example, what constitutes full-time employment (i.e., 40, >32, or, >30 hours per week)? How can full-time employment as a homemaker be verified? At what level does volunteer work become equivalent to paid employment? Many of these issues may be more academic than practical. Across studies, those in equivocal categories typically constitute a small proportion of the sample (<10%). From a practical methodological perspective, it may be more straightforward to report those who are *not* in community-based productive activity of any sort. Across samples, this group has typically been greater than 60% in natural history studies and less than 30% in interventional studies.

Repeated replication of results is a methodological strength of TBI vocational outcome research. Unlike many areas of investigation reported in this volume, studies reported here represent data on hundreds of individuals with TBI studied across a wide variety of socioeconomic and geographic settings at various times over a period of 30 years. While interventional studies as a group include fewer people than natural history studies, interventional research also represents relatively large and diverse samples. The consistency of findings across time, geography, and a diversity of participant characteristics provides a basis for the validity of these findings.

SUMMARY

Review of previous research describes the value for improving vocational outcomes of a system of intervention that uses a specific provider (VCC) who specializes in vocational rehabilitation for people with TBI to develop and coordinate systems and services that provide (1) case coordination, (2) early involvement in vocational planning, (3) appropriate medical and vocational rehabilitation interventions, (4) work trials, (5) temporary or long-term supported employment, (6) employer education and support, and (7) follow-up in the long term. This approach differs from traditional vocational rehabilitation in several important ways: (1) use of supported employment, as described by Wehman and colleagues (Wehman et al., 1990; Wehman, West et al., 1993), that is, job placement based on a match of client interests and potential skills to work requirements; on-site job training, advocacy, and work site modifications; and ongoing assessment and support for job maintenance; (2) the VCC as part of the medical center–based rehabilitation team, with the ability to access appropriate rehabilitation services to assist in developing social skills, cognitive compensation techniques, and other prevocational skills that support employment; (3) emphasis on the development of a network of naturally occurring community supports for employment including independent living and transportation services; (4) emphasis on employer education and follow-up; and (5) liaison with community based vocational services for traditional evaluation, training, and placement services as required. Methodological concerns in this area of research include the absence of comprehensive participant descriptions and definitions of employment. Nonetheless repeated replication of findings across settings, time, and a diversity of participants offers a basis for confidence in the validity of these findings.

Vocational Outcome Predictors

Traumatic Brain Injury Severity. The value of a measure of TBI severity (such as the GCS, length of unconsciousness, or duration of post-traumatic amnesia) for predicting outcome has been extensively documented in the literature (Cifu et al., 1997; Crepeau & Scherzer, 1993; Ezrachi, 1991; Levin, 1995). With the advent of roadside sedation, however, concern has been raised about the effect of early sedation on initial GCS scores (Zafonte et al., 1996). Intoxication at the time of injury also reduces GCS scores (Kelly et al, 1997). The presence of abnormalities on neuroimaging indicates a more severe injury than may be signified by the GCS alone (Williams et al., 1990). Future research should consider selecting the measure (or combination of measures) of injury severity that best predicts the outcome for the specific sample.

Impairment/Disability. Bush et al. (2003); and Novack et al. (2001) have advanced a model for long term outcome prediction in which early assessment of disability supplants initial TBI severity. Malec and associates reported that vocational outcomes are better for individuals with less impairment/disability, as measured by the MPAI, prior to admission to a postacute rehabilitation program (Malec, 2001; Malec & Degiorgio, 2002; Malec et al., 2000). Cope and colleagues (1991b) demonstrated a similar relationship between outcomes for their community re-integration program and impairment/disability as measured by the Disability Rating Scale.

Time Since Injury. A number of studies of both inpatient (Cope & Hall, 1982; Mackay et al., 1992; Sahgal & Heinemann, 1989; Tobis et al., 1982) and postacute TBI rehabilitation (Ashley et al., 1993; Fryer, 1987; Johnston, 1991; Malec, 2001; Malec & Degiorgio, 2002; Malec et al., 2000) have reported better vocational and other outcomes with early intervention. Several studies (Eames & Wood, 1985; Ezrachi, 1991; Mills et al., 1992; Prigatano et al., 1984), however, have found no relationship between time since injury and treatment outcome. The absence of an effect for time since injury on outcome in these latter studies may be explained by restricted ranges of time since injury within the small samples studied.

Impaired Self-awareness. Studies of the effect of impaired self-awareness on rehabilitation and vocational outcomes show mixed results (Crepeau & Scherzer, 1993; Ezrachi, 1991; Fordyce & Roueche, 1986; Lam et al., 1988; Malec & Moessner, 2000; Prigatano et al., 1994; Sherer, Bergloff, Levin et al., 1998). Crepeau and Scherzer (1993) commented on the difficulty of measuring self-awareness. Malec and Basford (1996) emphasized the need for more reliable, valid, and standardized measures of self-awareness. The Awareness Questionnaire developed by Sherer and colleagues (1995, 1996, 1998) has been more carefully studied and validated than other measures.

Substance Abuse. Prior studies have demonstrated that substance abuse negatively impacts TBI recovery and outcome (Corrigan, 1995; Corrigan et al., 1997; Kelly et al., 1997) and that people who abused alcohol prior to injury are at high risk of returning to a pattern of substance abuse postinjury (Kreutzer et al., 1996). The CAGE questions (see Table 10.4) comprise a brief screening instrument that has established validity in identifying people who abuse alcohol (Ewing, 1984).

Although other screening instruments, such as the Substance Abuse Subtle Screening Inventory-3 (SASSI; Arenth et al., 2001) have also been recommended, Fuller and colleagues (1994) reported that the CAGE questions were more sensitive and specific to alcohol problems with people with TBI than the SASSI. Using the four CAGE questions also creates significantly less burden for the responder than answering the 88-question SASSI.

Other Demographic and Preinjury Factors. Several studies (Brooks et al., 1987; Keyser-Marcus et al., 2002; McMordie et al., 1990; Ruff et al., 1993; Stambrook et al., 1990) and reviews (Crepeau & Scherzer, 1993; Malec & Basford, 1996) describe a negative relationship between age and vocational outcome after TBI.

Studies of the impact of preinjury level of education on vocational outcome have shown mixed results (Burke et al., 1988; Ezrachi, 1991; Fraser et al., 1988; Keyser-Marcus et al., 2002; Malec, 2001; Malec et al., 1992, 2000; Mills et al., 1992; Prigatano et al., 1984; Sherer, Bergloff, Levin et al., 1998). Even those studies that have reported a positive relationship between preinjury level of education and vocational outcomes have reported only a low correlation.

The relationship between pre- and postinjury employment has been variable in prior studies. In their review of the literature, Crepeau and Scherzer (1993) concluded that generally preinjury employment does not strongly predict postinjury employment. However, others (Brooks et al., 1987; Gollaher et al., 1998; Johnson, 1987) reported that workers with greater preinjury employment qualifications were more likely to be reemployed after injury. Using TBI Model System data, Keyser-Marcus and colleagues (2002) found a positive relationship between pre- and postinjury employment.

A preinjury history of psychiatric illness has generally not been related to outcome after mild TBI (Alves et al., 1993; Cicerone & Kalmar, 1995; Gerber & Schraa, 1995; Karzmark et al., 1995; MacMillan et al., 2002) However, MacMillan and colleagues (2002) reported that preinjury psychiatric history was related to employment after moderate to severe TBI.

Table 10.4. CAGE Screening Questions for Alcohol Problems

(A positive response to two or more questions suggests possible problem drinking.)
1. Have you ever felt that you ought to **C**ut down on your drinking?
2. Have people **A**nnoyed you by criticizing your drinking?
3. Have you ever felt bad or **G**uilty about your drinking?
4. Have you ever had a drink the first thing in the morning to steady your nerves or get rid of a hangover? (**E**ye opener)

Despite mixed support for the predictive value of this set of variables, future research should include these factors because of their potential contribution to outcome prediction, relative ease of acquisition, and importance in characterizing the sample of participants.

Environmental Factors. Many rehabilitation interventions focus on improving the abilities, adjustment, and compensation skills of the person who is disabled. As the disability community correctly points out, the social and physical environments in which people with disabilities live and work also need rehabilitation. Rather than coaching people with disabilities in how to adjust and compensate to an extraordinary degree in order to overcome societal barriers to their participation, developing a more accepting, accommodating, physically and psychologically barrier-free environment is, in many instances, a more reasonable (although often more challenging) approach to increasing community participation for people with disabilities. Research on the effect of the environment as well as participants (and the interaction of people and environments) on vocational outcome represents the *new paradigm* in rehabilitation research (Gill et al., 2003).

These same issues pertain to people disabled by TBI and to vocational rehabilitation. West (1995) has described and provided preliminary empirical data demonstrating how social environmental factors in the workplace, as well as financial incentives and disincentives, contribute to job maintenance for people with brain injury. Michaels and Risucci (1993) reported that vocational counselors tended to rate accommodations for people with TBI as *more problematic* than employers did. These same counselors tended to focus on the functional limitations of the person with TBI as obstacles to return to work, whereas employers indicated primary concern about actual job performance. Others (Bowe, 1993; Siegel & Gaylord-Ross, 1991) have detailed for other disability groups how both monetary and nonmonetary features of the workplace contribute to job maintenance. Such aspects of work include opportunities to develop social support and relationships, as well as benefits, opportunities for advancement, and financial compensation that are adequate not only to offset the costs of chronic medical care and disability-related expenses but also to sustain a sense of reward for work-related efforts. These factors, as well as accessibility and accommodation from the vocational services system itself, are important considerations in analyzing reasons and ways to improve vocational outcomes after TBI.

GAPS IN KNOWLEDGE AND METHODOLOGIC ISSUES

There is a large amount of evidence in the literature that, without a specialized approach to vocational rehabilitation, only a minority (less than 40%) of people with moderate to severe TBI enter or reenter CBE. Conversely, a number of studies and demonstration projects report much better outcomes, with 70%–80% or more of participants maintaining CBE for a substantial period of time after initial placement. Seven basic elements comprising the TBI-VCC Model are included in most of these model programs:

- Case coordination
- Early involvement in vocational planning
- Appropriate medical and rehabilitation interventions
- Work trials
- Temporary or long-term supported employment
- Employer education and support
- Long-term availability of follow-up

Perhaps the most critical element is the first: case coordination. The success of this approach to vocational intervention requires someone to be responsible to the person with TBI to assist in identifying, engaging with, and funding the other services needed to successfully obtain and maintain employment. In our experience, required services and funding are usually identifiable—but only with dogged ingenuity and considerable effort. An exceptional family member, friend, or the person with TBI may have the energy and system knowledge to coordinate needed services without professional assistance. However, in most cases, an expert in vocational rehabilitation after TBI will be extremely helpful, if not necessary, to assist the person with TBI in developing and implementing a successful self-directed vocational rehabilitation plan.

On a naive level, a state vocational rehabilitation counselor might seem to be the obvious choice for this role. However, a number of factors within the federal/state vocational rehabilitation system make it virtually impossible for state vocational counselors to effectively assume these responsibilities. Such factors include

1. An historical style of vocational rehabilitation that considers cognitive and behavioral problems resulting from TBI (or other neurologic or psychiatric disorders) to be motivational problems outside the realm of the vocational counselor or plan.
2. Order of selection criteria that give priority to serving people with severe physical disabilities but tend to minimize the impact of cognitive and behavioral disabilities.
3. An emphasis on job placement rather than job maintenance.
4. Minimal or no funds for long term supported employment.
5. A largely office-based, paperwork-burdened vocational practice that impedes active liaisons with medical, rehabilitation, and community service providers as well as potential employers and coworkers.

What Works Best for Whom?

Review of the literature reveals a number of factors that may affect the vocational outcome after TBI, including injury severity, severity of disability including specifically impaired self-awareness, time since injury, substance abuse, and other comorbid and premorbid factors. In evaluating vocational interventions, future interventional research should more clearly attempt to elaborate the basic TBI-VCC Model to address varying types and profiles of postinjury disability as well as premorbid and comorbid factors. As some of our previous research has suggested (Malec & Degiorgio, 2002), many individuals with even moderate disability can return to work with relatively limited intervention if this is begun within the first year after injury. The general model suggested in this chapter should not be construed as a "one-size-fits-all" model since the extent of services, supports, coordination, and follow-up can vary markedly among individuals. Future research should attempt to clarify the minimal extent of intervention required by people with various disability profiles after TBI for successful job placement and maintenance. This type of research has important implications for maximizing benefit while minimizing the cost of services.

Along these same lines, future research should focus on the specific effects and additional costs required by comorbid and premorbid factors for successful vocational outcomes. For example, it is extremely difficult to successfully maintain in community-based work a substance-dependent individual with limited education and no preinjury work history who largely relied on illegal means prior to injury for financial support. It must also be recognized, however, that many of the factors that make vocational rehabilitation difficult in such cases have nothing to do with TBI. These factors reflect socioeconomic and behavioral problems that would have served as significant obstacles to successful vocational rehabilitation even without the additional obstacles created by TBI. Future research to develop vocational rehabilitation methods for cases complicated by such premorbid and comorbid conditions should to be conducted with the recognition that such programs are not strictly *TBI rehabilitation* programs since they are required to address broader psychological, medical, and social issues that interfere with vocational rehabilitation. These types of programs serve a more complicated and challenging case that will no doubt require more extensive services for a successful outcome. Given the extensive obstacles to employment in many of these types of cases, more modest outcomes for programs targeted to these types of individuals would be expected.

Vocational rehabilitation after TBI might be conceived of as serving a range of participants, from those with relatively limited residual disabilities from TBI who can return to work with relatively minimal intervention and support, to those with more severe disabilities from TBI who require extensive rehabilitation, other interventions, and long-term support, to those with both significant disabilities due to TBI and significant premorbid/comorbid conditions and complications that create extreme obstacles to vocational success. Elaborating the general model for vocational rehabilitation after TBI and developing more specific methods that are designed to serve specific groups of people with TBI remain important challenges for future applied vocational research.

Not only level of intensity but also a number of other parameters that characterize various types of interventions should be examined, including the degree to which the intervention (1) results in reduced impairment of the individual served, (2) enhances activities, and (3) eliminates environmental and social obstacles to vocational participation. Many people apply for rehabilitation with the expectation that it will reduce impairment—for example, memory problems. In many of these cases, despite no change in impairment, a successful vocational outcome results from improving the participant's ability to engage in work and other activities through the use of compensation techniques and external support and by reducing obstacles, such as inappropriate employer and coworker expectations or ignorance. For instance, despite continuing memory problems, a vocational rehabilitation participant can learn to compensate by using a memory notebook and find success in a routinized job that places minimal demands on new learning and memory.

Future research in vocational rehabilitation should attempt to more clearly answer the question "What are the minimally necessary but sufficient conditions for successful vocational rehabilitation after TBI?" More completely stated, the question is "What are the minimally necessary but sufficient conditions for successful vocational rehabilitation at the lowest cost with people with various types and levels of disabilities and complicating conditions after TBI?" *Necessary but sufficient conditions* represent not only beneficial changes in the person with TBI (about which we know more) but also beneficial changes in the vocational rehabilitation system and in the workplace (about which and how to accomplish we know substantially less).

Measurement

As in many areas of TBI rehabilitation, measurement of both predictor and outcome variables remains problematic for vocational studies. A detailed discussion of measurement issues is beyond the scope of this chapter. Nonetheless, a number of reviews (Dijkers, 1997; Hall et al., 1996, 2001; Merbitz et al., 1989; Ware, 2003) have detailed the limitations of outcome measurement in rehabilitation and brain injury. The field of TBI rehabilitation, and vocational rehabilitation after TBI specifically, should work toward developing measures using contemporary measurement techniques (i.e., item response theory, Rasch analysis) that have demonstrated reliability and validity and will be consistently used across studies.

More consistent definitions of types of employment (for instance, competitive, supported) would assist in comparing outcomes across studies. More generally, accepted measures of overall disability and of specific types of disability (e.g., impaired self-awareness) will allow hypotheses about relationships between these predictors and outcomes to be examined. Valid measures of social and other elements of the workplace also require development to better understand the relationship of such factors to job maintenance and to evaluate interventions that target changes in such environmental features.

Methodology

Twenty years of data indicate that less than 40% of people with moderate to severe TBI return to work. Any intervention that demonstrates marked improvement on this historical benchmark is logically credible and efficacious, provided that it is conducted with a representative sample of people with moderate to severe TBI. A more powerful variation of this type of cohort design is represented by studies that include people with a long baseline of lack of success in vocational reintegration after TBI. Such studies use these individuals as their own controls. If a person who has been unable to return to work for many years after TBI finds community-based work through the intervention under study and maintains this work for a substantial period of time, that sequence of events (long baseline of failure, intervention, sustained period of success) provides convincing evidence of the efficacy of the intervention.

How long is a substantial period of success? Maintenance of continuous work for 1 year after placement has been used in many studies as a criterion for successful job maintenance and is recommended here as a standard for successful vocational reintegration. The longer the period of time that elapses after placement, the more opportunity there is for other factors (unrelated to TBI or the intervention under study) to influence job maintenance. While more sustained job maintenance is of interest, requiring longer maintenance than 1 year for positive evaluation of an intervention would seem to invite contamination of the appraisal of the outcome by extraneous and potentially irrelevant factors.

The type of social (person-environment) interventional research recommended in this chapter does not lend itself well to examination using a randomized controlled trial (RCT). While the general TBI-VCC Model (or a more specific elaboration of this model) underlying a proposed intervention should be consistent across participants in a given study, the complexity and variability of people served and their goals require that the model be individualized to each case. To attempt to specify and thereby control the intervention more precisely will very likely reduce the effect of the intervention. An additional consideration is that the complexity of and time required for vocational intervention (typically weeks to months) makes it extremely difficult to develop a believable placebo or sham control condition or to otherwise blind participants and those providing the intervention to the active treatment. It would be possible to compare an active TBI-VCC Model intervention to the current *standard of care* by random assignment. However, this type of design does not adequately control for nonspecific effects of providing the active treatment group with a novel additional intervention. With this lack of control for nonspecific effects, this type of RCT design does not appear to add substantially to demonstrations of the efficacy of specific vocational interventions that are already available in the literature.

Studies of specific vocational interventions reviewed previously demonstrate markedly improved vocational maintenance (70%–80% employed) for those served compared to the historic baseline of 30%–40% employed. Some of these studies included participants with a long baseline of vocational failure after brain injury. A potential selection bias (that is, selecting those cases most amenable to treatment) might occur as a potential source of error in such studies. However, the converse (that such studies rarely include people who have no need for vocational services) is undeniably true. Furthermore, some studies (Malec et al., 2000; Wall et al., 1998; Wehman, West et al., 1993) have reported an effect for this model of treatment even with participants whom other studies have identified as least likely to find employment without specialized intervention (that is, those with severe injuries who are several years postinjury and have a preinjury history of unemployment or who lack self-awareness). Such demonstrations of a positive treatment effect even with very difficult-to-treat participants argue strongly for the efficacy of the model. In this area of applied social interventional research, the possibility should be considered that additional demonstrations of *efficacy* (that is, that the intervention has an effect under controlled conditions) are less of a priority than studies of *effectiveness* (that is, studies assessing the impact on a population). Such studies would involve developing methods to implement, implementing methods based on the TBI-VCC Model in a defined community or region, and evaluating the long-term impact on the population served.

System Change

In reviewing this literature and appraising the current vocational service environment, it appears that *future research should focus not only on developing more specific elaborations of the TBI-VCC Model but also on developing methods to establish this model in the contemporary vocational and rehabilitation system.* The efficacy of TBI-VCC Model interventions that share the common elements outlined previously has been demonstrated in a number of centers and settings. Obstacles to the implementation of such a model have been discussed extensively in the vocational rehabilitation literature generally. *An important remaining unanswered question is how to effectively induce system change and test the effectiveness of this model of vocational rehabilitation after TBI in defined populations.*

UNANSWERED QUESTIONS

A large array of potential research questions could be generated in this area. However, in an attempt to provide a clearer focus for future research, only a few key questions will be proposed. Review of the literature and current gaps in knowledge suggest that future research questions concerned with system change (both in the federal/state vocational rehabilitation system and within specific workplace environments) should take precedence over further study of person change that potentiates vocational reintegration. We know much more about how to rehabilitate people than we do about how to rehabilitate systems and environments. In fact, review of the literature suggests that a general model for vocational rehabilitation of the person has been well established through previous research. Specific injury-related, premorbid, and comorbid characteristics of the person that create additional obstacles to vocational rehabilitation have also been extensively described. What is not well understood is how to introduce interventions with demonstrated efficacy into the current system and how to effectively address obstacles to such implementation.

Interventions have not been identified that will be successful even in the most complicated cases, that is, those with a number of premorbid and comorbid conditions that interfere with program engagement, job placement, and job maintenance. However, success in these complicated cases should not be a criterion for judging an intervention designed to assist people after TBI since interventions that are successful in these types of cases must address social problems (substance abuse, poverty, racial and ethnic discrimination) that have defied resolution for decades.

The fundamental question for vocational rehabilitation after TBI is:

1. What are the minimally necessary but sufficient conditions for successful vocational rehabilitation at the lowest cost with people with various types and levels of disabilities and complicating conditions after TBI?

More specifically, answering question 1 will require studies that answer question 2:

2. What type and extent of services are required for successful vocational rehabilitation for people with specific disability profiles after TBI at the lowest cost?

Necessary but sufficient conditions, as stated in question 1, include features of the system and workplace environments that create obstacles to implementation of efficacious person-oriented rehabilitation models. From this consideration, two additional extremely important questions emerge for future research:

3. How can recognition, acceptance, and implementation of efficacious and cost-effective person-oriented models for vocational rehabilitation after TBI be encouraged in the contemporary vocational and rehabilitation systems?
4. What methods will result in sustained changes in workplaces that support sustained employment in these environments for people with TBI?

RECOMMENDATIONS FOR FUTURE RESEARCH PRIORITIES

As described in the first section of this chapter, most research and other reviews indicate that the vast majority of people with *mild* TBI who were working at the time of injury return to work. For this reason, it is recommended that research in vocational rehabilitation after TBI be restricted to those with moderate to severe injuries or justify inclusion of milder cases based on documented significant cerebral pathology or residual disability. While there is much to be learned about optimizing return to work after moderate to severe TBI, the current state of the art and other factors examined previously in this chapter suggests that the six following areas receive priority.

1. Studies of methods to implement effective person-oriented vocational interventions after TBI within existing federal, state, and private agencies.
2. Studies that evaluate vocational interventions after TBI that are delivered with real-life variability, appropriate individualization, and in actual social and work environments to an identified population (effectiveness studies).
3. Studies of methods to modify the workplace, the more general social environment, and systems for financial and other work-life supports in ways that optimize vocational integration after TBI.
4. Studies applying vocational interventions after TBI in more complicated cases (such as those with additional comorbid and premorbid conditions) and in challenging circumstances (poverty, discrimination, lack of funding), recognizing that such methods address psychological, social, and medical issues that extend well beyond TBI rehabilitation.
5. Studies of vocational interventions aimed at more specifically matching the level and type of service to the severity and profile of disability after TBI.
6. Studies that include or develop reliable, valid, sensitive, and usable measures for prediction and evaluation of the vocational outcome and the workplace environment.

REFERENCES

Alves, W., Macciocchi, S.N., & Barth, J.T. (1993). Postconcussive symptoms after uncomplicated mild head injury. *Journal of Head Trauma Rehabilitation, 8,* 48–59.

Arenth, P.M., Bogner, J.A., Corrigan, J.D., & Schmidt, L. (2001). The utility of the Substance Abuse Subtle Screening Inventory-3 for use with individauls with brain injury. *Brain Injury, 15*(6), 499–510.

Ashley, M.J., Persel, C.S., & Krych, D.K. (1993). Changes in reimbursement climate: Relationship among outcome, cost, and payor type in the postacute rehabilitation environment. *Journal of Head Trauma Rehabilitation, 8*(4), 30–47.

Ben-Yishay, Y., & Prigatano, G.P. (1990). Cognitive remediation. In M. Rosenthal, E.R. Griffith, M.R. Bond, & J.D. Miller (Eds.), *Rehabilitation of the Adult and Child with Traumatic Brain Injury* (pp. 393–400). Philadelphia: F.A. Davis.

Ben-Yishay, Y., Silver, S.M., Piasetsky, E., & Rattok, J. (1987). Relationship between employability and vocational outcome after intensvie holistic cognitive rehabilitation. *Journal of Head Trauma Rehabilitation, 2*(1), 35–48.

Bowe, F. (1993). Statistics, politics, and employment of people with disabilities: Commentary. *Journal of Disability Policy Studies, 4,* 83–91.

Brooks, N., McKinlay, W., Symington, C., Beattie, A., & Campsie, L. (1987). Return to work within the first seven years of severe head injury. *Brain Injury, 1*(1), 5–19.

Bruckner, F.E., & Randle, A.P.H. (1972). Return to work after severe head injuries. *Rheumatological Physical Medicine, 2,* 344–348.

Burke, W.H., Wesolowski, M.D., & Guith, M.L. (1988). Comprehensive head injury rehabilitation: An outcome evaluation. *Brain Injury, 2,* 313–322.

Bush, B.A., Novack, T.A., Malec, J.F., Stringer, A.Y., Millis, S., & Madan, A. (2003). Validation of a model for evaluating outcome after traumatic brain injury. *Archives of Physical Medicine and Rehabilitation, 84*(12), 1803–1807.

Cicerone, K.D., & Kalmar, K. (1995). Persistent postconcussion syndrome: The structure of subjective complaints after mild traumatic brain injury. *Journal of Head Trauma Rehabilitation, 10*(3), 1–17.

Cifu, D.X., Keyser-Marcus, L., Lopez, E., Wehman, P., Kreutzer, J.S., Englander, J., & High, W. (1997). Acute predictors of successful return to work 1 year after traumatic brain injury: A multicenter analysis. *Archives of Physical Medicine and Rehabilitation, 78*(2), 125–131.

Cope, D.N., Cole, J.R., Hall, K.M., & Barkan, H. (1991a). Brain injury: Analysis of outcome in a post-acute rehabilitation system. Part 1: General analysis [see comments]. *Brain Injury, 5*(2), 111–125.

Cope, D.N., Cole, J.R., Hall, K.M., & Barkan, H. (1991b). Brain injury: Analysis of outcome in a post-acute rehabilitation system. Part 2: Subanalyses [see comments]. *Brain Injury, 5*(2), 127–139.

Cope, D.N., & Hall, K. (1982). Head injury rehabilitation: Benefit of early intervention. *Archives of Physical Medicine and Rehabilitation, 63*(9), 433–437.

Corrigan, J.D. (1995). Substance abuse as a mediating factor in outcome from traumatic brain injury. *Archives of Physical Medicine and Rehabilitation, 76*(4), 302–309.

Corrigan, J.D., Bogner, J.A., Mysiw, W.J., Clinchot, D., & Fugate, L. (1997). Systematic bias in outcome studies of persons with traumatic brain injury. *Archives of Physical Medicine and Rehabilitation, 78*(2), 132–137.

Corthell, D.W. (Ed.). (1990). *Traumatic Brain Injury and Vocational Rehabilitation.* Menomonie: University of Wisconsin–Stout.

Corthell, D.W., & Tooman, M. (1985). *Report from the Study Group on Rehabilitation of Traumatic Brain Injury.* Paper presented at the Twelfth Institute on Rehabilitation Issues, Louisville, KY.

Crepeau, F., & Scherzer, P. (1993). Predictors and indicators of work status after traumatic brain injury: A meta-analysis. *Neuropsychological Rehabilitation, 3,* 5–35.

Dacey, R., Dikmen, S., Temkin, N., McLean, A., Armsden, G., & Winn, H.R. (1991). Relative effects of brain and non-brain injuries on neuropsychological and psychosocial outcome. *Journal of Trauma—Injury Infection and Critical Care, 31*(2), 217–222.

Denny-Brown, D. (1945). Disability arising from closed head injury. *Journal of the American Medical Association, 127,* 429–436.

Dijkers, M. (1997). Measuring the long-term outcomes of traumatic brain injury: A review of Community Integration Questionnaire studies. *Journal of Head Trauma Rehabilitation, 12,* 74–91.

Dikmen, S.S., Temkin, N.R., Machamer, J.E., Holubkov, A.L., Fraser, R.T., & Winn, H.R. (1994). Employment following traumatic head injuries. *Archives of Neurology, 51*(2), 177–186.

Drudge, O.W., Williams, J.M., & Kessler, M. (1984). Recovery from severe closed head injuries: Repeat testings with the Halstead-Reitan neuropsychological battery. *Journal of Clinical Psychology, 40,* 259–265.

Eames, P., & Wood, R. (1985). Rehabilitation after severe brain injury: A follow-up study of a behavior modification approach. *Journal of Neurology, Neurosurgery and Psychiatry, 48,* 613–619.

Ellerd, D.A., & Moore, S.C. (1992). Follow-up at twelve and thirty months of persons with traumatic brain injury engaged in supported employment placements. *Journal of Applied Rehabilitation Counseling, 23*(3), 48–50.

Evans, R.W., & Jones, M.L. (1991). Integrating outcomes, value, and quality: An outcome validation system for post-acute rehabilitation programs. *Journal of Insurance Medicine, 3,* 192–196.

Ewing, J.A. (1984). Detecting alcoholism: The CAGE questionnaire. *Journal of the American Medical Association, 252,* 1905–1907.

Ezrachi, O. (1991). Predicting employment in traumatic brain injury following neuropsychological rehabilitation. *Journal of Head Trauma Rehabilitation, 6*(3), 71–84.

Fahy, T.J., Irving, M.G., & Millac, P. (1967). Severe head injuries: A six year follow-up. *Lancet, 2,* 475–479.

Fordyce, D.J., & Roueche, J.R. (1986). Changes in perspectives of disability among patients, staff, and relatives during rehabilitation of brain injury. *Rehabilitation Psychology, 31*(4), 217–229.

Fraser, R., Dikmen, S., McLean, A., Miller, B., & Temkin, N. (1988). Employability of head injury survivors: First year post-injury. *Rehabilitation Counseling Bulletin, 31,* 276–288.

Fryer, L. (1987). Cognitive rehabilitation and community readaptation: Outcomes of two program modules. *Journal of Head Trauma Rehabilitation, 2*(3), 51–63.

Fuller, M.G., Fishman, E., Taylor, C.A., & Wood, R.B. (1994). Screening patients with traumatic brain injuries for substance abuse. *Journal of Neuropsychiatry and Clinical Neurosciences, 6*(2), 143–146.

Gerber, D.J., & Schraa, J.C. (1995). Mild traumatic brain injury: Searching for the syndrome. *Journal of Head Trauma Rehabilitation, 10*(4), 28–40.

Gilchrist, E., & Wilkinson, M. (1979). Some factors determining prognosis in young people with severe head injuries. *Archives of Neurology, 36,* 355–359.

Gill, C.J., Kewman, D.G., & Brannon, R.W. (2003). Transforming psychological practice and society: Policies that reflect the new paradigm. *American Psychologist*, *58*(4),
305–312.

Gjone, R., Kristiansen, K., & Sponheim, N. (1972). Rehabilitation in severe head injuries. *Scandinavian Journal of Rehabilitation Medicine*, *4*, 2–4.

Godfrey, H.P., Bishara, S.N., Partridge, F.M., & Knight, R.G. (1993). Neuropsychological impairment and return to work following severe closed head injury: Implications
for clinical management. *New Zealand Medical Journal*, *106*(960), 301–303.

Gollaher, K., High, W., Sherer, M., Bergloff, P., Boake, C., Young, M.E., & Ivanhoe, C.
(1998). Prediction of employment outcome one to three years following traumatic brain
injury (TBI). *Brain Injury*, *12*(4), 255–263.

Hall, K.M., Bushnik, T., Lakisic-Kazazi, B., Wright, J., & Cantagallo, A. (2001). Assessing traumatic brain injury outcome measure for long-term follow-up of community-based individuals. *Archives of Physical Medicine and Rehabilitation*, *82*(3),
367–374.

Hall, K.M., Mann, N., High, W.M., Wright, J., Kreutzer, J.S., & Wood, D. (1996). Functional measures after traumatic brain injury: Ceiling effects of FIM, FIM+FAM, DRS,
and CIQ. *Journal of Head Trauma Rehabilitation*, *11*(5), 27–39.

Heiskanen, O., & Sipponen, P. (1970). Prognosis of severe brain injury. *Acta Neurologica
Scandinavica*, *46*, 343–348.

Hpay, H. (1971). Psychosocial effects of severe head injury. *International Symposium on
Head Injuries: 1970 Edinburgh and Madrid* (pp. 110–119). New York: Churchill
Livingstone.

Johnson, R. (1987). Return to work after severe head injury. *International Disability Studies*, *9*, 49–54.

Johnston, M.V. (1991). Outcomes of community re-entry programmes for brain injury
survivors. Part 2: Further investigations. *Brain Injury*, *5*(2), 155–168.

Karzmark, P., Hall, K., & Englander, J. (1995). Late-onset post-concussion symptoms after
mild brain injury: The role of premorbid, injury-related, environmental, and personality factors. *Brain Injury*, *9*(1), 21–26.

Kelly, M.P., Johnson, C.T., Knoller, N., Drubach, D.A., & Winslow, M.M. (1997). Substance abuse, traumatic brain injury, and neuropsychological outcome. *Brain Injury*,
11(6), 391–402.

Keyser-Marcus, L.A., Bricout, J.C., Wehman, P., Campbell, L.R., Cifu, D.X., Englander,
J., High, W., & Zafonte, R.D. (2002). Acute predictors of return to employment after
traumatic brain injury: A longitudinal follow-up. *Archives of Physical Medicine and
Rehabilitation*, *85*(5), 635–641.

Kolakowsky-Hayner, S.A., Miner, K.D., & Kreutzer, J.S. (2001). Long-term life quality
and family needs after traumatic brain injury. *Journal of Head Trauma Rehabilitation*, *16*(4), 374–385.

Kraft, J.F., Schwab, K.A., Salazar, A.M., & Brown, H.R. (1993). Occupational and educational achievements of head injured Vietnam veterans at 15-year follow-up. *Archives
of Physical Medicine and Rehabilitation*, *74*(6), 596–601.

Kreutzer, J.S., Marwitz, J.H., Walker, W., Sander, A., Sherer, M., Bogner, J., Fraser, R.,
& Bushnik, T. (2003). Moderating factors in return to work and job stability after traumatic brain injury. *Journal of Head Trauma Rehabilitation*, *18*(2), 128–138.

Kreutzer, J.S., Wehman, P., Morton, M.V., & Stonnington, H.H. (1991). Supported employment and compensatory strategies for enhancing vocational outcome folowing
traumatic brain injury. *International Disability Studies*, *13*, 162–171.

Kreutzer, J.S., Witol, A.D., & Marwitz, J.H. (1996). Alcohol and drug use among young persons with traumatic brain injury. *Journal of Learning Disabilities, 29*(6), 643–651.

Lam, C.S., McMahon, B.T., Priddy, D.A., & Gehred-Schultz, A. (1988). Deficit awareness and treatment performance among traumatic head injury adults. *Brain Injury, 2*(3), 235–242.

Levin, H.S. (1995). Prediction of recovery from traumatic brain injury. *Journal of Neurotrauma, 12*(5), 913–922.

Lewin, W.S. (1959). The management of prolonged unconsciousness after head injury. *Proceedings of the Royal Society of Medicine, 52,* 880–884.

Lewin, W.S. (1967). Severe head injuries. *Proceedings of the Royal Society of Medicine, 60,* 1208–1212.

Lewin, W.S (1976). Changing attitudes to the management of severe head injuries. *British Medical Journal, 2,* 1234–1239.

London, P.S. (1967). Some observations on the course of events after severe injury to the head. *Annals of the Royal College of Surgeons of England, 41,* 460–479.

Lyons, J.L., & Morse, A.R. (1988). A therapeutic work program for head-injured rehabilitation: An outcome evaluation. *American Journal of Occupational Therapy, 42,* 364–370.

MacIver, I., Lassman, L., Thompson, C., & McLeod, I. (1958). Treatment of severe head injuries. *Lancet, 2,* 544–550.

Mackay, L.E., Bernstein, B.A., Chapman, P.E., Morgan, A.S., & Milazzo, L.S. (1992). Early intervention in severe head injury: Long-term benefits of a formalized program. *Archives of Physical Medicine and Rehabilitation, 73*(7), 635–641.

MacMillan, P.J., Hart, R.P., Martelli, M.F., & Zasler, N.D. (2002). Pre-injury status and adaptation following traumatic brain injury. *Brain Injury, 16*(1), 41–49.

Malec, J.F. (2001). Impact of comprehensive day treatment on societal participation for persons with acquired brain injury. *Archives of Physical Medicine and Rehabilitation, 82,* 885–894.

Malec, J.F., & Basford, J.S. (1996). Postacute brain injury rehabilitation. *Archives of Physical Medicine and Rehabilitation, 77*(2), 198–207.

Malec, J.F., Buffington, A.L.H., Moessner, A. M., & Degiorgio, L. (2000). A medical/vocational case coordination system for persons with brain injury: An evaluation of employment outcomes. *Archives of Physical Medicine and Rehabilitation, 81,* 1007–1015.

Malec, J.F., & Degiorgio, L. (2002). Characteristics of successful and unsuccessful completers of three postacute brain injury rehabilitation pathways. *Archives of Physical Medicine and Rehabilitation, 83*(12), 1759–1764.

Malec, J.F., Kragness, M., Evans, R.W., Finlay, K.L., Kent, A., & Lezak, M. (2003). Further psychometric evaluation and revision of the Mayo-Portland Adaptability Inventory in a national sample. *Journal of Head Trauma Rehabilitation, 18*(6), 479–492.

Malec, J.F., & Lezak, M.D. (2003). *Manual for the Mayo-Portland Adaptability Inventory.* Available at www.tbimis.org/combi/mpai

Malec, J.F., & Moessner, A.M. (2000). Self-awareness, distress, and postacute rehabilitation outcome. *Rehabilitation Psychology, 45*(3), 227–241.

Malec, J.F., Schafer, D., & Jacket, M. (1992). Comprehensive-integrated postacute outpatient brain injury rehabilitation. *NeuroRehabilitation, 2*(3), 1–11.

Malec, J.F., Smigielski, J.S., DePompolo, R.W., & Thompson, J.M. (1993). Outcome evaluation and prediction in a comprehensive-integrated post-acute outpatient brain injury rehabilitation programme. *Brain Injury, 7*(1), 15–29.

Matheson, J.M. (1982). The vocational outcome of rehabilitation in fifty consecutive patients with severe head injuries. In J.F. Garrett (Ed.), *Australian Approaches to Rehabilitation in Neurotrauma and Spinal Cord Injury* (pp. 32–35). New York: World Rehabilitation Fund.

McKinlay, W., Brooks, D.N., & Bond, M.R. (1983). Postconcussional symptoms, financial compensation and outcome of severe blunt head injury. *Journal of Neurology, Neurosurgery and Psychiatry, 46*, 1084–1091.

McLean, A., Jr., Dikmen, S., Temkin, N., Wyler, A.R., & Gale, J.L. (1984). Psychosocial functioning at 1 month after head injury. *Neurosurgery, 14*, 393–399.

McMordie, W.R., Barker, S.L., & Paolo, T.M. (1990). Return to work (RTW) after head injury. *Brain Injury, 4*(1), 57–69.

Merbitz, C., Morris, J., & Grip, J. (1989). Ordinal scales and foundations of misinference. *Archives of Physical Medicine and Rehabilitation, 70*, 308–312.

Michaels, C.A., & Risucci, D.A. (1993). Employer and counselor perceptions of workplace accommodations for persons with traumatic brain injury. *Journal of Applied Rehabilitation Counseling, 24*(1), 38–45.

Miller, H., & Stern, G. (1965). The long-term prognosis of severe head injuries. *Lancet, 1*, 225–229.

Mills, V.M., Nesbeda, T., Katz, D.I., & Alexander, M.P. (1992). Outcomes for traumatically brain-injured patients following post-acute rehabilitation programmes. *Brain Injury, 6*(3), 219–228.

Novack, T.A., Bush, B.A., Meythaler, J.M., & Canupp, K. (2001). Outcome following traumatic brain injury: Contributions from premorbid, injury severity, and recovery variables. *Archives of Physical Medicine and Rehabilitation, 82*, 300–305.

Oddy, M., Coughlan, T., Terman, A., & Jenkins, D. (1985). Social adjustment after closed head injury: A further follow-up seven years after injury. *Journal of Neurology, Neurosurgery and Psychiatry, 48*, 564–568.

Oddy, M., & Humphrey, M. (1980). Social recovery during the year following severe head injury. *Journal of Neurology, Neurosurgery and Psychiatry, 43*, 798–802.

Oddy, M., Humphrey, M., & Uttley, D. (1978). Subjective impairment and social recovery after closed head injury. *Journal of Neurology, Neurosurgery and Psychiatry, 41*, 611–616.

O'Shaughnessy, E.J., Fowler, R.S., & Reid, V. (1984). Sequelae of mild closed head injuries. *Journal of Family Practice, 18*, 391–394.

Prigatano, G.P., Fordyce, D.J., Zeiner, H.K., Roueche, J.R., Pepping, M., & Wood, B.C. (1984). Neuropsychological rehabilitation after closed head injury in young adults. *Journal of Neurology, Neurosurgery and Psychiatry, 47*(5), 505–513.

Prigatano, G.P., Fordyce, D.J., Zeiner, H.K., Roueche, J.R., Pepping, M., & Wood, B.C. (1986). *Neuropsychological Rehabilitation After Brain Injury*. Baltimore: Johns Hopkins University Press.

Prigatano, G.P., Klonoff, P., O'Brien, K.P., Altman, I.M., Amin, K., Chiapello, D., Shepherd, J., Cunningham, M., & Mora, M. (1994). Productivity after neuropsychological oriented milieu rehabilitation. *Journal of Head Trauma Rehabilitation, 9*(1), 91–102.

Rao, N., & Kilgore, K.M. (1992). Predicting return to work in traumatic brain injury using assessment scales. *Archives of Physical Medicine and Rehabilitation, 73*(10), 911–916.

Reyes, R.L., Bhattacharyya, A.K., & Heller, D. (1981). Traumatic head injury: Restlessness and agitation as prognosticators of physical and psychologic improvement in patients. *Archives of Physical Medicine and Rehabilitation, 62*, 20–23.

Richardson, J.C. (1971). The late management of industrial head injuries. *International Symposium on Head Injuries: 1970 Edinburgh and Madrid* (pp. 127–131). New York: Churchill Livingstone.

Rimel, R.W., Giordani, B., Barth, J.T., Boll, T.J., & Jane, J.A. (1981). Disability caused by minor head injury. *Neurosurgery, 9,* 221–228.

Rimel, R.W., Giordani, B., Barth, J.T., & Jane, J.A. (1982). Moderate head injury: Completing the clinical spectrum of brain trauma. *Neurosurgery, 11,* 344–351.

Rowbotham, G., MacIver, I., Dickson, J., & Bousfield, M. (1954). Analysis of 1400 cases of acute injury to the head. *British Medical Journal, 1,* 726–730.

Ruff, R.M., Marshall, L.F., Crouch, J., Klauber, M.R., Levin, H.S., Barth, J., Kreutzer, J., Blunt, B.A., Foulkes, M.A., Eisenberg, H.M., et al. (1993). Predictors of outcome following severe head trauma: Follow-up data from the Traumatic Coma Data Bank. *Brain Injury, 7*(2), 101–111.

Rusk, H.A., Block, J.M., & Lowman, E.W. (1969). Rehabilitation following traumatic brain damage. *Medical Clinics of North America, 53,* 677–684.

Rusk, H.A., Lowman, E., & Block, J. (1966). Rehabilitation of the patient with head injuries. *Clinical Neurosurgery, 12,* 312–323.

Sahgal, V., & Heinemann, A. (1989). Recovery of function during inpatient rehabilitation for moderate traumatic brain injury. *Scandinavian Journal of Rehabilitation Medicine, 21,* 71–79.

Sherer, M., Bergloff, P., Boake, C., High, W.J., & Levin, E. (1998). The Awareness Questionnaire: Factor structure and internal consistency. *Brain Injury, 12*(1), 63–68.

Sherer, M., Bergloff, P., Levin, E., High, W.M., Oden, K.E., & Nick, T.G. (1998). Impaired awareness and employment outcome after traumatic brain injury. *Journal of Head Trauma Rehabilitation, 13*(5), 52–61.

Sherer, M., Boake, C., Clement, V., et al. (1996). Awareness of deficits after traumatic brain injury: Comparison of patient, family, and clinician ratings. *Journal of the International Neuropsychological Society, 2,* 17.

Sherer, M., Boake, C., Silver, B.V., et al. (1995). Assessing awareness of deficits following acquired brain injury: The Awareness Questionnaire. *Journal of the International Neuropsychological Society, 1,* 163.

Siegel, S., & Gaylord-Ross, R. (1991). Factors associated with employment success among youths with learning disabilities. *Journal of Learning Disabilities, 24,* 40–47.

Stambrook, M., Moore, A.D., Peters, L.C., Deviaene, C., & Hawryluk, G.A. (1990). Effects of mild, moderate and severe closed head injury on long-term vocational status. *Brain Injury, 4*(2), 183–190.

Steadman, J.H., & Graham, J.G. (1970). Head injuries: An analysis and follow-up study. *Proceedings of the Royal Society of Medicine, 63,* 23–28.

Stuss, D.T., Ely, P., Hugenholtz, H., Richard, M.T., LaRochelle, S., & Poirier, C.A. (1985). Subtle neuropsychological deficits in patients with good recovery after closed head injury. *Neurosurgery, 17,* 41–46.

Thomas, D.F., Menz, F.E., & McAlees, D.C. (Eds.). (1993). *Community-based Employment following Traumatic Brain Injury.* Menomonie: University of Wisconsin–Stout.

Thomsen, I.V. (1974). The patient with severe head injury and his family. *Scandinavian Journal of Rehabilitation Medicine, 6,* 180–183.

Thomsen, I.V. (1984). Late outcome of very severe blunt head trauma: A 10–15 year second follow-up. *Journal of Neurology, Neurosurgery and Psychiatry, 47,* 260–268.

Tobis, J.S., Puri, K.B., & Sheridan, J. (1982). Rehabilitation of the severely brain-injured patient. *Scandinavian Journal of Rehabilitation Medicine, 14,* 83–88.

VanZomeren, A.H., & Van den Berg, W. (1985). Residual complaints of patients two years after severe head injury. *Journal of Neurology, Neurosurgery and Psychiatry*, *48*, 21–28.

A vision for the future: TBI town meetings 1994. (1994). St. Paul: State of Minnesota Department of Human Services.

Wall, J.R., Rosenthal, M., & Niemczura, J.G. (1998). Community-based training after acquired brain injury: Preliminary findings. *Brain Injury*, *12*(3), 215–224.

Ware, J.E.J. (2003). Conceptualization and measurement of health-related quality of life: Comments on an evolving field. *Archives of Physical Medicine and Rehabilitation*, *84*(Suppl 2), S43–S51.

Weddel, R., Oddy, M., & Jenkins, D. (1980). Social adjustment after rehabilitation: A two year follow-up of patients with severe head injury. *Psychological Medicine*, *10*, 257–263.

Wehman, P., Kregel, J., Sherron, P., Nguyen, S., Kreutzer, J., Fry, R., & Zasler, N. (1993). Critical factors associated with the successful supported employment placement of patients with severe traumatic brain injury. *Brain Injury*, *7*(1), 31–44.

Wehman, P., Kreutzer, J.S., West, M.D., Sherron, P.D., Zasler, N.D., Groah, C.H., Stonnington, H.H., Burns, C.T., & Sale, P.R. (1990). Return to work for persons with traumatic brain injury: A supported employment approach. *Archives of Physical Medicine and Rehabilitation*, *71*(12), 1047–1052.

Wehman, P., Sherron, P., Kregel, J., Kreutzer, J., Tran, S., & Cifu, D.X. (1993). Return to work for persons following severe traumatic brain injury. *Archives of Physical Medicine and Rehabilitation*, *72*, 355–363.

Wehman, P., West, M., Fry, R., Sherron, P., Groah, C., & Kreutzer, J. (1989). Effect of supported employment on the vocational outcomes of persons with traumatic brain injury. *Journal of Applied Behavior Analysis*, *22*, 395–405.

Wehman, P., West, M., Sherron, P., Roah, C., & Kreutzer, J. (1993). Return to work: Supported employment strategies, costs, and outcome data. In D.F. Thomas, F.E. Menz, & D.C. McAlees (Eds.), *Community-Based Employment Following Traumatic Brain Injury*. Menomonie: University of Wisconsin-Stout.

West, M.D. (1995). Aspects of the workplace and return to work for persons with brain injury in supported employment. *Brain Injury*, *9*(3), 310–313.

Williams, D.H., Levin, H.S., & Eisenberg, H.M. (1990). Mild head injury classification. *Neurosurgery*, *27*(3), 422–428.

Wrightson, P., & Gronwall, D. (1981). Time off work and symptoms after minor head injury. *Injury*, *12*(6), 445–454.

Yasuda, S., Wehman, P., Targett, P., Cifu, D., & West, M. (2001). Return to work for persons with traumatic brain injury. *American Journal of Physical Medicine and Rehabilitation*, *80*(11), 852–864.

Zafonte, R.D., Hammond, F.M., Mann, N.R., Wood, D.L., Black, K.L., & Millis, S.R. (1996). Relationship between Glasgow Coma Scale and functional outcome. *American Journal of Physical Medicine and Rehabilitation*, *75*(5), 364–369.

IV

REHABILITATION WITH SPECIFIC POPULATIONS

11

Children with Cognitive, Behavioral, Communication, and Academic Disabilities

MARK YLVISAKER

Relatively little high-quality evidence is available that addresses interventions for children and adolescents with cognitive, academic, social, and/or behavioral disorders associated with traumatic brain injury (TBI). However, important intervention themes can be derived from the available research with this population combined with research with (nominally) different disability populations as well as nondisability populations. This synthesis of research findings across populations is the primary goal of this chapter. Following a summary of existing pediatric TBI evidence reviews, a description of issues related to TBI as a disability category, and a discussion of the concept of evidence in clinical decision making, the chapter reviews relevant evidence related to assessment and to cognitive, educational, social skills, and behavioral interventions, as well as family and teacher training and support. The chapter ends with a list of areas for future research.

EXISTING PEDIATRIC TRAUMATIC BRAIN INJURY EVIDENCE REVIEWS

A comprehensive review of evidence related to acute medical management of children with TBI was recently published simultaneously in three journals:

Pediatric Critical Care Medicine, Critical Care Medicine, and the *Journal of Trauma* (Carney et al., 2003). The review yielded a number of guidelines in domains of practice that fall outside the purview of this chapter.

Earlier, Carney, du Coudray and colleagues (1999), under a contract with the Agency for Health Care Policy and Research, reviewed evidence related to five questions in pediatric TBI rehabilitation (paraphrased):

1. Does early, intensive medical rehabilitation improve outcomes?
2. How many children with TBI receive special education designed for children with TBI?
3. Do those who receive TBI-specific special education have better outcomes?
4. Does early identification of the developmental stage at injury and at assessment, and the extent of arrest of normal development, improve prediction of subsequent needs and problems?
5. Does support for families enhance their ability to cope and reduce their burden?

The authors' conclusion was that "in general, studies have not been conducted with designs capable of providing evidence on the effectiveness of interventions for children and adolescents with TBI" (p. vi). This summary statement remains generally valid, with some exceptions discussed below, assuming that the domain of applicable studies is restricted to TBI. However, rational (i.e., evidence-based) decision making by clinicians and teachers can and should take into account other types of evidence, including results of studies of the effectiveness of intervention for children from related populations. Indeed, there is a massive amount of evidence relevant to clinical and educational decision making for children with TBI who need intervention or support because of cognitive, educational, behavioral, and/or social disability associated with their injury. Evidence from related populations should also guide hypothesis formulation for future TBI-related research.

TRAUMATIC BRAIN INJURY AS AN EDUCATIONAL DISABILITY CATEGORY

In 1990, TBI was added to federal special education law as an educational disability under the Individuals with Disabilities Education Act. Questions 2 and 3 of the 1999 Oregon Health Science University (OHSU) evidence review raise interesting concerns about the disability label: Is there such a thing as TBI-specific special education? If not, is it wise to organize interventions around—and restrict the domain of evidence to—this diagnostic label? A primary thesis of this chapter is that there is no such thing as TBI-specific special education because there is both extraordinary diversity within the population and substantial overlap in disability and need with other clinical/special education populations. Furthermore, many intervention themes and practices apply to all learners, with or without identified disabilities.

Table 11.1 lists many factors that may influence outcome following pediatric TBI. The extraordinary diversity in the population yields the undeniable conclusion that there can be no generally applicable "TBI assessment battery" or "TBI curriculum." Furthermore, the question "Is a given intervention effective for children with TBI?" is far too general to be meaningful. In addition, the ability and impairment profiles and needs of many children with TBI sufficiently resemble those of children with other disability labels that assessment and intervention strategies validated for those often more thoroughly studied populations are in many cases applicable to children with TBI. Thus evidence reviews relevant to clinical decision making must at the same time consider subgroups of children with TBI and also research conducted with nominally different disability populations that may be better studied.

Historically, the value of TBI as a disability category has been (1) that children who otherwise may not have qualified for services and supports under special education regulations can now receive them and (2) that professionals have begun to recognize central tendencies in the population that may offer general

Table 11.1. Factors That May Influence Outcome and Intervention

Preinjury Factors
- Age at injury
- Preinjury levels of knowledge and skills
- Possible preexisting neurologic/developmental disorders
- Social skills and social support network
- Adjustment/coping style
- Family adjustment

Injury Factors
- Nature and severity of the injury
- Site of focal brain damage
- Other injuries
- Early medical management

Postinjury Factors
- Time postinjury
- Physiologic recovery
- Psychologic/ behavioral adjustment
- Emotional/behavioral supports and management
- Family adjustment
- Other support systems, including school and friends
- Quality of ongoing rehabilitation and instruction
- Local resources
- Other factors

guidance for assessment and intervention planning. These central tendencies are largely a consequence of two features of TBI:

1. The vulnerability of prefrontal and limbic structures yields characteristic impairments in executive/self-regulatory functions, social perception, response to feedback, and learning and memory, all critical to success in school.
2. The fact that the disability is acquired after a period of normal development accounts for unusual profiles of ability and need, changing profiles over time, acute emotional and psychosocial needs, and a need to reconstruct a sense of self at a point in development when such construction is particularly difficult. This feature applies to all types of acquired brain injury, not just those injuries due to trauma.

Table 11.2 lists pediatric populations with special vulnerability in the domain of executive functions. The purpose of this list is to motivate a broad cross-population search for assessment and intervention strategies and for relevant research on their effectiveness. References to literature that supports the inclusion of the diagnoses in Table 11.2 can be found in Ylvisaker and Feeney (2002) and Marlowe (2002).

EVIDENCE-BASED CLINICAL AND EDUCATIONAL PRACTICE

Discussions of evidence-based practice are often restricted to the scientific processes involved in generating empirical support for general population evidence

Table 11.2. Pediatric Populations Vulnerable to Executive Function Impairment

Traumatic brain injury/frank frontal lobe injury
Attention deficit hyperactivity disorder
Autism (including Asperger's syndrome)
Fetal alcohol syndrome
Heavy cocaine exposure
Some types of epilepsy
Some types of meningitis
Early-treated phenylketonuria
Heavy lead burden
Hydrocephalus/spina bifida
Certain malignancies
Obsessive-compulsive disorder
Children from chaotic environments
Children with developmental disabilities/mental retardation
Children with learned helplessness of any origin

statements of the form "Treatment T is effective (or efficacious) for specific clinical population P" (Sackett et al., 2000). It is then assumed that responsible individual clinical decision making is guided by well-supported general population evidence statements. Sample-to-population inferences (the upward arrow in Fig. 11.1) are governed by demanding internal and external validity standards, yielding the conclusion that very few interventions for children or adults with TBI are evidence based, that is, supported by reasonably large numbers of Class I clinical trials with individuals with TBI (Carney, Chestnut et al., 1999, Carney, du Coudray et al., 1999).

Less attention has been given to the logic of clinical decision making (the lower right angle of the evidence triangle in Fig. 11.1). Ylvisaker and colleagues (2002) explored this logic in relation to evidence-based practice. Evidence that supports a *decision to act* (as opposed to an abstract proposition about a population) is a *reason* for that decision, and a reason is that which orders among alternative courses of action. From this perspective, evidence-based clinical and educational decision making is based on the question "Are there good and, on balance, persuasive *reasons* for the intervention decision and no persuasive reasons to refrain from the decision or select an alternative?"

Population evidence statements may be one reason for a clinical decision, but not always the best. The inference from a population evidence statement to an

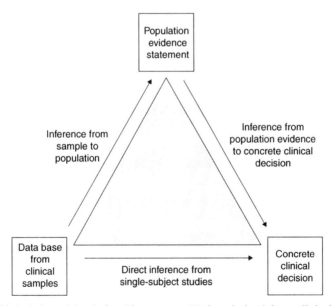

Figure 11.1. Inferential relationships among (1) data derived from clinical samples, (2) abstract population evidence statements, and (3) concrete decisions to treat specific individuals under specific circumstances. (Reproduced with permission from Ylvisaker et al., 2002.)

individual clinical decision is valid only if (1) the individual resembles those in the clinical trials who benefitted from the intervention and does not resemble those who did not benefit, refused entry, or were excluded from the trials; (2) the individual's life circumstances resemble those that obtained in the trials; (3) there are no interfering coexisting impairments; (4) the agent of intervention is similar in skill to those in the trials; (5) there are no preferable alternatives; and (6) requisite resources (including time) are available.

Stated positively, reasons (evidence) for a concrete clinical decision include the following, which can be combined in many ways:

- Population evidence statements, same population
- Population evidence statements, related population (on relevant variables)
- Results of trial intervention or dynamic, hypothesis-testing assessment with the individual
- Results of published single-subject experiments (similar individuals/circumstances)
- Relevant theory
- Negotiation/collaborative decision making with the individual and significant others
- Consistency with known constraints (e.g., time, money, patient and family compliance, environmental supports)
- No better alternative

Single-subject (SS) experiments, common in behaviorally oriented interventions, are generally considered weak (Class III) evidence for population evidence statements for the good reason that it is impossible to infer from one (or a small number) to all. Even accumulations of successful SS experiments or positive meta-analyses fail to support population evidence statements because of the subject selection bias inherent in SS research. For example, rarely do SS researchers report the results of experiments that had to be aborted for any number of possible reasons or that simply failed. However, a better way to conceptualize SS research in relation to clinical decision making is in terms of particular-to-particular inferences (the left-to-right arrow at the base of the evidence triangle in Figure 11.1): "If this individual in the SS report benefitted in experimentally verified ways from this intervention, then my client/student, who resembles this individual in all relevant respects, should also benefit, whatever the population evidence may suggest."

An analogy from a hard science (computer engineering) follows:

1. Crystals of silicon generally have n impurities/cm^3 (population mean).
2. There is normal variance around the mean.

3. The first crystal in a new consistent production batch has $n - 5$ impurities/cm^3.
4. Therefore, a second crystal from the same production batch will likely have $n - 5$ impurities (*not* n = the population mean).

In this case, it is irrational to use the validated population statement in making predictions about the individual crystal because better evidence is at hand. By analogy, if a clinician faces a decision for an individual who resembles the individual in a successful SS experiment, it may be more rational to choose the SS intervention than one guided by a general population evidence statement. In other words, what is normally considered Class III evidence may trump what is normally considered Class I evidence in individual cases.

This clinical reasoning is especially useful in the case of TBI because the individuals most in need of long-term clinical and special education services are often excluded from or outliers within clinical trials [e.g., individuals with serious behavioral challenges or psychiatric diagnoses, coexisting or preexisting impairments such as learning disabilities or attention deficit hyperactivity disorder (ADHD; Max et al., 2004), unusual life circumstances, and the like]. Thus, population evidence statements, no matter how well founded, may be *weak* evidence (reasons) for a clinical decision relative to other types of evidence (reasons). Traditional evidence reviews are, therefore, only one among many contributors to rational (i.e., evidence-based) clinical decision making. Indeed, the strongest evidence (reason) for a clinical decision is experimental validation *with that individual* (i.e., trial therapy, diagnostic teaching, or dynamic, hypothesis-testing assessment).

EVIDENCE FROM RELATED POPULATIONS

The practice of supporting a clinical decision for a member of one clinical population by citing evidence drawn from another population is often dismissed as an unacceptable *cross-population* inference. Indeed, invalid examples are easy to produce: "Tx T is effective for bacterial pneumonia; therefore, it should be effective for viral pneumonia" is clearly invalid and dangerous. However, apparent cross-population inferences are not necessarily invalid if:

1. Nominally different populations are functionally and pathologically identical. For example, adolescents with ADHD and TBI may properly be grouped in the same clinical population if the relevant diagnostic features are disinhibited and aggressive behavior associated with ventral frontal pathology.
2. The studied population is similar to the unstudied population in relation to the need for and the workings of the intervention. For example, TBI

and learning disability may be considered similar in relevant ways if the issue is teaching cognitive/academic strategies to nonstrategic students with learning problems but normal intelligence.

3. The intervention theme has proven to be valid across many studied populations and appears to be universally applicable. For example, all populations studied have demonstrated a need for cognitive/academic strategies to be taught intensively, long term, and in the context of relevant content.

With this discussion as background, the following assessment and intervention themes draw heavily on research with related populations as well as limited research with children with TBI. Certainly caution is in order when drawing on evidence from related populations. However, the argument in this section demonstrates that such evidence can be validly applied and therefore should be carefully considered in all evidence reviews.

THEME: CONTEXT SENSITIVITY OF ASSESSMENT

Determination of the need for special education services and supports traditionally depends heavily on standardized office-bound testing. In addition, discharge reports from hospitals tend to rely heavily on test results. Critical to the usefulness of these practices is the following question: Is it possible to validly identify children's needs, qualify them for special education services, and generate an effective intervention and support plan using standardized office-bound assessments? Research with children and adults with frontal lobe injury, as well as children with executive system impairment associated with other etiologies, strongly suggests a negative answer to this question (Gioia & Isquith, 2004).

Summaries of published studies of children with selective prefrontal injury indicate that ecological *invalidity* of standardized testing is sufficiently common to be a diagnostic indicator. "The dissociation between severe dysfunction in everyday activities and good performance on standardized cognitive tests provides both an important diagnostic indicator as well as a major challenge in the evaluation of persons with prefrontal dysfunction" (Anderson et al., 2000, p. 289). In the case of adults with TBI, specialists in neuropsychological rehabilitation have increasingly shown that office-bound testing is an inappropriate basis for intervention planning and outcome assessment because "there is no clear relationship between test performance and real-life skills" (Wilson, 2003, p. 26).

Reports of the invalidity of psychological and neuropsychological testing for diagnosis and intervention planning have long been available in related research literatures. For example, Gordon and Barkley (1998) cite the following rates of false-negative findings for individuals with ADHD (i.e., the percentage of indi-

viduals with properly diagnosed ADHD who scored within normal limits on the
purportedly diagnostic test):

- Wisconsin Card Sorting Test: 61%–89%
- Stroop Color-Word Naming: 53%
- Hand Movements Test: 63%
- Rey-Osterreith Complex Figure: 96%
- Trail Making A and B: 80%–82%
- Continuous Performance Test: 15%–52%
- Wechler Intelligence Scale for Children (WISC)-III: Freedom from
  Distractibility Factor: 48%–77%

These findings are especially relevant to TBI in that the hypothesized explanation for the high rate of false negatives is that individuals with executive function
impairment often perform adequately on highly structured tasks despite great difficulty regulating cognitive and social behavior in the unstructured real world.

Viewed positively, measures designed to obtain real-world information in an
objective and reliable manner have demonstrated strength in the research literature.
The recently developed *Behavioral Rating Inventory of Executive Functions* (BRIEF;
Gioia et al., 2000) has parent and teacher forms and was explicitly designed to overcome the ecological validity problems of office-bound testing. Domains addressed
by the inventory's eight scales cluster within two general indices: the Behavioral
Regulation Index (including inhibit, shift, and emotional control scales) and the
Metacognition Index (including initiate, plan/organize, organization of materials,
monitor, and working memory scales). A preschool version of this executive function (EF) rating inventory recently became available.

The BRIEF has already made a substantial contribution to the functional assessment of children with TBI. For example, Mangeot and colleagues (2002) found
substantial and generalized EF deficits 5 years after severe TBI in children and
adolescents. In addition, they found that BRIEF scores predicted the child's adaptive functioning and behavioral adjustment. The BRIEF scores were also correlated with parent psychological distress, perceived family burden, and general
family functioning. In contrast, neuropsychological test results were not strongly
related to real-world outcomes, underscoring concerns about their ecological validity. Similarly, Mahone and colleagues (2002) found that BRIEF scores correlated strongly with real-world measures and poorly with neuropsychological test
scores in their study of children with ADHD and Tourette syndrome.

For establishing an effective intervention and support program for children with
complex problems, dynamic hypothesis-testing assessment has long been supported in the special education and behavioral psychology literatures. With its
origins in the work of Vygotsky (1978) and elaboration by Feuerstein (1979) and
Lidz (1987), dynamic assessment has become a common practice in educational

psychology and special education with the goal of identifying the student's learning potential and the most effective educational supports and instructional practices. Understood as a disciplined experimental approach to creating an intervention and support plan, dynamic assessment is a close cousin to the active hypothesis-testing phase of functional behavior assessment (O'Neill et al., 1990), which has been shown to be useful in everyday school settings (Kern et al., 1994). Swanson and Lassier (2001) presented a meta-analysis of published studies of dynamic assessment in educational contexts.

Ylvisaker and Gioia (1998) and Ylvisaker and Feeney (1998) applied the practices of functional, dynamic hypothesis-testing assessment to TBI rehabilitation for children and adults. A cross-population inference from several non-TBI disability populations to TBI appears to be justified since the characteristic of children that renders dynamic hypothesis-testing assessment useful is the complexity of their ability profiles and of the multiple relations with context variables. In summary, although the validity of alternative assessment approaches and procedures with children with TBI is not well studied, there is considerable evidence from studies of (1) children with frank frontal lobe injury, (2) adults with TBI, and (3) children with related disorders (e.g., ADHD, behavior disorders) to support the conclusion that standardized office-bound testing must be supplemented by context-sensitive assessment procedures to make valid decisions about disability and needs, as well as by dynamic hypothesis-testing procedures to identify effective intervention and support strategies.

THEME: CONTEXT SENSITIVITY OF INTERVENTION

Cognitive Intervention: Negative Evidence

The first two decades of intensive program development in cognitive rehabilitation for individuals with TBI were dominated by an approach with the following features:

- Massed discrete-trial cognitive exercises
- Targeting separate components of cognition
- Using tasks independent of personally relevant application tasks/ contexts (content, settings, people)
- The goal of direct restoration of underlying cognitive processes

Is there evidence to support or reject this approach to cognitive retraining for children with TBI? First, recent reviews of impairment-oriented, exercise-based cognitive retraining for *adults* with TBI have not been promising (Carney, Chestnut et al., 1999). Direct memory retraining has received little empirical support

(Schacter & Glisky, 1986; Thoene, 1996; Wilson, 2002), and reviews of direct attention training have been mixed. The meta-analysis of Park and Ingles (2001) identified little generalized effect of such training, and the evidence reviews of Cicerone and colleagues (2000) and Sohlberg and colleagues (2003) found limited support for the training in *selected* TBI subpopulations.

Unfortunately, procedures for neuropsychological rehabilitation were developed with little appreciation for the large research base in special education and in studies of transfer of training for all disability and nondisability populations. Kavale and Mattson (1983) published a meta-analysis of 180 studies of the efficacy of *perceptual-motor* exercises used with students with varied cognitive and learning disabilities. The interventions were based on massed, hierarchically organized, discrete trial training exercises that in many cases were identical or similar to exercises later used in cognitive retraining programs for individuals with TBI. Furthermore, the theoretical intervention assumptions were the same: (1) that components of cognition and perception can be isolated and separately targeted with training exercises and (2) that learning and other disabilities can be remediated with massed, hierarchically organized application of these exercises, assuming that improvements in components will transfer to functional cognitive/perceptual tasks and to academic skills. These exercises were commonly used with children labeled *brain injured* from the 1940s through the 1970s.

The 180 studies in the meta-analysis included 637 effect sizes (due to multiple outcome measures in many studies) and yielded the following results:

- Perceptual-motor outcome: 233 effect sizes; mean effect size = .166 (6 percentile points improvement)
- Academic achievement: 283 effect sizes; mean effect size = .013 (no change)
- Cognitive/aptitude outcome: 95 effect sizes; mean effect size = .028 (1 percentile point improvement)

In addition to the general finding that there were no significant improvements on meaningful academic measures, Kavale and Mattson found that there were no specific clinical populations or age groups with substantial effects, and that studies rated *high* on internal validity had the *lowest* effect sizes (–.119).

Thus a great deal was known about the relative *ineffectiveness* of massed, decontextualized, process-specific cognitive and perceptual training exercises before this approach became popular in TBI rehabilitation in the 1970s and 1980s. Indeed, Mann (1979) ended a comprehensive narrative review of 200 years of research in cognitive process training as follows: "Process training has always made the Phoenix look like a bedraggled sparrow. You cannot kill it. It simply bides its time in exile after being dislodged by one of history's periodic attacks upon it and then returns, wearing disguises or carrying new noms de plume, as it were, but consisting of the same old ideas, doing business in the same old way" (p. 539).

Studies of Transfer of Cognitive Skill

A primary experimental motivator for context-sensitive approaches to cognition and learning has been studies of transfer. Important questions facing teachers and clinicians attempting to facilitate meaningful cognitive growth and improvement of function after brain injury are the following: Is far, general, deep, and durable transfer possible? If so, how can it be facilitated? If not, how can individuals be taught and supported to succeed in relevant settings and relevant content domains?

Histories of transfer research routinely cite Thorndike's work more than 100 years ago as pivotal. His experiments led to the famous theory of identical elements, according to which transfer is uncommon, but when it does occur, it is because of the large number of elements common to acquisition and application situations (Thorndike, 1906). For example, Thorndike showed that students with several years of study of Latin and mathematics were no better at organizational and reasoning tasks than those with no such training. These findings were contrary to the prevailing *doctrine of formal discipline*, which held that the forms or faculties of the mind (e.g., organized thinking, reasoning) could be trained or disciplined with specific curricular offerings (e.g., Latin and geometry), thereby improving performance on all tasks that require the processes that have been trained. This discredited educational principle associated with nineteenth-century faculty psychology bears a strong resemblance to the premises underlying cognitive retraining in the late twentieth century.

Detterman (1993) reviewed the subsequent 100 years of transfer experiments and drew a conclusion similar to Thorndike's: "The lesson learned from studies of transfer is that, if you want people to learn something, teach it to them. Don't teach something else and expect them to figure out what you really want them to do" (p. 21).

Limited transfer of cognitive training is predicted by many theories of cognition, including the classical Vygotsky/Luria sociocultural method (Vygotsky, 1934, 1978) as well as contemporary situated cognition theory (Clancey, 1997; Greeno, 1998), situated learning theories (Lave, 1996; Rogoff, 1990), standard information processing theory (Singley & Anderson, 1989), and behavioral theories of learning (Butterfield et al., 1993). Sternberg and Frensch (1993) outlined four mechanisms that facilitate transfer, again underscoring the importance of context-sensitive training:

1. *Encoding specificity*: Retrieval of information or procedures is facilitated by similarity of encoding and retrieval conditions. Therefore, flexible transfer is facilitated by encoding (training) in many varied

application contexts (based on Tulving's principle of encoding specificity derived from memory studies; Tulving & Thomson, 1973).

2. *Organization*: The way information is organized in memory affects
   transfer. For example, information encoded in narrative organization
   form will be applied most easily in narrative tasks. Similarly, cognitive
   strategies encoded as a routine component of functional tasks will more
   likely be applied to novel functional tasks in that domain than will
   strategies acquired during decontextualized cognitive exercises.

3. *Discrimination*: An item (information or strategy) will be applied in a
   new situation only if it is somehow tagged as relevant to the application situation. To be useful, cognitive strategies must be learned along
   with the conditions of their application, again recommending context-
   sensitive practice.

4. *Set*: Transfer occurs to the degree that individuals have a mental set to
   achieve transfer during the training and transfer tasks. Thus motivation
   is a factor in transfer, suggesting the use of tasks and content meaningful to the person being trained. This factor is also stressed by Flavell
   and colleagues (2002) in relation to the metacognitive behavior of all
   students.

Taken together, these conditions of transfer seem to converge on the conclusion
that attempts to improve cognitive functioning or performance of cognitively
demanding tasks must be sensitive to the individual's specific contexts of application and domains of relevant content.

Cognitive Intervention: Positive Evidence

To my knowledge, the only randomized, controlled trial of cognitive intervention for children with TBI was conducted in Brazil at the SARAH rehabilitation
hospitals (Braga & Campos da Paz, 2000; Braga et al., in press). The participants were children with moderate to severe TBI between 5 and 12 years of age
and at least 6 months postinjury. They were randomly assigned to one of two
conditions: (1) direct, intensive, conventional, clinician-delivered treatment in
a clinical setting ($n = 44$) and (2) indirect parent intervention (with intensive
parent training and support) largely within the context of everyday home and
family routines ($n = 43$). Both groups received individually customized intervention for 1 year. Cognitive outcome, as measured by the WISC-III, demonstrated a greater than one standard deviation superiority for the indirect,
contextualized delivery group.

Interpretation of this finding is complicated by the following concerns: (1) It
is impossible to know if the independent variable is context per se, intensity of
intervention, integration of services, comfort level of the child, or parents'

adjustment and empowerment that may have resulted from their engagement in their child's treatment; (2) the Wechsler tests are generally considered an inadequate measure of cognitive functioning and improvement in children with TBI; and (3) there were no measures of educational outcome or psychosocial adjustment. However, placed in the context of research with adults with TBI, 100 years of transfer research, and substantial research with other special education populations, Braga and colleagues' findings suggest the need to contextualize cognitive interventions for children with TBI.

Educational Strategy Intervention

The field of educational intervention is vast. Many instructional strategies have been validated across disability and nondisability populations alike and have been applied to students with TBI (Glang et al., 1997). The goal in this section is simply to add to the evolving themes of this chapter by citing research reviews showing that effective academic strategy interventions have the following features (Pressley, 1995):

- *Context sensitivity*: Cognitive/educational interventions need to be delivered within the context of relevant curricular content.
- *Direct and intensive instruction*: Academic skills require direct instruction along with a large number and variety of authentic application trials.
- *Long-term*: The shaping of effective cognitive and academic habits and skills requires *years* of high-quality instruction and successful practice.
- *Intensive*: Intervention needs to be part of the daily regimen.
- *Personally meaningful, with a focus on correct attribution*: Students need to know that they are responsible for their academic success and that their strategic efforts will have a meaningful payoff.

Early strategy intervention was often short term and delivered outside of the context of the student's curricular content. Resnick's (1987) narrative review documents the disappointing results of these early efforts: "Most of the training was successful in producing immediate gains in performance, but people typically ceased using the cognitive techniques they had been taught as soon as the specific conditions of training were removed . . . they had acquired no general *habit* of using it or capacity to judge for themselves when it is useful" (p. 39).

Recent curriculum-embedded approaches to strategy intervention have been more successful. In their narrative review of research on cognitive strategy approaches to improving reading comprehension in students with varied disabilities, Baker and colleagues (2002) described this progression:

Early attempts to teach cognitive strategies focused on generic skills without sufficient attention to how they are executed in specific academic domains. We now know that much strategy use is domain specific. Generalization of strategy learning to learning content in other domains is often difficult. Teaching generic strategies divorced from teaching academic content tends to result in students failing to apply these strategies when it really counts. . . .

Attempts to understand why students failed to transfer skills across classroom settings led to an important insight. Each academic discipline has its unique ways of reasoning that must be understood as part of successfully learning that content. For students with learning difficulties, acquiring strategies to succeed in multiple settings requires being taught in these settings, even when the instruction focuses more on general learning strategies than on strategies tied specifically to subject-area content. (p. 67)

Summaries of the recent Rand Reading Study Group review of research in reading instruction have highlighted similar themes (funded by the U.S. Department of Education Office of Educational Research and Improvement). Based on that comprehensive evidence review, Sweet and Snow (2002) offered 10 principles of instruction. Principles 3 and 6 are especially relevant to the current theme that cognitive and academic strategy intervention for all populations needs to be both direct and embedded.

Principle 3: "The explicitness with which teachers teach these strategies makes a difference in learner outcomes, especially for students who are low achieving and who profit from greater explicitness."

Principle 6: "Teachers who provide comprehension strategy instruction deeply connected within the context of subject matter learning, such as history and science, foster comprehension development."

The same themes were demonstrated in a meta-analysis of 180 group studies (1537 effect sizes) of strategy intervention in special education generally (Swanson, 1999). Swanson concluded that there was ample evidence for a Combined Model that integrates direct intensive instruction with curriculum-embedded strategy intervention in teaching students with learning problems (independent of etiology).

These well-documented themes are highly relevant to discussions of TBI rehabilitation in light of the frequency with which rehabilitation professionals recommend a focus on remediation of underlying cognitive and academic process deficits *before* the student resumes academic pursuits with relevant academic tasks and materials. In addition, strategy intervention research with individuals (children and adults) with TBI has often been short term (e.g., 4 to 8 weeks or less) and not connected to personally relevant real-world content and activities. For example, Levine and colleagues (2000) positively described the effectiveness of a goal management strategy training program for adults with TBI that included only *1 hour* of training in a laboratory setting using tasks unrelated to the individuals' everyday lives. Furthermore, outcome was measured with artificial paper-pencil tasks that were not related to the participants' real-world activities. Experimental treatment designs of this sort (i.e., brief intervention in a laboratory setting, artificial outcome measures, no measures of meaningful generalization or maintenance) were common in educational psychology in the 1960s and 1970s and have long since been shown to yield misleadingly optimistic results. Attempts to teach strategies independent of their application within relevant content (academic content in the case of students) have repeatedly been shown to fail the litmus tests of transfer and maintenance with many disability populations and are highly unlikely to be successful with students with cognitive impairment after TBI. Like most investigators in the field of neuropsychological rehabilitation, Levine and colleagues failed to mention the enormous body of research that supports this negative conclusion.

Validated strategy intervention procedures have been described by several investigators in educational psychology (Block & Pressley, 2002; Brown et al., 1996; Guthrie et al., 2000; Meichenbaum & Beimiller, 1998; Palinscar & Brown, 1989; Pressley, 2002) and special education (Deshler & Schumaker, 1988; Gersten et al., 2001; Wehmeyer et al., 2000). Furthermore, Borkowski has repeatedly highlighted the important point that an intervention focus on correct attribution for success and failure, and attention to the student's sense of personal identity as a potentially successful strategic student, are both critical additions to strategy intervention for struggling students (Borkowski et al., 1988, 1990, 1996, 2000). Ylvisaker and Feeney (2002) argued that assistance in constructing an effective sense of self is particularly important in the case of young people with acquired brain injury, and they described intervention procedures designed to assist with this process (Ylvisaker & Feeney, 2000).

Social Skills Intervention

Many reviews of outcome following pediatric and adult TBI have highlighted the important role of social competence and behavioral self-regulation in successful reintegration into school, family, and social networks and the frequency with which these competencies are impaired (McDonald, 2003). For students with and without identified disability, "the ability to interact successfully with peers and significant adults is one of the most important aspects of students' development. The degree to which students are able to establish and maintain satisfactory interpersonal relationships, gain peer acceptance, establish and maintain friendships, and terminate negative or pernicious interpersonal relationships defines social competence and predicts adequate long-term psychological and social adjustment" (Gresham et al., 2001, p. 331).

Over the past 30 years, a model of social skills training has dominated clinic- and school-based social skills intervention. The model assumes that knowledge of social rules, roles, and routines is lacking or insufficient and must therefore be taught directly. Most approaches use a preset curriculum that targets discrete social behaviors within a training context (classroom or clinic). Traditional behavioral teaching procedures are used, including modeling, role playing, scripting, shaping, and reinforcing, ideally accompanied or followed by transfer activities. However, often too few deliberate efforts at transfer and maintenance are implemented.

This model has come to be referred to generically as *social skills training* (SST) and has been subjected to a large number of experimental investigations across many populations, including special education populations. Gresham and colleagues (2001) reviewed narrative reviews and meta-analyses of this extensive research literature, concluding that "SST has not produced large, socially important, long-term, or generalized changes in the social competence of students with high-incidence disabilities" (p. 331). Specifically, they described two meta-analyses. The first included 99 studies of SST applied to students with emotional and behavioral disturbance, with a small mean effect size of .20. The second included 53 studies of SST applied to students with learning disabilities, with a similarly small mean effect size of .21. In general, meta-analyses and narrative reviews of experiments with several populations using decontextualized social skills training suggest minimal effect on real-world behavior, peer social skills ratings, and maintenance of new social behaviors over extended periods of time.

There exist no published well-controlled group studies of the effectiveness of any specific approach to SST for children with TBI. However, the findings from related populations are critically important for TBI rehabilitation professionals for three reasons. First, SST programs (or *pragmatics/functional communication groups*) continue to be a staple of pediatric rehabilitation. Second, individuals with TBI often retain declarative knowledge of social rules, roles, and routines, reducing their need for traditional SST despite difficulty applying this knowledge effectively in social contexts. Third, social competence deficits after TBI are often based on self-regulatory or executive function impairment (versus gaps in social knowledge), requiring *point-of-participation* (i.e., contextualized) intervention and support. Thus, knowledge of population central tendencies combines with large amounts of evidence from related populations to yield a reasonable hypothesis that context-sensitive, natural environment coaching approaches hold greater potential than traditional SST, a conclusion previously drawn in the case of students with executive system impairment associated with ADHD (Pfiffner & Barkley, 1998). In addition, clinical attention to impaired social perception (McDonald, 2003) and systematic efforts to train communication partners have begun to receive the attention they deserve in the TBI clinical (e.g., Feeney & Ylvisaker, 1995, 2003) and research literatures (e.g., Togher et al., 2004).

Behavioral Intervention

There exist no published well-controlled group studies of the effectiveness of any specific behavioral intervention for children with behavior disorders after TBI. Thus it is again relevant to identify themes from related literatures and from a growing number of single subject studies of children with TBI.

Attention deficit hyperactivity disorder and TBI are closely related diagnostic categories neuropsychologically (likely involvement of ventral prefrontal cortex) and symptomatically (including disinhibition often associated with aggressive behavior). Cognitive-behavioral interventions have a long clinical and research history in the field of ADHD. Early reviews were not promising. Abikoff's (1991) narrative review of 13 studies in which cognitive-behavior modification (CBM; Meichenbaum, 1977) was used to reduce aggressive behavior in individuals with ADHD suggested that initial gains were not generalized or maintained over time. A generalization effect was observed in only 2 of the 13 interventions, which were for the most part short-term and delivered in a clinical setting. Dush and colleagues' (1989) meta-analysis of CBM experiments with aggressive individuals (varied clinical populations, including ADHD) yielded a low .18 effect size.

More recently, Robinson and colleagues (1999) conducted a meta-analysis of studies in which CBM was used to treat the aggression of adolescents with ADHD. They wisely restricted the scope of their analysis to studies *implemented in everyday school settings*. Twelve studies (with 36 effect size measures) yielded a mean effect size of .64, or a 24 percentile rank increase for the CBM subjects compared to controls. It is tempting to interpret this positive result—particularly in contrast to earlier pessimistic reviews—as underscoring the importance of embedding intervention in the routines of everyday life, particularly for children and adolescents with executive function impairment.

Wade and colleagues (in press) reported the results of a randomized, controlled clinical trial comparing standard care (SC: $N = 16$, procedures not described) in pediatric rehabilitation units with a fairly intensive family-centered, problem-solving intervention (FPS: $N = 16$). The FPS group received seven standardized sessions and up to four additional individualized sessions as needed. The sessions, which involved parents, the child with TBI, and possibly siblings, were spread over 6 months and offered the family coaching in identifying and solving the behavioral and cognitive/academic problems that often arise after pediatric TBI. The FPS sessions covered many domains of content but focused heavily on behavioral issues, using a general antecedent-focused, positive behavior supports framework. Results suggest that the program was well received by parents and children alike; both parents and children noted increased knowledge and skills, and improved relationships compared to the SC group; and parents in the FPS group reported greater improvements in child behavior. This study offers preliminary data from a controlled group study supporting a contextualized, executive system–

oriented, positive, proactive, and family-centered approach to serving children with behavior problems after TBI.

Ylvisaker and Feeney have combined themes from context-sensitive CBM, support-oriented cognitive and executive function intervention, and the theory and practice of positive behavior supports in their work with children and adolescents with poorly regulated behavior after TBI. (See Ylvisaker et al., 2003, for a discussion of the theoretical and empirical supports for this approach.) The emphasis on cognitive and behavioral antecedent supports is based in part on the repeated finding that individuals with ventral prefrontal damage (common in TBI) learn at best inefficiently from the consequences of their behavior (Bechera et al., 1994, 1996; Damasio, 1994; Rolls, 1998, 2000; Schlund, 2002a, 2002b). This finding is especially important in light of the fact that most school-based behavior management programs are organized almost exclusively around the consequences of behavior. Similarly, classroom instruction tends to be organized around demands for performance followed by feedback. Thus students with TBI may routinely receive interventions that are incompatible with their primary neuropsychological impairment.

Ylvisaker and Feeney have presented the results of several successful single-subject experiments and case studies with young children and adolescents with severe behavior disorders after TBI (Feeney & Ylvisaker, 1995, 2003; Ylvisaker & Feeney, 1998) and have recently submitted several more for publication. Multi-component interventions include the following procedures, all delivered within the student's everyday routines:

- *Cognitive/executive function Focus*: graphic advance organizers for complex tasks
- *Cognitive/behavioral focus:* do-ability of tasks; removal of time pressure
- *Cognitive/behavioral focus:* assurance of success, possibly including errorless learning via apprenticeship teaching procedures
- *Behavioral/communication focus*: facilitation of positive communication alternatives to negative behavior
- *Behavioral/communication focus*: facilitation of positive ("nonnagging and nonscolding") communication from everyday communication partners, including teaching staff
- *Behavioral focus*: ensuring positive behavioral momentum before difficult tasks
- *Executive function focus*: involvement of student in planning
- *Executive function focus*: systematic use of an everyday *goal-plan-do-review* routine

As stated earlier, successful single-subject experiments, regardless of their number, are not capable of supporting a population evidence statement. In contrast, they offer useful intervention hypotheses to clinicians and teachers who serve children and adolescents whose behavioral difficulties, neuropsychological profiles, and life circumstances resemble in relevant ways those of the children whose successful outcomes have been documented in single-subject experiments. That is, these experiments are evidence in the sense of good reasons for clinical decisions.

THEME: TEACHER TRAINING

In light of decreasing lengths of stay in children's hospitals and rehabilitation centers, and the persisting and evolving nature of disability after childhood TBI, schools are unquestionably the primary location for pediatric rehabilitation; educators and school-based related services providers are the primary providers of rehabilitation services. Unfortunately, preservice training programs rarely offer more than a cursory introduction to this complex disability group.

Many state departments of education have produced TBI manuals for teachers and have offered 1- and 2-day training sessions to facilitate a basic understanding of the population. However, there is a substantial body of evidence for the conclusion that teacher training outside the context of classroom practice has little impact on everyday instruction and behavior management (Joyce & Showers, 1980, 1982).

Ylvisaker and colleagues (2001) surveyed 10 TBI professionals, each of whom had at least 10 years' experience training and supporting educators through public education funding grants. According to this panel of specialists, training and support for educators (teachers, educational assistants, and related service providers) must include context-sensitive coaching that:

- relates in practical ways to their everyday interaction with students
- is ongoing
- involves specific teacher assignments and intervention experiments, with concrete feedback, including collaborative problem solving
- is broadly consistent with the school's culture and existing constraints on teachers' time, and meets the objectives of those seeking help
- ultimately results in improvements in the student's performance

A similar conclusion was reached in the case of training programs designed to improve teaching and behavior management for students with ADHD (Shapiro et al., 1996). It remains to be determined whether this goal mandates on-site consultation by a TBI specialist or can be achieved more efficiently with teams of specially trained peer consultants within educational districts or by means of Internet-based teleconsulting.

THEME: FAMILY TRAINING AND SUPPORT

It is well established in the research literature that TBI in a child creates significant stress for families (Wade et al., 2002). Furthermore, the child's long-term outcome and the family's adjustment are interrelated (Taylor et al., 1999, 2001), supporting the hypothesis that the success of intervention programs designed to assist families in their adjustment may also improve the child's outcome.

Drotar's (1997) narrative review of family intervention across several pediatric clinical populations revealed considerable experimental evidence that intervention focused on problem solving and stress management improves the family outcome. To date there have been few experimental studies of family intervention in children with TBI. In a pilot comparative study, Singer and colleagues (1994) found that explicit stress management training was more effective in reducing symptoms of depression and anxiety than participation in family information and sharing groups. Wade (2003) reported that parents and siblings of children with TBI expressed great satisfaction with and enjoyment of a relatively short-term intervention designed to teach families collaborative problem-solving strategies. Wade and colleagues (in press) further reported that this family-centered, problem-solving intervention yielded statistically superior outcomes, compared to those of a standard intervention control group, in the following areas: knowledge of TBI, problem-solving skills, family relationships, and child behavior (as reported by the parent). The positive effect sizes for internalizing symptoms in the child, depression/anxiety, and withdrawal in the child were all reported to be large. Thus, interventions directed at collaborative family problem solving may be of benefit for the parents but, more important, of substantial benefit for the child.

Braga and colleagues' RCT (described above) demonstrated that with intensive training and support, parents can acquire the competence and confidence needed to organize everyday routines in the home in a way that effectively facilitates their child's ongoing cognitive and physical developmental achievements after TBI. In their study, children in the parent-delivered intervention group had cognitive and physical outcomes superior to those in the clinician-delivered intervention group. Interestingly, educational level of the parents was not a factor that influenced child outcome. Unfortunately, there was no direct measure of family adjustment or perceived burden.

SUMMARY AND OUTSTANDING RESEARCH QUESTIONS

As Carney, du Coudray, and colleagues (1999), observed, very few high-quality intervention studies have been conducted with children and adolescents with cognitive, behavioral, academic, and social disability after TBI. However, if investigators are willing to survey the research landscape broadly, they will find a large amount of relevant evidence to guide hypothesis formulation for future studies. Similarly, if clinicians and teachers are willing to survey the intervention research landscape broadly, they will find a large amount of relevant evidence to guide their clinical and educational decision making. Heightened attention to this research base would likely have resulted in substantially improved services to children and adolescents with TBI over the past 25 years.

When all is said and done, good clinical and educational decisions are not made on the basis of diagnostic labels, but rather on the basis of the individual's presenting strengths and needs, context barriers and potential supports, and informed, disciplined, person-specific hypothesis testing. Many intervention strategies have been validated across all tested populations and are thus reasonable hypotheses for children with TBI. Other strategies have been validated for children with profiles of ability and need similar in relevant ways to profiles common after TBI and are also reasonable hypotheses. Yet other apparently attractive intervention approaches (e.g., those insensitive to well-documented transfer and maintenance themes) have been *invalidated* across a wide spectrum of clinical and special education populations, and are thus unattractive clinical, educational, or research choices.

Having frankly acknowledged this large research base, this chapter concludes with a list of questions that are research priorities building on the existing knowledge base (Table 11.3). Consistent with the theme of the chapter, two of the recurring questions are these: (1) What are the most effective procedures for ensuring that clinicians and teachers are aware of relevant research-based practices as they make decisions about serving individuals with TBI? (2) What are the most effective procedures for ensuring that investigators are aware of relevant research findings in clinical and educational domains that heretofore have infrequently informed TBI research? A well-funded pediatric TBI research and training center would help to achieve these research goals.

Table 11.3. Outstanding Questions in Pediatric Traumatic Brain Injury (TBI): Cognition, Social Skills, Behavior, and Education

Early Rehabilitation
1. What is the impact of early rehabilitation on long-term outcome?
2. What is a reasonable duration of inpatient rehabilitation? What are reasonable criteria for discharge, taking into account the preparedness of the family and school?
3. What is the most effective primary focus of inpatient rehabilitation?
   a. Direct therapy to the child?
   b. Preparation of the family/school?

Transitions
1. What are best practices for:
   a. Hospital-to-home/school transition?
   b. School year-to-school year transitions?
   c. School-to-work (and adult life) transitions?
2. What is the best organization of case management (clinical/educational effectiveness and cost-effectiveness)

Family Intervention and Support
1. What are the best procedures for family problem-solving intervention and ongoing support?
   a. Specific procedures, intensity, and duration of family intervention?
   b. Role of family peer supports?
   c. Role of video self-modeling in family training?
   d. Best procedures for training families in child advocacy?
   e. Best procedures for training service providers in effective collaboration with families?

Educator Training and Support
1. What are effective procedures for organizing student-specific, classroom-based consulting?
   a. Teams of trained peer consultants?
   b. Direct access to a full-time TBI specialist/consultant?
   c. Internet-based teleconsulting?
2. What are effective procedures for training and supporting educational assistants?
3. What are effective procedures for disseminating education-related TBI information?
   a. Preservice courses?
   b. Internet-based courses?
   c. Clearinghouses for materials?
4. What are effective procedures for creating classroom habits of ongoing disciplined but flexible hypothesis testing for planning and modifying intervention?

Assessment
1. What are valid assessment procedures for establishing qualification for services (ecological validity of assessment)?
2. What are effective procedures for organizing dynamic/hypothesis-testing assessment for designing intervention/support programs?
3. What are effective procedures for training school psychologists and special education managers in TBI-related assessment themes?

Educational Intervention and Support
1. What are effective procedures for integrating best practices from research with related disability and non-disability populations?
2. What characteristics of children with TBI are associated with specific research-based intervention/support approaches?

(*continued*)

Table 11.3. Continued

Cognitive and Executive Function Intervention and Support
1. What are effective procedures for integrating best practices from research with related disability and nondisability populations?
2. What are effective procedures for identifying the best mix of impairment-oriented, activity/participation-oriented, and context/environmental support–oriented approaches?
3. What are effective procedures for context-sensitive executive system (self-regulation) intervention?
4. What are effective procedures for assisting students with the construction of a positive and motivating sense of self, consistent with educational potential and demands?

Behavioral Intervention and Support
1. What are effective procedures for integrating best practices from research with related disability and nondisability populations?
2. What is an effective mix of positive behavior support procedures (including antecedent supports) and traditional contingency management?
3. What are the neuropsychological and behavioral indicators for an antecedent support-oriented approach to behavior management?
4. What are effective procedures for facilitating student self-management?

Social Skills Intervention and Support
1. What are effective procedures for integrating best practices from research with related disability and nondisability populations?
2. What are effective procedures for context-sensitive (point-of-participation) intervention and support?
3. What are effective procedures for facilitating accurate social perception and interpretation?
4. What are effective procedures for orienting and training everyday communication partners?

REFERENCES

Abikoff, H. (1991). Cognitive training in ADHD children: Less to it than meets the eye. *Journal of Learning Disabilities, 24,* 205–209.

Anderson, S.W., Damasio, H., Tranel, D., & Damasio, A.R. (2000). Long-term sequelae of prefrontal cortex damage acquired in early childhood. *Developmental Neuropsychology, 18*(3), 281–296.

Baker, S., Gersten, R., & Scanlon, D. (2002). Procedural facilitators and cognitive strategies: Tools for unraveling the mysteries of comprehension and the writing process, and for providing meaningful access to the general curriculum. *Learning Disabilities Research and Practice, 17*(1), 65–77.

Bechera, A., Damasio, A., Damasio, H., & Anderson, S. (1994). Insensitivity to future consequences following damage to human prefrontal cortex. *Cognition, 50,* 7–15.

Bechera, A., Tranel, D., Damasio, H., & Damasio, A. (1996). Failure to respond autonomically to anticipated future outcomes following damage to prefrontal cortex. *Cerebral Cortex, 6,* 215–225.

Block, C.C., & Pressley, M. (Eds.). (2002). *Comprehension Instruction: Research-Based Best Practices.* New York: Guilford Press.

Borkowski, J.G., & Burke, J.E. (1996). Theories, models, and measurements of executive functioning: An information processing perspective. In G.R. Lyon & N.A. Krasnegor (Eds.), *Attention, Memory, and Executive Function* (pp. 235–261). Baltimore: Paul H. Brookes.

Borkowski, J.G., Carr, M., Rellinger, E., & Pressley, M. (1990). Self-regulated cognition: Interdependence of metacognition, attributions, and self-esteem. In B.F. Jones & L. Idol (Eds.), *Dimensions of Thinking and Cognitive Development* (pp. 53–92). Hillsdale, NJ: Erlbaum.

Borkowski, J.G., Chan, K.S., & Muthukrishna, N. (2000). A process-oriented model of metacognition: Links between motivation and executive functioning. In G. Shraw (Ed.), *Issues in Measurement of Metacognition.* Lincoln: University of Nebraska Press.

Borkowski, J.G., Weyhing, R.S., & Carr, M. (1988). Effects of attributional training on strategy-based reading comprehension in learning disabled students. *Journal of Educational Psychology, 80,* 46–53.

Braga, L.W., & Campos da Paz, A. (2000). Neuropsychological pediatric rehabilitation. In A.L. Christensen & B. Uzzell (Eds.), *International Handbook of Neuropsychological Rehabilitation.* New York: Kluwer Academic/Plenum.

Braga, L.W., Campos da Paz, A., & Ylvisaker, M. (in press). Direct clinician-delivered versus indirect family-supported rehabilitation of children with traumatic brain injury: A randomized controlled trial. *Brain Injury.*

Brown, R., Pressley, M., Van Meter, P., & Schuder, T. (1996). A quasi-experimental validation of transactional strategies instruction with low-achieving second grade readers. *Journal of Educational Psychology, 88,* 18–37.

Butterfield, E.C., Slocum, T.A., & Nelson, G.D. (1993). Cognitive and behavioral analyses of teaching and transfer: Are they different? In D.K. Detterman & R.J. Sternberg, (Eds.), *Transfer on Trial: Intelligence, Cognition, and Instruction* (pp. 192–257). Norwood, NJ: Ablex.

Carney, N., Chesnut, R., & Kochanek, P. (2003). Guidelines for the acute medical management of severe traumatic brain injury in infants, children, and adolescents. *Pediatric Critical Care Medicine, 4*(3), supplement, s1–s71.

Carney, N., Chesnut, R., Maynard, H., Mann, N. C., Patterson, P., & Helfand, M. (1999). Effect of cognitive rehabilitation on outcomes for persons with traumatic brain injury: A systematic review. *Journal of Head Trauma Rehabilitation, 14*(3), 277–307.

Carney, N., du Coudray, H., Davis-O'Reilly, C., et al. (1999, September). Rehabilitation for traumatic brain injury in children and adolescents. Evidence Report No. 2, Supplement. Rockvile, MD: Agency for Health Care Policy and Research.

Cicerone, K.D., et al. (2000). Evidence-based cognitive rehabilitation: Recommendations for clinical practice. *Archives of Physical Medicine and Rehabilitation, 81,* 1596–1615.

Clancey, W.J. (1997). *Situated Cognition: On Human Knowledge and Computer Representations.* Cambridge: Cambridge University Press.

Damasio, A.R. (1994). *Descartes' Error: Emotion, Reason, and the Human Brain.* New York: Avon Books.

Deshler, D.D., & Schumaker, J.B. (1988). An instructional model for teaching students how to learn. In J.L. Graden, J.E. Zins, & M.J. Curtis (Eds.), *Alternative Educational Delivery Systems: Enhancing Instructional Options for All Students* (pp. 391–411). Washington, DC: National Association of School Psychologists.

Detterman, D.K. (1993). The case for the prosecution: Transfer as an epiphenomenon. In D.K. Detterman & R.J. Sternberg (Eds.), *Transfer on Trial: Intelligence, Cognition, and Instruction* (pp. 1–24). Norwood, NJ: Ablex.

Drotar, D. (1997). Relating parent and family functioning to the psychological adjustment of children with chronic health conditions: What have we learned? What do we need to know? *Journal of Pediatric Psychology, 22,* 149–165.

Dush, D.M., Hirt, M.L., & Schroeder,H.E. (1989). Self-statement modification in the treatment of child behavior disorders: A meta-analysis. *Psychological Bulletin, 106,* 97–106.

Feeney, T., & Ylvisaker, M. (1995). Choice and routine: Antecedent behavioral interventions for adolescents with severe traumatic brain injury. *Journal of Head Trauma Rehabilitation, 10*(3), 67–82.

Feeney, T., & Ylvisaker, M. (2003). Context-sensitive behavioral supports for young children with TBI: Short-term effects and long-term outcome. *Journal of Head Trauma Rehabilitation, 18*(1), 33–51.

Feuerstein, R. (1979). *The Dynamic Assessment of Retarded Performers: The Learning Potential Assessment Device, Theory, Instruments, and Techniques.* Baltimore: University Park Press.

Flavell, J.H., Miller, P.H., & Miller, S.A. (2002). *Cognitive Development* (4th ed.). Upper Saddle River, NJ: Prentice Hall.

Gersten, R., Fuchs, L.S., Williams, J.P., & Baker, S. (2001). Teaching reading comprehension strategies to students with learning disabilities: A review of research. *Review of Educational Research, 71*(2), 279–320.

Gioia, G., & Isquith, P.K. (2004). Ecological assessment of executive function in pediatric traumatic brain injury. *Developmental Neuropsychology, 25*(1&2), 135–158.

Gioia, G.A., Isquith, P.K., Guy, S.C., & Kenworthy, L. (2000). *Behavior Rating Inventory of Executive Function.* Odessa, FL: Psychological Assessment Resources, Inc.

Glang, A., Singer, G., & Todis, B. (Eds.). (1997). *Children with Acquired Brain Injury: The School's Response.* Baltimore: Paul H. Brookes.

Gordon, M., & Barkley, R.A. (1998). Tests and observational measures. In R.A. Barkley (Ed.), *Attention Deficit Hyperactivity Disorder: A Handbook for Diagnosis and Treatment* (pp. 294–311). New York: Guilford Press.

Greeno, J.G., & the Middle School Mathematics Through Applications Projects Group. (1998). The situativity of knowing, learning, and research. *American Psychologist, 53*(1), 5–26.

Gresham, F.M.., Sugai, G., & Horner, R.H. (2001). Interpreting outcomes of social skills training for students with high-incidence disabilities. *Exceptional Children, 67*(3), 331–344.

Guthrie, J.T., Wigfield, A., & VonSecker, C. (2000). Effects of integrated instruction on motivation and strategy use in reading. *Journal of Educational Psychology, 92,* 331–341.

Joyce, B., & Showers, B. (1980). Improving inservice training: The message of research. *Educational Leadership, 37,* 379–385.

Joyce, B., & Showers, B. (1982). The coaching of teaching. *Educational Leadership, 40,* 4–10.

Kavale, K., & Mattson, P. (1983). "One jumped off the balance beam": Meta-analysis of perceptual-motor training. *Journal of Learning Disabilities, 16,* 165–173.

Kern, L., Childs, K.E., Dunlap, G., Clarke, S., & Falk, G.D. (1994). Using assessment based curricular intervention to improve the classroom behavior of a student with emotional and behavioral challenges. *Journal of Applied Behavior Analysis, 27,* 7–19.

Lave, J. (1996). The practice of learning. In S.Chaiklin, & J. Lave (Eds.), *Understanding Practice: Perspectives on Activity and Context* (pp. 3–32). New York: Cambridge University Press.

Levine, B., Robertson, I.H., Clare, L., Carter, G., Hong, J., Wilson, B.A., Duncan, J., & Stuss, D. (2000). Rehabilitation of executive functioning: An experimental-clinical validation of Goal Management Training. *Journal of the International Neuropsychological Society, 6,* 299–312.

Lidz, C.S. (1987). *Dynamic Assessment: An Interactional Approach to Evaluating Learning Potential.* New York: Guilford Press.

Mahone, E.M., Cirino, P.T., Cutting, L.E., Cerrone, P.M., Hagekthorn, K.M., Hiemenz, J.R., Singer, H.S., & Denckla, M.B. (2002). Validity of the Behavior Rating Inventory of Executive Function in children with ADHD and/or Tourette syndrome. *Archives of Clinical Neuropsychology, 17*(7), 643–662.

Mangeot, S., Armstrong, K., Colvin, A.N., Yeates, K.O., & Taylor, H.G. (2002). Long-term executive function deficits in children with traumatic brain injuries: Assessment using the Behavior Rating Inventory of Executive Functions (BRIEF). *Child Neuropsychology, 8*(4). 271–284.

Mann, L. (1979). *On the Trail of Process: A Historical Perspective on Cognitive Processes and Their Training.* New York: Grune and Stratton.

Marlowe, W.B. (2002). Commentary on Ylvisaker, M. and Feeney, T. Executive functions, self-regulation, and learned optimism in pediatric rehabilitation: A review and implications for intervention. *Pediatric Rehabilitation, 6*(1), 57–60.

Max, J.E., Lansing, A.E., Koele, S.L., Castillo, C.S, Bokura, H., & Schachar, R. (2004). Attention deficit hyperactivity disorder in children and adolescents following traumatic brain injury. *Developmental Neuropsychology, 25*(1&2), 150–177.

McDonald, S. (2003). Traumatic brain and psychosocial function: Let's get social. *Brain Impairment, 4,* 36–47.

Meichenbaum, D. (1977). *Cognitive behavior Modification: An Integrative Approach.* New York: Plenum Press.

Meichenbaum, D., & Biemiller, A. (1998). *Nurturing Independent Learners: Helping Students Take Charge of Their Learning.* Cambridge, MA: Brookline Books.

O'Neill, R.E., Horner, R.H., Albin, R.W., Storey, K., & Sprague, J.R. (1990). *Functional Analysis of Problem Behavior: A Practical Assessment guide.* Sycamore, IL: Sycamore Publishing.

Palinscar, A.S., & Brown, A.L. (1989). Classroom dialogues to promote self-regulated comprehension. In J. Brophy (Ed.), *Teaching for Understanding and Self-Regulated Learning* (Vol. 1, pp. 35–71). Greenwich, CT: JAI Press.

Park, N.W., & Ingles, J.L. (2001). Effectiveness of attention rehabilitation after an acquired brain injury: A meta-analysis. *Neuropsychology, 15*(2), 199–210.

Pfiffner, L.J., & Barkley, R.A. (1998). Treatment of ADHD in school settings. In R.A. Barkley (Ed.), *Attention Deficit Hyperactivity Disorder: A Handbook for Diagnosis and Treatment* (pp. 458–490). New York: Guilford Press.

Pressley, M. (1995). *Cognitive Strategy Instruction That Really Improves Children's Academic Performance.* Cambridge, MA: Brookline Books.

Pressley, M. (2002). *Reading Instruction That Works: The Case for Balanced Teaching* (2nd ed.). New York: Guilford Press.

Resnick, L.B. (1987). *Education and Learning to Think*. Washington, DC: National Academy Press.

Robinson, T.R., Smith, S.W., Miller, M.D., & Brownell, M.T. (1999). Cognitive behavior modification of hyperactivity-impulsivity and aggression: A meta-analysis of school-based studies. *Journal of Educational Psychology, 91*, 195–203.

Rogoff, B. (1990). *Apprenticeship in Thinking: Cognitive Development in Social Context*. New York: Oxford University Press.

Rolls, E.T. (1998). The orbitofrontal cortex. In A.C. Roberts, T.W. Robbins, & L. Weiskrantz (Eds.), *The Prefrontal Cortex: Executive and Cognitive Functions* (pp. 67–86). Oxford: Oxford University Press.

Rolls, E.T. (2000). The orbitofrontal cortex and reward. *Cerebral Cortex, 10*(3), 284–294.

Sackett, D. L., Straus, S. E., Richardson, W. S., Rosenberg, W., & Haynes, R. B. (2000). *Evidence-Based Medicine* (2nd ed.). New York: Churchill Livingstone.

Schacter, D.L., & Glisky, E.L. (1986). Memory remediation: Restoration, alleviation, and the acquisition of domain-specific knowledge. In B. Uzzell & Y. Gross (Eds.), *Clinical Neuropsychology of Intervention* (pp. 257–282). Boston: Martinus Nijhoff.

Schlund, M.W. (2002a). The effects of brain injury on choice and sensitivity to remote consequences: Deficits in discriminating response–consequences relations. *Brain Injury, 16*, 347–357.

Schlund, M.W. (2002b). Effects of acquired brain injury on adaptive choice and the role of reduced sensitivity to contingencies. *Brain Injury, 16*, 527–535.

Shapiro, E.S., DuPaul, G.J., Bradley, K.L., & Bailey, L.T. (1996). A school-based consultation program for service delivery to middle school students with attention deficit hyperactivity disorder. *Journal of Emotional and Behavioral Disorders, 4*(2), 73–81.

Singer, G.H.S., Glang, A., Nixon, C., Cooley, E., Kerns, K.A., Williams, D., & Powers, L.E. (1994). A comparison of two psychosocial interventions for parents of children with acquired brain injury. An exploratory study. *Journal of Head Trauma Rehabilitation, 9*, 38–49.

Singley, M., & Anderson, J.R. (1989). *Transfer of Cognitive Skill*. Cambridge, MA: Harvard University Press.

Sohlberg, M.M., Avery, J., Kennedy, M. Ylvisaker, M., Coehlo, C., Turkstra, L., & Yorkston, K. (2003). Practice guidelines for direct attention training. *Journal of Medical Speech-Language Pathology, 11*(3), 19–39.

Sternberg, R.J., & Frensch, P.A. (1993). Mechanisms of transfer. In D.K. Detterman & R.J. Sternberg (Eds.), *Transfer on Trial: Intelligence, Cognition, and Instruction* (pp. 25–38). Norwood, NJ: Ablex.

Swanson, H.L. (1999). Instructional components that predict treatment outcomes for students with learning disabilities: Support for a combined strategy and direct instruction model. *Learning Disabilities Research and Practice, 14*(3), 129–140.

Swanson, H.L., & Lassier, C.M. (2001). A selective synthesis of the experimental literature on dynamic assessment. *Review of Educational Research, 71*(2), 321–363.

Sweet, A.P., & Snow, C. (2002). Reconceptualizing reading comprehension. In C.C. Block, L.B. Gambrell, & M. Pressley (Eds.), *Improving Comprehension Instruction: Rethinking Research, Theory, and Classroom Practice* (pp. 17–53). San Francisco: Wiley (Jossey-Bass).

Taylor, H.G., Yeates, K.O., Wade, S.L., Drotar, D., Klein, S., & Stancin, T. (1999). Influences on first-year recovery from traumatic brain injury in children. *Neuropsychology, 13* , 76–89.

Taylor, H.G., Yeates, K.O., Wade, S.L., Drotar, D., Stancin, T., & Burant, C. (2001). Bidirectional child–family influences on outcomes of traumatic brain injury in children. *Journal of the International Neuropsychological Society, 7*, 755–767.

Thoene, A. (1996). Memory rehabilitation—recent developments and future directions. *Restorative Neurology and Neuroscience, 9*, 125–140.

Thorndike, E.L. (1906). *Principles of Teaching.* New York: A.G. Seiler.

Togher, L., McDonald, S., Code, C., & Grant, S. (2004). Training communication partners of people with traumatic brain injury: A randomised control study. *Aphasiology, 18*(4), 313–335.

Tulving, E., & Thomson, D.M. (1973). Encoding specificity and retrieval processes in episodic memory. *Psychological Review, 80*, 352–373.

Vygotsky, L.S. (1934/1962). *Thought and Language* (A. Kozulin, Trans). Cambridge, MA: MIT Press.

Vygotsky, L.S. (1978). *Mind in Society: The Development of Higher Psychological Processes* (M. Cole, V. John-Steiner, S. Scribner, & E. Souberman, Eds. & Trans.). Cambridge, MA: Harvard University Press.

Wade, S.L. (2003, February). *A Family Problem Solving Intervention for Child Brain Injury: Initial Findings.* Abstract presented at the annual meeting of the International Neuropsychological Society, Orlando, FL.

Wade, S.L., Michaud, L., & Maines, T. (in press). Putting the pieces together: Preliminary efficacy of a family problem-solving intervention for children with traumatic brain injury. *Journal of Head Trauma Rehabilitation.*

Wade, S.L., Taylor, H.G., Drotar, D., Stancin, T., Yeates, K.O., & Minich, N.M. (2002). A prospective study of long-term caregiver and family adaptation following brain injury in children. *Journal of Head Trauma Rehabilitation, 17*(2), 96–111.

Wehmeyer, M.L., Palmer, S.B., Agran, M., Mithaug, D.E., & Martin, J.E. (2000). Promoting causal agency: The self-determined learning model of instruction. *Exceptional Children, 66*(4), 439–453.

Wilson, B.A. (2002). Towards a comprehensive model of cognitive rehabilitation. *Neuropsychological Rehabilitation, 12*(2), 97–110.

Wilson, B.A. (2003). Goal planning rather than neuropsychological tests should be used to structure and evaluate cognitive rehabilitation. *Brain Impairment, 4*(1), 25–30.

Ylvisaker, M., Coelho, C., Kennedy, M., Sohlberg, M.M., Turkstra, L., Avery, J., & Yorkston, K. (2002). Reflections on evidence-based practice and rational clinical decision making. *Journal of Medical Speech-Language Pathology, 10*(3), xxv–xxxiii.

Ylvisaker, M., & Feeney, T. (1998). *Collaborative Brain Injury Intervention: Positive Everyday Routines.* San Diego, CA: Singular.

Ylvisaker, M., & Feeney, T. (2000). Construction of identity after traumatic brain injury. *Brain Impairment, 1*, 12–28.

Ylvisaker, M., & Feeney, T. (2002). Executive functions, self-regulation, and learned optimism in pediatric rehabilitation: A review and implications for intervention. *Pediatric Rehabilitation, 5*(2), 51–70.

Ylvisaker, M., & Gioia, G. (1998). Comprehensive cognitive assessment. In M. Ylvisaker (Ed.), *Traumatic Brain Injury Rehabilitation: Children and Adolescents* (rev. ed., pp. 159–179). Boston: Butterworth-Heinemann.

Ylvisaker, M., Jacobs, H., & Feeney, T. (2003). Positive supports for people who experi-
    ence disability following brain injury: A review. *Journal of Head Trauma Rehabilita-
    tion, 18*(1), 7–32.
Ylvisaker, M., Todis, B., Glang, A., Urbanczyk, B., Franklin, C., DePompei, R., Feeney,
    T., Maher Maxwell, N., Pearson, S., & Tyler, J. (2001). Educating students with TBI:
    Themes and recommendations. *Journal of Head Trauma Rehabilitation, 16*(1),
    76–93.

12

Older Adults

FELICIA C. GOLDSTEIN

Unlike the extensive literature on children and young adults summarized in this volume, little is known about the rehabilitation needs of older persons who sustain traumatic brain injuries (TBI). A search of MEDLINE and PsychInfo from 1996 to the present, using the keywords *rehabilitation and elderly* or *rehabilitation and older adults*, revealed a plethora of papers on orthopedic injuries, cardiac disease, and stroke, but no papers that specifically addressed older adults with TBI. A more extensive and broader search dating back to 1966 produced similar results. When the terms *head injury* and *TBI* in *elderly* or *older adults* were used, the search indicated a handful of papers addressing their neurologic and neuropsychological complications, neuropsychological effects, or functional outcome, but none addressing the topic of rehabilitation per se.

This lack of systematic investigation of older adults with TBI raises the question of whether or not head injury in this population represents a significant health problem to even warrant investigation. The epidemiologic literature clearly indicates that the answer to this question is "yes." Based on the Centers for Disease Control and Prevention guidelines for identifying cases of TBI, Thurman et al. (1999) found that the incidence rates were highest among persons 75 years of age and older (191.1 per 100,000) and among persons 15–24 years (145.1 per 100,000). Thirty-five million people in the United States were 65 years of age or older in 2000, representing a 12% increase over the past decade (United States Census,

2000). With the continuing rise in the number of elderly patients, we can anticipate an even greater need for postacute rehabilitation services in the future.

Given the dearth of current information on older persons with TBI, the number of questions that need to be addressed is limitless. Below, some beginning
issues are raised as a starting point for research in this area.

GAPS IN OUR CURRENT KNOWLEDGE

What Other Risk Factors, Apart from Age, Influence Outcome and Rehabilitation Potential in Older Adults with Traumatic Brain Injury?

As shown in Table 12.1, the literature on TBI has focused on the relationship
between age and outcome and has clearly demonstrated that advanced age is an
important predictor of mortality. Compared to young adults, older patients with
TBI, despite having similar Glasgow Coma Scale (GCS) scores (Teasdale &
Jennett, 1974), are more likely to die from their injuries. A recent study of adults
admitted to Level I trauma centers found that age and severity of injury were the
two strongest predictors of mortality (Mosenthal et al., 2002). The mortality rate
for the elderly was twice that of young patients, and there was a progressive increase in mortality after age 50.

The functional outcomes of patients who do survive are worse than those of
younger patients. Investigations have detected a decreased probability of a good
recovery, or at least moderate disability, in older patients (Alberico et al., 1987;
Katz & Alexander, 1994; Pennings et al., 1993; Rothweiler et al., 1998; Susman
et al., 2002). Rothweiler and colleagues (1998) observed that with increasing age,
there was a corresponding decrease in the probability of a good recovery on the
Glasgow Outcome Scale (Jennett & Bond, 1975). Based on data from the New
York State Trauma Registry, Susman et al. (2002) found that a larger percentage
of patients 65 years of age and older had poorer outcomes on the Functional Independence Measure (Granger et al., 1992). In addition, 54% of elderly patients were
discharged to extended care facilities compared to only 26% of younger adults.
This poorer prognosis may begin in middle-aged adults. Dikmen and Machamer
(1995) observed a decline in a good functional recovery at age 50 and older in
patients with GCS scores of 3–15. The findings were not due to older patients
sustaining more severe injuries. Patients 50 years old were twice as likely as those
of age 40 to be discharged to an institution or group home, and only 25%–33%
were working at 1 year versus over 50% of patients below 50 years old (Rothweiler
et al., 1998).

While the available research has clearly identified age as an important predictor, however, it has tended to exclude other potential influences that are intertwined
with age and that may cause variability in outcome and rehabilitation needs.

Table 12.1. Glasgow Outcome Scale as a Function of Age in Representative Studies of Traumatic Brain Injury*

INVESTIGATORS	N	SAMPLE CHARACTERISTICS	FINDINGS
Alberico et al. (1987)	330	Patients 0–80 yr old; prospective series of hospitalized patients with GCS scores of 7 or less for at least 6 hr; outcome at 1 yr	*GR*: 0–20 yr = 45%, 21–40 yr =35%, 41–60 yr = 15%, 61–80 yr = 5% *Dead*: 0–20 yr = 25%, 21–40 yr = 32%, 41–60 yr = 50%, 61–80 yr = 70%
Dikmen et al. (1995)	466	Patients <20–70 yr old; prospective series of hospitalized patients with GCS scores of 3–15; time to follow commands <1 hr–29 days; outcome at 1 yr	*GR*: <20–29 yr = >75%, 30–39 yr = 70%, 40–49 yr = 60%, 50–59 yr = 30%, 60–69 yr = 25%, ≥ 70 yr = 20%
Gomez et al. (2000)	810	Patients ≥14 yr old; admitted to a hospital; GCS scores of 8 or less; outcome at 6 mo	*GR/MD*: 15–25 yr = 47%; 26–35 yr = 40%; 36–45 yr = 30%; 46–55 yr = 32%; 56–65 yr = 15%; >65 yr = 8% *Dead*: 15–25 yr = 41%; 26–35 yr = 47%; 36–45 yr = 56%; 46–55 yr = 38%; 56–65 yr = 65%; >65 yr = 87%
Jennett et al. (1976)	600	Patients 0–60 yr old; prospective series of patients in coma for 6 hr	*GR/MD*: 0–19 yr = 56%, 20–59 yr = 39%, ≥ 60 yr = 5% *Dead*: 0–19 yr = 37%, 20–59 yr = 53%, ≥ 60 yr = 88%
Katz & Alexander (1994)	243	Patients 8–89 yr old; admitted to rehabilitation; coma >1 hr (*n* = 97); outcome at 1 yr	*GR*: <20 yr = 55%, 20–39 yr = 40%, 40–59 yr = 10%, ≥60 yr = 43% *MD*: <20 yr = 38%, 20–39 yr = 50%, 40–59 yr = 78%, ≥60 yr = 10% *SD*: <20 yr = 8%, 20–39 yr = 10%, 40–59 yr = 10%, ≥60 yr = 43%
Mosenthal et al. (2002)	694	Patients 0–≥80 yr old; retrospective analysis of patients admitted to Level I trauma centers; GCS scores of 3–15; outcome at discharge	*SD/Veg*: 0–<64 yr = 5%; ≥65 yr = 13% *Dead*: 0–<65 yr = 14%; ≥65 yr = 30%

(continued)

Table 12.1. Continued

INVESTIGATORS	N	SAMPLE CHARACTERISTICS	FINDINGS
Pennings et al. (1993)	92	Patients 20–40 and ≥60 yr old; admitted to a hospital and alive 6 hr after admission; GCS scores of 5 or less; outcome at discharge	*GR/MD*: 20–40 yr = 38%, ≥60 yr = 2% *SD*: 20–40 yr = 18%, ≥60 yr = 5% *Veg/Dead*: 20–40 yr = 44%, ≥60 yr = 93%
Pentland et al. (1986)	2,019	Patients <65 and >65 yrs old; prospective series of hospitalized patients; GCS scores of 3–14; outcome at discharge or at 1 mo	*GR/MD*: GCS scores of 3–7: <65 yr = 22%, >65 yr = 4%; GCS scores of 8–12: <65 yr = 86%, >65 yr = 46%; GCS scores of 13–14: <65 yr = 99%, >65 yr = 96%; *SD/Veg/Dead*: GCS scores of 3–7: <65 yr = 78%, >65 yr = 96%; GCS scores of 8–12: <65 yr = 14%, >65 yr = 55%; GCS scores of 13–14: <65 yr = 1%, >65 yr = 4%
Rothweiler et al. (1998)	411	Patients 18–89 yr old; prospective series of hospitalized patients; GCS scores of 3–15; outcome at 1 yr	*GR*: Time to follow commands (TFC) ≥14 days: 18–29 yr = 18%, 30–39 yr = 30%, 40–49 yr = 0%, 50–59 yr = 15%, >60 yr = 8% TFC 25 hr–13 days: 18–29 yr = 80%, 30–39 yr = 70%, 40–49 yr = 100%, 50–59 yr = 18%, ≥60 yr = 0% TFC 24 hr or less: 18–29 yr = 95%, 30–39 yr = 80%, 40–49 yr = 81%, 50–59 yr = 75%, ≥60 yr = 40%
Vollmer et al. (1991)	661	Patients ≥15 yr old; prospective sample of hospitalized patients with traumatic coma; outcome at 6 mo	*GR/MD*: 16–25 yr = 49%, 26–35 yr = 48%, 36–45 yr = 33%, 46–55 yr = 22%, ≥56 yr = 9% *SD/Veg/Dead*: 16–25 yr = 50%, 26–35 yr = 52%, 36–45 yr = 66%, 46–55 yr = 77%, ≥56 yr = 91%

*Figures cited in the table are estimates when data were presented in graph form.
GCS, Glasgow Coma Scale; GR, good recovery (resumption of normal activities with some possible minor deficits); MD, moderate disability (disabled but independent in daily activities); SD, Severe Disability (dependent on others for daily support); Veg, Vegetative.

One major gap in our current knowledge is an understanding of these additional factors. A focus on age alone may mask the actual critical predictors for rehabilitation success. These additional factors separate older adults from young patients; thus, the construct of age may actually be a surrogate marker for these influences. Preinjury factors that must be considered in any prediction model of outcome include medical comorbidities and preexisting cognitive and functional status. Falls are a common mechanism of injury in older patients (Susman et al., 2002), and these are associated with numerous risk factors including medical comorbidities and medication side effects, deconditioning, and cognitive impairment (Leipzig et al., 1999; Tinetti et al., 1993). Extrainjury factors such as available social supports and living arrangements are also important to consider. For example, Lawes (2002) examined the reasons for hospital admission for head-injured patients who were 75 years of age and older. Approximately half of the patients sustaining mild TBI were admitted because they lived alone or needed further assistance at home rather than due to complications related to their head injuries. Additional gauges of a successful outcome such as return to employment may be meaningless in older persons, many of whom have likely retired at the time of their injury. All of these factors may set the goals of a rehabilitation program and determine which patients will eventually return to independent living.

Is a Good Outcome Possible in Older Adults with Traumatic Brain Injury?

Another major gap in our knowledge concerns whether a good outcome is even possible in older adults who sustain TBI. There is some evidence that older patients are capable of a positive outcome, and that similar to the findings in young patients, there is a dose–response relationship with severity of injury. Mosenthal et al. (2002) noted a decrease in mortality from TBI with a corresponding decrease in injury severity. While over 60% of patients 65 years of age and older with GCS scores of 3–8 died, 45% of those with GCS scores of 9–13 and only 5% of those with GCS scores of 14–15 died. Rothweiler et al. (1998) separately examined the outcome of patients with mild TBI (GCS scores of 13–15 and no head injury complications) and found a "good recovery" in 40% of patients 60 years of age and older. Other investigators have found good outcomes in up to 28% of patients with moderate TBI and in up to 80% of patients with mild TBI (Kotwica & Jakubowski, 1992; Ross et al., 1992).

As part of a two-center study funded by the National Institute on Disability and Rehabilitation Research, we examined the cognitive functioning of adults who were 50 years of age and older when they sustained mild and moderate TBI (Goldstein et al., 1994, 1996, 1999, 2001; Levin et al., 1997). Patients were prospectively recruited from acute care neurosurgery services and received a comprehensive battery of cognitive measures. Our overall findings indicate that there is a continuum of recovery based on the initial severity of injury. As shown in Table 12.2, at approximately 1 month postinjury, the performance of patients with mild TBI did not differ significantly from demographically comparable community residing controls on any cognitive measures except on a letter fluency task during which the patients generated fewer words. In contrast, the mildly injured patients performed significantly better than the moderately injured patients in terms of visuomotor processing speed and set shifting, verbal memory, confrontation naming, and reasoning and hypothesis generation.

Although the patients with mild TBI as a group performed better than those with moderate TBI, there was considerable variability in outcome. The previous analyses examined cognitive outcomes as a function of overall group differences

Table 12.2. Cognitive Test Scores for Patients with Mild and Moderate Traumatic Brain Injury (TBI) and Controls*

	MILD TBI n = 18 MEAN (SD)	MODERATE TBI n = 17 MEAN (SD)	CONTROLS n = 14 MEAN (SD)
Attention			
Automatic (Square Root Transformation)			
Alphabet (secs)	2.9 (1.1)	2.7 (.3)	2.5 (.6)
Sequencing numbers (secs)	4.5 (1.4)a	5.9 (1.7)a,b	4.3 (.8)b
Effortful (Square Root Transformation)			
Serial threes (secs)	5.2 (1.8)	6.1 (2.3)a	4.3 (1.3)a
Alternation of #'s and letters (secs)	6.7 (2.1)a	11.0 (4.6)a,b	6.1 (1.8)b
Memory			
CVLT (# wds. out of 45)	35.6 (5.1)a	29.9 (5.3)a,b	36.5 (4.9)b
CRM (correct out of 100)	87.8 (7.0)	82.0 (8.2)	87.1 (8.2)
Language			
Visual Naming (points out of 60)	52.0 (4.9)a	45.1 (8.5)a,b	54.6 (4.5)b
COWA (total words for three letters)	32.3 (7.7)a,c	20.8 (8.0)a,b	39.0 (10.2)b,c
Executive Functioning			
Similarities (points out of 28)	17.5 (6.0)a	12.3 (6.4)a,b	20.9 (3.8)b
MCST (categories out of 6)	4.9 (1.7)a	2.6 (1.8)a,b	5.1 (1.3)b

*A common superscript indicates a significant ($p < .05$) difference between groups by Newman-Keuls. CRM, Continuous Recognition Memory; COWA, Controlled Oral Word Association; CVLT, California Verbal Learning Test; MCST, Modified Card Sorting Test.

on the various measures. In order to look at individual differences, we transformed each patient's cognitive scores into standard scores based on the control group's functioning. A z score was calculated by taking a patient's raw test score, subtracting the control group's mean, and then dividing this result by the control group's standard deviation on the same measure. We derived a mean composite z score that reflected a patient's functioning in a particular cognitive domain.

Figure 12.1 shows the mean z score of each patient with mild and moderate TBI in the executive functioning domain. Across all cognitive domains, there was considerable variability in outcome, with some moderately injured patients performing within normal limits. We visually examined whether the same mildly and moderately injured patients who were impaired in one domain were consistently impaired in the other domains; no pattern emerged. In other words, a patient with mild or moderate TBI who was impaired in one area such as executive functioning was not necessarily impaired across others.

Our findings are consistent with investigations in young adults (Dikmen et al., 1986, 1995, 2001; Levin et al., 1987; McLean et al., 1983; Ponsford et al., 2000) that uncomplicated mild head injury in adults 50 years and older does not produce clinically significant persistent cognitive deficits. While our findings are limited to premorbidly healthy and independently functioning individuals, and thus cannot be generalized to the population at large, they suggest the potential for a positive outcome even in patients with moderate TBI.

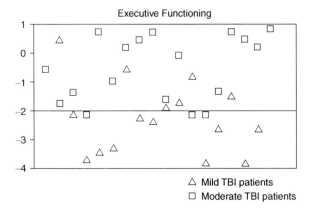

Figure 12.1. Scatterplot of the z scores of patients with mild and moderate traumatic brain injury (TBI) in the executive functioning domain. The *boxes* represent the performance of individual patients with mild TBI, and the *triangles* represent the performance of individual patients with moderate TBI.

What Are the Rehabilitation Needs of Older Adults with Traumatic Brain Injury?

A third gap in our knowledge is an understanding of the specific rehabilitation needs of older adults with TBI. The literature has used global indicators such as the Glasgow Outcome Scale and the Functional Independence Measure, as opposed to more fine-grained measures that would provide information about preserved and impaired abilities. It is not sufficient to rely on the findings in younger patients and to assume that these same areas are similarly affected in older patients. For example, there is evidence that patients 50 years of age and older exhibit more pronounced changes in working memory, reasoning, information processing speed, and episodic memory (Verheaghen & Salthouse, 1997). These changes in cognitive abilities, in turn, have been correlated with structural (e.g., reduced volume) and metabolic (increased activation) changes in the frontal and medial temporal lobes (Cabeza et al., 1997; Grady et al., 1994; Moscovitch & Winocur, 1995). These brain regions are frequent sites of contusions and hematomas after TBI in younger adults and may be vulnerable to disconnections that result from diffuse axonal injury, ischemic injury, and secondary insults (Levin et al., 1991, 1992). Such age-related processes may interact to produce a unique set of deficits that require different rehabilitation approaches in the elderly.

Older patients with TBI may also be especially vulnerable to psychiatric morbidity that could influence their rehabilitation potential. Goldstein et al. (2001) observed depression in one-third of older adults with mild and moderate TBI, indicating that it is an important secondary condition that requires diagnosis and treatment since it may lead to significant disability and a poor quality of life. In addition, mildly and moderately injured patients with higher Geriatric Depression Scale scores (Ysevage et al., 1983), indicating greater depression, were rated by their significant others as showing a postinjury decline in social functioning and activities of daily functioning. Four of 22 patients who were not initially depressed at 1 month postinjury endorsed symptoms of new onset depression at 7 months (Levin et al., 1997). Extrainjury factors such as the unavailability of social support may make some older patients with TBI especially vulnerable.

Finally, should the timing and intensity of rehabilitation differ for older adults with TBI? The current approach is to immediately transfer patients who are capable of obeying commands from the acute care setting to a rehabilitation program. This approach, however, may be untenable for the older patient, who, compared to the young patient, may require a longer period of in-hospital recovery past the resolution of the impaired ability to follow commands, a graduated rehabilitation program emphasizing a less intensive therapy schedule, and the adjustment of discharge goals to better suit the older person's needs. These ideas have not been formally tested with older patients with TBI but clearly are in need of investigation.

Are Older Adults with Traumatic Brain Injury Being Referred for Postacute Rehabilitation?

A fundamental question raised by the lack of studies on older patients with TBI is whether they are even being referred for postacute rehabilitation. In other words, is there a belief among health care providers that older adults with TBI cannot benefit from rehabilitation? A letter to the editor published in a journal in 1987 stated, "The main problem for elderly patients is that they have a reduced cerebral reserve to withstand even minor injury" (Gailbraith, 1987). More recently, Ritchie et al. (2000) recommended "conservative treatment" of TBI patients 65 years of age and older with GCS scores of <11 due to the fact that they had either high mortality rates or poor outcomes on hospital discharge. The literature portrays a pessimistic view of outcome, which, in turn, may affect whether postinjury rehabilitation is even attempted. In a study based in Scotland, Grant et al. (2000) reported that age was a significant factor in determining whether patients with head injuries were transferred from accident and emergency departments to neurosurgical units. They found that despite having similar GCS scores of 9–15, the odds of a patient's being transferred significantly decreased as a function of increasing age. While the authors acknowledged that they could not determine the exact reasons for this difference (e.g., the older patients may have had deteriorating conditions that made transfer less tenable), they suggested the possibility of *ageism* as a factor contributing to less aggressive management of the older patient. The optimistic findings of our preliminary investigations may encourage health care providers to offer an array of services, including outpatient rehabilitation, to the older adult with TBI.

PRIORITIES FOR RESEARCH

This chapter has provided an overview of the current state of knowledge concerning the outcome and rehabilitation needs of older adults sustaining TBI. It should be clear from the lack of systematic research in this area that the field is in its infancy. Some suggested areas of future investigation include studies describing the cognitive and behavioral sequelae that occur in older patients, the intra- and extra-severity features that influence these outcomes, and the expected recovery curves of these functions. Perhaps even more fundamental, however, is the need for studies demonstrating that the older patient with TBI can in fact benefit from rehabilitation, as these studies, in turn, may change providers' attitudes and referrals. As Marilyn Ferguson wrote in 1981, "Of all the self-fulfilling prophecies in our culture, the assumption that aging means decline and poor health is probably the deadliest." It is up to future investigators in the field to change this perception regarding head-injured patients.

REFERENCES

Alberico, A.M., Ward, J.D., Choi, S., Marmarou, A., & Young, H.F. (1987). Outcome after severe head injury: Relationship to mass lesions, diffuse injury, and ICP course in pediatric and adult patients. *Journal of Neurosurgery, 67,* 648–656.

Cabeza, R., Grady, C.L., Nyberg, L., McIntosh, A.R., Tulving, E., Kapur, S., Jennings, J.M., Houle, S., & Craik, F.I. (1997). Age-related differences in neural activity during memory encoding and retrieval: A positron emission tomography study. *Journal of Neuroscience, 17,* 391–400.

Dikmen, S., & Machamer, J.E. (1995). Neurobehavioral outcomes and their determinants. *The Journal of Head Trauma Rehabilitation, 10,* 74–86.

Dikmen, S., Machamer, J., & Temkin, N. (2001). Mild head injury: Facts and artifacts. *Journal of Clinical and Experimental Neuropsychology, 23,* 729–738.

Dikmen, S., McLean, A., & Temkin, N. (1986). Neuropsychological and psychosocial consequences of minor head injury. *Journal of Neurology, Neurosurgery, and Psychiatry, 49,* 1227–1232.

Dikmen, S.S., Ross, B.L., Machamer, J.E., & Temkin, N.R. (1995). One year psychosocial outcome in head injury. *Journal of the International Neuropsychological Society, 1,* 67–77.

Ferguson, M. (1981). *The Aquarian Conspiracy.* Los Angeles: Tarcher.

Galbraith, S. (1987). Head injuries in the elderly. *British Medical Journal, 294,* 325.

Goldstein, F.C., Levin, H.S., Goldman, W.P., Clark, A.N., & Kenehan-Altonen, T. (2001). Cognitive and neurobehavioral functioning after mild and moderate traumatic brain injury. *Journal of the International Neuropsychological Society, 7,* 373–383.

Goldstein, F.C., Levin, H.S., Goldman, W.P., Kalechstein, A.D., Clark, A.N., & Kenehan-Altonen, T. (1999). Cognitive and behavioral sequelae of closed head injury in older adults according to their significant others. *The Journal of Neuropsychiatry and Clinical Neurosciences, 11,* 38–44.

Goldstein, F.C., Levin, H.S., Presley, R.M., Searcy, J., Colohan, A.R.T., Eisenberg, H.M., Jann, B., & Kusnerik-Bertolino, L. (1994). Neurobehavioral consequences of closed head injury in older adults. *Journal of Neurology, Neurosurgery, and Psychiatry, 57,* 961–966.

Goldstein, F.C., Levin, H.S., Roberts, V.J., Goldman, W.P., Kalechstein, A.S., Winslow, M., & Goldstein, S.J. (1996). Neuropsychological effects of closed head injury in older adults: A comparison with Alzheimer's disease. *Neuropsychology, 10,* 147–154.

Gomez, P.A., Lobato, R.D., Boto, G.R., De la Lama, A., Gonzalez, P.J., & de la Cruz, J. (2000). Age and outcome after severe head injury. *Acta Neurochirurgica, 142,* 373–381.

Grady, C.L., Maisog, J.M., Horwitz, B., Ungerleider, L.G., Mentis, M.J., Salerno, J.A., Pietrini, P., Wagner, E., & Haxby, J.V. (1994). Age-related changes in cortical blood flow activation during visual processing of faces and location. *The Journal of Neuroscience, 14,* 1450–1462.

Granger, C.V., & Hamilton, B.B. UDS report. (1992). The uniform data system for medical rehabilitation report of first admissions for 1992. *American Journal of Physical Medicine and Rehabilitation, 71,* 108–113.

Grant, P.T., Henry, J.M., & McNaughton, G.W. (2000). The management of elderly blunt trauma victims in Scotland: Evidence of ageism? *Injury, 31,* 519–528.

Jennett, B., & Bond, M.R. (1975). Assessment of outcome after severe brain damage. *Lancet, 1,* 480–484.

Jennett, B., Teasdale, G., Braakman, R., Minderhoud, J., & Knill-Jones, R. (1976). Predicting outcome in individual patients after severe head injury. *Lancet, 1*, 1031–1034.

Katz, D.I., & Alexander, M.P. (1994). Traumatic brain injury: Predicting course of recovery and outcome for patients admitted to rehabilitation. *Archives of Neurology, 51*, 661–670.

Kotwica, Z., & Jakubowski, J.K. (1992). Acute head injuries in the elderly. An analysis of 136 consecutive patients. *Acta Neurochirurgica, 118*, 98–102.

Lawes, D. (2002). A retrospective review of emergency admission for head injury in the over 75s. *Injury, 33*, 349–351.

Leipzig, R.M., Cumming, R.G., & Tinetti, E. (1999). Drugs and falls in older people: A systematic review and meta-analysis: 1. Psychotropic drugs. *Journal of the American Geriatrics Society, 47*, 30–39.

Levin, H.S., Goldstein, F.C., & MacKenzie, E. (1997). Depression as a secondary condition following mild and moderate traumatic brain injury. *Seminars in Clinical Neuropsychiatry, 2*, 207–215.

Levin, H.S., Goldstein, F.C., Williams, D.H., & Eisenberg, H.M. (1991). The contribution of frontal lobe lesions to the neurobehavioral outcome of closed head injury. In H.S. Levin, A.L. Benton, & H.M. Eisenberg (Eds.), *Frontal Lobe Function and Dysfunction* (pp. 318–338). New York: Oxford University Press.

Levin, H.S., Mattis, S., Ruff, R.M., Eisenberg, H.M., Marshall, L.F., Tabaddor, K., High, W.M., Jr., & Frankowski, R.F. (1987). Neurobehavioral outcome following minor head injury: A three center study. *Journal of Neurosurgery, 66*, 234–243.

Levin, H.S., Williams, D.H., Eisenberg, H.M., High, W.M., Jr., & Guinto, F.C., Jr. (1992). Serial magnetic resonance imaging and neurobehavioral findings after mild to moderate closed head injury. *Journal of Neurology, Neurosurgery and Psychiatry, 55*, 255–262.

McLean, A., Temkin, N.R., Dikmen, S., & Wyler, A.R. (1983). The behavioral sequelae of head injury. *Journal of Clinical Neuropsychology, 5*, 361–376.

Moscovitch, M., & Winocur, G. (1995). Frontal lobes, memory, and aging. *Annals of the New York Academy of Sciences, 769*, 119–150.

Mosenthal, A.C., Lavery, R.F., Addis, M., Kaul, S., Ross, S., Marburger, R., Deitch, E.A., & Livingston, D.H. (2002). Isolated traumatic brain injury: Age is an independent predictor of mortality and early outcome. *Journal of Trauma, 52*, 907–911.

Pennings, J.L., Bachulis, B.L., Simons, C.T., & Slazinski, T. (1993). Survival after severe brain injury in the aged. *Archives of Surgery, 128*, 787–794.

Pentland, B., Jones, P.A., Roy, C.W., & Miller, J.D. (1986). Head injury in the elderly. *Age and Ageing, 15*, 193–202.

Ponsford, J., Willmott, C., Rothwell, A., Cameron, P., Kelly, A.M., Nelms, R., Curran, C., & Ng, K. (2000). Factors influencing outcome following mild traumatic brain injury in adults. *Journal of the International Neuropsychological Society, 6*, 568–579.

Ritchie, P.D., Cameron, P.A., Ugoni, A.M., & Kaye, A.H. (2000). A study of the functional outcome and mortality in elderly patients with head injuries. *Journal of Clinical Neuroscience, 7*, 301–304.

Ross, A.M., Pitts, L.H., & Kobayashi, S. (1992). Prognosticators of outcome after major head injury in the elderly. *Journal of Neuroscience Nursing, 24*, 88–93.

Rothweiler, B.R., Temkin, N.R., & Dikmen, S.S. (1998). Aging effect on psychosocial outcome in traumatic brain injury. *Archives of Physical Medicine and Rehabilitation, 79*, 881–887.

Susman, M., DiRusso, S.M., Sullivan, T., Risucci, D., Nealon, P., Cuff, S., Haider, A., & Benzil, D. (2002). Traumatic brain injury in the elderly: Increased mortality and worse functional outcome at discharge despite lower injury severity. *Journal of Trauma*, *53*, 219–224.

Teasdale, G., & Jennett, B. (1974). Assessment of coma and impaired consciousness: A practical scale. *Lancet*, *2*, 281–284.

Thurman, D.J., Alverson, C., Dunn, K.A., Guerrero, J., & Sniezek, J.E. (1999). Traumatic brain injury in the United States: A public health perspective. *Journal of Head Trauma Rehabilitation*, *14*, 602–615.

Tinetti, M.E., Liu, W.L., & Claus, E.B. (1993). Predictors and prognosis of inability to get up after falls among elderly persons. *Journal of the American Medical Association*, *269*, 65–70.

United States Census Bureau. (2000). *The 65 Years and Over Population*. Washington, DC: U.S. Department of Commerce, Economics, and Statistics Administration.

Verhaeghen, P., & Salthouse, T.A. (1997). Meta-analyses of age–cognition relations in adulthood: Estimates of linear and nonlinear age effects and structural models. *Psychological Bulletin*, *122*, 231–249.

Vollmer, D.G., Torner, J.C., Jane, J.A., Sadovnic, B., Charlebois, D., Eisenberg, H.M., Foulkes, M.A., Marmarou, A., & Marshall, L.F. (1991). Age and outcome following traumatic coma: Why do older patients fare worse? *Journal of Neurosurgery*, *75*, S37–S49.

Ysevage, J.A., Brink, T.L., Lum, O., Huang, V., Adey, M., & Leirer, N.O. (1983). Development and validation of a geriatric depression screening scale: A preliminary report. *Journal of Psychiatric Research*, *17*, 37–49.

13

Multicultural Perspectives

JAY M. UOMOTO

Traumatic brain injury (TBI) is a biopsychosocial phenomenon that encompasses biological, psychological, interpersonal, cultural, and community perspectives. These realms interact with each other in conceptualizing the experience of any given person with TBI. The sociocultural context in which a TBI occurs is likely to affect both the process of rehabilitation and the long-term outcome of survivors of this injury. The causes, incidence, and prevalence rates, and the rehabilitation of the person with TBI, all can be examined from a multicultural perspective. The goal of this chapter is to examine the relevant literature on multicultural aspects of TBI and provide directions for further research that has potential import for both rehabilitative and preventive efforts.

To begin with, the construct of culture is broad in its meaning and covers the beliefs, social norms, and social characteristics of a group (Wong et al., 2000). Persons with TBI may define themselves from a number of cultural perspectives (e.g., Western vs. Eastern, Protestant vs. Catholic, urban vs. rural). United States residents clearly live in a society with multiple cultures by which the individual is influenced. This chapter focuses on multiculturalism expressed as ethnicity. In this regard, this chapter uses the American Psychological Association's (APA) definition of ethnicity as referring to a person's "acceptance of group mores and practices of one's culture of origin and the concomitant sense of belonging" (APA, 2003, p. 380). The concept of *multiculturalism* and, interchangeably, that of *diversity* connote broader categories including socioeconomic status, sexual orientation, gender, and religious affiliation, as well as disability status. A comprehensive review of these perspectives is beyond the scope of this chapter. According to Wong et al. (2000), *ethnicity* refers to group membership "based on common descent, physical characteristics, and heritage" (p. 7). These authors go on to state that, commonly, ethnic groups in the United States are often broken down into five major groups: Caucasian, African American, Hispanic/Latino, American Indian/Alaskan Natives, and Asian/Pacific Islander. These categories are relevant for the current discussion and will be used to examine the subject matter of this chapter.

CURRENT KNOWLEDGE BASE

Epidemiology

Population-based epidemiologic investigations of TBI are few in number relative to those concerning other diseases and disorders, yet there is consistency among available investigations that clearly underscores the incidence, prevalence, and cost of TBI in the United States (Kraus & McArthur, 1996; Thurman et al., 1999). Few studies have thoroughly examined the prevalence and incident rates of TBI in various ethnic populations. This is a general finding in the field of neuroepidemiology regarding many neurologic disorders (Kurtzke & Jurland, 1983); only a few of these studies target specific ethnic populations (e.g., Molgaard et al., 1990). In the past, databases to study the epidemiology of TBI were sometimes incomplete in ways necessary to evaluate such variables as race or ethnicity. For example, in the often quoted San Diego County study by Kraus and colleagues (1984, 1988), in 36% of those studied, or 1198 out of 3358 cases of TBI, race or ethnicity was not identifiable. Of the remaining 2160 cases, only 20% were nonwhite, and the authors did not conduct further analysis of ethnic variables. Therefore, conclusions could not be drawn regarding the ethnic aspects of obtained incidence rates or mechanisms of injury in their initial report. They later reported on a smaller subset of their study population in an investigation of median family income against sociodemographic variables including race and ethnicity (Kraus et al., 1986). The incidence of TBI decreased with increasing median family income for Caucasians, African Americans, and American Indians/Asians but increased with increasing income for Hispanics. The authors concluded that after accounting for median family income, race and ethnicity did not appreciably change the incidence rate. There was no further discussion of the differential findings for Hispanics versus other ethnic groups concerning median family income.

These findings can be compared to those of Cooper and colleagues (1983), who studied the epidemiology of TBI in the Bronx, New York. African American males had the highest rate of TBI in their study; violent causes were highly prevalent in this group. These investigators inferred that the national incidence rate of TBI in African Americans was 262 per 100,000 and that of Hispanic Americans was approximately 278 per 100,000. Compared to the typical incidence rate of TBI in the general population of 200 per 100,000 (Kalsbeek et al., 1981; Kraus, 1978), the incidence rates for African Americans and Hispanics in the Cooper et al. study reflect an overrepresentation of these ethnic groups relative to the general population. Even higher rates of TBI among African Americans (approximately 400 per 100,000) were found by Whitman et al. (1984), who compared inner-city blacks with suburban-dwelling whites in the Chicago metropolitan area. These comparisons underscore the importance of studying the factors that contribute to these alarming incidence rates among ethnic populations.

In comparison to other ethnic groups, the Centers for Disease Control and Prevention (CDC, 1999) reported African Americans to have a higher than normal risk of dying as a result of firearm related TBI. Death rates attributable to transportation-related TBI and to falls were equivalent among whites and African Americans. Based on TBI death rate data compiled by the National Center for Health Statistics for the years 1980 to 1994, the CDC also reported disproportionately high death rates in the African American population (25.5 per 100,000) compared to whites (19.0 per 100,000) and to other ethnic groups combined (15.3 per 100,000). Again, ethnic variation is characteristic of incidence and prevalent rates of TBI in the United States.

Recent epidemiologic investigations have included race/ethnicity as predictive variables, particularly in examining TBIs that occur as a result of violence or what has been termed *intentional traumatic brain injury* (Wagner, Sasser et al., 2000). In their study, Wagner et al. gathered data obtained through the Carolinas Medical Center (a Level I trauma center in the Charlotte, North Carolina, metropolitan area) Trauma Registry and identified a sample of 2637 patients who had sustained a TBI. Among the 31% of their sample who were nonwhite, 77% were African American and 15% were Hispanic. The intentional mechanism of injury consisted largely of gunshot wounds and assaults with a blunt instrument. Minority status was associated with intentional injury (2.35 odds ratio), closely followed by drug use and alcohol consumption as significant predictors (1.70 and 1.69 odds ratios, respectively). Race was not predictive of fatal intentional TBI, however. The authors concluded that further examination is necessary to determine the underlying factors that account for associations between race and intentional brain injury. Their findings are consistent with those of other similar studies of intentional injuries (see the review by Sosin et al., 1995). To examine the association between TBI and violent crime, Turkstra and colleagues (2003) used a within-subjects design to compare 20 African American males who were convicted of domestic violence with 20 who had no criminal convictions. The variable of ethnicity was held constant by the within-subjects design, and the findings accepted the null position of no differences in occurrence of TBI between the two groups. The authors commented, however, on the overrepresentation of African Americans in groups of offenders, suggesting interaction effects between socioeconomic status and race that may shed light on the fact that lower-income African American males have higher rates of TBI.

A comprehensive database on TBI related hospital discharges has been developed through federal funding due to passage of the Traumatic Brain Injury Act of 1996 (Public Law 104-166). The funds provided for TBI surveillance across a 14-state region, and a report on data gathered in 1997 was recently issued (Langlois et al., 2003). Applying age adjustments, American Indian/Alaskan Native and African American populations were found to have the highest hospital discharge rate (75.3 and 74.4 per 100,000, respectively) for TBI. These figures compare with the slightly lower rates of discharge for Caucasians (62.9 per 100,000) and Asian/Pacific Islanders (34.8 per 100,000). Thus, there is a high rate of TBI not only among African Americans, but also among American Indian/Alaskan Natives. The report states that these findings may be conservative since race data were not available for about 11% of the TBI hospital discharges. Other ethnicity related findings include the following: African Americans (followed closely by American Indian/Alaska Natives) had the highest TBI discharge rate for assaults (approximately four times that of whites). The rate of motor vehicle pedestrian-related TBIs among African American males was about three times that of whites. The high rate of TBI among American Indian/Alaska Natives likely resulted from the fact that the State of Alaska was included in the dataset. Such findings highlight the critical need to include a wide sampling of geographic regions that more closely represent United States Census characteristics from a multicultural perspective. The report sounds a cautionary note regarding conclusions about race as a risk factor for TBI, stating that race may be a marker for other socioeconomic or other moderating variables that may account for the ethnic differences noted above.

Multicultural Variations in Neurobehavioral Sequelae

No two TBIs are alike, particularly given the spectrum of physiologic, cognitive, affective, and interpersonal sequelae that can occur after injury. Although common biopsychosocial sequelae are routinely expected in TBI (e.g., diffuse axonal injury, vulnerability to frontal and temporal brain region lesions, behavioral disinhibition and dysexecutive symptoms, impairment in communication pragmatics), cultural variations in expression and experience of these sequelae likely occur. To date, few empirical studies have systematically examined cultural variations in the neurobehavioral sequelae of TBI. Most accounts of cultural differences in neurobehavioral sequelae have been in the form of case descriptions providing important qualitative data that are useful to the clinical practice of the health-care provider. Finding what might be universally observed after TBI across different ethnic groups would be considered an examination of *etic* dimensions of functioning. Those neurobehavioral characteristics that arise or are influenced by a person's ethnic culture would be examples of *emic* aspects of such sequelae. The emic–etic distinction is derived from the cultural anthropological literature and has been applied, for instance, to multicultural neuropsychological test interpretation (Evans et al., 2000). Chan and Manly (2002) measured the dysexecutive syndrome cross-culturally. They found the use of a standardized checklist of such symptoms to be empirically validated in a Hong Kong Chinese–speaking sample. Thus, similar dysexecutive problems may be seen more universally across cultures. This example of an etic approach to understanding the phenomena has been more frequently applied in the true cross-cultural context rather than in a multicultural setting in the United States. The unique experiences of African American women who sustain brain injuries as a result of domestic violence have been studied and described by Banks and Ackerman (2002). Their description of an African American woman who was involved in a motor vehicle accident and had been a victim of physical abuse by a boyfriend, together with analysis of neuropsychological test results, illuminates many of the emic issues relative to the care and psychotherapy of that individual.

Illness and injury can be conceptualized within the context of culture. The *Diagnostic and Statistical Manual of Mental Disorders* (*DSM-IV-TR*; American Psychiatric Association, 2000) devotes a significant section to culture-bound syndromes. Based upon cross-cultural and international psychiatric research, these syndromes have significance for the diagnostic process in mental illness, particularly for persons who have immigrated to the United States. This is also true of persons whose family upbringing and developmental history include a worldview similar to those of the culture of origin. In TBI, the conceptualization of illness and recovery can have significant cultural and worldview overtones (e.g., Culhane-Pera & Vawter, 1998). In the clinical context, mental status assessment of affect and mood after brain injury often requires the analysis of any cultural significance of an observation (Takushi & Uomoto, 2000). For example, Asian patients may not necessarily exhibit or report mood or affective disturbance even though they may experience symptoms of low mood. Uomoto and Wong (2000) reported on a Russian male who sustained a work-related TBI and who subsequently reported concerns about being reported to the KGB. Although this observed behavior could be considered a manifestation of paranoid ideation, it was discovered later in this patient's rehabilitation stay that he had worked in a printing business in Moscow and had written underground publications critical of the government. Here, an emic understanding of the symptom complex was critical in the clinical decision-making process during this patient's postacute rehabilitation program. Although these clinical examples emphasize the case-specific nature of cultural variations in neurobehavioral difficulties, empirical verification and knowledge are sparse in the TBI rehabilitation literature.

Some of what can be known about multicultural variations in the neuro-behavioral expression of TBI can be gleaned from the cross-cultural brain injury literature. A good example of this type of research was conducted by Prigatano and Leathem (1993), who studied anosognosia in New Zealanders of Maori and English ancestry. They found that while impaired awareness was common in both cultures (an etic finding), patients of Maori ancestry tended not to overestimate their competencies in comparison to the English group (an emic finding). Culture had a significant influence on how anosognosia was behavioral expressed. However, anosognosia is universal in persons with brain injury since frontal-subcortical circuits are commonly involved. In a similar study, Prigatano and colleagues (1997) used a similar research methodology in studying a sample of Japanese national patients with TBI and stroke. They concluded that impaired awareness appears across cultures in brain injury, whereas self-reports of behavioral competencies may vary with the cultural context.

Studies on cross-cultural aspects of stress and coping in family caregivers of those with brain injury (e.g., Man, 2002) show patterns of reported stress and burden comparable to those in the U.S. literature. However, familial coping may have culturally specific characteristics, such as the experience of social embarrassment in Japanese families compared to British families (Watanabe et al., 2001).

A qualitative research methodology was employed by Simpson et al. (2000) to study cultural variations in the TBI rehabilitation process. They conducted semistructured interviews with 39 patients and family members from Italian, Lebanese, and Vietnamese backgrounds who received services at a brain injury unit in Sydney, Australia. In these interviews, which verbatim quotes were coded through an inductive thematic analysis according to commonly established qualitative data analysis designs. Their analysis led to the discovery of themes within the sample that appear universally consistent across cultures: burden of care, prizing the friendliness of health professionals; reports of common physical, cognitive, and personality sequelae after TBI; stigma, shame, and social isolation. Although these general themes appear common across cultures, there remains an empirical question: Are there specific cultural variations in each of these themes in ethnic minority patients who sustain TBI?

In sum, a task and challenge in TBI rehabilitation is similar to that in psychiatry, where multicultural and cross-cultural diagnosis and treatment will require a clear understanding of both intracultural (emic) and cross-cultural (etic) conceptual frameworks and how they might converge for any given patient (Westermeyer, 1985).

Outcome of Traumatic Brain Injury Rehabilitation

Numerous outcome studies exist in the area of TBI recovery and rehabilitation. While this literature is too voluminous to cover in this chapter, key studies are examined here to provide an overview of significant multicultural findings as an impetus for future research. Many of these findings are derived from data collected through the National Institute for Disability and Rehabilitation Research (NIDRR)–funded Traumatic Brain Injury Model Systems.

One of the seminal studies on TBI outcome that examined multicultural perspectives is that of Rosenthal and colleagues (1996), who reported on ethnicity data on 586 patients admitted through the TBI Model Systems between 1989 and 1995. These data were collapsed across African American, Hispanic, and Asian/Pacific Islander groups due to the small number of patients in the latter two groups. Thus, comparisons were made between "minority" and white groups. The minority percentage of the total sample was relatively high (46.6%), attributable to the catchment areas of the four Model Systems that were involved in this study. Essentially no significant differences were detected between the two groups on the Functional Independence Measure (FIM) or on the Disability Rating Scale (DRS) upon discharge. At the 1-year follow up, FIM scores were also similar between the minority and white groups. Two scales of the Community Integration Questionnaire (CIQ), Productivity and Social Integration, were different, with the minority group having lower scores (i.e., poorer role performance in the community). These group differences held after multiple regression analyses controlled for etiology of TBI, severity of injury, age, gender, and functional status at discharge from acute rehabilitation services.

These investigators raised important questions about the explanation of these community integration differences in the minority group, suggesting that there may be preinjury discrepancies persisting through the time of the follow-up assessment that relate to socioeconomic differences. They stated, for example, that a low percentage of those in the minority group were employed prior to the TBI (46%) compared to the white group (60%). They also pointed to the overall rate of preinjury employment in the TBI Model Systems (53%). Preinjury educational attainment differences were also offered as a potentially explanatory variable for these group differences. Another explanation involved the notion of poor access to rehabilitative care by minority group members relative to whites in the sample. Inequities in health-care service delivery may also be a potential contributor to the obtained findings, according to these investigators. They noted that the frequency of seizures was higher in the minority group and suggested that poorer access to medical care by minority group members may account for this result. They concluded that future research may assist in determining "whether better access to postacute service delivery or different models are needed to optimize outcome in this segment of the population with brain injuries" (p. 56).

A recent analysis of similar data collected by Wagner, Hammond and colleagues (2000) at the Carolinas Medical Center between September 1997 and May 1998 found results similar to these of the Rosenthal et al. (1996) report. Minority status, along with other predictors (payer source, violence, premorbid disability, psychiatric disorder, premorbid substance use, lower educational status, premorbid unemployment), was associated with lower CIQ scores. These investigators also concluded that information regarding preinjury community integration status is needed to better understand the ethnic differences found in their analysis.

A population of primarily African Americans was studied with regard to functional outcomes through the Virginia Brain Injury Model System at the Medical College of Virginia by Burnett et al. (2000). The authors used a within-subjects design. Their sample of 87 participants included 94.3% African Americans and 5.7% Hispanics who had completed inpatient rehabilitation programs. Most sample members were single men with an average age of 35 years. A significant portion of the sample (50.5%) reported preinjury moderate to heavy alcohol use, and a lower percentage (34.2%) reported preinjury illicit drug use. The causes of TBI in this sample were similar to those of the general population, with transportation-related causes being the most frequent (48.8%). However, consistent with findings presented earlier in this chapter, violence-related causes were second in frequency (approaching 35%). Functional outcomes via FIM and DRS measures appeared similar to those in earlier studies (e.g., Rosenthal et al., 1996). The study design did not allow for comparisons across ethnicity or against a white sample; however, the authors underscored the need to study ethnic differences in functional outcomes.

A comprehensive ethnographic analysis of recent TBI Model Systems data undertaken by Burnett and colleageus (2003) extends the aforementioned findings. Studied were 2020 persons with TBI seen between October 1988 and April 2000 who completed acute rehabilitation programs through one of the Model Systems rehabilitation centers. As with previous studies, ethnicity was collapsed into two groups: minority and nonminorities. Nonminorities comprised 57.8% (n = 1168) of the sample and minorities 42.2% (n = 852). Demographic characteristics were similar to that in other studies. That is, a higher proportion of minorities in this study were unmarried and male, unemployed before injury, and had less than a high school education than nonminorities prior to the TBI. Minorities had suffered a greater proportion (33.4%) of violence-related TBIs than nonminorities (11.4%); a similar pattern characterized pedestrian-related TBIs (11.4% vs. 6.4%). Minorities received fewer therapy services and spent less time in therapy than nonminorities. The mean length of stay was shorter for minorities (31.2 days) compared to nonminorities (34.6 days). Minorities had lower FIM efficiency scores (1.7 vs. 1.8). However, despite what appear to be poorer rehabilitation process findings (e.g., less intensive therapy, lower efficiency scores), the data demonstrated no significant differences in costs for rehabilitation services, discharge disposition, employment status, FIM scores, or FIM change scores. The authors postulate these differences may reflect team functioning variations, but they underscore the importance of examining "socioeconomic variables (access to services), analyses of patient-provider quality of care assessments, careful documentation of acute rehabilitation therapy intensity, and the comparative effect of medical-surgical LOS before rehabilitation admission, as well as long-term (1-5-y) outcome measures" (p. 267). They advocate for improved funding and efforts to bridge the "ethnic divide" (p. 267) seen in these and similar outcome findings among ethnic TBI groups.

Ethnic differences in vocational outcomes after TBI were examined by Johnstone, Mount et al. (2003). Because of the financial loss associated with any given TBI, these investigators sought to determine if racial differences exist in terms of vocational service provision and eventual vocational success. A small sample of African Americans ($n = 13$) was compared with Caucasians ($n = 62$) with TBI who sought services through the Missouri Division of Vocational Rehabilitation (DVR). No significant differences were found between the two groups on injury severity or on DVR service provision, except that the African Americans tended to receive more transportation services than the Caucasians. There were no statistical differences between the groups on ratings of vocational success upon case closure. The authors concluded that African Americans can benefit and be vocationally successful if provided with vocational services. They noted, however, that the African Americans tended to access such services later than the Caucasians, emphasizing the need for efforts to direct all persons with TBI earlier to vocational services.

Predictors of rehabilitation service used by African Americans with disabilities were examined by Asbury et al. (1994) based on literature demonstrating that ethnic minorities may be reluctant to access rehabilitation services. In their within-group study, 186 African Americans with either physical, cognitive, emotional, or sensory disabilities were recruited from disability- and rehabilitation-related facilities and agencies. The four significant predictors of rehabilitation service use by this population were, in order of influence, race/ethnicity of the service provider, perception of service provider capability, attitude toward employment, and perceptions of the rehabilitation process. Ethnic match between patient and provider, along with provider capability, appear to be important factors enhancing rehabilitation service use by the African American population according to this study.

The issue of patient–provider ethnic match has been investigated in parallel research that has examined the length of treatment for ethnic minority group members who obtain services through community mental health centers (Sue et al., 1991). Here ethnic match was related to a greater number of therapy sessions attended. Applying these findings to vocational outcomes in ethnic groups, it may be important to direct efforts toward culturally relevant rehabilitation services (e.g., patient–provider cultural match) paired with capable service provision to enhance vocational and other functional successes in ethnic minority patients with TBI. This is particularly apropos in light of the finding that the provision of specific vocational services appears to be the best predictor of a successful vocational outcome (Johnstone, Vessell et al. 2003).

Finally, the TBI Model Systems data provided an updated examination of violence-related TBI. In their report, Hanks and colleagues (2003) documented once again the high rate of violent TBI among African Americans. Minorities as a group (collapsing African American, Hispanic, Asian/Pacific Islander, Native American, and other racial groups) showed a significantly higher frequency of violent versus nonviolent TBI (74% vs. 46% for whites). In contrast to functional outcome results in the general TBI population mentioned above, this study found minorities to have poorer scores on the DRS and the Total FIM at discharge, and these differences held after a 1-year and 2-year follow-ups. The productivity subscale (a measure of employment and participation in volunteer and educational activities) of the CIQ also showed differences between minority and nonminority groups at follow-up intervals. Thus, among persons with violence-related TBIs, ethnic differences are evident with regard to frequency and to functional outcomes.

CRITIQUE AND METHODOLOGIC ISSUES

As can be inferred from this brief review of relevant studies on ethnicity and TBI rehabilitation, the literature is sparse. Few multicultural epidemiologic assays of TBI characteristics exist, though more recent investigations have made significant contributions to understanding ethnic variations in rates and causes in the United States. Few studies also exist on the rehabilitation process and the potential physiologic, cognitive, functional, vocational, and community outcomes in ethnic groups. The NIDRR-sponsored TBI Model System centers have generated the majority of data on ethnicity and brain injury, but there have been too few ethnic participants to allow for cross-ethnic and within-ethnic group comparisons. This paucity of knowledge provides the background for the following comments. The purpose of these comments is not to criticize prior studies, but to point out limitations that call for specific remedies and recommendations for future research.

Poor Representation of Ethnic Participants

One of the greatest difficulties in conducting multicultural research is that culture includes a broad range of variables. While ethnicity may be a marker for aspects of culture in a particular ethnic group, broad categories such as Hispanic/Latino or Asian/Pacific Islander are apt to lose much of the diversity that resides within those categories. Puente and Ardila (2000) point out that Hispanics are an extremely heterogeneous ethnic group, including those who reside in the Americas as well as those who hail from the Iberian Peninsula. Those who live in the Americas include people brought up in North America, Mexico, Central America and South America. Asian/Pacific Islanders are an equally diverse ethnically, including immigrants from Southeast Asian countries (e.g., Cambodia, Laos, Vietnam),

Koreans, Filipinos, Japanese, Chinese, and those from the Pacific rim (e.g., Samoa, Hawaii). There is likely to be significant within-group variability within each of these groups in terms of beliefs, customs, and worldviews that impact their conceptualization of TBI, recovery expectations, and view of rehabilitation services. Many individuals from diverse ethnic backgrounds may also have little contact with Western medical service delivery systems in general, making them potentially reluctanct to participate in, for example, specialized programs such as postacute brain injury programs that offer milieu approaches to neurorehabilitation. This is not to say that those from the majority culture may not also have reluctance (i.e., there may be an etic dimension of general reluctance to engage in unfamiliar rehabilitation therapies); however, the source of that reluctance may have culture underpinnings. Individuals from ethnic groups may not participate in research studies for cultural reasons or they may not be readily accessible (e.g., not engaged in rehabilitation to be evaluated through the TBI Model Systems) for enrollment in a study. The CDC-sponsored TBI surveillance project (Langlois et al., 2003) is a good example of the importance of ethnic group inclusion where resultant findings on American Indian/Alaska Native rates of TBI were previously not well known, particularly regarding more violent causes of injury, similar to the pattern found in studies involving African Americans.

One significant reason for the underrepresentation of ethnic groups in studies on TBI may be loss to follow-up. Corrigan et al. (2003) poignantly remark that from one-third to one-half of subjects in outcomes studies of TBI are not included in analyses because they are difficult to track at follow-up intervals. As might be expected, therefore, those who are tracked and are represented in TBI outcome studies may be a biased sample, whose characteristics are known only partially by an analysis of the demographics of those who represent the "lost to follow-up" group. In their examination of three database set samples (the Ohio State Suboptimal Outcome Study, the TBI Model Systems national database, and the Colorado TBI Registry and Follow-Up System), the investigators reported a 41.4% to 42.0% rate of subject loss at the 1-year follow-up. Those lost to follow-up (1) were socioeconomically disadvantaged (i.e., racial and ethnic minorities, less education, unemployed, dependent on public funding for payment of medical bills), (2) had a preinjury history of substance abuse, and (3) had violence-related TBI. The reseachers concluded that the "level of attrition should concern all researchers with a stake in long-term outcome research and should be an incentive to seek out methods to improve our ability to draw valid conclusions and to generalize from our samples to the population of persons with TBI" (p. 159). Appropos of the current discussion, these disquieting findings also point to the need to understand more fully the interaction of cultural, socioeconomic, and psychosocial factors in order to chart some directions for improving inclusion of ethnic groups in studies on TBI.

Another potential source of bias in studies on TBI is the commonly employed method of collapsing across ethnic groups to form two dichotomous variables,

minorities and nonminorities. Studies such as those of Rosenthal et al. (1996) and
Wagner, Sasser, et al. (2000) are aware of the importance of minority status to
findings on community integration and intentional brain injury (respectively).
However, reseachers are forced to collapse various ethnic/racial groups due to
the small numbers of the ethnic samples. While this allows for an analysis of
the data, the results may not directly apply to any ethnic group specifically. The
overrepresentation of African Americans who sustain violence-related TBIs,
therefore, may be less a problem of minority status in general than a result of
other issues such as socioeconomic status, access to quality education, or availability of social supports in the community. These latter variables may not necessarily be tied to any one ethnic group but may be potent moderating or mediating
variables that lead to the conclusion about the linkage between minority status
and TBI outcomes. Kaufman et al. (1997) warn researchers about the residual confounding effects of socioeconomic status that may potentially change the conclusions regarding effects of race on epidemiologic studies, thus biasing results in
the end. The early study by Kraus et al. (1986) provides hints of interethnic group
variation in TBI epidemiology. Their findings of differential patterns of median
family income were related to rates of TBI in Hispanics versus African Americans and American Indians/Asians, yet the literature to date is silent on the sources
of and contributors to this interethnic variation. The "minority" grouping classi-
fies this variable as nominal data and therefore does not allow it to show within-
group variation. This is true for most empirical investigations of minority status
as a predictor variable. It may limit our understanding of interethnic group differences, as well as intragroup variation in a specific culture or ethnic group.

Need for Acculturation Measures in Research on Traumatic Brain Injury

The issue of within-group variation is difficult to assess and difficult to fully account for in comprehensive designs in TBI research. Aside from the smaller sizes
of ethnic samples in TBI research that naturally lower statistical power, the addition of acculturation measurement adds further complexity to research designs
by adding another source of variance and error in prediction equations and algo-
rithms for modeling relationships between variables. That said, one potential
missing link in examining ethnic differences in TBI is the level of acculturation
of the ethnic participant. *Acculturation* refers to the extent to which individuals
use the language, values, and practices of their own ethnic community compared
to those of the majority culture (Manly et al., 1998). Stephenson (2000) comments
that the measurement of acculturation in research designs "serves as a tool to
delineate the relative contributions of dominant and ethnic society experiences in
observed differences between groups in research, assessment, and clinical presentation" (p. 77). She goes on to state that, for example, "a racial minority individual may be more immersed in dominant American society than a first-generation

White European immigrant. It would seem that all individuals, regardless of race or ethnic group affiliation, should undergo some process of change in order to adapt to a society different from their society of origin" (p. 78). These views have yet to be applied in TBI outcomes research. It may be a methodologic advance to apply a measure of acculturation specific to ethnic group membership that may better explain observed relationships that have been found to date.

Need for Examining Moderator and Mediator Effects

In much of the research literature in TBI, ethnicity and race have been used primarily as independent predictor variables. As noted above, since ethnicity most frequently appears as a dichotomous nominal variable, it is used as a grouping variable within which characteristics of TBI are compared (e.g., rates of violent causes, risk ratios for causes). As noted above, however, interaction effects with other variables (e.g., socioeconomic status) are posited to account for some of the findings that implicate ethnic differences, yet no studies to date have examined such interactions in detail with regard to TBI characteristics or outcome. Missing from previous studies, therefore, is the impact of moderator and mediator variables that may provide explanatory linkages between ethnicity and TBI-related outcomes. We know, for example, that African Americans have a higher rate than whites of violence-related TBI, but we do not yet understand the socioeconomic or sociocultural variables that either moderate or mediate this relationship. Holmbeck (1997) defines a *moderator variable* as

> one that affects the relationship between two variables, so that the nature of the impact of the predictor on the criterion varies according to the level or value of the moderator. . . . A moderator interacts with a predictor variable in such a way as to have an impact on the level of a dependent variable. (p. 599)

Holmbeck states that a mediator variable "specifies how (or the mechanism by which) a given effect occurs" (p. 599). Figure 13.1 describes the way moderators and mediators may be influential in TBI research. In a moderator variable model,

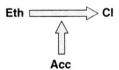

Figure 13.1. Hypothesized moderator model for modifying the relationship between ethnicity (Eth) and community integration (CI) where acculturation (Acc) is a moderating variable.

ethnic group membership (Eth) may be predictive of community integration (CI); however, the acculturation (Acc) of members of a specific ethnic group may increase or decrease the level of community integration.

There may be differential effects based on aspects of CI (home integration, productivity, social integration) that are modified by acculturation. As Langlois et al. (2003) have suggested, socioeconomic status may be a potential mediator; therefore, the interactive effect of ethnicity and socioeconomic status could explain the greatest amount of variance in CI (Fig.13.2).

One study that illustrates the impact of a moderating variable is that of Yeates et al. (2002). They found that race (African American vs. white) moderated group differences (orthopedic injury vs. TBI) in parental distress and perceived family burden, and this effect was independent of socioeconomic status. These approaches to a systematic evaluation of ethnic and racial differences in TBI outcomes may lead to a deeper understanding of predictive factors. Future studies will need to identify and evaluate the impact of potential buffers and accelerants to achieve a deeper understanding of ethnic minority influences on TBI outcomes. Clearly, a knowledge base has been established on which further studies can expand.

REMAINING CRITICAL QUESTIONS IN MULTICULTURAL RESEARCH ON TRAUMATIC BRAIN INJURY

Traumatic brain injury research is still in the early stages of development, given that the most comprehensive analysis of national TBI databases has occurred only within the past two decades. Of those studies, few have thoroughly examined ethnic influences in data gathered on etiology, recovery, and rehabilitation outcomes. Progress in psychotherapy for minorities has had a parallel developmental history. In a seminal article, Sue (1988) provides an account of the history of psychotherapeutic service delivery research for ethnic minorities. *Methodologic limitations of previous studies* and *lack on consensus of ethnic outcomes of treatment* were among the key issues in ethnic minority research that were highlighted as concerns for future research. I believe that these same issues remain paramount in order to capitalize on earlier findings on ethnic differences in TBI research.

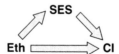

Figure 13.2. Hypothesized mediator model for the relationship between ethnicity (Eth) and community integration (CI) where socioeconomic status (SES) acts as a mediating variable.

Methodologic Limitations

It will be important to address some of the limitations of previous multicultural research in TBI. It is particularly important to ascertain the true rates of incidence and prevalence of TBI among a variety of ethnic groups. There is a paucity of findings on the epidemiology of TBI across and within these groups. Researchers to date have been unable to break these groups down into smaller subsets due to the very small numbers of individuals enrolled in such investigations. Okazaki and Sue (1995) note that an important methodologic distinction should be made between individual differences and group differences given the heterogeneity within ethnic groups.

Another related area that requires significant study is the causes of the high rates of violence-related TBI in African Americans and American Indians/Alaska Natives. It has been shown that socioeconomic factors, substance abuse, and education may play a role, and these will require extensive investigation. Because the enrollment of ethnic group subjects is low relative to that of whites in TBI research, there are few empirical investigations explaining the underuse of rehabilitation services by minority group members. It is also unclear to what extent ethnic minority groups use indigenous care providers or to what extent familial supports and culturally specific community resources may play a role in the underuse of traditional rehabilitation services. While prior studies acknowledge that many of those in ethnic groups rely more frequently on public funding (e.g., Medicaid) and therefore have poorer long-term access to services, the exact numbers and the quantifiable impact remain open questions.

Outcomes of Rehabilitation Services

Studies of the long-term outcome and recovery from TBI are available, but few comment on ethnic differences in outcome, again largely due to the small sample sizes and high attrition rate among those in such studies. It could be contended that those who are not lost to follow-up might represent a biased sample of ethnic minorities—hypothesized as having significant biopsychosocial resilience. As a select sample, they may represent truncated variance on predictor variables within the group itself and, sociodemographically, may have characteristics similar to those in the nonminority group (i.e., more education, better funding sources, and higher median income). As a result, differences between minorities and nonminorities on predictors of outcome may not be minimized. Okazaki and Sue (1995) also emphasize the need to elaborate on discussions of samples (including acculturation, generational status, self-identification, and ethnic/cultural composition of the neighborhood and community) of ethnic minorities. In TBI research, there is no detailed information on samples of minority group participants in published studies. For example, it may be helpful to know if Japanese

Americans enrolled in a study belonged to Issei (first-generation), Nisei (second-generation), Sansei (third-generation), or Yonsei (fourth-generation) subgroups, since each has a unique sociocultural background, acculturation and assimilation patterns, and economic history. Such variables could be important in the analysis of causes of TBI and long-term outcomes. Each ethnic group may have unique histories of prejudice, racism, sociocultural vulnerabilities, and modes of resilience that could be examined. Although alluded to in many TBI studies, no systematic investigation exists of larger sociocultural determinants of the treatment response, the impact of patient–provider ethnic match on rehabilitative therapy, or specific cultural strengths that enhance or improve long-term outcomes.

Rehabilitation therapy plays a significant role in treatment outcomes in the same way that psychotherapy orientation and process variables are vital in the examination of treatment outcomes for psychotherapy and counseling. The social climate, interprofessional relations, team practices, and managerial practices, all part of interdisciplinary rehabilitation team functioning, have been found to result in differential outcomes in stroke (Strasser et al., 1994). Team processes are a critical aspect of neurorehabilitation, and cultural factors may play a significant role in TBI outcomes. Niemeier and colleagues (2003) call for cultural competence in professional education and training of rehabilitation professionals, as well as the need to maintain such competence via continuing education of practitioners in rehabilitation settings. There continues to be a need for studies and program evaluations of cultural competencies and their impact on TBI rehabilitation outcomes.

RECOMMENDATIONS FOR FUTURE RESEARCH PRIORITIES

In a sobering statement in his keynote address at the National Multicultural Conference and Summit of 1999, Sue noted the following about the state of science in psychological research with ethnic minorities:

> I believe that there is a lack of psychological research on ethnic minority populations; that research on ethnic minority groups is uneven, with much of it at a relatively low level; and that funding for ethnic minority research has been woefully inadequate. The reasons for these problems are subtle and systemic. Science and scientific methods are not the culprit. Rather, the culprit is how science has been practiced—an effect caused by the selective enforcement of the principles of science. This selective enforcement of the principles of science emphasizes internal validity over external validity, which discourages the growth and development of ethnic minority research. As a consequence, steps must be taken in psychology to rectify the situation, not only in the interest of ethnic minority populations, but also in the promotion of better science. (p. 1070)

With these comments in mind, the following recommendations are made that seek to emphasize external validity, or "the extent to which one can generalize the results of the research to the populations and settings of interest" (Sue, 1999, p. 1072):

1. Large scale epidemiologic studies on TBI are needed on specific ethnic minority groups, with emphasis upon detailing within-group variations on such factors as acculturation, generational status, socioeconomic, and community contextual variables (e.g., access to culture specific community resources, availability of culturally competent practitioners). The purpose of these data will be to better define specific areas of vulnerability, risk, and resiliency factors for specific subgroups within ethnic minorities, thus potentially leading to better culture-specific rehabilitation services. It will be important to make comparisons across ethnic groups and with majority culture study participants in order to ascertain emic and etic dimensions of TBI causes, mechanisms, risks, and protective factors to better generalize results appropriately in constructing prevention, early intervention, and rehabilitation services.

2. Long-term outcome studies on neurophysiologic, neuropsychological, neurobehavioral, and interpersonal outcomes, functional activity, and community integration are needed for many ethnic groups and subsets within these groups. This will likely require intensive efforts at sample identification. Such studies will need to consider the common problem of attrition among ethnic minority subjects, with systematic efforts made to retain such subjects at follow-up. Identification of strategies that reduce attrition and facility retention throughout longer-term outcome studies may itself be a research priority. Examination of the use of culturally competent and sensitive interviewers, proactive engagement and endorsement of research by gatekeepers in the ethnic community, and enlistment and employment of ethnic minority research staff recruited from the community from which participants are drawn may potentially be as beneficial as subject recruitment and retention strategies.

3. Service use patterns and barriers (e.g., economic) to accessing the continuum of care in TBI rehabilitation in ethnic minority groups should be examined. Results of such research are needed to show health service delivery systems how to better serve ethnic patients with TBI, as well as those with other disabilities. Finding strategies that result in earlier and more complete TBI rehabilitation service use is an important goal of this line of research.

4. To better address the immediate needs of those who have sustained TBI and require rehabilitation, funding priority might be given to initiating systematic professional education and training in cultural

competencies specific to TBI rehabilitation. As with studies of ethnic minority group use of community mental health services, it will be important to use a "culturally responsive" approach (Sue et al., 1991). This approach may stress the training of health care providers to a culturally competent standard to work effectively with culturally dissimilar patients, use bilingual/bicultural health-care providers, and establish and test services that are specifically responsive to ethnic minorities. Evaluation of training efforts on the eventual effectiveness of rehabilitation practitioners with a variety of ethnic minority patients with TBI may be a necessary and ongoing priority to meet service delivery needs.

REFERENCES

American Psychiatric Association. (2000). *Diagnostic and Statistical Manual of Mental Disorders, Text Revision* (4th ed.). Washington, DC: American Psychiatric Press.

American Psychological Association. (2003). Guidelines on multicultural education, training, research, practice, and organizational change for psychologists. *American Psychologist, 58,* 377–402.

Asbury, C.A., Walker, S., Belgrave, F.Z., Maholmes, V., & Green, L. (1994). Psychosocial, cultural, and accessibility factors associated with participation of African-Americans in rehabilitation. *Rehabilitation Psychology, 39,* 113–121.

Banks, M.E., & Ackerman, R.J. (2002). Special issue: Violence in the lives of Black women: Battered, Black, and blue. *Women and Therapy, 25*(3/4), 133–143.

Burnett, D.M., Kolakowsky-Hayner, S.A., Slater, D., Stringer, A., Bushnik, T., Zafonte, R., & Cifu, D.X. (2003). Ethnographic analysis of traumatic brain injury patients in the national Model Systems database. *Archives of Physical Medicine and Rehabilitation, 84,* 263–267.

Burnett, D.M., Silver, T.M., Kolakowsky-Hayner, S.A., & Cifu, D.X. (2000). Functional outcome for African Americans and Hispanics treated at a traumatic brain injury model systems centre. *Brain Injury, 14,* 712–718.

Centers for Disease Control and Prevention, National Center for Injury Prevention and Control. (1999). Traumatic brain injury in the United States: A report to Congress. Atlanta: Author. Available at http://www.cdc.gov/ncipc/factsheets/tbi.htm Accessed August 29, 2003.

Chan, R.C.K., & Manly, T. (2002). The application of "dysexecutive syndrome" measures across cultures: Performance and checklist assessment in neurologically healthy and traumatically brain-injured Hong Kong Chinese volunteers. *Journal of the International Neuropsychological Society, 8,* 771–780.

Cooper, K.D., Tabaddor, K., Hauser, W.A., Shulman, K., Feiner, C., & Factor, P.R. (1983). The epidemiology of head injury in the Bronx. *Neuroepidemiology, 2,* 70–88.

Corrigan, J.D., Harrison-Felix, C., Bogner, J., Dijkers, M., Terrill, M.S., & Whiteneck, G. (2003). Systematic bias in traumatic brain injury outcome studies because of loss to follow-up. *Archives of Physical Medicine and Rehabilitation, 84,* 153–160.

Culhane-Pera, K.A., & Vawter, D.E. (1998). A study of healthcare professionals' perspectives about a cross-cultural ethical conflict involving a Hmong patient and her family. *Journal of Clinical Ethics, 9,* 179–190.

Evans, J.D., Miller, S.W., Byrd, D.A., & Heaton, R.K. (2000). Cross-cultural applications of the Halstead-Reitan batteries. In E. Fletcher-Janzen, T.L., Strickland, & C.R. Reynolds (Eds.), *Handbook of Cross-Cultural Neuropsychology* (pp. 287–303). New York: Kluwer Academic/Plenum.

Hanks, R.A., Wood, D.L., Millis, S., Harrison-Felix, C., Pierce, C.A., Rosenthal, M., Bushnik, T., High, W.M., Jr., & Kreutzer, J. (2003). Violent traumatic brain injury: Occurrence, patient characteristics, and risk factors from the Traumatic Brain Injury Model Systems Project. *Archives of Physical Medicine and Rehabilitation, 84,* 249–254.

Holmbeck, G.N. (1997). Toward terminological, conceptual, and statistical clarity in the study of mediators and moderators: Examples from the child-clinical and pediatric psychology literatures. *Journal of Consulting and Clinical Psychology, 65,* 599–610.

Johnstone, B., Mount, D., Gaines, T., Goldfader, P., Bounds, T., & Pitts, O. (2003a). Race differences in a sample of vocational rehabilitation clients with traumatic brain injury. *Brain Injury, 17,* 95–104.

Johnstone, B., Vessell, R., Bounds, T., Hoskins, S., & Sherman, A. (2003b). Predictors of success for state vocational rehabilitation clients with traumatic brain injury. *Archives of Physical Medicine and Rehabilitation, 84,* 161–167.

Kalsbeek, W., McLaurin, R., Harris, B., & Miller, J. (1981). Disability after severe head injury: Observations on use of the Glasgow Outcome scale. *Journal of Neurology, Neurosurgery, and Psychiatry, 4,* 285–293.

Kaufman, J.S., Cooper, R.S., & McGee, D.L. (1997). Socioeconomic status and health in blacks and whites: The problem of residual confounding and the resiliency of race. *Epidemiology, 8,* 621–628.

Kraus, J.F. (1978). Epidemiological features of head and spinal cord injury. *Advances in Neurology, 19,* 261–279.

Kraus, J.F., Black, M.A., Hessol, N., Ley, P., Rokaw, W., Sullivan, C., Bowers, S., Knowlton, S., & Marshall, L. (1984). The incidence of acute brain injury and serious impairment in a defined population. *American Journal of Epidemiology, 119,* 186–201.

Kraus, J.F., Fife, D., Ramstein, K., Conroy, C., & Cox, P. (1986). The relationship of family income to the incidence, external causes, and outcomes of serious brain injury, San Diego County, California. *American Journal of Public Health, 76,* 1345–1347.

Kraus, J.F., & McArthur, D.L. (1996). Epidemiologic aspects of brain injury. *Neurologic Clinics, 14,* 435–450.

Kraus, J.F., & Nourjah, P. (1988). The epidemiology of mild, uncomplicated brain injury. *Journal of Trauma, 28,* 1637–1643.

Kurtzke, J.F., & Kurland, L.T. (1983). The epidemiology of neurologic disease. In A.B. Baker (Ed.), *Clinical Neurology* (pp. 1–143). Philadelphia: Harper & Row.

Langlois, J.A., Kegler, S.R., Butler, J.A., Gotsch, K.E., Johnson, R.L., Reichard, A.A., Webb, K.W., Coronado, V.G., Selassie, A.W., & Thurman, D.J. (2003). Traumatic brain injury–related hospital discharges: Results from a 14-state surveillance system, 1997. *Mortality and Morbidity Weekly Reports Surveillance, 52,* 1–20.

Man, D.W. (2002). Hong Kong family caregivers' stress and coping for people with brain injury. *International Journal of Rehabilitation Research, 25,* 287–295.

Manly, J.J., Miller, W., Heaton, R.K., Byrd, D., Reilly, J., Velasquez, R.J., Sacuezo, D.P., & Grant, I. (1998). The effect of African American acculturation on neuropsychological test performance in normal and HIV positive individuals. *Journal of the International Neuropsychological Society, 4,* 291–302.

Molgaard, C.B., Stanford, E. P., Morton, D.J., Ryden, L.A., Schubert, K.R., & Golbeck,

A.L. (1990). Epidemiology of head trauma and neurocognitive impairment in a multi-ethnic population. *Neuroepidemiology, 9,* 233–242.

Niemeier, J.P., Burnett, D.M., & Whitaker, D.A. (2003). Cultural competence in the multidisciplinary rehabilitation setting: Are we falling short of meeting needs? *Archives of Physical Medicine and Rehabilitation, 84,* 1240–1245.

Okazaki, S., & Sue, S. (1995). Methodological issues in assessment research with ethnic minorities. *Psychological Assessment, 7,* 367–375.

Prigatano, G.P., & Leathem, J.M. (1993). Awareness of behavioral limitations after traumatic brain injury: A cross-cultural study of New Zealand Maoris and non-Maoris. *The Clinical Neuropsychologist, 7,* 123–135.

Prigatano, G.P., Ogano, M., & Amakusa, B. (1997). A cross-cultural study on impaired self-awareness in Japanese patients with brain dysfunction. *Neuropsychiatry, Neuropsychology, and Behavioral Neurology, 10,* 135–143.

Puente, A. E., & Ardila, A. (2000). Neuropsychological assessment of Hispanics. In E. Fletcher-Janzen, T.L., Strickland, & C.R. Reynolds (Eds.), *Handbook of Cross-Cultural Neuropsychology* (pp. 87–104). New York: Kluwer Academic/Plenum.

Rosenthal, M., Dijkers, M., Harrison-Felix, C., Nabors, N., Witol, A.D., Young, M.E., & Englander, J.S. (1996). Impact of minority status on functional outcome and community integration following traumatic brain injury. *Journal of Head Trauma Rehabilitation, 11,* 40–57.

Simpson, G., Mohr, R., & Redman, A. (2000). Cultural variations in the understanding of traumatic brain injury and brain injury rehabilitation. *Brain Injury, 14,* 125–140.

Sosin, D.M., Sniezek, J.E., & Waxweiler, R.J (1995). Trends in death associated with traumatic brain injury, 1979 through 1992: Success and failure. *Journal of the American Medical Association, 273,* 1778–1780.

Stephenson, M. (2000). Development and validation of the Stephenson Multigroup Acculturation Scale. *Psychological Assessment, 12,* 77–88.

Strasser, D.C., Falconer, J.A., & Martino-Saltzman, D. (1994). The rehabilitation team: Staff perceptions of the hospital environment, the interdisciplinary team environment, and interprofessional relations. *Archives of Physical Medicine and Rehabilitation, 75,* 177–182.

Sue, S. (1988). Psychotherapeutic services to ethnic minorities: Two decades of research findings. *American Psychologist, 43,* 301–308.

Sue, S. (1999). Science, ethnicity, and bias: Where have we gone wrong? *American Psychologist, 54,* 1070–1077.

Sue, S., Fujino, D.C., Hu, L., Takeuchi, D.T., & Zane, N.W.S. (1991). Community mental health services for ethnic minority groups: A test of the cultural responsiveness hypothesis. *Journal of Consulting and Clinical Psychology, 59,* 533–540.

Takushi, R., & Uomoto, J.M. (2000). The clinical interview from a multicultural perspective. In L. A. Suzuki, J.G. Ponterotto, & P.J. Meller (Eds.), *The Handbook of Multicultural Assessment: Clinical, Psychological, and Educational Applications* (2nd ed., pp. 47–66). San Francisco: Jossey-Bass.

Thurman, D.J., Alverson, C., Dunn, K.A., Guerrero, J., & Sniezek, J.E. (1999). Traumatic brain injury in the United States: A public health perspective. *Journal of Head Trauma Rehabilitation, 12,* 602–615.

Turkstra, L., Jones, D., & Toler, H.L. (2003). Brain injury and violent crime. *Brain Injury, 17,* 39–47.

Uomoto, J.M., & Wong, T.M. (2000). Multicultural perspectives on the neuropsychology of brain injury assessment and rehabilitation. In E. Fletcher-Janzen, T.L., Strickland,

& C.R. Reynolds (Eds.), *Handbook of Cross-Cultural Neuropsychology* (pp. 169–184). New York: Kluwer Academic/Plenum.

Wagner, A.K., Hammond, F.M., Sasser, H.C., Wiercisiewski, D., & Norton, H.J. (2000). Use of injury severity variables in determining disability and community integration after traumatic brain injury. *Journal of Trauma, 49*, 411–419.

Wagner, A.K., Sasser, H.C., Hammond, F.M., Wiercisiewski, D., & Alexander, J. (2000). Intentional traumatic brain injury: Epidemiology, risk factors, and associations with injury severity and mortality. *Journal of Trauma, 49*, 404–410.

Watanabe, Y., Shiel, A., McLellan, D.L., Kurihara, M., & Hayashi, K. (2001). The impact of traumatic brain injury on family members living with patients: A preliminary study in Japan and the UK. *Disability and Rehabilitation, 23*, 370–378.

Westermeyer, J. (1985). Psychiatric diagnosis across cultural boundaries. *American Journal of Psychiatry, 142*, 798–805.

Whitman, S., Coonley-Hoganson, R., & Desai, B.T. (1984). Comparative head trauma experience in two socioeconomically different Chicago-area communities: A population study. *American Journal of Epidemiology, 4*, 570–580.

Wong, T.M., Strickland, T.L., Fletcher-Janzen, E., Ardila, A., & Reynolds, C.R. (2000). Theoretical and practical issues in the neuropsychological assessment and treatment of culturally dissimilar patients. In E. Fletcher-Janzen, T.L. Strickland, & C.R. Reynolds (Eds.), *Handbook of Cross-Cultural Neuropsychology* (pp. 3–18). New York: Kluwer Academic/Plenum.

Yeates, K.O., Taylor, H.G., Woodrome, S.E., Wade, S.L., Stancin, T., & Drotar, D. (2002). Race as a moderator of parent and family outcomes following pediatric traumatic brain injury. *Journal of Pediatric Psychology, 27*, 393–403.

V

MEDICAL TOPICS

14

Pharmacologic Management
of Spastic Hypertonia

GERARD E. FRANCISCO

Spastic hypertonia is a costly complication of traumatic brain injury (TBI) that contributes to the loss of motor abilities. Along with associated impairments, it results in functional limitations, such as inability to use the hand in daily activities and difficulty with transfers and gait. When severe, it may cause pain and lead to contractures and other permanent deformities. Lance (1980) defined spasticity as "motor disorder characterized by a velocity-dependent increase in tonic stretch reflexes with exaggerated tendon jerks, resulting from hyperexcitability of the stretch reflex, as one component of the upper motor neuron syndrome." While this is the most commonly used definition, it does not accurately describe the entire spectrum of motor disorders observed in clinical practice. Indeed, recent investigations suggest that spastic hypertonia may not be the sole cause of these impairments and functional limitations. (Ada et al., 1998; Gracies, 2001; Gracies et al., 2002; Levin et al., 2000; Sgouros & Seri, 2002) Rather, the abnormalities associated with the upper motor neuron syndrome—dystonia, cocontraction of agonists and antagonists, clonus, weakness, incoordination—are also believed to play important, if not predominant, roles. Although the root cause of this problem has not been well established, therapeutic efforts have focused on peripheral (e.g., altering muscle properties through physical techniques) and central strategies (e.g., influencing neurotransmission through gamma-aminobutyric acid–mediated medications and modifying reciprocal inhibition through chemodenervation).

When brought to the attention of a clinician, the impact of spastic hypertonia and associated abnormalities on a TBI survivor's function and well-being are embodied by physical deformities and performance deficiencies. Thus, it is logical to direct treatment not only to the underlying pathologic phenomena at the central nervous system level, but also to the resulting physical abnormalities. In addition to medications, physical interventions (e.g., sustained stretch) and surgical procedures have been used. Frequently, these modalities are used concurrently in order to achieve a satisfactory treatment outcome.

The choice of treatment largely depends on the severity (i.e., the resultant physical deformities) and significance (i.e., the impact on an individual's abilities and well-being, regardless of severity) of spastic hypertonia. Although these are the most important determinants of treatment goals, other considerations include topographic involvement (i.e., focal vs. generalized spastic hypertonia), disease etiology, previous response to therapies, ability to tolerate medication side effects, duration of disease, and cost. Astute clinicians take these multiple factors into consideration when designing treatment for a TBI survivor encumbered by spastic hypertonia.

While it cannot be denied that various treatment modalities are successful in clinical practice, there is relatively little evidence from well-designed investigations to support them. In particular, few studies have specifically investigated the effectiveness of spastic hypertonia treatment in persons with TBI. This chapter reviews these investigations and summarizes their findings. Recommendations for considerations for future studies are also made.

METHOD

Literature Search Strategy

A literature search using MEDLINE was used to identify all trials from 1967 to 2003 that evaluated pharmacologic treatment of spastic hypertonia in TBI. Key terms used were *brain injuries*, *head injuries*, and *spasticity*. The names of specific medications were also used in the search. In an effort to be exhaustive, both prospective and retrospective studies were considered, as were studies that used either experimental or quasi-experimental designs. Also considered were investigations in which different diagnostic populations were enrolled in the same trial. Since this procedure revealed few double-blind, placebo-controlled trials, case series were also included, but single case reports and abstracts were excluded.

Every effort was made to identify all articles in English that dealt with pharmacologic treatment of lower limb spastic hypertonia in adults. Of the 1167 citations and abstracts assessed for suitability, 90 were considered for a semifinal review. Among the excluded papers were review articles, single case series, and those that did not address the primary interest of this chapter: management of spastic hypertonia in TBI. A final evaluation excluded small case series. It was felt that including papers that investigated certain drugs (specifically, oral spasmolytics, phenol, and intrathecal baclofen) would be beneficial to identify gaps and opportunities in research. This final review resulted in the 34 studies used in the preparation of this report.

This chapter will discuss each drug category and, within each section, will summarize and critique the study design, method, and treatment outcomes. Lastly, comments about the state of the science of spasticity management in TBI, and recommendations for future studies, will be made.

Oral Medications

Study Design and Methods

Only three studies (Basmajian et al., 1984; Bes et al., 1988; Meythaler et al., 2001) of oral spasmolytics were included in this review, two of which were double-blind, randomized, placebo-controlled, crossover investigations (Basmajian et al., 1984; Meythaler et al., 2001). One study (Bes et al., 1998) was a comparative evaluation of the efficacy of diazepam versus ketazolam versus placebo. In the other study (Meythaler et al., 2001), the efficacy of tizanidine against placebo was evaluated. The remaining investigation compared the efficacy of tizanidine against diazepam (Bes, 1988).

Samples

Not one of the studies was exclusive to TBI survivors, and none reported a separate analysis of the subsample of TBI subjects. Thus, the results of the studies are difficult to generalize to the TBI population. Sample sizes were small (range, 2–16). The total number of TBI participants in all three studies was 26 out of 173 subjects.

Beyond the usual demographic data, some important patient characteristics were not reported, such as ambulatory status at study entry. The studies did not report disease duration. Thus, improvement cannot be clearly attributed to treatment, since natural recovery may have played a role. Similarly, chronic complications (e.g., contractures) may have accounted for the observed poor response to treatment in some cases.

Interventions

Doses of the medications varied among the studies but were all within the range of clinical use. None of the studies gave a detailed description of concomitant or subsequent physiotherapy or use of other physical modalities.

Outcome Measures

Only one study (Meythaler et al., 2001) used a formal assessment tool for muscle hypertonia (Ashworth Scale; Ashworth, 1964] in addition to goniometric measurement. Other assessment measures used included patient self-ratings and objective measures. The latter included muscle strength assessment, clonus and spasm frequency, and electrophysiologic monitoring. None of these measures have been validated in the TBI population. Only the Ashworth score has been tested for reliability; its interrater reliability is in question (Blackburn et al., 2002; Bohannon & Smith, 1987).

As in many studies of management of spastic hypertonia in various patient populations, the most commonly used outcome measures assessed impairment rather than function. Only one investigation (Bes et al., 1988) attempted to study the impact of treatment on ambulation. Moreover, the accompanying signs and symptoms of the upper motor neuron syndrome—cocontraction of agonist and antagonist muscle groups, incoordination—were largely ignored. It must be pointed out, however, that the majority of the studies of oral medications reviewed antedate the investigations that have suggested the important roles of the various deficits coexisting with spastic hypertonia.

Assessments were performed about every 1–2 weeks, but the duration of follow-up assessment was short, with most studies terminating after 6–12 weeks. The longest study was conducted over a 16-week period (Meythaler et al., 2001). Thus, while some medications showed superiority over placebo in decreasing hypertonia and improving range of motion, the effects of their long-term use are unknown.

Results

Diazepam, ketazolam, and tizanidine showed effects that were superior to placebo on various outcome measures. Table 14.1 summarizes the results of each study cited.

Nerve Blocks

Study Design and Methods

Only six studies (Albert et al., 2002; Chua & Kong, 2000; Garland et al., 1984; Keenan et al., 1987, 1990; Moore & Anderson, 1991) on neurolysis for spasticity management were included in this review. All were case series reporting results of neurolysis using etidocaine, phenol, or ethyl alcohol.

Samples

Similar to studies on oral medications, investigations on nerve blocks used samples of mixed diagnoses. Disease duration ranged from 1 to 134 months.

Table 14.1. Oral Medications

STUDY	STUDY DESIGN	INTERVENTION GROUPS/INTERVENTION	INTERVAL POST-TBI	TREATMENT DURATION	FOLLOW-UP	OUTCOME MEASURES	RESULTS
Bes et al. (1988)	Randomized, double-blind, parallel group	$N = 105$ hemiplegics (16 cranial trauma, 89 stroke) Two groups well matched for sex, age, height, and body weight: Tizanidine (5 TBI) started at 6 mg/d and titrated up to maximum of 24 mg/d within 2 wk (mean dosage at week 8: 17.08 mg/d) Diazepam (11 TBI) started at 7.5 mg/d and titrated up to maximum of 30 mg/d (mean dosage at week 8: 19.52 mg/d)	Not reported, but mean duration of difficult walking was 20.08 ± 5.59 and 23.06 ± 4.43 mo for the tizanidine and diazepam groups, respectively	8 wk	Varied for different measures, but in general, before and after treatment	Duration of muscle contraction in the stretch reflex Angle at which contraction occurred Clonus Biceps and quadriceps strength assessed before treatment, and at wk 2 and 8 (but only for those with abnormalities before start of treatment) Walking distance on flat and rough ground Subjective (investigator's impression of improvement)	15 subjects on tizanidine and 6 on diazepam dropped out due to side effects Tizanidine group improved walking distance on flat ground; 3 of 11 bedridden subjects on tizanidine and 2 of 4 bedridden subjects on diazepam became ambulatory Both groups demonstrated improvement in duration of muscle contractions, and in the angle at which contractions occurred, but there was no statistically significant difference between them *(continued)*

Table 14.1. Continued

STUDY	STUDY DESIGN	INTERVENTION GROUPS/INTERVENTION	INTERVAL POST-TBI	TREATMENT DURATION	FOLLOW-UP	OUTCOME MEASURES	RESULTS
							Clonus improved in 48.3% and 40% of those on tizanidine and diazepam, respectively
							Drugs had no effect on muscle strength
							Drowsiness and fatigue were most commonly reported side effects in both groups
							Comment: Results were based on entire sample, not on TBI subjects alone
Basmajian et al. (1984)	Randomized, double-blind, crossover	2 TBI survivors out of 50 subjects, but neither completed the study Three treatment conditions: ketazolam 10 and 20 mg/d (1 wk each)	Not reported	45 days; 14 days for active treatment, separated by 1 day for washout	Weekly, at start and end of each treatment condition	Used an ordinal rating scale (0 = nil to 4 = marked) Subjective (pain, motor status, spasms) Objective (resistance to	Ketazolam and diazepam groups conditions better than placebo groups on most outcomes ($p < .05$) but no significant difference between ketazolam and diazepam groups

		Diazepam 5 and 10 mg/d (1 wk each) Placebo (2 wk)		Group A: ketazolam→ diazepam→ placebo Group B: diazepam→ ketazolam→ placebo	passive stretching, ROM, deep tendon reflexes, pathologic reflexes, clonus, associated movements, muscle power, activities of daily living) Technical (electromyography of quadriceps muscle group on the worse side)	Comment: Results were based on entire sample, not on TBI subjects alone
Meythaler et al. (2001)	Randomized, double-blind, placebo-controlled, crossover	8 TBI survivors among 17 subjects Two treatment conditions: Placebo Tizanidine 4 mg qHS titrated to goal of 12–36 mg/d	Not reported	16 wk total 6 wk drug titration→ 1 wk taper→ 1 wk washout→ 6 wks placebo titration→ 1 wk taper→ 1 wk washout	Spasm score Reflex score Assessed at start, wks 2, 4, 6, and 8 of each treatment condition	Only 6 tolerated up to nine tizanidine pills (36 mg/d), while 11 tolerated all nine placebo pills Somnolence in 41% of those on tizanidine and none in the placebo group *Tizanidine phase* Wk 4: Improved AS ($p < .0001$), spasm ($p = .0464$), and reflex ($p = .0883$) scores *(continued)*

Table 14.1. Continued

STUDY	STUDY DESIGN	INTERVENTION GROUPS/INTERVENTION	INTERVAL POST–TBI	TREATMENT DURATION	FOLLOW-UP	OUTCOME MEASURES	RESULTS
							Placebo phase Wk 4: Improved AS scores ($p = .0006$), but magnitude less than that of tizanidine
							Tizanidine superior to placebo at wk 4 ($p = .0006$) and wk 6 ($p < .0001$). No difference in effect on muscle strength between placebo and tizanidine
							Comment: Results were based on entire sample, not on TBI subjects alone

AS, Ashworth Scale; ROM, range of motion; TBI, traumatic brain injury.

Sample sizes were small. Across all studies, there were 77 TBI survivors out of 101 subjects.

Interventions

One study used etidocaine 1%, 2 cm^3 for femoral nerve block (Albert et al., 2002). Thus the effect of this treatment was short-term due to the pharmacodynamic property of the drug. Chua and Kong (2000) used ethyl alcohol of varying concentrations (50%–100%) to block the sciatic nerve. The potential effect of different alcohol concentrations could not be ascertained from the data reported. Nerves blocked in other studies include the musculocutaneous (Keenan et al., 1990), ulnar (Garland et al., 1984; Keenan et al., 1987), and tibial (Moore & Anderson, 1991) nerves.

Outcome Measures

Two studies (Albert et al., 2002; Chua & Kong) used either the Ashworth Scale or its modification as the primary measure. Other impairment measures used included range of motion, velocity of voluntary knee extension, and clonus duration.

Results

Etidocaine nerve block of the femoral nerve resulted in reduction of quadriceps tone (Albert et al., 2002). Alcohol neurolysis of the sciatic nerve caused an improvement in modified Ashworth scores up to 6 months postintervention and, in some subjects, improvement in ambulation quality and wheelchair positioning (Chua & Kong, 2000). Similar observations were noted when the musculocutaneous (Keenan et al., 1990), ulnar (Garland et al., 1984; Keenan et al., 1987), and tibial (Moore & Anderson, 1991) nerves were blocked with phenol. The results are summarized in Table 14.2.

Chemodenervation

Study Design and Methods

Four randomized, double-blind, placebo-controlled, parallel group trials (Burbaud et al., 1996; Childers et al., 1996; Richardson et al., 2000; Smith et al., 2000), one randomized, single-blinded study (Francisco et al., 2002), and seven case series (Dengler et al., 1992; Dunne et al., 1995; Pavesi et al., 1998; Pierson et al., 1996; Reiter et al., 1998; Suputtitada, 2002; Yablon et al., 1996) on botulinum toxin A were reviewed. Only one case series on the use of botulinum toxin B has been published (Brashear et al., 2003). That study used a diagnostically mixed sample and investigated treatment effects only in the upper limbs.

Table 14.2. Phenol, Alcohol and Anesthetic Nerve Blocks

STUDY	STUDY DESIGN	INTERVENTIONAL GROUPS AND INTERVENTION	INTERVAL POST-TBI	TREATMENT DURATION	FOLLOW-UP	OUTCOME MEASURES	RESULTS
Garland et al. (1984)	Case series	11 TBI survivors received percutaneous blocks of the motor branches of the median and ulnar nerves using phenol 3% or 5%	3–14 mo (mean, 5.8 mo)	8 patients received only one injection, while 2 received two injections, and 1 received three injections	Not specified	Active and passive ROM	Mean increase in wrist extension resting angle was 25 degrees Only complications reported were minor tenderness and swelling at the injection site
Keenan et al. (1990)	Case series	17 TBI survivors underwent a total of 23 musculocutaneous nerve blocks	Not reported	15 patients received injections only once; 2 required reinjection due to a poor response after the first one	Mean follow-up duration was 21 mo	ROM	Elbow ROM improved by a mean of 53 degrees. Mean resting position decreased from 120 degrees of flexion to 69 degrees Mean duration of effectiveness of block was 5 mo

Study	Design	Subjects/Treatment	Time post-TBI	Frequency	Assessment	Outcome Measures	Results
Chua et al. (2000)	Case series	3 TBI survivors out of 8 subjects with hemiplegia and severe knee flexor spasticity. Ethyl alcohol 50%–100% (with 1% lidocaine) injected to sciatic nerve using repetitive mono-polar electric stimulation	1–5 mo post-TBI	One-time treatment	Assessed before and 1, 3, and 6 mo after treatment	MAS; Passive knee extension ROM; Visual assessment of gait	MAS scores of knee flexors improved significantly at 1 ($p < .005$), 3 ($p < .01$), and 6 ($p < .02$) mo postinjection. 2 out of 3 TBI subjects had functional improvement. Comment: Results were based on entire sample, not on TBI subjects alone
Albert et al. (2002)	Case series, open label	2 TBI survivors out of 12 subjects with hemiplegia disabled by quadriceps overactivity. Etidocaine 1%, 2 cm^3 was injected to block the branch of the femoral nerve to either the vastus intermedius or lateralis. Block was efficient when maximum motor response of the muscles was at least 50% lower than the initial value upon supramaximal stimulation of the femoral nerve	Not reported	One-time treatment	Before and after the block (how long after the block?)	AS; Voluntary knee extension velocity; Gait analysis (velocity and length of stride)	Decrease in quadriceps spasticity, but results were difficult to interpret based on the data reported. Comment: Results were based on entire sample, not on TBI subjects alone

AS, Ashworth Scale; MAS, Modified Ashworth Scale; ROM, range of motion; TBI, traumatic brain injury.

Samples

Collectively, there were 82 TBI survivors among 289 subjects in all 12 studies. The four randomized, double-blind, placebo-controlled, parallel group trials (Burbaud et al., 1996; Childers et al., 1996; Richardson et al., 2000; Smith et al., 2000) accounted for only 20 of the TBI subjects. Only two of the case series studied TBI survivors exclusively (Pavesi et al., 1998; Yablon et al., 1996). Disease duration varied widely within a given study. Onset of disease prior to intervention ranged from 1 month to 22 years. One study (Dengler et al., 1992) did not report this information. Since many studies with mixed samples did not analyze the subsample of TBI survivors separately, the outcome data are for subjects with all diagnoses combined. As with most spastic hypertonia interventional studies, the main entry criterion was impairment severity.

Interventions

Currently, botulinum toxin is manufactured and marketed either as Botox-A or Dysport. Although both preparations are expressed in units, their potencies differ unit per unit. It is estimated that 1 unit of Botox is equivalent to 3 to 4 units of Dysport. Both are available in Europe, but only Botox-A is commercially available in the United States as of this writing. Nine studies used Botox-A (Childers et al., 1996; Dunne et al., 1995; Francisco et al., 2002; Pavesi et al., 1998; Pierson et al., 1996; Reiter et al., 1998; Richardson et al., 2000; Suputtitada, 2002; Yablon et al., 1996), and the remaining three used Dysport. (Burbaud et al., 1996; Dengler et al., 1992; Smith et al., 2000). Botox-A doses ranged from 20 to 500 units. Dysport doses used in the studies ranged from 500 to 1500 units. One study (Dengler et al., 1992) reported Dysport doses ranging from 2.5 to 25 ng.

Most studies used fixed doses of the toxin. Six (Dengler et al., 1992; Dunne et al., 1995; Pierson et al., 1996; Richardson et al., 2000; Reiter et al., 1998; Suputtitada, 2002) allowed the use of different doses. One Dysport study (Smith, 2001) compared three different doses of the drug to placebo. Commonly injected muscles were the biceps, flexor carpi and flexor digitorum, gastrocnemius, soleus, and tibialis posterior. Many studies predetermined the muscles to be injected (Childers et al., 1996; Francisco et al., 2002; Reiter et al., 1998; Smith, 2000; Suputtitada, 2002). Injection techniques reported were variable and included electromyographic guidance and electrical stimulation to identify motor points. Study methods and intervention groups are summarized in Table 14.3.

Outcome Measures

Once again, the primary outcome measure of most studies is the Ashworth Scale or its modified form. Several other studies used ambulation, usually measured as gait velocity, as a secondary measure.

Except for one report (Suputtitada, 2002) on the long-term effects (up to 2 years) of repeated toxin injections, the studies were limited to one-time treatment.

Post-treatment assessment in most studies was performed between 4 and 12 weeks. One study (Burbaud et al., 1996) performed a follow-up at 120 days postinjection and another (Dunne et al., 1995) up to 6 months post-treatment, a time period that goes beyond the usual duration of effect of botulinum toxin A in many clinical settings.

Results

All the studies showed that botulinum toxin, whether Botox-A or Dysport, was effective in decreasing spastic hypertonia and, in certain subjects, improving gait speed. Interestingly, it also appeared that adjunctive ankle taping enhanced the effects of botulinum toxin (Reiter et al., 1998). Most studies included subjects with various diagnoses, but a separate analysis for the TBI subsample was not carried out. Therefore, results represent the outcomes combined over disease etiologies. Details of the study results are summarized in Table 14.3.

Intrathecal Therapies

Study Design and Methods

Fifteen studies were considered for review (Avellino & Loeser, 2000; Becker et al., 1997, 2000; Cuny et al., 2001; Dario et al., 2002; Francois et al., 2001; Lazorthes et al., 1990; Meythaler et al., 1996, 1997, 1999a, 1999b; Rawicki, 1999; Remy-Neris et al., 2003; Rifici et al., 1994; Saltuari et al., 1989). Four studies (Meythaler et al., 1996, 1997, 1999a, 1999b) were randomized, double-blind, placebo-controlled, crossover trials, and the rest were case series. It must be pointed out that the studies that employed the randomized, double-blind, placebo-controlled, crossover design did so in only one phase of the study (intrathecal baclofen bolus injection during the screening trial) and then employed an open-label design (Meythaler, 1996, 1997, 1999a, 1999b).

Samples

Collectively, 99 TBI survivors were studied in the 15 reports. Disease duration ranged from 1 month to 14 years prior to study entry. Only four studies were devoted exclusively to TBI survivors (Avellino & Loeser, 2000; Cuny et al., 2001; Meythaler et al., 1997; Saltuari et al., 1989).

Interventions

Thus far, baclofen is the only medication used in studies investigating the effects of intrathecal therapies in TBI-related spastic hypertonia. Elsewhere in the literature, medications such as clonidine (Remy-Nerys et al., 2001), morphine (Erickson et al., 1989; Gatscher et al., 2001), and fentanyl (Chabal et al., 1992) have been reported in the spinal cord population.

Table 14.3. Botulinum Toxin

STUDY	STUDY DESIGN	INTERVENTIONAL GROUPS AND INTERVENTION	INTERVAL POST-TBI	FOLLOW-UP	OUTCOME MEASURES	RESULTS
Dengler et al. (1992)	Retrospective	5 TBI survivors among 10 subjects who received Dysport 2.5–25 ng (mean, 23.5 ng)	13 mo (range, 4–30 mo) Comment: Based on entire sample, not on TBI subjects alone	4 wk	AS ROM Pain Scale	Improved AS (7/10) and ROM (4/6) Decreased pain (4/4) Comment: Results were based on entire sample, not on TBI subjects alone
Dunne et al. (1995)	Case series, open label, single blind	1 TBI survivor among 40 subjects who were injected with Botox to either the upper (mean dose 175 u; range, 70–270) or lower limb (mean dose 221 u; range 100–500 u)	Not reported	Two baseline assessments 3–4 wks apart, and then at 4–6 wks, or 4–6 mo post-injection	MAS Spasm Frequency Scale Lindmark's modified motor assessment Joint angle measurement Pain Score	Results difficult to interpret because of mixed diagnosis and different limbs. Also, follow-up times were different Reported improvement in MAS, pain, ROM, and function Comment: Results were based on entire sample, not on TBI subjects alone

Reference	Design	Subjects	Age	Follow-up	Outcome measures	Results
Burbaud et al. (1996)	Randomized, double-blind, placebo-controlled, parallel group	4 TBI survivors out of 23 who received either placebo or 1000 Dysport plus therapy	Mean, 23.5 mo (range = 3.5–120 mo) Comment: Based on entire sample, not on TBI subjects alone	120 d	MAS; Gait velocity; Fugl-Meyer Scale; Subjective response of subjects	MAS, Fugl-Meyer, and subjective reports were significantly improved, while gait velocity showed trend toward improvement. Comment: Results were based on entire sample, not on TBI subjects alone
Pierson et al. (1996)	Retrospective	17 TBI survivors among 39 subjects; 17 of 39 subjects had lower limb Botox injections (how many TBI survivors?)	1 mo–6 yr Comment: Results were based on entire sample, not on TBI subjects alone	Not applicable (N/A)	AS; ROM; Brace wear; Gait velocity; Pain Scale	Improved AS, ROM, brace wear tolerance. Gait velocity improved by about 14%. Pain: 10/13 improved. Comment: Results were based on entire sample not on TBI subjects alone
Childers et al. (1996)	Randomized, double-blind, placebo-controlled, parallel group	2 TBI survivors out of 17 subjects who received Botox 50 unit in the gastrocnemius: Group A: injected proximally in a site near the muscle origin; Group B: injected distally at three sites along the midbelly	2.42–5.17 yr	Two baseline assessments 1 wk apart, and then at 1 and 4 wk postinjection	MAS; Fugl-Myer Scale; Ankle ROM; Timed 50 ft fastest walk	MAS improved in Group B at wk 4. No statistically significant difference in outcome between the two groups. Comment: Results were based on entire sample, not on TBI subjects alone. Note: the 2 TBI patients had worsening of MAS scores at wk 4, although ROM scores improved

(*continued*)

Table 14.3. Continued

STUDY	STUDY DESIGN	INTERVENTIONAL GROUPS AND INTERVENTION	INTERVAL POST-TBI	FOLLOW-UP	OUTCOME MEASURES	RESULTS
Reiter et al. (1998)	Case series, open label	2 TBI survivors among 17 subjects who received a mean dose of 165 u Botox (range, 100–210 u)	Mean 28.4 mo Comment: Based on entire sample, not on TBI subjects alone	6 mo	ROM MAS MRC Motor Scale Motricity Index Visual Analog Scale FAT FIM Nottingham Health profile (pain, energy level, physical disabilities)	Improved ROM and MAS in elbow and wrist; MRC, Visual Analog Scale and Nottingham profile improved Comment: Results were based on entire sample and not on TBI subjects only
Yablon et al. (1996)	Case series, open label	21 TBI survivors who received 20–40 u Botox under EMG guidance	142 d–89 mo	12 wk	PROM MAS	ROM and MAS significantly improved
Pavesi et al. (1998)	Case series, open label	6 TBI survivors who received various doses (mean 96 u) of Botox to upper limb muscles. 3 received 1 injection only, while the other 3 received a second injection 1.5–3.5 mo after the first.	Spasticity present for a mean of 4.5 mo (range, (4–6 mo)	1 wk, 1, 3, 6, and 12 mo after each injection Mean follow-up 10 mo (range 4–19 mo)	MAS ROM Clinical evaluation of postural improvement, voluntary movement and changes in limb function	Improved MAS and ROM Functional improvement noted (recovery of ability to write, dress and eat independently)

Reference	Design	Sample/Intervention	Comments	Duration	Outcome Measures	Results
Smith et al. (2000)	Randomized, double-blind, placebo-controlled, parallel group	2 TBI survivors out of 21 subjects who received Dysportin spastic elbow, wrist and finger muscles: Group A: placebo Group B: 500 u Group C: 1000 u Group D: 1500 u	Difficult to abstract from the report because of mixed diagnoses	6 and 12 wk	MAS ROM Posture Disability measures (Frenchay Arm Test; upper body dressing time) Patient-reported Global Assessment Scale	Decreased MAS and improved ROM at 6 wk; effect gone by 12 wk Higher doses resulted in greater MAS reduction but did not appear to affect duration Comment: Results based on entire sample, not on TBI subjects alone
Richardson et al. (2001)	Randomized, double-blind, placebo-controlled, parallel group	12 TBI survivors among 52 subjects who received either placebo or Botox 300–500 u to the upper and lower extremities, followed by therapy	Mean 35 mo (range, 3 mo – 22 yr) Comment: Results were based on entire sample, not on TBI subjects alone	12 wk	AS ROM Timed ambulation (10 min) Goal Attainment Scale Rivermead Motor Assessment Nine-hole peg test Subject problem rating	AS improved in both groups but more in Botox group ROM increased in Botox group Time ambulation and nine-hole peg test unchanged Goal attainment improved for both groups Rivermead scores and subject problem ratings of better lower limb function in Botox group Comment: Results were based on entire sample, not on TBI subjects alone

(continued)

Table 14.3. Continued

STUDY	STUDY DESIGN	INTERVENTIONAL GROUPS AND INTERVENTION	INTERVAL POST-TBI	FOLLOW-UP	OUTCOME MEASURES	RESULTS
Suputtitada (2002)	Case series, open label	6 TBI survivors among 20 subjects who received Botox in the toe flexors or great toe extensor. Those with AS score of 2 received 25 u, AS = 3, received 50 u, and AS = 4, received 75 u	6–12 mo	Baseline, 2 and 4 wk post-treatment, and every month thereafter until MAS scores returned to baseline	MAS Visual analog scale for pain Visual analog scale for function	Improvement in all outcome measures. Most benefited up to 5–6 mo, some up to 2 yr Comment: Results were based on entire sample, not on TBI subjects alone
Francisco et al. (2002)	Randomized, single-blinded, parallel group	3 TBI survivors out of 13 subjects who received Botox in the wrist and finger flexors: Group A: 240 u (100 u/ml) Group B: 240 u (50 u/ml) (Note: 60 u each to the flexor carpi radialis, flexor carpi ulnaris, flexor digitorum superficialis, and flexor digitorum profundus)	Mean disease duration: Group A: 50.4 mo Group B: 27.7 mo Comment: Based on entire sample, not on TBI subjects alone	4, 8, 12 wk	MAS Clinician Global Rating Scale Patient/Caregiver Global Rating Scale	No difference between groups, but significant improvement in MAS scores at 4, 8, and 12 wk ($p < .05$)

AS, Ashworth Scale; FIM, Functional Independence Measure; MAS, modified Ashworth Scale; PROM, passive range of motion; ROM, range of motion; TBI, traumatic brain injury.

Most of the studies assessed the effects of both a single intrathecal baclofen bolus and the continuous intrathecal infusion of baclofen via an implanted pump. Some of the case series investigated only the effects of a single bolus-intrathecal injection of baclofen or continuous infusion through an external catheter. Although some studies acknowledged that the patients received physiotherapy after pump implantation, the frequency, intensity, and type of physiotherapy were not reported.

Outcome Measures

The Ashworth score was the main outcome measure for most studies. Other measures of impairment used were reflex and spasm frequency scores. While many studies noted unexpected functional improvements after intrathecal baclofen therapy, only one case series used a functional measure—gait analysis—as a predetermined outcome measure (Remy-Neris et al., 2003).

Apart from reporting the impact on related impairments, such as clonus, studies did not systematically measure other phenomena that accompany spastic hypertonia, such as agonist-antagonist cocontraction and reduction of motor control and coordination.

The longest follow-up duration in the studies was up to 10 years (Rawicki, 1999). However, subjects in that study had varied follow-up periods. In one randomized trial, the endpoint was at 12 months (Meythaler et al., 1999b).

Results

All studies reported a decrease in spastic hypertonia and related impairments. Additionally, the case series that specifically investigated the effects of bolus intrathecal baclofen on function found an improvement in gait speed and other ambulation parameters (Remy-Neris et al., 2003). Details of the study results are outlined in Table 14.4.

SUMMARY

Study Design and Method

Although spastic hypertonia is a frequent complication of TBI, there are only a few studies addressing its pathophysiology, natural history, and management. Among these, randomized controlled trials (RCTs), the so-called gold standard of clinical studies, are rare. While it is tempting to recommend that more studies using this design should be conducted in the future, one must first consider its limitations, especially in light of the challenges imposed by the natural evolution, assessment, and management of spastic hypertonia in clinical practice. Many motor problems associated with TBI that are characterized by muscle

Table 14.4. Intrathecal Baclofen

STUDY	STUDY DESIGN	INTERVENTIONAL GROUPS	INTERVAL POST-TBI	FOLLOW-UP	OUTCOME MEASURES	RESULTS
Saltuari et al. (1992)	Case series, open label	6 TBI survivors ("traumatic apallic syndrome") out of 9 subjects who received ITB pump after intrathecal bolus of baclofen Tip of catheter at least at T8–T9	2–32 mo	11 d–29 mo	AS Reflexes Bladder function	Varied improvement in outcome measures from subject to subject
Rifici et al. (1994)	Case series, open label	8 TBI survivors (GCS not reported) Tip of catheter at T10	2–32 mo	0.3–10.6 mo	AS Reflex score	AS and reflex scores improved
Meythaler et al. (1996)	Randomized, double-blind, placebo-controlled, crossover	10 TBI survivors (GCS not reported) out of 11 subjects with spasticity and dystonia of at least 6 mo duration, who received intrathecal bolus injection of either baclofen 50 µg or placebo (saline) via a lumbar puncture Crossover was at 48 hr after initial treatment	Not reported, but patients included if spastic hypertonia in the lower limbs (MAS ≥3; average spasm score ≥2) is present for ≥1 yr	1, 2, 4, and 6 hr postinjection	AS Reflex score Spasm score	Statistically significant improvement in upper and lower limb AS, reflex, and spasm scores with active drug administration but not with placebo Maximum effect noted at 4 hr

Study	Design	Subjects	Duration	Assessment	Measures	Results
Becker et al (1997)	Case series, open label	9 TBI survivors (GCS not reported) out of 18 subjects with spasticity. (6 had severe TBI, while the other 3 had "multiple trauma with head injury but brain damage predominantly resulted from hypoxia" Tip of catheter not reported	1–62 mo	Up to 34 mo	AS Spasm score	Improved AS and spasm scores
Meythaler et al. (1997)	Randomized, double-blind, placebo-controlled, crossover (screening phase), then open label after ITB pump implantation	9 TBI survivors (GCS not reported) out of 12 subjects with spasticity and dystonia of at least 6 mo duration, who received intrathecal bolus injection of either baclofen or placebo (saline) via a lumbar puncture during the screening phase, followed by ITB pump implantation Tip of catheter in mid-thoracic area	>6 mo	Assessment done prior to intrathecal bolus injection and at 3 mo after ITB pump implantation	AS Reflex core Spasm score	Average ITB pump dose 183.8 µg/d (range, 100–412 µg/d) Statistically significant improvement in average upper and lower limb AS, spasm, and reflex scores ($p < .0001$), although magnitude of improvement in the upper limbs was less

(continued)

Table 14.4. Continued

STUDY	STUDY DESIGN	INTERVENTIONAL GROUPS	INTERVAL POST-TBI	FOLLOW-UP	OUTCOME MEASURES	RESULTS
Becker et al. (2000)	Case series, open label	1 TBI survivor (GCS not reported) out of 4 subjects with severe dysautonomia. The TBI subject received intrathecal infusion of baclofen 400 μg/d via a lumbar catheter Tip of catheter not reported	Not reported	TBI subject: up to 5 mo	Signs of dysautonomia	Dysautonomia resolved
Lazorthes et al. (1990)	Case series, open label	1 TBI survivor out of 18 subjects, who received ITB pump Tip of catheter not reported	Not reported	3–37 mo for all. 9 mo for TBI subject	AS Muscle spasms frequency (no formal scale) Function (descriptive)	AS improved in all Painful spasms improved in 16/18 Variable functional improvement Comment: Results were based on entire sample, not on TBI subject alone

Study	Study Design	Subjects	Duration		Outcome Measures	Results
Rawicki (1999)	Case series, open label	13 TBI subjects out of 18 subjects, who received intrathecal bolus injection of either baclofen or placebo (saline) via a lumbar puncture during the screening phase, followed by ITB pump implantation Tip of catheter not reported	5 mo–13 yr	1–10 yr postimplant	MAS Penn Spasm Scale score Snow Hygiene Scale score FIM transfer scale score Subjects divided into two groups: Group 1: Goal was to improve nursing care Group B: Goal was to improve function	Improvement in MAS, hygiene score, and spasm scores in both groups ($p < .001–.038$). Transfer scores improved in group B only
Meythaler et al. (1999a)	Randomized, double-blind, placebo-controlled, crossover (screening phase), then, open label after ITB pump implantation	3 TBI survivors (GCS not reported) out of 6 with spastic hemiplegia, who received intrathecal bolus injection of either baclofen or placebo (saline) via a lumbar puncture during the screening phase, followed by ITB pump implantation Tip of catheter in midthoracic area	>6 mo	Assessment done prior to intrathecal bolus injection and at 3 mo after ITB pump implantation	AS Reflex score Spasm score	Average ITB pump dose 268 µg/d Statistically significant improvement in average lower limb AS ($p < .0001$), reflex scores ($p = 0208$), and average upper limb AS ($p = .0002$) No change in strength on nonhemiplegic side Comment: Results were based on entire sample, not on TBI subjects alone

(continued)

Table 14.4. Continued

STUDY	STUDY DESIGN	INTERVENTIONAL GROUPS	INTERVAL POST-TBI	FOLLOW-UP	OUTCOME MEASURES	RESULTS
Meythaler et al. (1999b)	Randomized, double-blind, placebo-controlled, crossover (screening phase), then open label after ITB pump implantation	17 TBI survivors (GCS not reported); spasticity and dystonia of at least 6 mo duration, who received intrathecal bolus injection of either baclofen or placebo (saline) via a lumbar puncture during the screening phase, followed by ITB pump implantation Tip of catheter in midthoracic area	>6 mo	Assessment done prior to intrathecal bolus injection and at 1 yr after ITB pump implantation	AS Reflex core Spasm score	Average ITB pump dose 302 µg/d Statistically significant improvement in average upper and lower limb AS, spasm, and reflex scores ($p < .0001$)
Avellino & Loeser (2000)	Case series, open label	5 TBI survivors out of 62 subjects who received ITB pump Tip of catheter not reported	Not reported	Mean 28.3 mo (range 3–81 mo) for all Mean 11.8 mo for TBI subjects	AS Spasm score	Improved AS and spasm scores Comment: Results were based on entire sample, not on TBI subjects alone
Cuny et al. (2001)	Case series, open label	4 TBI survivors (GCS 4–7), who received continuous intrathecal infusion of baclofen	23–68 d	Variable	Dysautonomic signs Scale for the first initial stages of	Decrease in dysautonomic episodes correlated with baclofen dose Improved recovery scores

					Outcome	Results
		via a catheter over 6 d, followed by ITB pump implantation if dysautonomia recurred Tip of catheter not reported		head injury coma recovery		AS improved within 48 hr and at 6 mo Signs of dysautonomia improved
Francois et al. (2001)	Case series, open label	4 TBI survivors (GCS 3–4), who received continuous intrathecal infusion of baclofen 25 mg via a catheter, followed by ITB pump implantation Tip of catheter not reported	Mean 25 d (range, 21–31 d)	Within 48 hr of initiation of catheter infusion and up to 6 mo after ITB pump placement	AS	
Dario et al. (2002)	Case series, open label	6 TBI survivors out of 14 subjects, who received bolus intrathecal infusion of baclofen followed by ITB pump implantation Tip of catheter at T7–T9	≥6 yr	Up to mean 23.5 mo (range, 6–65 mo)	AS Spasm score	Improved AS ($p < .05$) and spasm ($p < .001$) scores

(continued)

Table 14.4. Continued

STUDY	STUDY DESIGN	INTERVENTIONAL GROUPS	INTERVAL POST-TBI	FOLLOW-UP	OUTCOME MEASURES	RESULTS
Remy-Neris et al. (2003)	Case series, open label	3 TBI survivors among 7 subjects with spastic hemiplegia involving quadriceps and triceps surae Bolus intrathecal baclofen injection only	1–14 yr	Before and 4 hr after bolus intrathecal injection of baclofen via a lumbar puncture	AS of quadriceps and triceps surae Preferred and maximal walking speed measured by motion analysis system with two force plates EMG of leg muscles	Significant improvement in AS ($p < .05$) and maximal walking speed ($p < .05$) Preferred walking speed was unchanged Minimal knee extension and maximal ankle flexion were the only kinematic data that significantly improved ($p < .05$) Comment: Results were based on entire sample, not on TBI subjects alone

AS, Ashworth Scale; EMG, electromyography; GCS, Glasgow Coma Scale; ITB, intrathecal baclofen therapy; MAS, modified Ashworth Scale; TBI, traumatic brain injury.

tightness, abnormal posturing, and deficits in movement are described as being due to spastic hypertonia. However, one must consider the important question "Is spastic hypertonia solely responsible for deformities and functional penalties, or are other phenomena contributing to the problem?" The ability to clearly define the impact of spastic hypertonia and the other accompanying deficits (i.e., cocontraction of agonist and antagonist muscle groups, weakness, incoordination, loss of motor control) will be helpful in designing studies that will employ accurate outcome measures and render appropriate treatment.

While RCTs have strong internal validity, their external validity is diminished by the use of stringent enrollment criteria and treatment protocols. This assumes that all subjects have the same characteristics. In reality, subjects who present with spastic hypertonia or other motor abnormalities have varying types, degrees, and durations of deformities. They also have different intervention goals (improve perineal hygiene vs. facilitate wearing of orthosis vs. enhance gait). Strict inclusion/exclusion criteria and the use of a rigorous preset treatment algorithm (thereby ignoring the unique needs of a specific individual) limit generalizability of the results of RCTs in all clinical situations, since they do not reflect actual clinical practice. For instance, ankle equinovarus is usually due to abnormalities of the gastrocnemius-soleus complex and the tibialis posterior. However, in some individuals, abnormalities of the tibialis anterior, flexor digitorum longus, and extensor hallucis longus may contribute to the deformity. In a stringent treatment protocol, only one or two muscles will be treated, for example with botulinum toxin injection. Thus it is conceivable that the difference in outcomes may not be due to the actual response to the drug, but rather to the difference in pretreatment muscle involvement.

Potentially useful complements of—not substitutes for—RCTs are observational studies involving a large number of individuals, which are more representative of patients with a specific condition. This design is less restrictive than RCTs and does not exclude many conditions frequently encountered in clinical practice. Referring back to the example in the previous paragraph, an observational study will allow injection of whatever muscle requires it in the clinician's judgment. While this predisposes the study to treatment variability that will definitely account for differences in outcome, it permits the investigation of actual clinical practices. Perhaps a way to control this variability in treatment is to anticipate and incorporate it in a treatment algorithm that clearly defines *allowable protocol deviations* and specifies the type and amount of confounding therapies (e.g., physical therapy in addition to the main experimental treatment, such as Botox injections). Whyte and Hart (2003) advocate the use of a detailed manual to guide researchers in delivering an experimental treatment and other active therapy ingredients.

Patient Selection

In order to make better sense of treatment outcomes, future studies should report subject characteristics more clearly. Several factors may influence a person's response to a specific therapy. For instance, severity of spastic hypertonia, disease duration, functional capabilities and potential, and patient motivation all play a role in therapeutic outcome.

Disease duration is also an important consideration. If enrolled too early in the recovery process, a patient may have a good treatment outcome (e.g., enhancement of function) not due to intervention, but rather to natural recovery. Conversely, when a patient is enrolled many years after TBI and onset of spastic hypertonia, failure to demonstrate a positive change may not be due to nonresponse to treatment, but rather to comorbidities such as contractures. Learned nonuse of the limbs (Taub et al., 1994), similar to what has been observed to develop over time in stroke survivors, may also account for failure to achieve functional progress after intervention. The studies reviewed cannot answer the question "How early should drug treatment be rendered?" This is an important issue, since many spasmolytic drugs have potential negative effects on cognitive recovery due to their effects on the GABAergic and alpha-adrenergic systems (Goldstein, 1998) and muscle paralysis. Hence, the risk-benefit ratio of any therapy should always be considered. One way to study this would be to compare an intervention's short- and long-term efficacy in two comparable groups of TBI subjects, one receiving early and the other delayed treatment.

Many studies enrolled mixed diagnostic groups. Future studies should limit enrollment to those with one diagnosis in order to make the results generalizable to a specific patient population.

Treatment Outcome Measures

Currently, the bulk of the published literature assumes that spastic hypertonia, a velocity-dependent abnormal increase in muscle tone, is the chief cause of the condition to be treated. Yet, the most commonly used measure to assess muscle tone, the Ashworth Scale (Ashworth, 1964), does not reflect the status of other spastic hypertonia–related phenomena. In this respect, the Tardieu Scale (Gracies et al., 2000) may be a better alternative because it considers the velocity of joint movement. However, it also has limitations since it is an impractical measure for certain muscles (e.g., toe flexors) and its interrater reliability in TBI patients has not yet been investigated. A recent study (Blackburn et al., 2002) demonstrated the poor interrater reliability of the Ashworth Scale, except when the score is 0 (no muscle tone abnormality). Other commonly used outcome measures, such as the spasm frequency score and global impression scales, have not been validated in this patient population.

Laboratory assessment tools, such as electrophysiologic monitoring or motion analysis, provide a more objective measure but are not readily available to most clinicians. Also, these tests can help only to the extent that the problem demonstrated is due to spastic hypertonia and not one of the associated motor abnormalities. Clearly, there is a need to develop clinical outcome measures that are simple to administer, valid, and have good intra- and interrater reliability. They should also be ecologically valid (i.e., the outcomes measured should have an impact on real-life situations).

Most studies use measures of tone impairment (e.g., the Ashworth Scale) as the primary outcome measure. However, one must bear in mind that patients do not complain of these impairments, but instead seek help to improve function. A statistically significant decrease in Ashworth scores has no value to TBI survivors unless it translates into an improvement in the ability to walk or use the hand. Thus, a priority for future studies is to refocus attention on functional outcomes rather than impairments. In this regard, individualized assessments, such as the Canadian Occupational Performance Measure (Law et al., 1990), where the patient and the clinician agree on the treatment goals, merit consideration.

Intervention

There have been only a few trials of oral medications in the past few years (Meythaler et al., 2001), perhaps because these drugs are not well tolerated by many TBI survivors due to sedation. For those patients who can overcome this adverse effect, certain medications may be helpful in alleviating spastic hypertonia, but their efficacy compared to that of other treatment options has not yet been evaluated. Perhaps it is time that an oral medication be compared head-to-head with either botulinum toxin or intrathecal baclofen therapies in order to determine if oral drugs have a role in the management of spastic hypertonia.

The long-term effectiveness of phenol and alcohol neurolysis must also be studied, especially because the only other injection therapy for spastic hypertonia, with botulinum toxin, is costly. Similarly, the efficacy and cost effectiveness of repeated injections of botulinum toxin need to be evaluated. The toxin appears to work best only when spastic hypertonia is focal and limited to a few muscles. Thus, its role in TBI survivors with generalized spasticity must be delineated further. None of the existing studies on botulinum toxin have addressed these issues.

Although hundreds of articles on botulinum toxin A for spastic hypertonia have been published in the past few years, only a few of them used an experimental design. Case series have served as the basis for many clinical practices. The toxin has been widely used clinically in the last decade, yet answers to some questions are still needed: What is the optimum dose of botulinum toxin for a specific muscle at a certain degree of spastic hypertonia? Does dilution of the toxin impact the result? What is the role of postinjection physiotherapy and physical modalities in enhancing the treatment outcome?

In the handful of studies on dosing, it appears that higher doses of the toxin result in greater muscle tone reduction. However, this information is limited to only a few muscles, such as the elbow flexors, wrist and finger flexors, and ankle plantarflexors, which are most frequently studied. The doses used for other muscles are largely empiric, based on a clinician's opinion and experience.

Many studies look at the effect of botulinum toxin on only one or two muscles. If functional improvement is an intended outcome, then other muscle groups must also be studied. For instance, many lower limb studies focus solely on the ankle plantarflexors. Spastic hemiplegic gait is due not only to abnormalities around the ankle joint, but also to muscle weakness or muscle hypertonia in the knee and hip regions. Thus, a failure to demonstrate functional improvement may be more likely because not all abnormal muscle groups were treated. This is a typical scenario when strict treatment protocols are used in studies, where only a certain dose can be injected into predetermined muscles. An attractive alternative is to investigate the effect of treatment when all abnormal muscles are injected. Doing so allows for a better assessment of treatment impact on function, but one must recognize its limitation in that a nonstandardized intervention was used.

Studies of combination therapies are needed to determine if this approach is more effective and less costly than monotherapy. It is common clinical practice to combine pharmacologic and nonpharmacologic interventions. For example, patients with severe spastic hypertonia may benefit from intrathecal baclofen therapy to manage the lower limbs, yet may need injections of either phenol or botulinum toxin for certain muscles in the upper limb or shoulder girdle. In other situations, some patients may benefit from a combination of phenol and botulinum toxin therapy for the treatment of proximal and distal spastic muscles, respectively, in the same limb. Some patients also benefit from receiving oral medications for sustained control of hypertonia, but may need an additional botulinum toxin injection to one muscle recalcitrant to the oral drug or because of poor tolerance of adverse effects associated with further dose increases. These treatment approaches, while used widely, are yet to be subjected to formal study.

In clinical practice, many patients receive physiotherapy following pharmacologic intervention, regardless of what drug was used. Hence the role of physiotherapy—both traditional methods, such as serial casting, stretching, and strengthening, and more contemporary strategies, such as constraint-induced movement therapy (Taub et al., 1999)—and partial weight treadmill training (Werner et al., 2002)—need to be elucidated further. The majority of studies done in spastic hypertonia management in TBI have focused on casting. In general, casting has been beneficial in increasing the range of motion, but its role in enhancing function and its actual influence on spastic hypertonia have not been demonstrated (Mortenson & Eng, 2003).

In summary, while significant advances have been made in investigating the effects of various pharmacologic agents for lower limb spastic hypertonia in TBI, there is still a multitude of opportunities for studying the true clinical impact of these treatment modalities. Future studies should not be limited to interventional investigations. Further investigations on the pathophysiology of spastic hypertonia and its associated impairments, the development of valid and reliable assessment measures, and a shift of focus of treatment goals from reducing impairments to enhancing function should complement interventional trials in order to make the results more meaningful and applicable in real-life situations.

REFERENCES

Ada, L., Vattanasilp, W., O'Dwyer, N.J., et al. (1998). Does spasticity contributes to walking dysfunction after stroke? *Journal of Neurology, Neurosurgery, and Psychiatry, 64*, 628–635.

Albert, T.A., Yelnik, A., Bonan, I., et al. (2002). Effectiveness of femoral nerve selective block in patients with spasticity: Preliminary results. *Archives of Physical Medicine and Rehabilitation, 83*, 692.

Ashworth B. (1964). Preliminary trial of carisoprodol in multiple sclerosis. *Practitioner, 192*, 540–543.

Avellino, A.M., & Loeser, J.D. (2000). Intrathecal baclofen for the treatment of intractable spasticity of spine or brain etiology. *Neuromodulation, 3*, 75–81.

Basmajian, J.V., Shakardass, K., Russell, D., et al. (1984). Ketazolam treatment for spasticity: Double-blind study of a new drug. *Archives of Physical Medicine and Rehabilitation, 65*, 698–701.

Becker, R., Alberti, O., & Bauer, B.L. (1997). Continuous intrathecal baclofen infusion in severe spasticity after traumatic or hypoxic brain injury. *Journal of Neurology, 244*, 160–166.

Becker, R., Benes, L., Sure, U., et al. (2000). Intrathecal baclofen alleviates autonomic dysfunction in severe brain injury. *Journal of Clinical Neurosciences, 7*, 316–319.

Bes, A., Eyssette, M., Pierrot-Deseiglligny, et al. (1988). A multi-center, double-blind trial of tizanidine, a new antispastic agent, in spasticity associated with hemiplegia. *Current Medical Residents Opinion, 10*, 709–718.

Blackburn, M., van Vliet, P., & Mockett, S.P. (2002). Reliability of measurements obtained with the Modified Ashworth Scale in the lower extremities of people with stroke. *Physical Therapy, 82*, 25–34.

Bohannon, R.W., & Smith, M.B. (1987). Interrater reliability of a modified Ashworth scale of muscle spasticity. *Physical Therapy, 67*, 206–207.

Brashear, A., McAfee, A.l., Kuhn, E.R., et al. (2003). Treatment with botulinum toxin type B for upper-limb spasticity. *Archives of Physical Medicine and Rehabilitation, 84*, 103–107.

Burbaud, P., Wiart, L., Dubos, J.L., et al. (1996). A randomized, double-blind, placebo controlled trial of botulinum toxin in the treatment of spastic foot in hemiparetic patients. *Journal of Neurology, Neurosurgery, and Psychiatry, 61*, 265–269.

Chabal, C., Jacobson, L., & Terman, G. (1992). Intrathecal fentanyl alleviates spasticity in the presence of tolerance to intrathecal baclofen. *Anesthesiology, 76*(Pt 2), 312.

Childers, M.K., Stacy, M., & Cooke, D.L. (1996). Comparison of two injection techniques using botulinum toxin in the treatment of spastic hemiplegia. *American Journal of Physical Medicine and Rehabilitation, 75,* 462.

Chua, K.S.G., & Kong, K.-H. (2000). Alcohol neurolysis of the sciatic nerve in the treatment of hemiplegic knee flexor spasticity: Clinical outcomes. *Archives of Physical Medicine and Rehabilitation, 81,* 1432–1435.

Cuny, E., Richer, E., & Castel, J.P. (2001). Dysautonomia syndrome in the acute recovery phase after traumatic brain injury: Relief with intrathecal baclofen therapy. *Brain Injury, 15,* 917–925.

Dario, A., Di Stefano, M.G., Grossi, A., et al. (2002). Long-term intrathecal baclofen infusion in supraspinal spasticity of adulthood, *Acta Neurologica Scandinavica, 105,* 83.

Dengler, R., Neyer, U., Wohlfarth, K., et al. (1992). Local botulinum toxin in the treatment of spastic drop foot. *Journal of Neurology, 239,* 375–378.

Dunne, J.W., Heye, N., & Dunne, S.L. (1995). Treatment of chronic limb spasticity with botulinum toxin A. *Journal of Neurology, Neurosurgery, and Psychiatry, 58,* 232–235.

Erickson, D.l., Lo, J., & Michaelson, M. (1989). Control of intractable spasticity with intrathecal morphine sulfate. *Neurosurgery, 24*(Pt 2), 236.

Francisco, G.E., Boake, C., & Vaughn, A. (2002). Botulinum toxin in upper limb spasticity after acquired brain injury. *American Journal of Physical Medicine and Rehabilitation, 81,* 355–363.

Francois, B., Vacher, P., Roustan, J., et al. (2001). Intrathecal baclofen after traumatic brain injury: Early treatment using a new technique to prevent spasticity. *Journal of Trauma, Infection, and Critical Care, 50,* 158–161.

Garland, D.E., Lilling, M., & Keenan, M.A. (1984). Percutaneous phenol blocks to motor points of spastic forearm muscles in head-injured adults. *Archives of Physical Medicine and Rehabilitation, 65,* 243–245.

Gatscher, S., Becker, R., & Bertanlanffy H. (2001). Combined intrathecal baclofen and morphine infusion for the treatment of spasticity related pain and central deafferentation pain. *Acta Neurochirurgica, 72*(Suppl), 75–76.

Goldstein, L.B. (1998). Potential effects of common drugs on stroke recovery. *Archives of Neurology, 55,* 454–456

Gracies, J.M. (2001). Pathophysiology of impairment in patients with spasticity and use of stretch as a treatment of spastic hypertonia. *Physical Medicine and Rehabilitation Clinics of North America, 12,* 747–768.

Gracies, J.M., Marosszeky, J.E., Renton, R., et al. (2000). Short-term effects of dynamic Lycra splints on upper limb in hemiplegic patients. *Archives of Physical Medicine and Rehabilitation, 81,* 1547.

Gracies, J.M., Weisz, D.J., Yang, B.Y., et al. (2002). Spastic co-contraction and movement speed: effects of botulinum toxin type A injection into an agonist. *Annals of Neurology, Suppl 1,* S89.

Keenan, M.A., Todderud, E.P., Henderson, R., & Botte, M. (1987). Management of intrinsic spasticity in the hand with phenol injection or neurectomy of the motor branch of the ulnar nerve. *Journal of Hand Surgery, 12,* 734–739.

Keenan, M.A.E., Tomas, E.S., Stone, L., et al. (1990). Percutaneous phenol block of the musculocutaneous nerve to control elbow flexor spasticity. *Journal of Hand Surgery, 15A,* 340–346.

Lance, J.W. (1980). Symposium synopsis. In R.G. Feldman, R.R. Young, & W.P. Koella (Eds.), *Spasticity Disordered Motor Control* (pp 487–489). Chicago: Year Book.

Law, M., Baptiste, S., McColl, M., et al. (1990). The Canadian occupational performance measure: An outcome measure for occupational therapy. *Canadian Journal of Occupational Therapy, 57*, 82–7.

Lazorthes, Y., Caute-Sallerin, B., Verdie, J.C., et al. (1990). Chronic intrathecal baclofen administration for control of severe spasticity. *Journal of Neurosurgery, 72*, 393–402.

Levin, M.F., Selles, R.W., Verheul, M.H.G., et al. (2000). Deficits in the coordination of agonist and antagonist muscles in stroke patients: Implications for normal motor control. *Brain Research, 853*, 352–369.

Meythaler, J.M., DeVivo, M.J., & Hadley, M. (1996). Prospective study on the use of bolus intrathecal baclofen for spastic hypertonia due to acquired brain injury. *Archives of Physical Medicine and Rehabilitation, 77*, 461–466.

Meythaler, J.M., Guin-Renfroe, S., Grabb, P., & Hadley, M.N. (1999a). Long term continuously infused intrathecal baclofen for spastic–dystonic hypertonia in traumatic brain injury: 1 year experience. *Archives of Physical Medicine and Rehabilitation, 80*, 13–19.

Meythaler, J.M., Guin-Renfroe, S., & Hadley, M.N. (1999b). Continuously infused intrathecal baclofen for spastic/dystonic hemiplegia: A preliminary report. *American Journal of Physical Medicine and Rehabilitation, 78*, 247–254.

Meythaler, J.M., Guin-Renfroe, S., Johnson, A., et al. (2001). Prospective assessment of tizanidine for spasticity due to acquired brain injury. *Archives of Physical Medicine and Rehabilitation, 82*, 1155–1163.

Meythaler, J.M., McCary, A.N., & Hadley, M. (1997) Prospective assessment of continuous intrathecal infusion of baclofen for spasticity caused by acquired brain injury: A preliminary report. *Journal of Neurosurgery, 87*, 415–419.

Moore, T.J., & Anderson, R.B. (1991). The use of open phenol blocks to the motor branches of the tibial nerve in adult acquired spasticity. *Foot and Ankle, 4*, 219–221.

Mortenson, P.A., & Eng, J. (2003). The use of casts in the management of joint mobility and hypertonia following brain injury in adults: A systematic review. *Physical Therapy, 83*, 648–658.

Pavesi, G., Brianti, R., Medici, D., & Mammi, P. (1998). Botulinum toxin type A in the treatment of upper limb spasticity among patients with traumatic brain injury. *Journal of Neurology, Neurosurgery and Psychiatry, 64*, 419–420.

Pierson, S.H., Katz, D.I., & Tarsy, D. (1996). Botulinum toxin A in the treatment of spasticity: Functional implications and treatment selection. *Archives of Physical Medicine and Rehabilitation, 77*, 717.

Rawicki, B. (1999). Treatment of cerebral origin spasticity with continuous intrathecal baclofen delivered via an implantable pump: Long-term follow up review of 18 patients. *Journal of Neurosurgery, 91*, 733–736.

Reiter, F., Danni, M., Lagalla, G., et al. (1998). Low-dose botulinum toxin with ankle taping for the treatment of spastic equinovarus foot after stroke. *Archives of Physical Medicine and Rehabilitation, 79*, 532–535.

Reiter, F., Danni, M., Lagalla, G., et al. (1999). Low-dose botulinum toxin with ankle taping for the treatment of spastic equinovarus foot after stroke. *Archives of Physical Medicine and Rehabilitation, 79*, 532–535.

Remy-Neris, O., Denys, P., & Bussel, B. (2001). Intrathecal clonidine for controlling spastic hypertonia. *Physical Medicine and Rehabilitation Clinics of North American, 12*, 939–951.

Remy-Neris, O., Tiffrau, V., Bouilland, S., et al. (2003). Intrathecal baclofen in subjects with spastic hemiplegia: Assessment of the antispastic effect during gait. *Archives of Physical Medicine and Rehabilitation, 84,* 643–650.

Richardson, D., Sheean, G., Werring, D., et al. (2000). Evaluating the role of botulinum toxin in the management of focal hypertonia in adults. *Journal of Neurology, Neurosurgery, and Psychiatry, 69,* 499.

Rifici, C., Kofler, M., Kronenberg, A., et al. (1994). Intrathecal baclofen application in patients with supraspinal spasticity secondary to severe traumatic brain injury. *Functional Neurology, 9,* 29–34.

Saltuari, L., Schmutzhard, E., Kofler, M., et al. (1989). Intrathecal baclofen for intractable spasticity due to severe brain injury. *Lancet, 2*(8661), 503–4.

Sgouros, S., & Seri, S. (2002). The effects on intrathecal baclofen on muscle co-contraction in children with spasticity of cerebral origin. *Pediatric Neurosurgery, 37,* 225–230.

Smith, S.J., Ellis, E., White, S., & Moore, A.P. (2000). A double-blind placebo-controlled study of botulinum toxin in upper limb spasticity after stroke or head injury. *Clinical Rehabilitation, 14,* 5–13.

Suputtitada, A. (2002). Local botulinum toxin type A injections in the treatment of spastic toes. *American Journal of Physical Medicine and Rehabilitation, 81,* 770–775.

Taub, E., Crago, J.E., Burgio, L.D., et al. (1994). An operant approach to rehabilitation medicine: Overcoming learned nonuse by shaping. *Journal of Experimental and Analytical Behavior, 61,* 281–293.

Taub, E., Uswatte, G., & Pidikiti, R.D. (1999). Constrained-induced movement therapy: A new family of techniques with broad application to physical rehabilitation: A clinical review. *Journal of Rehabilitation and Resident Development, 36,* 237–251.

Werner, C., von Frankenberg, S., Treig, T., et al. (2002). Treadmill training with partial body weight support and an electromechanical gait trainer for restoration of gait in subacute stroke patients: A randomized crossover study. *Stroke, 33,* 2895–2901.

Whyte, J., & Hart, T. (2003). It's more than a black box: It's a Russian doll: Defining rehabilitation treatments. *American Journal of Physical Medicine and Rehabilitation, 82,* 639–652.

Yablon, S.A., Agana, B.T., Ivanhoe, C.B., et al. (1996). Botulinum toxin in severe upper extremity spasticity among patients with traumatic brain injury: An open-label trial. *Neurology, 47,* 939.

15

Rehabilitation of Patients with Disorders of Consciousness

JOSEPH T. GIACINO

Among individuals who sustain severe traumatic brain injury (TBI), a significant percentage experience prolonged or permanent disorders of consciousness
(DOC). The reliability of published data is suspect; however, 10%–15% of those
admitted to a hospital with severe TBI are discharged in a vegetative state. Of
these, only 50% recover consciousness over the next 1 to 3 years (Levin &
Eisenberg, 1996). Prevalence estimates for the vegetative state range from 15,000
to 40,000 (Multi-Society Task Force on PVS, 1994; National Consensus Development Panel on Rehabilitation, 1999), with as many as 280,000 additional
individuals believed to be in the minimally conscious state in the United States
(Strauss et al., 2000). Lifetime costs of care may approach $2 million per case
(Spudis, 1991). Despite these staggering figures, rehabilitative interventions for
persons with DOC have been largely ignored by clinicians and understudied by
researchers. Some have attributed this to the notion of *therapeutic nihilism* (Fins,
2003). This is the belief that persons with very severe brain injury are beyond
the reach of available treatment; therefore, there is little justification to recommend intervention or, as the case may be, to fund treatment research involving
these individuals. It is likely that therapeutic nihilism has fueled the diagnostic
inaccuracy, prognostic ambiguity, and empirically weak research that define the
context in which individuals with DOC currently exist.

While diagnostic guidelines have recently been published for the vegetative state (Quality Standards Subcommittee, 1995) and the minimally conscious state (Giacino et al., 2002), guidelines for rehabilitative treatment of persons with DOC do not exist. Consequently, clinical decision making is often based on anecdotal experience and other subjective criteria. The aim of this chapter is to provide an evidence-based review of the effectiveness of rehabilitative interventions designed for persons with DOC. The strength of the existing evidence will be systematically evaluated according to preexisting criteria. The discussion will conclude by identifying important clinical research questions and will offer recommendations for future research.

DEFINITION OF TERMS

The major DOCs include coma, the vegetative state and the minimally conscious state. Delirium, which is commonly included in discussions of DOC, is not considered here, as it is typically a transient state. *Coma* is a state of complete self and environmental unawareness during which the eyes remain continuously closed even when vigorous stimulation is applied (Plum & Posner, 1982). Spontaneous or stimulus-induced eye-opening signals emergence from coma and usually occurs within 4 weeks of onset. The *vegetative state* (VS) is marked by periods of wakefulness without any indication of command-following, communication, or purposeful movement (MSTF on PVS, 1994). It is considered permanent after 12 months following TBI and after 3 months following nontraumatic causes (Quality Standards Subcommittee, 1995). The *minimally conscious state* (MCS) is characterized by inconsistent but clearly recognizable behavioral signs of consciousness (Giacino et al., 2002). The diagnosis of MCS requires reproducible evidence of command-following, discernible yes/no responses, intelligible verbalization, or movements and affective behaviors provoked by relevant environmental stimuli that cannot be accounted for by reflexive activity (e.g., visual tracking, directed reaching, contingent smiling/crying). Prognostic data are sparse, but MCS is believed to be permanent when the condition persists for 12 months or longer.

EVIDENCE REVIEW PROCESS

The evidence review process employed in this investigation was guided by the procedure developed by the Quality Standards Subcommittee of the American Academy of Neurology (AAN, 2003). The AAN evidence classification system relies on a well-established process designed to rigorously evaluate the strength of the available literature. Upon completion of the evidence review, explicit recommendations are formulated to guide clinical practice. In the section that follows, the components of the current review process are explicated to allow the reader to evaluate the conclusions reached.

Study Inclusion/Exclusion Criteria

To qualify for review, studies had to meet all of the following criteria:

- Subjects must have sustained a TBI. If subjects with non-TBI were also included, results must have been analyzed separately for both groups.
- Subjects' diagnosis at the time of treatment must have been reported as coma, VS, or MCS.
- In the absence of a clinical diagnosis, subjects must have received a score on a standardized rating scale consistent with the definition of coma, VS, or MCS [i.e., Glasgow Coma Scale (GCS) $\leq = 9$, Disability Rating Scale (DRS) $\geq = 15$, Rancho Level II–III].
- The intervention studied must have been one that is typically used in a rehabilitation setting.
- Studies including pediatric cases were excluded.
- Studies including cases with concomitant spinal cord injury were excluded.
- Review articles and position papers were excluded.

Search Strategy

A MEDLINE search of articles published in English between 1987 and 2003 was conducted. Search terms included *traumatic brain injury, vegetative state, persistent vegetative state, minimally conscious state, rehabilitation, sensory stimulation, hyperbaric oxygen,* and *deep brain stimulation.* These terms were entered in various combinations to maximize retrieval of relevant studies. Abstracts were screened by two reviewers, and qualifying full-text articles were reviewed by the author using data extraction and evaluation forms used by the Agency for Healthcare Research and Quality (West et al., 2002). To supplement the MEDLINE search, reference lists were reviewed from the articles retrieved and from other sources (e.g., prior review articles).

Evidence Classification

Articles were divided into one of four classes of evidence, depending on the design of the study, according to the AAN framework. *Class I* evidence includes randomized, controlled trials in a representative population with masked outcome assessment, well-defined outcome measures, sufficiently detailed inclusion/exclusion criteria, adequate accounting of dropouts/crossovers, and comparable control groups. *Class II* is composed of prospective studies of matched cohorts that meet all of the Class I criteria except random subject allocation *or* randomized controlled trials that lack one of the required Class I criteria. *Class III* studies represent all other controlled clinical trials (e.g., natural history controls, subjects serving as their own controls) administered in a representative population with outcome assessment conducted independent of patient treatment. *Class IV* consists of those studies not assessing outcome independent of treatment and include uncontrolled case series, case reports, and expert opinion.

Strength of Recommendations

In keeping with AAN guidelines, treatment recommendations were made at one of four levels, based on the strength of the existing evidence. A *Level A* recommendation indicates that the treatment has been established as effective, ineffective, or harmful for a given condition in a specified population. Pooled results from two or more Class I studies demonstrating a consistent, significant, and important effect were required to assign a Level A recommendation. *Level B* indicates that a particular treatment is probably effective, ineffective, or harmful for a given condition in a specified population. One Class I study showing a significant and important effect, or pooled results from at least two distinct Class II studies demonstrating a consistent, significant, and important effect were required to achieve a Level B recommendation. A *Level C* recommendation denotes that a treatment is possibly effective, ineffective, or harmful for a given condition in a specified population. To obtain a Level C recommendation, the treatment must have been supported by a single Class II study showing a significant and important effect or the pooled results from at least two distinct Class III studies demonstrating a consistent, significant, and important effect. Treatments were designated as *Level U* when the data were incomplete or conflicting, thus precluding an evidence-based recommendation.

EVIDENCE SUMMARY

Studies that qualified for inclusion were reviewed across nine parameters: (1) description of subjects, (2) sample size, (3) description of the intervention, (4) time of the intervention, (5) duration of the intervention, (6) research design, (7) outcome measures, (8) assessment schedule, and (9) results. Five types of rehabilitation interventions were identified as treatments intended for patients with DOC: pharmacologic interventions, sensory stimulation/regulation, physical management procedures, hyperbaric oxygen therapy, and deep brain stimulation. To facilitate the review, each study was grouped into one of these five categories and evidence summary tables were constructed for each treatment area.

Pharmacologic Interventions

The first group of studies were composed of those in which medications were administered to facilitate recovery of arousal, cognition, or behavioral responsiveness. These studies, summarized in Table 15.1, were categorized as, "Pharmacologic Interventions." Seven studies qualified for review, based on the inclusion and exclusion criteria. There were no Class I studies. One Class II and two Class IV studies reported that amantadine hydrochloride (AH) was effective in improving behavioral responsiveness and accelerating the rate of cognitive and functional recovery in samples comprised largely of patients in MCS. The Class II study used a prospective, randomized, double-blind, placebo-controlled crossover trial to determine the effectiveness of AH (100 mg bid) in 35 patients with DRS scores between 15 and 22 at 1 to 6 weeks postinjury (Meythaler et al., 2002). There was more rapid cognitive and functional improvement during the on-drug phase, regardless of whether subjects received AH or placebo first. At the 3- and 6-month follow-ups, there was no significant difference between treatment groups. No significant adverse events were reported at any time. Both Class IV studies reported marked improvements in functional capacity tied to initiation of amantadine (200 mg bid) in postacute MCS patients (i.e., 55–266 days postinjury) (Nickels et al., 1994; Zafonte et al., 1998).

One Class III investigated the effectiveness of bromocriptine (2.5 mg bid), in association with multidisciplinary rehabilitation, in improving the functional outcome in a series of five patients in VS (Passler & Riggs, 2001). The authors reported that physical and cognitive recovery at 12 months postinjury was greater in the bromocriptine-treated patients relative to a group of historical controls (Giacino & Kalmar, 1997).

Three Class IV studies described improvements in arousal, speech, and consistency of command-following in patients with behavioral underresponsiveness following treatment with methylphenidate (12.5 mg bid) (DiPasquale & Whyte, 1996), tricyclic antidepressants (amitriptyline: 50 mg qd; desipramine: 50–75 mg qd); Reinhard et al., 1996), or lamotrigine (200–350 mg qd; Chatham-Showalter & Netsky-Kimmel, 2000). Two of these studies were single-subject case reports (i.e., subjects as their own controls) with one to three patients, and the third was an uncontrolled case series.

Sensory Stimulation/Sensory Regulation

A second group of studies, summarized in Table 15.2, employed various forms of sensory stimulation (SS) or regulation (SR) to facilitate recovery. Sensory stimulation treatments typically apply different forms of sensory stimuli at varying frequencies, intensities, and durations in an effort to elicit neurologic and behavioral responses. Treatments involving SR intentionally limit the frequency, intensity,

Table 15.1. Pharmacologic Interventions Evidence Summary

STUDY	SUBJECTS	n	TYPE OF INTERVENTION	TIME OF INTERVENTION	DURATION OF INTERVENTION	DESIGN	OUTCOME MEASURES	ASSESSMENT POINTS	RESULTS
Meythaler et al. (2002)	Mean DRS = 15–22 (diagnoses not specified)	35	Amantadine (200 mg qd)	4d–6 wks	6 wk	Prospective randomized, double-blind, placebo-controlled, crossover trial	DRS; GOS; GOAT; ABS; MMSE; FIMCOG; side effects	6 wks, 12 wks, 6 mo	More rapid functional improvement on drug vs. off drug on all measures except GOAT and ABS; No significant difference between groups at 12 wk or 6 mo; no adverse events
Passler & Riggs (2001)	VS	5	Bromocriptine (2.5 mg bid) + "basic stimulation approach"	Not reported (mean time postinjury = 39 d)	2–6 mo	Case series w/comparison to historical controls	DRS, CRS, FIM, BRISC	DRS: 1, 3, 6, 12 mo; FIM: 1 and 12 mo; CRS, BRISC: variable	Degree of functional recovery at 12 mo greater than expected based on historical controls
Chatham-Showalter & Netsky-Kimmel (2000)	Mean RLA scale score = 2.6 (diagnoses not specified)	13 (TBI = 6)	Lamotrigine (final dose: M = 200–350 mg qd)	Mean = 74 d	Not reported	Retrospective case series	Clinician judgment; discharge site	Discharge	More patients showed cognitive improvement and were discharged to the community than expected based on authors' experience

Study	n	Diagnosis	Medication (dose)	Duration	Time since injury	Design	Measures	Comparison	Outcome
Reinhard et al. (1996)	3	Severe brain injury with arousal and initiation problems (diagnoses not specified)	Amitriptyline (50 mg qd); desipramine (50–75 mg, qd)	2 mo; 6 mo; 19 mos	1 mo; 5 mo; "several" mo	Single-subject (ABAB) case reports	Clinician observation	Varied	Improvement in arousal and behavior (e.g., command-following, speech) following drug initiation and decline after drug discontinuation
DiPasquale & Whyte (1996)	1	VS?	Methylphenidate (12.5 mg bid)	3 mo	Not reported	Single-subject case report (subject as own control)	Differential rate of command-following	Pre-post drug	Significant increase in command-following consistency and accuracy on drug
Nickels et al. (1994)	9	"Moderate to severe under-responsiveness (n = 8/9) (diagnoses not specified)	Amantadine (50–200 mg bid)	30–266 d	Not reported	Retrospective chart review	Informal measures of functional, neuro-behavioral, and cognitive status; side effects	Predrug, during drug, postdrug	Treatment effect reported in 8/9 subjects
Zafonte et al. (1998)	1	MCS	Amantadine (200 mg bid)	5 mo	8 mo	Single-subject case report (ABA)	Coma-Near Coma scale	Every 5 for 65	Dose-dependent relationship between amantadine and CNC score

ABS, Agitated Behavior Scale; BRISC, Barry Rehabilitation Inpatient Screening of Cognition; CNC, Coma–Near Coma Scale; CRS, coma recovery scale; DRS, Disability Rating Scale; FIM, Functional Independence Measure; FIMCOG, Functional Independence Measure–Cognitive Scale; GOAT, Galveston Orientation and Amnesia Test; GOS, Glasgow Outcome Scale; MMSE, Mini-Mental State Examination; RLA, Rancho Los Amigos Scale.

Table 15.2. Sensory Stimulation: Evidence Summary

STUDY	SUBJECTS	n	TYPE OF INTERVENTION	TIME OF INTERVENTION	DURATION OF INTERVENTION	DESIGN	OUTCOME MEASURE	ASSESSMENT POINTS	RESULTS
Johnson et al. (1993)	Coma/VS (GCS ≤ 8)	14	Multimodal SS (20 min/d)	Within 24 hr post-injury	Treatment group: mean = 8.1 d; placebo group: mean = 3.7 d	Prospective, randomized clinical trial	Biochemical markers; skin conductance; heart rateone	Pre-post stimulation	Significant between-group stimulation effect noted at 6 d post-injury on biochemical marker only; no difference in biochemical or physiologic measures between survivors and deceased
Mitchell et al. (1990)	Coma (mean GCS = 5)	24	Multimodal SS (1–2 hr/d for 6 d/wk)	2–12 d postinjury	4 wk	Prospective cohort study with matched controls	Mean weekly GCS score; mean duration of coma	Weeks 1, 2, 3, 4	Duration of coma significantly shorter in treatment group
Kater (1989)	Group 1: GCS = 3–6; Group 2: GCS = 7–10; Group 3: GCS = 11–14 (diagnoses not specified)	30	Multimodal SS (90 min/d for 6 d/wk)	2 wk postinjury	1–3 mo	Prospective cohort study	RLA scale	2 wk and 3 mo post-injury	RLA score significantly higher at 3 mo postinjury in treatment group; greatest difference noted in moderate severity group
Pierce et al. (1990)	Coma/VS	31	Multimodal SS (8 hr/d for 7 days/wk)	2 wk postinjury	Until acceptance into inpatient rehabilitation program	Case series w/comparison to historical controls	Time to command-following; GOS score at 10–12 mos postinjury	Daily during ICU stay and twice weekly afterward	No difference between groups in coma duration or GOS outcome at 1 year

Study	Diagnosis	N	Intervention	Time postinjury	Duration	Design	Measures	Timing of measurement	Results
Schinner et al. (1995)	Coma (GCS = 4–7; 11 subjects medically paralyzed)	15	Alternating auditory stimulation (earplugs, music, ICU noise; q 15 min)	36–48 hr postinjury	Not reported	Single-subject alternating treatment design	Pressure ICP; CPP	Before, during, and after stimulation	No significant difference in pre-post measures of ICP or CPP
Wilson et al. (1991)	VS	4 (TBI = 3)	Alternating multimodal or unimodal SS (10 min/d)	2–22 mo postinjury	Not reported for 2/3 TBI subjects	Single-subject alternating treatment, repeated-measures design	Eyelid (open/closed) and movement (yes/no) status poststimulation	Time sampling (q 10 sec for 10 min before/after stimulation)	Significant increase in post-treatment eyeopening and/or movement after multimodal stimulation
Wilson et al. (1993)	VS	7	Alternating multimodal or unimodal SS (10 min/d)	5–47 mo postinjury	15 d	Single-subject alternating treatment, repeated-measures design	Eyelid (open/closed) and movement (yes/no) status poststimulation	Time sampling (q 10 sec for 10 min before/after stimulation)	Stimulation increased arousal in 4/7 subjects; no consistent relationship between type of stimulation and response
Hall et al. (1992)	Coma (GCS ≤ 8)	6	Alternating (weekly) directed (SDS: structured, multimodal) or nondirected (NDS: unstructured, auditory) stimulation (30 min/d)	11–23 d postinjury	4–6 wk	Single-subject alternating treatment repeated-measures design	(SSAM). WNNSP, GCS, RLA	At the end of each treatment session	Scores on all three measures increased progressively over course of study; eye movement and motor scores higher following SDS

(continued)

Table 15.2. Continued

STUDY	SUBJECTS	n	TYPE OF INTERVENTION	TIME OF INTERVENTION	DURATION OF INTERVENTION	DESIGN	OUTCOME MEASURE	ASSESSMENT POINTS	RESULTS
Wood et al. (1992)	VS	8	CS (n = 4) or SR (n = 4)	31–73 d postinjury	CS: mean = 126 d SR: mean = 89 d	Retrospective case-comparison study (unmasked)	GCS; RLA; (LOS); discharge placement	Admission and discharge;	GCS and RLA scores higher in SR group on discharge; LOS longer in CS group; 4/4 SR single subject discharged to acute rehab v. 1/4 CS Single subjects
Wood et al. (1993)	RLA II/III (diagnoses not specified)	15 (TBI = 10)	SR	Mean = 70 d	Mean = 78 d	Case series with comparison to historical controls (Traumatic Coma DataBank)	GCS; RLA; SRH scale Response scale	Admission, weekly, discharge	Significant improvement in GCS, RLA, and SRH scores on discharge; no difference in mean gain scores between TBI and non-TBI subjects on any scale; outcome at 5 mo more favorable in SR group v. historical controls

Study	RLA level (Diagnoses)	N	Intervention	Time postinjury	Frequency/Duration	Design	Outcome measures	Timing	Results
Rader et al. (1989)	RLA II/III (Diagnoses not specified)	19 (TBI =14)	SSAM administered 1 hr/d for 4 d/wk	Mean = 12 mo postinjury	3 mo	Uncontrolled case series (pre-test–post-test design)	SSAM General Responsiveness score	Before and after stimulation program (4 mo)	No significant difference in General Responsiveness score at 3 mo post-test
Jones et al. (1994)	RLA II (diagnoses not specified)	1	Audiotapes of family/friend conversation, music, and nature sounds	42 d postinjury	Two 20-min sessions/d for 14 consecutive d	Single-subject alternating treatment, repeated measures design	Pulse rate; respiration rate; frequency of body and facial movement	Two-min pre-stimulation baseline, immediately after stimulation presented, 2 min post-stimulation	Mean scores on all four outcome measures consistently highest following exposure to family/friend voices

CPP, cerebral perfusion pressure; CS, conventional sensory stimulation; GCS, Glasgow Coma scale; GOS, Glasgow Outcome Scale; ICP, intracranial pressure; ICU, intensive care unit; NDS, nondirected stimulation; RLA, Rancho Los Amigos scale; SDs, directed multi-sensory stimulation; SR, sensory regulation; SRH, Stimulus-Response Hirarchy; SS, sensory stimulation; SSAM, Sensory Stimulation Assessment Measure; TBI, traumatic brain injury; VS, vegetative state; WNSSP, Western Neurosensory Stimulation Profile.

and duration of stimulation the patient is exposed to in order to accommodate the limited processing capacity of the severely damaged brain.

Studies investigating the effects of SS/SR comprised the largest group, with 12 studies qualifying for review. There were no Class I studies. One Class II, three Class III, and one Class IV study explored the effectiveness of multimodal stimulation (i.e., all five senses stimulated) on physiologic, neurobehavioral, and functional measures of patients in coma and VS. The Class II prospective, randomized, controlled trial found a significant between-group difference on only one of six physiologic indicators in 14 comatose patients at 6 days postinjury (Johnson et al., 1993). No difference was found for biochemical or physiologic markers between patients who survived or died in either treatment group. Two of the three Class III studies (Kater, 1989; Mitchell et al., 1990) suggested that multimodal stimulation reduced the duration of coma or the level of disability on the Rancho Los Amigos (RLA) scale at 3 months post-injury, while the third class III (Pierce et al., 1990) study found no such effects.

Two Class IV studies of patients in coma and VS reported greater change on physiologic and neurobehavioral measures in response to multimodal versus unimodal (i.e., stimulation of one sensory channel only) stimulation (Hall et al., 1992; Wilson, 1991), while a third Class IV study did not find a consistent difference in these responses when subjects were exposed to both forms of stimulation (Wilson et al.,1993).

One class III (Wood et al., 1992) and one Class IV (Wood et al., 1993) study conducted by the same group reported that SR led to more favorable neurologic and functional outcomes in patients in VS and MCS on the Glasgow Coma Scale (GCS) (Teasdale & Jennett, 1974) and Glasgow Outcome Scales (GOS) (Jennett & Bond, 1975), respectively, when compared to SS.

Two Class IV studies exposed patients in coma to either meaningful (e.g., familiar voices, music) or nonmeaningful (e.g., intensive call unit noises, nature sounds) auditory stimuli using a repeated measures alternating-treatment design. The effects of the stimuli on physiologic (i.e., intracranial pressure, cerebral perfusim pressure, pulse/respiratory rate) and behavioral (i.e., frequency of body and facial movements) indices were measured. One study reported significant increases in both parameters following presentation of meaningful stimuli (Jones et al., 1994), while the second study failed to find any significant differences (Schinner et al., 1995).

Physical Management

The third category consisted of studies that used traditional physical rehabilitation procedures designed to preserve the physiologic integrity of the body through physical conditioning and prevention of secondary complications. These studies focused primarily on the influence of range-of-motion exercises, positioning protocols, suctioning, and hygiene management on physical, cognitive, and functional outcomes. Multisensory stimulation was also included as part of the treatment regimen. Only two studies qualified for inclusion in the physical management category, each of which is summarized in Table 15.3.

There were no Class I or II studies in this category. One Class III study retrospectively investigated the effect of an early "formalized," multidisciplinary rehabilitation by comparing a group of 38 patients in coma who received this intervention within 2 days of injury to a concurrent no-treatment matched control group that was hospitalized in another facility (Mackay et al., 1992). The authors reported that the duration of coma and the length of rehabilitation stay of patients in the formalized program were approximately one-third those of patients in the control group. The difference between groups remained significant after controlling for initial GCS score. The authors also reported that 94% of the treatment group were discharged home compared to 57% of the controls. One Class IV study using a similar health maintenance intervention reported that 34% (11/32) of patients in VS improved to the severe disability category of the GOS and "began to respond specifically to environmental stimuli" between 3 and 6 months postinjury (Timmons et al., 1987).

A few studies were identified that investigated the effectiveness of passive range of motion, prolonged muscle stretch, and serial casting interventions. While some of these studies appeared to include individuals with DOC, it was not possible to determine this number or the specific diagnoses of the patients studied. Moreover, outcome assessment was limited to goniometric measures in all but one study. In view of these limitations, these studies are not reviewed here. The interested reader is referred to an evidence-based review of these interventions by Leong (2002) that discusses the implications of the results of this review for children in VS and MCS.

Hyperbaric Oxygen Therapy

Studies involving the use of *hyperbaric oxygen therapy* (HBO) formed the fourth intervention category. This treatment has become increasingly popular as an alternative for patients with DOC, due, in part, to aggressive marketing by some of its proponents. In HBO, oxygen is administered at a pressure greater than sea-level in a specially equipped chamber. This permits inhalation of highly concentrated oxygen and increases cerebral vasoconstriction, which, in turn, decreases cerebral blood flow. These changes are believed to reduce intracranial pressure and stabilize cerebral metabolism. Advocates suggest that HBO also promotes growth of microvasculature and restores the functional integrity of damaged but still viable neurons (Neubauer et al., 1990).

One Class I, one Class III, and one Class IV study of HBO qualified for review. These studies are summarized in Table 15.4. The Class I study reported a

Table15.3. Physical Management: Evidence Summary

STUDY	SUBJECTS	n	TYPE OF INTERVENTION	TIME OF INTERVENTION	DURATION OF INTERVENTION	DESIGN	OUTCOME MEASURE	ASSESSMENT POINTS	RESULTS
Mackay et al. (1992)	GCS = 3–8 (diagnoses not specified)	38	Formalized early intervention program (TBI-F: multidisciplinary trauma rehabilitation + family support) v. traditional acute care services (TBI-NF)	TBI-F = 2 d postinjury; TBI-NF = 23 d postinjury	TBI-F = 158 d; TBI-NF = 304 d (both groups received the same intervention following admission to rehabilitation at 51 (TBI-F) to 64 (TBI-NF) d51 postinjury	Retrospective comparison of treatment group to matched controls	Ratings on physical/motor, sensory/ perceptual, and cognitive /linguistic parameters; length of coma; acute LOS; rehabilitation LOS; total LOS; RLA-acute discharge; RLA—rehabilitation discharge; % of subjects discharged home	Acute discharge and rehab discharge	Ratings on specific outcome measures significantly lower in TBI-F group at rehabilitation discharge; length of coma, LOS, and RLA outcomes significantly better in TBI-F group after controlling for initial GCS; 94% of TBI-F subjects v. 57% of TBI-NF subjects discharged home

| Timmons et al. (1987) | RLA II/III (Diagnoses not specified) | 47 | Physical rehabilitation (e.g., hygiene, suctioning, positioning, ranging) + multisensory stimulation | < 6 mo postinjury | 28 d | Retrospective case series | GOS; RLA; functional rating index | GOS/RLA: 3, 6, 12 mo post-injury; rating index: rehabilitation admission and 12 mo postinjury | 44% improved in at least one functional area by 12 mo; 34% of VS subjects recovered consciousness between 3 and 6 mo; 83% of RLA III subjects improved on rating index after 6 mo v. 31% of RLA II subjects; subjects admitted to rehabilitation earlier showed greater functional improvement |

GCS, Glasgow Coma Scale; GOS, Glasgow Outcome Scale; LOS, length of stay; RLA, Rancho Los Amigos scale; TBI-F, traumatic brain injury–formalized rehabilitation; TBI-NF, traumatic bran injury–traditional rehabilitation.

Table 15.4. Hyperbaric Oxygen: Evidence Summary

STUDY	SUBJECTS	N	TYPE OF INTERVENTION	TIME OF INTERVENTION	DURATION OF INTERVENTION	DESIGN	OUTCOME MEASURE	ASSESSMENT POINTS	RESULTS
Rockswold et al. (1992)	GCS ≤ = 9 (diagnoses not specified)	168	Administration of 100% O_2 at 1.5 A TA for 60 min	6–24 hr postinjury	Max = 2 wk	Prospective, randomized, masked, controlled trial (controls not sham-treated)	GOS	6, 12 and 18 mo postinjury	Mortality significantly lower in HBO group (17% v. 32%); no difference between groups in number of subjects with moderate-good outcomes at 12 mo postinjury
Haijun et al. (2001)	Mean GCS = 5	55	Administration of 100% O_2 for 40–60 min over 30–40 sessions	3 d postinjury (following surgery)	12–16 d	Prospective, randomized, controlled trial	GCS; brain electrical activity mapping; GOS	3 d, 2 wk, 2 mo and 6 mo postinjury	Significant improvements in GCS, BEAM, and GOS at all four intervals in HBO group only
Rockswold et al. (2001)	Mean GCS = 6 (Diagnoses not specified)	37	Administration of 100% O_2 at 1.5 ATA for 60 min	Mean = 23 hr postinjury	Up to 7 d (max = 7 treatments/patient)	Prospective three-group pre-test-post-test design (subjects grouped by pre-HBO CBF rate: reduced. normal. raised	CBF: arterio venous O_2 difference; $CMRO_2$: CSF lactate ; ICP	1 hr before and 1 and 6 hr post-HBO	$CMRO_2$ significantly increased and CSF lactate significantly decreased in subjects with reduced or normal pretreatment CBF indicating improved cerebral metabolism post-HBO; pretreatment elevations in ICP and CBF normalized post-HBO: treatment effect lost between sessions

BEAM, brain electrical activity mapping; CBF, cerebral blood flow; $CMRO_2$, cerebral metabolic rate of oxygen; CSF, cerebrospinal fluid; GCS, Glasgow Coma Scale; GOS, Glasgow Outcome Scale; HBO, hyperbaric oxygen therapy; ICP, intracerebral pressure.

significant decrease in mortality but not morbidity subsequent to HBO (Rocks-wold et al., 1992). The Class III study found indications of improvement in neurobehavioral, electrophysiologic, and functional measures (Ren et al., 2001), and the Class IV study showed significant improvements in cerebral metabo-lism (Rockswold et al., 2001). In the Class I study, 168 patients with GCS scores ≤ 9 were randomized to an HBO or a no-treatment control group (Rockswold et al., 1992). The HBO group received thirty to forty 60-minute sessions of 100% oxygen at 1.5 ATA beginning within 24 hours of injury. Both groups received standard neurosurgical intensive care. The control group did not receive sham-HBO treatment. The mortality rate at 12 months postinjury was significantly lower in the HBO group (17% vs. 32%), with the largest difference noted in patients with GCS scores of 4–6 (17% vs. 42%). There was no between-group difference in the number of patients with a moderate to good outcomes on the GOS at 12 months postinjury.

The Class III study, a prospective, randomized, controlled trial, employed a similar HBO protocol (Ren et al., 2001). This study reported that GCS and brain electrical activity mapping (BEAM) scores were significantly higher in the HBO group after 2 weeks of treatment compared to the scores of a matched control group. The percentage of subjects that fell in the good recovery and mild disability cate-gories of the GOS was also significantly higher in the HBO group (84% vs. 30%). In the Class IV study, patient outcomes were not assessed (Rockswold et al., 2001). However, the authors reported significant increases in the cerebral metabolic rate of oxygen ($CMRO_2$) and significant decreases in cerebrospinal fluid (CSF) lac-tate after HBO in 37 comatose patients with normal or reduced cerebral blood flow (CBF). This effect was not sustained between treatment sessions.

Deep Brain Stimulation

Two studies of *deep brain stimulation* (DBS) met criteria for inclusion in the re-view. These studies are summarized in Table 15.5. In DBS, electrical pulses are transmitted by electrodes implanted in structures within the ascending reticular activating system (usually thalamic and midbrain nuclei) to promote activation of higher cortical structures. This treatment is premised on the assumption that preserved cortical functions cannot be recruited adequately because of damage to reticular structures. Electrical stimulation may help reengage these quiescent cor-tical structures and thus restore functional capability.

This category was represented by two Class IV studies. Both studies were un-controlled case series that included patients with TBI and non-TBI. In each study, DBS was applied to the midbrain tegmentum or centromedian nucleus of the thala-mus of patients who were reportedly in persistent VS. The stimulation was ad-ministered at a frequency of either 25 or 50 Hz for 30 minutes every 2 to 3 hours and lasted at least 12 months in some cases. Subjects were at least 3 months

Table 15.5. Deep Brain Stimulation: Evidence Summary

SUDY	SUBJECTS	N	TYPE OF INTERVENTION	TIME OF INTERVENTION	DURATION OF INTERVENTION	DESIGN	OUTCOME MEASURE	ASSESSMENT POINTS	RESULTS
Yamamoto et al. (2001)	PVS	20 (TBI = 9)	DBS (25 Hz) applied to mid-brain tegmentum or centromedian nucleus of thalamus (q 2–3 hr for 30 min)	≤ 3 mths postinjury	Not reported (subjects received DBS for at least 12 mo)	Uncontrolled case series	Neurological Grading Score	Monthly after initiating DBS (length of time post injury upon completion of DBS reported)	2/9 TBI subjects emerged from PVS (i.e., capable of producing sound or obeying orders); subjects who emerged had recordable ABR wave V, SEP N20, pain-related P250, and desynchronized EEG
Tsubokawa et al. (1990)	PVS	8 (TBI = 3)	DBS (50 Hz) applied to mid-brain tegmentum or centromedian nucleus of thalamus (q 2 hr for 30 min)	> 6 mo postinjury	Not reported (some subjects received DBS for at least 12 mo)	Uncontrolled case series	Neurological Grading Score	Monthly after initiating DBS (length of time post injury upon completion of DBS reported)	1 TBI subject emerged from PVS (i.e., capable of producing sound or obeying orders), 1 showed incomplete recovery (i.e., oral intake) and 1 showed no recovery

ABR, auditory brain stem evoked response; DBS, deep brain stimulation; EEG, electroencephalogram; PVS, persistent vegetative state; SEP, somatosensory evoked potential; TBI, traumatic brain injury.

postinjury in one study and a minimum of 6 months postinjury in the other. In one study, two of the nine subjects with TBI emerged from VS within 12 months of starting DBS (Tsubokawa et al., 1990). In the second study, one patient recovered the ability to "produce sound" and follow commands, a second regained the capacity for oral intake, and the third showed no recovery (Yamamoto et al., 2001).

QUALITY OF THE EVIDENCE

After a descriptive review of the evidence was completed, the quality of each study was evaluated across eight domains based on recommendations suggested by the Agency for Healthcare Research and Quality (West et al., 2002). This is a critical step in the evidence review process, as it contributes heavily to the strength of the recommendations made concerning the treatment of interest. The domains assessed in the current review included (1) method of subject allocation, (2) concealment strategy, (3) inclusion/exclusion criteria, (4) description of the intervention, (5) equivalence of the comparison group, (6) reliability and validity of outcome measure(s), (7) functional relevance of outcome measure(s), and (8) appropriateness of conclusions. The adequacy of each domain was judged dichotomously (i.e., yes/no). A rating of "not applicable (N/A)" was assigned when the domain was not pertinent to the study. When the information provided was insufficient to make a determination, this was listed as "not reported." The number of quality criteria met in each study was summed to provide an indication of the overall quality of the study. Although all studies were assigned a yes/no rating as to whether the study constituted a randomized, controlled trial (RCT), this rating was not considered in the sum of the quality criteria met if the study was not intended to be an RCT. This reduced the maximum number of criteria attainable to six or seven for the Class III and IV studies, depending on the design of the study. Finally, the average number of quality criteria met for studies within each class of evidence was determined for the five areas of treatment. These data provide a general index of the overall quality of the evidence supporting the effectiveness of each treatment intervention. Table 15.6 provides a summary of the quality ratings for each domain in the 26 studies reviewed.

Pharmacologic Interventions

No Class I drug studies were identified. The prospective, randomized, controlled trial of amantadine by Meythaler and colleagues (2002) met six of the eight quality criteria and was methodologically the most rigorous in this category. However, this study was downgraded to Class II because the results are mitigated by two methodologic problems. First, the group that received AH first was less severely disabled prior to treatment than the placebo group and may have achieved

Table 15.6. Study Quality Rating Criteria

STUDY	RANDOMIZED CLINICAL TRIAL	MASKED	STUDY POPULATION/ INCLUSION/ EXCLUSION CRITERIA WELL-DEFINED	INTERVENTIONS CLEARLY DETAILED FOR ALL SUBJECTS	COMPARISON GROUP EQUIVALENT	OUTCOME MEASURE(S) RELIABLE/ VALID	OUTCOME MEASURE(S) FUNCTIONALLY RELEVANT	CONCLUSIONS APPROPRIATE RELATIVE TO DESIGN /RESULTS	CLASS OF EVIDENCE	NO. OF QUALITY CRITERIA MET
Drug Interventions										
Meythaler et al. (2002)	Yes	Yes	Yes	Yes	No	Yes	Yes	No	II	6/8
Passler & Riggs (2001)	No	No	Yes	Yes	No	Yes	Yes	Yes	III	5/7
Chatham-Showalter & Netsky-Kimmel (2000)	No	No	No	No	N/A	No	No	No	IV	0/6
Reinhardet et al. (1996)	No	No	No	Yes	N/A	No	Yes	Yes	IV	3/6
DiPasquale & Whyte (1996)	No	Yes	No	No	N/A	Yes	Yes	Yes	IV	4/6
Nickels et al. (1994)	No	No	No	No	N/A	No	Yes	No	IV	1/6

Study										
Zafonte et al. (1998)	No	No	Yes	Yes	N/A	Yes	Yes	Yes	IV	5/6
Sensory Stimulation										
Johnson et al. (1993)	Yes	No	Yes	No	No	No	No	Yes	II	3/8
Mitchell. et al. (1990)	No	No	No	Yes	Not reported	Yes	Yes	No	III	3/7
Kater (1989)	No	No	No	No	Not reported	Yes	Yes	No	III	2/7
Pierce. et al. (1990)	No	No	Yes	No	No	Yes	Yes	No	III	3/7
Wood et al. (1993)	No	No	Yes	No	Not Reported	Yes (2/3)	Yes	No	III	3/7
Wood. et al. (1992)	No	No	Yes	No	No	Yes	Yes	No	IV	3/7
Hall et al. (1992)	No	No	Yes	Yes	N/A	Yes	Yes	Yes	IV	5/6
Schinner et al. (1995)	No	No	No	Yes	N/A	No	No	No	IV	1/6

(continued)

Table 15.6. Continued

STUDY	RANDOMIZED CLINICAL TRIAL	MASKED	STUDY POPULATION/ INCLUSION/ EXCLUSION CRITERIA WELL-DEFINED	INTERVENTIONS CLEARLY DETAILED FOR ALL SUBJECTS	COMPARISON GROUP EQUIVALENT	OUTCOME MEASURE(S) RELIABLE/ VALID	OUTCOME MEASURE(S) FUNCTIONALLY RELEVANT	CONCLUSIONS APPROPRIATE RELATIVE TO DESIGN /RESULTS	CLASS OF EVIDENCE	NO. OF QUALITY CRITERIA MET
Wilson, et al. (1991)	No	No	No	Yes	N/A	No	No	Yes	IV	2/6
Wilson, et al. (1993)	No	No	No	Yes	N/A	No	No	Yes	IV	2/6
Rader et al. 1989	No	No	Yes	No	N/A	Yes	Yes	Yes	IV	4/6
Jones et al. (1994)	No	No	No	Yes	N/A	Yes	No	Yes	IV	3/6
Physical Management										
Mackay et al. (1992)	No	No	Yes	No	Yes	Yes (1/4)	Yes	Yes	III	5/7

Timmons et al. (1987)	No	No	No	No	N/A	Yes	Yes	No	IV	2/6
Hyperbaric Oxygen										
Rockswold et al. (1992)	Yes	Yes	Yes	Yes	Yes	Yes	Yes	Yes	I	8/8
Haijun et al. (2001)	Yes	No	No	Yes	Yes	Yes (2/3)	Yes	Yes	III	6/8
Rockswold et al. (2001)	No	No	Yes	Yes	Not reported	Not reported	No	Yes	IV	3/7
Deep Brain Stimulation										
Yamamoto et al. (2001)	No	No	No	No	N/A	No	Yes	No	IV	1/6
Tsubokawa et al. (1990)	No	No	No	Yes	N/A	No	Yes	No	IV	2/6

more favorable outcomes independent of treatment. Second, because a crossover design was used early in the course of recovery, the group that received AH first had improved substantially at the point of crossover, which limited their opportunity to improve to the same extent as the comparison group during the second phase of treatment. By the time the group treated with AH first reached crossover, the range of possible improvement on the DRS had narrowed from 15 points (during the AH phase) to 5 points (during the placebo phase).

The sole Class III study by Passler and Riggs (2001) met five of seven criteria; however, the small sample size, questionable comparability of the historical control group, and failure to adequately address the influence of spontaneous recovery on the outcome limit the strength of this study. The five Class IV studies met an average of three of the six criteria. Some of these studies failed to meet any criteria (Chatham-Showalter & Netsky-Kimmel, 2000), while others represented relatively well-designed single subject trials (Zafonte et al., 1998). Most did not adequately describe the subjects or interventions and relied on untested outcome measures.

Sensory Stimulation/Regulation

There were no Class I studies addressing SS or SR. The prospective, randomized, controlled trial of multimodal SS by Johnson and colleagues (1993) represents a weak Class II study, having met only three of eight quality criteria. This study was unmasked, subjects were not well defined, treatment and assessment windows were very short, and the outcome measures were of limited utility.

The four Class III studies met three of seven criteria, and the seven Class IV studies met three of six criteria on average. The conclusions of two of the Class III studies were based on gross comparisons to historical control groups (Pierce et al., 1990; Wood et al., 1992). Surprisingly, in one of the Class IV studies, 11 of the 15 patients were either chemically paralyzed or sedated during exposure to the treatment (Jones et al., 1994). None of these studies were masked, approximately 50% provided inadequate subject and treatment descriptions, and information concerning the equivalence of the comparison group was often missing.

Physical Management

The physical management studies that qualified for review were limited to one Class III and one Class IV study. The Class III study met five of seven criteria, but the results were based on a retrospective chart review and the authors provided only a cursory description of the treatment intervention (Mackay et al., 1992). The class IV study, based on a retrospective chart review, met only two of six criteria and did not consider spontaneous recovery as a possible cause of the functional improvements noted (Timmons et al., 1987).

Hyperbaric Oxygen Therapy

The sole Class I study of HBO completed by Rockswold's group (1992) met all eight quality criteria. Of the 26 studies reviewed, this was the only one that conducted a power analysis to determine the treatment effect size. The control group was not sham-treated in this study, which represents a potential limitation. The prospective, randomized, controlled trial by Ren and colleagues (2001) was downgraded to a Class III study because it was conducted unmasked, the subject were not well described, and it is not clear that the groups were equivalent prior to treatment. The Class IV study met two of six criteria and did not include patient outcome data, as the investigation was not designed as a treatment study (Rockswold et al., 2001).

Deep Brain Stimulation

Only two Class IV studies of DBS qualified for review. Both were uncontrolled case series. Of the six criteria considered, one study met one criterion (Tsubokawa et al., 1990) and the second met only two criteria (Yamamoto et al., 2001). Numerous methodologic weaknesses were noted in both studies, including insufficient information to confirm the subjects' diagnoses, use of subjectively scored outcome measures devised by the authors, and failure to consider the influence of spontaneous recovery. Qualitative analysis of these studies clearly challenges the claim that DBS was responsible for the cases of late emergence from VS reported by both groups of authors.

Of the five treatment areas reviewed, only pharmacologic interventions and HBO were supported by at least one Class I or II study. No area had more than one good-quality Class I or II study. Collapsing across treatment areas, more than 60% of the studies reviewed were Class IV and most had significant design flaws.

Recommendations

The following recommendations are made based on analysis of the class and quality of existing evidence for the five areas of treatment reviewed. The reader is reminded that these recommendations are based on studies that qualified for review according to the previously described inclusion and exclusion criteria. Consequently, some published studies in each area may not have been extracted. The reader is also cautioned that all studies were classified by a single rater (i.e., the author) and, therefore, may not be free of bias.

- Amantadine hydrochloride is *possibly effective* for facilitating rate of recovery without adverse effects in patients with DRS scores ≥ 15 when administered during the first 12 weeks postinjury (Level C).

- Bromocriptine, methylphenidate, tricyclic antidepressants, and lamotrigine are unproven treatments in patients with DOC. *Data are inadequate* to make an evidence-based recommendation concerning these medications (Level U).
- Multimodal SS is *possibly ineffective* in inducing changes in heart rate, skin conductance, and neurotransmitter levels in comatose patients (Level C).
- Multimodal SS, unimodal SS, and SR are unproven treatments for reducing the duration of coma or improving the functional outcome of patients in coma, VS, and RLA Level III. *Data are inadequate and inconsistent* regarding these interventions, precluding an evidence-based recommendation (Level U).
- Physical rehabilitation procedures (e.g., passive range of movement, positioning protocols, hygiene management) are unproven for promoting physical, cognitive, or functional outcomes in patients functioning at RLA Levels II and III. *Data are inadequate* to make an evidence-based recommendation concerning these interventions (Level U).
- Hyperbaric oxygen therapy is *probably effective* in reducing mortality in patients with GCS scores ≤ 9 when applied within 24 hours of injury (Level B).
- Hyperbaric oxygen therapy is *probably ineffective* in reducing severity of disability (i.e., number of patients severely disabled or in VS) at 12 months postinjury when applied within 24 hours of injury (Level B).
- Deep brain stimulation is an unproven treatment for facilitating recovery of consciousness in patients in VS. *Data are inadequate* to make an evidence-based recommendation concerning this intervention (Level U).

PRESSING QUESTIONS

When one considers how meager our understanding of consciousness is, it is not surprising that there are no proven rehabilitative treatments for individuals with DOC. There are relatively few medical disorders for which effective treatments were developed prior to understanding their pathophysiology. In DOC, this is a daunting task that requires a systematic and multidimensional approach. A brief discussion of some of the critical questions that are key to understanding DOC follows.

Can Functional Neuroimaging Procedures Inform Our Understanding of the Neurophysiology of Consciousness?

Over the past 5 years, there has been burgeoning interest in new applications of functional neuroimaging. This trend has extended to the study of DOC. Metabolic profiles of patients in VS and MCS have been investigated using single photon emission computed tomography (SPECT), positron emission tomography (PET), and functional magnetic resonance imaging (fMRI). As one example, Laureys and coworkers (1999) performed FDG-PET studies in a patient who developed VS after carbon monoxide poisoning. Positron emission tomography scans were completed during VS and after recovery of consciousness, with subsequent comparison to normal controls. Global glucose utilization remained the same during and after VS; however, significant changes in regional glucose metabolism were noted in parieto-occipital association cortices subsequent to recovery. Based on these findings, the authors suggested that posterior association cortices are critical to conscious awareness. Functional neuroimaging studies such as this are expected to provide new insights into the neural substrate underlying normal and altered levels of consciousness.

What Is the Natural History of Recovery from the Vegetative State and the Minimally Conscious State?

The effectiveness of a treatment intervention must be referenced against a recovery curve that reflects the natural history of the disorder targeted for treatment. This is particularly troubling for rehabilitation research, as patients are most accessible during the initial 12 weeks postinjury, when the rate of spontaneous recovery is highest. At present, there is no modal natural history curve that can serve as a referent against which rehabilitative interventions can be compared. In addition, most clinical trials in rehabilitation have been conducted in the context of a standard rehabilitation program. This makes it difficult to separate the effects of a specific treatment (e.g., medication) from those attributable to the background treatment (e.g., routine physical, occupational, and speech therapies) and from spontaneous recovery.

How Effective Are Existing Assessment Methods for Measuring Recovery and Response to Treatment?

Rehabilitation lacks standard measurement instruments for assessing patients with DOC. Consequently, there is little consistency across studies in the selection of neurobehavioral assessment and outcome measures. This inconsistency limits the degree to which the results of treatment effectiveness studies can be pooled and generally compromises the rehabilitation literature. This situation is in stark contrast to that of the neurosurgical literature, which has adopted the GCS and GOS as standard measures for diagnostic and prognostic assessment during the acute stage of recovery. Although these tools are not without limitations, their shortcomings are common across studies.

In rehabilitation, studies of patients with DOC most commonly rely on the DRS and RLA scales as primary outcome measures. These measures appear to have assumed this role by default, as neither instrument was designed for this purpose and there is some evidence questioning their performance in this population (Giacino et al., 2004; Gouvier et al., 1987). In view of concerns that the GOS, RLA scale, and DRS may not be sensitive enough to detect the subtle changes in behavioral responsiveness characteristic of patients with DOC, numerous specialized neurobehavioral rating scales have been developed (Ansell & Keenan, 1989; Giacino et al., 1991; Gill-Thwaites, 1997; Johnston et al., 1996; Rader et al., 1989; Rappaport et al., 1992). Unfortunately, most of these measures were standardized on small, heterogeneous samples, fail to meet criteria for interval measurement, and do not have well-established clinical utility.

Behaviorally based assessment methods are an essential component of diagnostic and outcome assessment; however, the data they produce represent indirect evidence of neural function. Behavioral assessment of consciousness is often confounded by underarousal, sensorimotor impairment, and other extraneous factors. Studies have begun to use functional neuroimaging protocols to supplement behavioral measures in an effort to provide a more direct window into the underpinnings of consciousness. Using F-fluorodeoxyglucose position emission tomography (FDG-PET) imaging, Schiff and colleagues (1999) found evidence of a metabolically active speech circuit in a well-studied patient who was in VS for 20 years but intermittently emitted intelligible single words without any other sign of meaningful communication or behavioral activity. This viable speech circuit was surrounded by large regions of inactive cortex, which presumably accounted for the patient's preserved capacity to generate words devoid of meaning or purpose. A number of other studies involving patients in VS have demonstrated preserved auditory (Laureys et al., 2000), somatosensory (Laureys et al., 2002), and visual processing (Menon et al., 1998) in the absence of behavioral evidence of intact function in these areas.

Is It Possible to Facilitate Recovery of Consciousness and Improve the Functional Outcome?

The answer to this question is contingent, in large part, on answers to the preceding ones. The first step is to determine which patient variables may influence recovery and response to treatment. Recent evidence suggests that the outcome in patients with DOC is partially determined by the level of consciousness (i.e., VS vs. MCS; Giacino & Kalmar, 1997), lesion location (i.e., cortex vs. thalamus vs. brain stem; Jennett et al., 2001; Kampfl et al., 1998), and pace of recovery during the first 16 weeks postinjury (based on week-to-week changes in DRS score; Katz et al., 2002). These preliminary results will need to be confirmed in larger studies. As data accumulate in support of specific rehabilitative treatments, a new set of issues will arise. Foremost among these will be the need to determine which treatments are best for which patients. Present-day rehabilitation continues to espouse a "one size fits all" philosophy in spite of mounting evidence that widely disparate patterns of brain injury underlie similar-appearing behavioral presentations (Jennett et al., 2001; Schiff et al., 2002).

RESEARCH PRIORITIES

To advance our knowledge of the mechanisms underlying DOC and to identify effective interventions to promote recovery, the practice of rehabilitation research must shift from small single-center studies to large multicenter clinical trials. Few, if any, rehabilitation centers have access to a sufficient sample size, and most lack the resources to conduct well-designed clinical trials. Unlike other medical conditions, recovery from TBI is influenced by many variables, all of which need to be controlled or accounted for. Failure to build in adequate controls for these covariates significantly limits generalizability of the results and diminishes the clinical importance of the study. One strategy to prevent this problem is to substratify the study population, but this usually requires a significant increase in sample size to maintain adequate power. Research collaborations and partnerships will need to be developed and fostered to accomplish this objective.

Measurement tools are the bedrock of research. Neurorehabilitation specialists have developed numerous assessment instruments, but few have been psychometrically scrutinized. In DOC, most measures have been virtually ignored. Research emphasis should be placed on ascertaining the reliability/validity, sensitivity/specificity, and positive/negative predictive value of existing assessment methods. The results of these studies will help determine which measures can be accepted as standards, which require modification, and which should be abandoned.

As functional neuroimaging techniques enter the mainstream, rehabilitation researchers will have increased opportunities to gain a better understanding of the pathophysiology of DOC. Functional neuroimaging can now be exploited to spawn a new generation of hypotheses concerning the relationship between behavior and neural activity. Potential research foci include correlational studies of behavior and cerebral metabolism, time series analyses of metabolic profiles of patients who eventually recover consciousness, and multiple baseline single-subject studies of treatment-related changes in metabolic activity.

Logistically, the pace of research would be increased by establishing a central clearinghouse for rehabilitation research involving patients with DOC. Once constructed, this database would rapidly expand and could be mined on a continuous basis. The TBI Model Systems database, funded by the National Institute on Disability and Rehabilitation Research, provides the basic framework from which this type of databank might be developed.

ACKNOWLEDGMENTS
The author would like to thank Ms. Jenny Jansson for her many scheduled and unscheduled hours of assistance with the evidence retrieval and abstract review process. I also wish to thank Mrs. Lena Feld, Medical Librarian, for her usual persistence and timeliness in responding to a multitude of requests for material and consultative support.

REFERENCES

American Academy of Neurology. (2003). Practice guideline development process. Available at http://www.aan.com/professionals/practice/development.cfm.

Ansell, B.J., & Keenan, J.E. (1989). The Western Neuro Sensory Stimulation Profile: A tool for assessing slow-to-recover head-injured patients. *Archives of Physical Medicine and Rehabilitation, 70,* 104–108.

Chatham-Showalter, P.E., & Netsky-Kimmel, D. (2000). Stimulating consciousness and cognition following severe brain injury: A new potential clinical use for lamotrigine. *Brain Injury, 14*(11), 997–1001.

DiPasquale, M. C., & Whyte, J. (1996). The use of quantitative data in treatment planning for minimally conscious patients. *Journal of Head Trauma Rehabilitation, 11*(6), 9–17.

Fins, J.J. (2003). Constructing an ethical stereotaxy for severe brain injury: Balancing risks, benefits and access. *Nature Reviews/Neuroscience, 4,* 323–327.

Giacino, J.T., Ashwal, S.A., Childs, N., Cranford, R., Jennett, B., Katz, D.I., Kelly, J., Rosenberg, J., Whyte, J., Zafonte, R.A., & Zasler, N.D. (2002). The minimally conscious state: Definition and diagnostic criteria. *Neurology, 58,* 349–353.

Giacino, J.T., & Kalmar, K. (1997). The vegetative and minimally conscious states: A comparison of clinical features and functional outcome. *Journal of Head Trauma Rehabilitation, 12*(4), 36–51.

Giacino, J.T., Kalmar, K., & Whyte, J. (2004). The JFK Coma Recovery Scale-Revised: Measurement characteristics and diagnostic utility. *Archives of Physical Medicine and Rehabilitation, 85,* 2020–2029.

Giacino, J.T., Kezmarsky, M.A., DeLuca, J., & Cicerone, K.D. (1991). Monitoring rate of recovery to predict outcome in minimally responsive patients. *Archives of Physical Medicine and Rehabilitation, 72,* 897–901.

Gill-Thwaites, H. (1997). The Sensory Modality Assessment Rehabilitation Technique—a tool for assessment and treatment of patients with severe brain injury in a vegetative state. *Brain Injury, 11*(10), 723–734.

Gouvier, W.D., Blanton, P.D., LaPorte, K.K., & Nepomuceno, C. (1987). Reliability and validity of the Disability Rating Scale and the levels of cognitive functioning scale in monitoring recovery from severe head injury. *Archives of Physical Medicine and Rehabilitation, 68,* 94–97.

Haijun, R., Wang, W., Zhaoming, G.E. (2001). Glasgow Coma Scale, brain electrical activity mapping and Glasgow Outcome Scale after hyperbaric oxygen treatment. *Chinese Journal of Traumatology, 4*(4), 239–241.

Hall, M.E., MacDonald, S., & Young, G.C. (1992). The effectiveness of directed multisensory stimulation versus nondirected stimulation in comatose CHI patients: Pilot study of a single subject design. *Brain Injury, 6*(5), 435–445.

Jennett, B., Adams, J.H., Murray, L.S., & Graham, D.I. (2001). Neuropathology in vegetative and severely disabled patients after head injury. *Neurology, 56,* 486–489.

Jennett, B., & Bond, M. (1975). Assessment of outcome after severe brain damage: A practical scale. *Lancet, 1*(7905), 480–484.

Johnson, D.A., Roethig-Johnston, K., & Richards, D. (1993). Biochemical and physiological parameters of recovery in acute severe head injury: Responses to multisensory stimulation. *Brain Injury 7(6)*, 491–499.

Johnston, M.D., Thomas, L., & Stanczak, D.E. (1996). Construct validity of the Comprehensive Level of Consciousness Scale: A comparison of behavioral and neurodiagnostic measures. *Archives of Clinical Neuropsychology, 11*(8), 703–711.

Jones, R., Hux, K, Morton-Anderson, K.A., & Knepper, L. (1994). Auditory stimulation effect on a comatose survivor of traumatic brain injury. *Archives of Physical Medicine and Rehabilitation, 75*, 164–171.

Kampfl, A., Schmutzhard, E., Franz, G., Pfausler, B., Haring, H.P., Ullmer, H., Felber, F., Golaszewski, S., & Aichner F. (1998). Prediction of recovery from post-traumatic vegetative state with cerebral magnetic-resonance imaging. *Lancet, 351*, 1763–1767.

Kater, K.M. (1989). Response of head-injured patients to sensory stimulation. *Western Journal of Nursing Research, 11*(1), 20–33.

Katz, D.I., Whyte, J., DiPasquale, M., Giacino, J.T., Kalmar, K., Maurer, P., Eifert, B., Childs, N., Mercer, W., Moheban, C., Hoover, E., Novak, P., VanWie, S., & Long, D. (2002). Prognosis and effects of medications on recovery from prolonged unconsciousness after traumatic brain injury. *Neurology, 58*(Suppl 3), A6.

Laureys, S., Faymonville, M.E., Degueldre, C., Del Fiore, G., Damas, P., Lambermont, B., Jannsens, N., Aerts, J., Franck, G., Luxen, A., Moonen, G., Lamy, M., & Maquet, P. (2000). Auditory processing in the vegetative state. *Brain, 123*, 1589–1681.

Laureys, S., Faymonville, M.E., Peigneux, P., Damas, P., Lambermont, B., Del Fiore, G., Degueldre, M.E., Aerts, J., Luxen, A., Franck, G., Lamy, M., Moonen, G., & Maquet, P. (2002). Cortical processing of noxious somatosensory stimuli in the persistent vegetative state. *Neuroimage, 17*, 732–741.

Laureys, S., Lemarie, C., Maquet, P., Phillips, C., & Frank, G. (1999). Cerebral metabolism during vegetative state and after recovery to consciousness. *Journal of Neurology, Neurosurgery, and Psychiatry, 67*, 121–122.

Leong, B. (2002). Critical review of passive muscle stretch: Implications for the treatment of children in vegetative and minimally conscious states. *Brain Injury, 16*(2), 169–183.

Levin, H.S., & Eisenberg, H.M. (1996). Vegetative state after head injury: Findings from the Traumatic Coma Data Bank. In: H.S. Levin, A.L. Benton, J.P. Muizelaar, & H.M. Eisenberg (Eds.), *Catastrophic Brain Injury* (pp. 35–49). New York: Oxford University Press.

Mackay, L.E., Bernstein, B.B., Chapman, P.E., Morgan, A.S., & Milazzo, L.S. (1992). Early intervention in severe head injury: Long-term benefits of a formalized program. *Archives of Physical Medicine and Rehabilitation, 73*, 635–641.

Menon, D.K., Owen, A.M., Williams, E.J., Minhas, P.S., Allen, C.M.C., Boniface, S.J., Pickard, J.D., & the Wolfson Brain Imaging Centre Team. (1998). Cortical processing in persistent vegetative state. *Lancet, 352*, 200.

Meythaler, J.M., Brunner, R.C., Johnson, A., & Novack, T.A. (2002). Amantadine to improve neurorecovery in traumatic brain injury–associated diffuse axonal injury: A pilot double-blind randomized trial. *Journal of Head Trauma Rehabilitation, 17*(4), 300–313.

Mitchell, S., Bradley, V.A., Welch, J.L., & Britton, P.G. (1990). Coma arousal procedure: A therapeutic intervention in the treatment of head injury. *Brain Injury, 3*, 273–279.

Multi-Society Task Force Report on PVS. (1994). Medical aspects of the persistent vegetative state. *New England Journal of Medicine, 330,* 1499–1508, 1572–1579.

National Consensus Development Panel on Rehabilitation of Persons with Traumatic Brain Injury. (1999). Rehabilitation of persons with traumatic brain injury. *Journal of the American Medical Association, 282*(10), 974–983.

Neubauer, R.A., Gottlieb, S.F., & Kaga, R.L. (1990). Enhancing "idling neurons." *Lancet, 335*(8688), 542.

Nickels, J.L., Schneider, W.N., Dombovy, M.L., & Wong, T.M. (1994). Clinical use of amantadine in brain injury rehabilitation. *Brain Injury, 8*(8), 709–718.

Passler, M.A., & Riggs, R.V. (2001). Positive outcomes in traumatic brain injury—Vegetative state: Patients treated with bromocriptine. *Archives of Physical Medicine and Rehabilitation, 82,* 311–315.

Pierce, J.P., Lyle, D.M., Quine, S., Evans, N.J., Morris, J., & Fearnside, M.R. (1990). The effectiveness of coma arousal intervention. *Brain Injury, 4*(2),191–197.

Plum, F., & Posner, J. (1982). *The Diagnosis of Stupor and Coma* (3rd ed.). Philadelphia: F.A. Davis.

Quality Standards Subcommittee of the American Academy of Neurology. (1995). Practice parameter: Assessment and management of persons in the persistent vegetative state. *Neurology, 45,* 1015–1018.

Rader, M.A., Alston, J.B., & Ellis, D.W. (1989). Sensory stimulation of severely brain-injured patients. *Brain Injury, 3*(2), 141–147.

Rappaport, M., Dougherty, A.M., & Kelting, D.L. (1992). Evaluation of coma and vegetative states. *Archives of Physical Medicine and Rehabilitation, 73,* 628–634.

Reinhard, D.L., Whyte, J., & Sandel, M.E. (1996). Improved arousal and initiation following tricyclic antidepressant use in severe brain injury. *Archives of Physical Medicine and Rehabilitation, 77,* 80–83.

Ren, J., Wang, W., & Ge, Z. (2001). Glasgow Outcome Scale, brain electric activity mapping and Glasgow Outcome scale after hyperbaric oxygen treatment of severe brain injury. *Chinese Journal of Traumatology, 4*(4), 239–241.

Rockswold, G.L., Ford, S.E., Anderson, D.C., Bergman, T.A., & Sherman, R.E. (1992). Results of a prospective randomized trial for treatment of severely brain-injured patients with hyperbaric oxygen. *Journal of Neurosurgery, 76,* 929–934.

Rockswold, S.B., Rockswold, G.L., Vargo, J.M., Erickson, C.A., Sutton, R.L., Bergman, T.A., & Biros, M.H. (2001). Effects of hyperbaric oxygenation therapy on cerebral metabolism and intracranial pressure in severely brain injured patients. *Journal of Neurosurgery, 94,* 403–411.

Schiff, N.D., Ribary, U., Plum, F., Llinas, R. (1999). Words without mind. *Journal of Cognitive Neuroscience, 11*(6), 650–656.

Schiff, N.D., Ribary, U., Rodriquez-Moreno, D., Beattie, B., Kronberg, E., Blasberg, R., Giacino, J., McCagg, C., Fins, J.J., Llinas, R., & Plum, F. (2002). Residual cerebral activity and behavioral fragments can remain in the persistently vegetative brain. *Brain, 125,* 1210–1234.

Schinner, K.M., Chishlm, A.H., Grap, M.J., Siva, P., Hallinan, M., & LaVoice-Hawkins, A.M. (1995). Effects of auditory stimuli on intracranial pressure and cerebral perfusion pressure in traumatic brain injury. *Journal of Neuroscience Nursing, 27*(6), 348–354.

Spudis, E.V. (1991). The persistent vegetative state—1990. *Journal of Neurological Sciences, 102,* 128–136.

Strauss D.J., Ashwal S., Day, S.M., & Shavelle, R.M. (2000). Life expectancy of children in vegetative and minimally conscious states. *Pediatric Neurology, 23*(4), 1–8.

Teasdale, G., & Jennett B. (1974). Assessment of coma and impaired consciousness. *Lancet*, 2, 81–84.

Timmons, M., Gasquoine, L., & Scibak, J.W. (1987). Functional changes with rehabilitation of very severe traumatic brain injury survivors. *Journal of Head Trauma Rehabilitation*, 2(3), 64–67.

Tsubokawa, T., Yamamoto, T., Katayama, Y., Hirayama, T., Maejima, S., & Moriya, T. (1990). Deep brain stimulation in a persistent vegetative state: Follow-up results and selection of candidates. *Brain Injury*, 4(4), 315–327.

West, S., King, V., Carey, T.S., et al. (2002, April). *Systems to Rate the Strength of Scientific Evidence. Evidence Report/Technology Assessment No. 47* (prepared by the Research Triangle Institute—University of North Carolina Evidence-based Practice Center under Contract No. 290-97-0011). AHRQ Publication No. 02-E016. Rockville, MD: Agency for Healthcare Research and Quality. April 2002.

Wilson, S.L., & McMillan, T.M. (1993). A review of the evidence for the effectiveness of sensory stimulation treatment for coma and vegetative states. *Neuropsychological Rehabilitation*, 3(2), 149–160.

Wilson, S.L., Powell, G.E., Elliott, K., & Thwaites, H. (1991). Sensory stimulation in prolonged coma: Four single case studies. *Brain Injury*, 4(5), 393–400.

Wilson, S.L., Powell, G.E., Elliot, K., & Thwaites, H. (1993). Evaluation of sensory stimulation as a treatment for prolonged coma: Seven single experimental case studies. *Neuropsychological Rehabilitation*, 3(2), 191–201.

Wood, R.L., Winkowski, T., & Miller, J. (1993). Sensory regulation as a method to promote recovery in patients with altered states of consciousness. *Neuropsychological Rehabilitation*, 3(2), 177–190.

Wood, R. L., Winkowski, T.B., Miller, J.L., Miller, J.L., Tierney, L., & Goldman, L. (1992). Evaluating sensory regulation as a method to improve awareness in patients with altered states of consciousness: A pilot study. *Brain Injury*, 6(5), 411–418.

Yamamoto, T., Katayama, Y., Oshima, H., Fukaya, C., Kawamata, T., & Tsubokawa, T. (2001). Deep brain stimulation therapy for a persistent vegetative state. *Acta Neurochirurigica* 79(Suppl), 79–82.

Zafonte, R.D., Watanabe, T., & Mann, N.R. (1998). Amantadine: A potential treatment for the minimally conscious state. *Brain Injury*, 12(7), 617–621.

16

Neuroimaging and Rehabilitation

HARVEY S. LEVIN and RANDALL S. SCHEIBEL

Neuroimaging studies are relevant to traumatic brain injury (TBI) rehabilitation because they can address issues such as reorganization of function, including changes associated with interventions such as training techniques. The results of neuroimaging can also be useful in evaluating the efficacy of an intervention in addition to elucidating the mechanism of action. For the purposes of this chapter, neuroimaging studies pertinent to rehabilitation of patients with TBI can be broadly divided between anatomic or structural imaging and functional brain imaging. Although the literature on structural brain imaging of TBI has been reviewed by Bigler (1999, 2001), it is presented briefly here. The sections on functional brain imaging are organized according to studies addressing cerebral hypometabolism and executive function after TBI, changes in distributed activation associated with cognitive performance, and studies reporting changes in the allocation of neural resources in relation to task demands following mild TBI. Although methodologic issues in functional imaging are discussed, a review focused on this topic is available (Hillary et al., 2002).

STRUCTURAL BRAIN IMAGING

Studies can be distinguished by severity of TBI, adult versus pediatric age range, and chronicity of injury. Prior to the mid-1980s, investigations used computed tomography (CT), whereas magnetic resonance imaging (MRI) has since predominated in studies of postacute TBI. Neuroimaging studies of acute TBI have generally addressed prediction, particularly in relation to survival after severe TBI (Eisenberg et al., 1990). Investigation of the quality of survival and neurobehavioral recovery has disclosed that structural imaging findings obtained following the acute phase of TBI are more closely associated with outcome than imaging data collected during the initial weeks following injury (Bigler, 1999). In addition, measurement of diffuse brain injury has generally had a stronger relation to neurobehavioral recovery than the presence and volume of focal brain lesions (Bigler, 1999).

Diffuse Brain Injury

The ventricle-brain ratio (VBR), which is typically computed based on the area of the lateral ventricles in relation to the volume of brain parenchyma, provides a measure of diffuse injury severity primarily reflecting loss of cerebral white matter. The VBR obtained in adults several months or longer after TBI is related to the cognitive and behavioral outcome of TBI (Bigler, 2001). A related finding based primarily on cross-sectional data is that the whole brain volume decreases after severe TBI in adults, with most of the tissue loss occurring within the first year (Bigler, 1999).

To investigate reduced growth of cerebral white matter after severe TBI in children, Levin et al. (2000) performed MRI at 3 and 36 months postinjury and compared the volume of the corpus callosum to findings in children who had sustained mild TBI. As shown in Figure 16.1, growth of the corpus callosum was reduced in the severe TBI group. This reduction was generalized rather than confined to a specific region and was related to the functional outcome. It is plausible that development of other white matter connections is similarly affected by severe TBI. This could be investigated by diffusion tensor imaging (DTI), which evaluates the integrity of cerebral white matter by measuring the movement of water molecules parallel to fiber tracts relative to their relatively restricted movement perpendicular to the tracts (Klingberg et al., 1999). Disruption of white matter fibers is reflected by the quantitative indices used in DTI research.

Focal Brain Lesions and Cognitive Deficit

The relation of lesion volume to the neurobehavioral sequelae of TBI has varied across studies. In general, the findings have been less consistent than the effects of TBI severity, as reflected by the Glasgow Coma Scale (GCS; Teasdale & Jennett, 1974). In a study of adolescents and adults who sustained mild to moderate impairment of consciousness, Levin et al. (1992) analyzed MRI findings obtained within the first week and 3 months later in relation to performance on measures

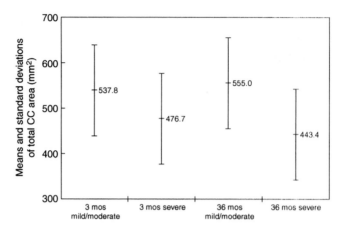

Figure 16.1. Mean and standard deviation of total corpus callosum (CC) area obtained on MRI at 3 months and 36 months postinjury and plotted by severity of TBI group. Interaction of group with occasion is reflected by the reduction in total CC after severe TBI in contrast to the increased CC area over time after mild to injury. (From Levin et al., 2000.)

of executive function and memory. Although most of the focal lesions were in the frontotemporal region, there was a lack of specificity in the relation of neuropsychological deficit to lesion site. For example, an episodic memory deficit was no more likely to occur with temporal lobe lesions than with frontal lesions. However, the cognitive performance at 3 months postinjury by patients who had a brain lesion on the initial MRI tended to fall below the level of the subgroup without acute brain lesions. Levin et al. inferred that the presence of a brain lesion on MRI during the first week after injury was a risk factor for residual cognitive impairment but was nonspecific regarding the type of impairment.

In a pediatric TBI study of children who underwent MRI on the average of 2 years after TBI, Levin et al. (1993) analyzed frontal and extrafrontal lesion volume in relation to executive function and other cognitive skills. The patients were school-age children in whom a broad spectrum of injury severity was represented. Using hierarchical regression analysis, Levin et al. (1993) found that the volume of frontal lesion incremented the GCS score and the child's age in predicting cognitive performance (Fig. 16.2). Although the volume of extrafrontal lesions had a weak relation to cognitive performance, there were fewer lesions in posterior cortical sites than in frontal cortex.

In a later volumetric study of brain lesions in children following TBI, Levin et al. (2001) used the Porteus Maze Test to investigate problem solving. The results confirmed that frontal lesion volume was related to maze learning and that the effect was primarily due to inferior frontal rather than dorsolateral lesion sites.

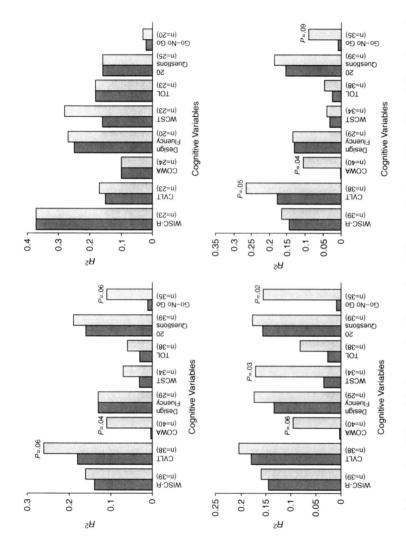

Figure 16–2. Summary of the results of hierarchical regression that evaluated the contributions of frontal (*top left*) and extrafrontal (*top right*) lesions to making incremental the variance in cognitive test scores explained by the lowest postresuscitation Glasgow Coma Scale score. The regressions were repeated to evaluate specifically the contributions of left frontal (*bottom left*) and right frontal (*bottom right*) lesions. Closed bars indicate R2: hatched bars, incremental R2. WISC-R, Wechsler Intelligence Scale for Children-Revised; CVLT, California Verbal Learning Test; COWA, Controlled Oral Word Association; WCST, Wisconsin Card Sorting Test; and TOL, Tower of London. (From Levin et al., 1993.)

The investigators postulated that inhibitory deficit arising from inferior frontal lesions (Casey et al., 1997) contributed to the errors in maze learning such as entering blind alleys.

However, the distinct contribution of frontal lesions to cognitive impairment has not been a consistent finding across studies. Slomine et al. (2002) analyzed lesion site and volume using MRI at 3 months following TBI in children. Cognitive outcome measures included letter fluency and the Wisconsin Card Sorting test. They found that site of lesion was unrelated to residual cognitive deficit. With only partial overlap in the cognitive measures used in the study by Slomine et al. (2002) compared with the report from Levin and coworkers (1997), it is difficult to explain the disparity in findings.

Focal Lesions and Psychosocial Outcome of Traumatic Brain Injury

Orbitofrontal and ventromedial frontal lesions have been implicated in psychosocial and behavioral disturbance in adults and children (Barrash et al., 2000; Blair & Cipolotti, 2000; Eslinger et al., 1992). Disruption of the dispositional linkage between knowledge about situations and events and emotions paired with these situations and events has been postulated to explain the psychosocial sequelae associated with these frontal lesions (Damasio, 1996). According to the somatic marker theory, these linkages are essential for reactivating emotions when a similar situation recurs (e.g., reaction by a supervisor to arriving late for an appointment), thus alerting the individual that appropriate action should be taken (e.g., allowing more time for travel due to anxiety about being late). Right orbitofrontal lesions have also been specifically implicated in response reversal based on processing of social cues, such as inhibiting anger and aggression in response to expressions of fear or submission by others (Blair, et al., 1999).

Although bilateral frontal lesions are common in moderate to severe TBI (Levin et al., 1997), MRI has identified subgroups of patients with lesions confined to the left or right frontal region. To investigate the effects of unilateral frontal lesions on psychosocial outcome of TBI, Levin et al. (2004) administered the Vineland Adaptive Behavioral Scales (VABS); (Sparrow et al., 1984) to the parents of matched groups of 22 children with and without unilateral frontal lesions on MRI who were imaged at least 3 months postinjury. Children with frontal lesions had worse scores on the Daily Living and Socialization domains and a higher frequency of maladaptive behavior on the VABS than children without frontal lesions. Volume of frontal lesion was related to the Socialization domain. However, side of lesion had no effect. In a related study, the authors found that the psychosocial outcomes of TBI associated with a unilateral extrafrontal lesion did not differ from those of a matched group of 18 nonlesional pediatric TBI patients. Taken together, the two studies converge in showing that unilateral frontal but not extrafrontal lesions contribute to the psychosocial outcome of TBI in children.

Depth of Focal Brain Lesions

According to a model of TBI severity effects proposed by Ommaya and Gennarelli (1974), the depth of focal lesions is a function of the traumatic forces imparted to the freely moving head. Based on a centripetal model of injury, cortical structural and functional disconnections are primarily affected by injuries with less rotational acceleration and milder impairment of consciousness. In contrast, more severe traumatic forces produce deeper lesions involving the subcortical white matter and deep central gray that are associated with more severe neurobehavioral sequelae than cortical lesions. By grouping children according to their deepest lesion on MRI at least 3 months postinjury, Levin et al. (1997) showed that the functional outcome, as measured by the Glasgow Outcome Scale (GOS; Teasdale & Jennett, 1974) modified for children, was inversely related to lesion depth. Although many patients with subcortical or deep central gray lesions also had cortical lesions, Levin et al. noted that total lesion size did not explain the difference in outcome associated with lesion depth. This pattern of findings was corroborated by Grados et al. (2001) in a more recent study that used a slightly different scheme of classifying depth of lesion.

Brain Regional Volumes in Patients with Traumatic Brain Injury

Due to potential distortion of neuroanatomic landmarks by TBI (e.g., large lesions, herniation due to raised intracranial pressure), manual tracing of regions is the preferred approach for studies of brain regional volumes. In pediatric TBI studies, the added dimension of developmental changes in brain region volumes provides additional justification for the manual tracing of brain regions. However, this is time-consuming and labor-intensive relative to semiautomated methods (Ashburner & Friston, 2000). Using manual tracing of prefrontal cortex in children who had sustained severe diffuse TBI, Berryhill et al. (1995) found that the volume of prefrontal gray matter relative to cerebrospinal fluid was reduced relative to that of age-matched children who had sustained mild TBI. However, the study did not report absolute volumetric measurement, and an uninjured control group was not included.

FUNCTIONAL BRAIN IMAGING

Structural versus Functional Brain Imaging

Neurobehavioral sequelae of TBI have been reported in patients with diffuse injury despite the absence of structural brain lesions and no evidence of obvious pathology on CT scanning during the intensive care phase of treatment (Levin et al., 1990). However, functional brain imaging has disclosed evidence of cerebral dysfunction related to cognitive and behavioral sequelae of TBI even in patients without structural lesions on anatomic MRI. Fontaine et al. (1999) used positron emission tomography (PET) to study regional cerebral glucose metabolism (rCMRGlu) at rest in 13 adults between 1 and 12 months following severe diffuse TBI. This methodology provided an absolute measure of glucose metabolism, but the link to cognitive function was limited to correlations with performance on tasks completed outside the imaging environment rather than activating tasks during scanning. Results of PET showed hypometabolism, a characteristic feature associated with reduced cerebral blood flow during at least the initial months following severe TBI. Significant correlations between rCMRGlu and verbal fluency, digit cancellation, inhibition of prepotent responses on the Stroop, test, and performance on the Modified Card Sorting Task were obtained for prefrontal cortex and anterior cingulate. Episodic memory was correlated with metabolism in left prefrontal cortex and anterior cingulate, whereas clinical ratings of executive function (e.g., planning, self-insight) using the Neurobehavioral Rating Scale–Revised were correlated with prefrontal and anterior cingulate rCMRGlu. Overall these findings highlight the contribution of functional brain imaging to elucidating the mechanisms mediating neurobehavioral disturbance following TBI.

Evidence for More Dispersed Brain Activation by Cognitive Tasks

Using H_2 ^{15}O PET rather than glucose is less invasive and can be repeated to compare the pattern of activation while performing a cognitive task relative to a control condition. Levine et al. (2002) used this methodology to study brain activation associated with episodic memory retrieval in six males who had sustained moderate to severe TBI about 4 years earlier. A paired-associate verbal learning task was given in which the patient was asked to generate an association between word pairs during the encoding condition and, when given the first word of each pair during the retrieval condition, to retrieve the linked word that had been presented. Subtraction of the activation produced during encoding from the retrieval condition showed right insular/ventrolateral frontal and frontopolar activation in both the TBI and uninjured control groups. The brain injured participants also had activation in the contralateral homologues of these areas, the right lenticular and left cerebellar regions. Interaction analyses showed that TBI patients had more activation of the right anterior cingulate, bilateral occipital region, and area 10 bilaterally, whereas controls showed more activation of right area 9 (dorsolateral frontal). In contrast, the healthy controls exhibited activation of the right angular gyrus, bilateral thalami, and left caudate and putamen that was not present in the TBI group.

Levine et al. (2002) interpreted the increased dispersion of activation in the patients as a compensatory mechanism for reduced mnemonic efficiency associated with deafferentation due to axonal injury and neuroplastic changes reflecting axonal sprouting and synaptogenesis. Serial functional imaging could provide additional evidence to support the view that the altered pattern of brain activation reflects the recovery process. It is also conceivable that interventions during rehabilitation and postinjury experience could affect brain activation by engagement of episodic memory. Limitations of the Levine et al. study, which are shared by most functional imaging investigations of brain injured populations, include reduced performance by the patients, which could possibly account for at least a portion of the group differences in activation pattern.

Functional magnetic resonance imaging (fMRI) offers a noninvasive approach to functional brain imaging and enables investigators to identify brain regions that become activated during performance of specific tasks. With block design fMRI, the areas of task-relevant activation are identified by subtracting the activation produced by a control condition that has sensory features comparable to those of the experimental task but lacks a key cognitive operation such as a demand on memory. Methodologic issues include control of head movement; artifacts in imaging the orbitofrontal region, which is especially vulnerable to trauma; and exclusion of patients with metallic surgical implants (Hillary et al., 2002). In common with PET, activation measured by fMRI could also reflect the difficulty experienced by a subject. Thus, control for level of performance could potentially attenuate observed group differences.

To investigate changes in cerebral representation of working memory following TBI, Christodoulou et al. (2001) studied nine adults (mean of 51 months postinjury) who had sustained moderate to severe TBI and seven controls using a version of the paced auditory serial addition that involved adding each number presented to the immediately preceding number and lifting a finger when the sum was equal to 10. This task was selected because of its demand on working memory—that is, a limited capacity for storage and manipulation of information (Baddeley, 1992)—that is mediated by a distributed circuit typically involving dorsolateral and ventrolateral prefrontal cortex in addition to posterior cortical regions. The activation found in the control group was focused in the middle frontal gyrus and middle temporal gyrus, with left greater than right hemisphere involvement, a pattern consistent with the fMRI literature (Collette & Van der Linden, 2002) and the verbal nature of this task. In contrast to the pattern exhibited by the controls, the patients' activation was more dispersed, with right greater than left hemisphere involvement. Christodoulou et al. (2001) interpreted this recruitment of additional brain regions in the TBI group as evidence for a compensatory mechanism due to the reduced efficiency of the prefrontal and temporal regions. Limitations of this study included a dissimilar control condition (imagine brushing one's teeth) that differed in sensory stimulation and different levels of paced auditory addition performance by the two groups. Increased subjective difficulty and/or frustration experienced by the TBI patients could have altered their pattern of brain activation, a nonspecific effect that is not necessarily related to the cognitive skill under investigation (Bookheimer, 2000).

Our group (Scheibel et al., 2003) reported fMRI findings for a 46-year-old male who had sustained a severe diffuse TBI 1 year prior to a study that included both working memory and inhibition tasks. Working memory was studied because it is mediated by a prefrontally guided neural network and because of its importance for complex cognitive skills such as reading comprehension and everyday tasks that require an individual to hold and manipulate information, such as listening to a list of items to see if any are missing and if they are in the correct sequence. The N-back working memory task allows parametric manipulation of memory load, including conditions that enable patients who have sustained a severe TBI to perform above chance without experiencing marked frustration. The activation procedures used by Scheibel et al. included an N-back working memory task for faces in which the patient responded when the face presented was identical to the immediately preceding face (one-back) or the face presented prior to the immediately preceding face (two-back). (This study did not include a 3-back condition.) The control condition required the subject to respond when a male face was presented, thus minimizing the demand on working memory while presenting similar visual stimuli that required attention. The uninjured controls exhibited primarily right frontal activation under the memory load conditions relative to zero-back, whereas the TBI patients exhibited bilateral frontal activation that involved a greater extent of frontal cortex relative to the controls. Performance data were obtained for one of the controls, which showed fewer omission errors compared with the patient.

Scheibel et al. (2003) also administered an inhibition task during the same study in which the participant pressed the key corresponding to the direction of a blue arrow (noninhibition condition). However, on trials in which the color of the arrow was red, the correct response was to press the key on the side opposite to the direction of the arrow, that is, to override the prepotent response. Both the TBI patient and a matched control showed more activation under the inhibition condition than the noninhibition condition. Similar to the N-back task, the patient had a larger percentage of frontal tissue activated during the inhibition condition than the control subject. Although the TBI patient performed above chance after the rate of stimulus presentation was slowed relative to the condition used with the control participant, he nevertheless had a larger increase in errors than the control under the inhibition condition. Consistent with the reports by Levine et al. (2002) and the Christodoulou et al. (2001) study, it is possible that the activation data of our patient also reflect remodeling of the neural network mediating working memory and inhibition.

Integration of Positron Emission Tomography, Functional Magnetic Resonance Imaging, and Magnetic Resonance Spectroscopic Imaging Data

Integrating the fMRI data and PET findings, the cognitive activation studies to date indicate residual frontal dysfunction in patients who sustain severe TBI, including cases with and without acute focal lesions. Consistent with this interpretation, magnetic resonance spectroscopic (MRS) imaging of TBI patients has disclosed metabolic dysfunction, as reflected by reduced N-acetylaspartate and a tendency toward increased choline in normal-appearing frontal and occipital tissue (Brooks et al., 2000; Friedman et al., 1999; Garnett et al., 2000).

Functional Brain Imaging After Mild Traumatic Brain Injury

Investigation of alterations in the pattern of brain activation in patients recovering from mild TBI is especially informative because the structural imaging findings are typically normal. McAllister et al. (1999) studied 12 adults with postconcussional symptoms at 6 to 10 days postinjury using an auditory version of the N-back working memory task. Although the groups did not differ in working memory performance during scanning, and although both patients and controls showed bilateral frontoparietal activation with increasing memory load, there were differences in the modulation of brain activation. Uninjured control subjects had more activation under the one-back condition relative to the zero-back condition than the patients, whereas the mild TBI group showed greater activation than controls when the activation under one-back was subtracted from two-back.

In a related study (McAllister et al., 2001), these investigators compared fMRI findings of 18 mild TBI patients with 12 controls using the auditory N-back task extended to a three-back memory load. In comparison with the control group, the mild TBI patients had a larger increase in activation under the two-back relative to the one-back condition, whereas the increased activation for three-back was greater in the uninjured control group. McAllister et al. postulated that the processing resources of the mild TBI patients peaked at two-back, an interpretation that would not appear to explain the group differences in their initial study, in which the patients had increased activation for two-back versus one-back subtraction.

In contrast to the functional brain imaging studies of patients following moderate to severe TBI, the key finding in the mild TBI studies is a change in modulation of activation rather than recruitment of additional brain regions. This alteration in modulation of activation could be due to neurotransmitter changes associated with mild TBI (McAllister et al., 1999, 2001). Further investigation is indicated to determine whether the modulation of brain activation after mild TBI changes over time to the pattern seen in uninjured controls and to evaluate whether this change is related to resolution of postconcussional symptoms. In addition, inclusion of patients who sustain general traumatic injuries without TBI would provide a control for risk factors (e.g., impulsivity) and posttraumatic stress associated with traumatic injury that could independently affect the patterns of brain activation.

METHODOLOGIC CRITIQUE

Neuroimaging studies have demonstrated a dissociation between structural and functional abnormalities in patients recovering from TBI. Functional MRI, PET, and MRS converge in showing cerebral dysfunction in normal-appearing cortical tissue, including patients without focal brain lesions. What is not known is how these areas of brain dysfunction following TBI change over time and whether they are sensitive to interventions such as training or pharmacologic treatment. There is also a need to integrate structural imaging techniques such as DTI with fMRI to elucidate the relation of white matter integrity in various brain regions to the extent and distribution of activation during performance of cognitive tasks. Methodologic problems also need to be addressed, including the matching of performance by patients and controls. It is also important to include neurologically intact patients with extracranial injuries in functional imaging studies because their preinjury risk factors, such as impulsivity, could contribute to the pattern of brain activation. There is also a dearth of data concerning the impact of TBI on developmental changes in brain activation associated with cognitive tasks.

SUGGESTIONS FOR FUTURE RESEARCH

Future studies could more closely integrate functional brain imaging with rehabilitative interventions. Such investigations could include changes in the extent and distribution of activation associated with working memory and inhibition in TBI patients following cognitive rehabilitation. Similar studies could also address changes associated with speech and language therapy in patients with communication disorders such as difficulty extracting the important information in discourse processing. Although reorganization of motor function is generally more relevant to stroke than TBI, it is appropriate to consider in the subgroup of TBI patients who undergo physical therapy due to hemiparesis or other motor deficits. Amelioration of emotional disturbance such as depression is often an important treatment goal during rehabilitation. In view of the extensive functional imaging research pertaining to mood disorder and regulation, it would be informative to investigate changes in the cortical and subcortical representation of affect related to treatment. Finally, recent advances in the neurobiology of social cognition could be applied to studying changes in the cerebral representation of processing the feelings and intentions imputed to others as TBI patients undergo rehabilitation for socially inappropriate behavior.

ACKNOWLEDGMENT

Preparation of this chapter and the author's research were supported in part by Grants NS21889 and NS42772 from the NINDS. I am indebted to Stacey K. Martin for editorial assistance.

REFERENCES

Ashburner, J., & Friston, K.J. (2000). Voxel-based morphometry—the methods. *Neuroimage*, *11*, 805–821.

Baddeley, A. (1992). Working memory. *Science*, *255*, 556–559.

Barrash, J., Tranel, D., & Anderson, S.W. (2000). Acquired personality disturbances associated with bilateral damage to the ventromedial prefrontal region. *Developmental Neuropsychology*, *18*, 355–381.

Berryhill, P., Lilly, M.A., Levin, H.S., Hillman, G.R., Mendelsohn, D., Brunder, D.G. et al. (1995). Frontal lobe changes after severe diffuse closed head injury in children: A volumetric study of magnetic resonance imaging. *Neurosurgery*, *37*, 392–399.

Bigler, E.D. (1999). Neuroimaging in pediatric traumatic head injury: Diagnostic considerations and relationships to neurobehavioral outcome. *Journal of Head and Trauma Rehabilitation*, *14*, 406–423.

Bigler, E.D. (2001). Quantitative magnetic resonance imaging in traumatic brain injury. *Journal of Head and Trauma Rehabilitation*, *16*, 117–134.

Blair, R.J., & Cipolotti, L. (2000). Impaired social response reversal. A case of "acquired sociopathy." *Brain*, *123*(Pt 6), 1122–1141.

Blair, R.J., Morris, J.S., Frith, C.D., Perrett, D.I., & Dolan, R.J. (1999). Dissociable neural responses to facial expressions of sadness and anger. *Brain*, *122* (*Pt 5*), 883–893.

Bookheimer, S.Y. (2000). Methodological issues in pediatric neuroimaging. *Mental Retardation and Developmental. Disabilities Research Review*, *6*, 161–165.

Brooks, W.M., Stidley, C.A., Petropoulos, H., Jung, R.E., Weers, D.C., Friedman, S.D., et al. (2000). Metabolic and cognitive response to human traumatic brain injury: a quantitative proton magnetic resonance study. *Journal of Neurotrauma*, *17*, 629–640.

Casey, B.J., Castellanos, F.X., Giedd, J.N., Marsh, W.L., Hamburger, S.D., Schubert, A.B. et al. (1997). Implication of right frontostriatal circuitry in response inhibition and attention-deficit/hyperactivity disorder. *Journal of the American Academy of Child and Adolescent Psychiatry*, *36*, 374–383.

Christodoulou, C., DeLuca, J., Ricker, J.H., Madigan, N.K., Bly, B.M., Lange, G., et al. (2001). Functional magnetic resonance imaging of working memory impairment after traumatic brain injury. *Journal of Neurology, Neurosurgery, and Psychiatry*, *71*, 161–168.

Collette, F., & Van der Linden, M. (2002). Brain imaging of the central executive component of working memory. *Neuroscience Biobehavioral Reviews*, *26*, 105–125.

Damasio, A.R. (1996). The somatic marker hypothesis and the possible functions of the prefrontal cortex. *Philosophical Transactions of the Royal Society of London B, Biological Sciences*, *351*, 1413–1420.

Eisenberg, H.M., Gary, H.E., Aldrich, E.F., et al. (1990). Initial CT findings in 753 patients with severe head injury. A report from the NIH Traumatic Coma Data Bank. *Journal of Neurosurgery*, *73*, 688–698.

Eslinger, P.J., Grattan, L.M., Damasio, H., & Damasio, A.R. (1992). Developmental consequences of childhood frontal lobe damage. *Archives Neurology*, *49*, 764–769.

Fontaine, A., Azouvi, P., Remy, P., Bussel, B., & Samson Y. (1999). Functional anatomy of neuropsychological deficits after severe traumatic brain injury. *American Academy of Neurology*, *53*, 1963–1968.

Friedman, S.D., Brooks, W.M., Jung, R.E., Chiulli, S.J., Sloan, J.H., Montoya, B.T., et al. (1999). Quantitative proton MRS predicts outcome after traumatic brain injury. *Neurology*, *52*, 1384–1391.

Garnett, M.R., Blamire, A.M., Corkill, R.G., Cadoux-Hudson, T.A., Rajagopalan, B., & Styles, P. (2000). Early proton magnetic resonance spectroscopy in normal-appearing brain correlates with outcome in patients following traumatic brain injury. *Brain, 123*(Pt 10), 2046–2054.

Grados, M.A., Slomine, B.S., Gerring, J.P., Vasa, R., Bryan, N., & Denckla, M.B. (2001). Depth of lesion model in children and adolescents with moderate to severe traumatic brain injury: Use of SPGR MRI to predict severity and outcome. *Journal of Neurology, Neurosurgery, and Psychiatry, 70*, 350–358.

Hillary, F.G., Steffener, J., Biswal, B.B., Lange, G., DeLuca, J., & Ashburner, J. (2002). Functional magnetic resonance imaging technology and traumatic brain injury rehabilitation: Guidelines for methodological and conceptual pitfalls. *Journal of Head Trauma Rehabilitation, 17*, 411–430.

Klingberg, T., Vaidya, C.J., Gabrieli, J.D., Moseley, M.E., & Hedehus, M. (1999). Myelination and organization of the frontal white matter in children: A diffusion tensor MRI study. *NeuroReport, 10*, 2817–2821.

Levin, H.S., Benavidez, D.A., Verger-Maestre, K., Perachio, N., Song, J., Mendelsohn, D. et al. (2000). Reduction of corpus callosum growth after severe traumatic brain injury in children. *Neurology, 54*, 647–653.

Levin, H.S., Culhane, K.A., Mendelsohn, D., Lilly, M.A., Bruce, D., Fletcher, J.H.M. et al. (1993). Cognition in relation to magnetic resonance imaging in head injured children and adolescents. *Archives of Neurology, 50*, 897–905.

Levin, H.S., Gary H.E., Jr., Eisenberg, H.M., Ruff, R.M., Barth, J.T., Kreutzer, J., et al. (1990). Neurobehavioral outcome 1 year after severe head injury: Experience of the Traumatic Coma Data Bank. *Journal of Neurosurgery, 73*, 699–709.

Levin, H.S., Mendelsohn, D., Lilly, M.A., Yeakley, J., Song, J., Scheibel, R.S., et al. (1997). Magnetic resonance imaging in relation to functional outcome of pediatric closed head injury: A test of the Ommaya-Gennarelli model. *Neurosurgery, 40*, 432–440.

Levin, H.S., Song, J., Ewing-Cobbs, L., & Roberson, G. (2001). Porteus Maze performance following traumatic brain injury in children. *Neuropsychology, 15*, 557–567.

Levin, H.S., Williams D.H., Eisenberg, H.M., High, W.M. Jr., & Guinto, F.C., Jr. (1992). Serial magnetic resonance imaging and neurobehavioral findings after mild to moderate closed head injury. *Journal of Neurology, Neurosurgery, and Psychiatry, 55*, 255–262.

Levin, H.S., Zhang, L., Dennis, M., Ewing-Cobbs, L., Schachar, R., Max, J., et al. (2004). Psychosocial outcome of TBI in children with unilateral frontal lesions. *Journal of the International Neuropsychological Society, 10*, 305–316.

Levine, B., Cabeza, R., McIntosh, A.R., Black, S.E., Grady, C.L., & Stuss, D.T. (2002). Functional reorganisation of memory after traumatic brain injury: A study with H(2) (15) 0 positron emission tomography. *Journal of Neurology, Neurosurgery, and Psychiatry, 73*, 173–181.

McAllister, T.W., Saykin, A.J., Flashman, L.A., Sparling, M.B., Johnson, S.C., Guerin, S.J., et al. (1999). Brain activation during working memory 1 month after mild traumatic brain injury: A functional MRI study. *Neurology, 53*, 1300–1308.

McAllister, T.W., Sparling, M.B., Flashman, L.A., Guerin, S.J., Mamourian, A.C., & Saykin, A.J. (2001). Differential working memory load effects after mild traumatic brain injury. *Neuroimage, 14*, 1004–1012.

Ommaya, A.K., & Gennarelli, T.A. (1974). Cerebral concussion and traumatic unconsciousness. Correlation of experimental and clinical observations of blunt head injuries. *Brain, 97*, 633–654.

Scheibel, R.S., Pearson, D.A., Faria, L.P., Kotrla, K.J., Aylward, E., Bachevalier, J., et al. (2003). An fMRI study of executive functioning after severe diffuse TBI. *Brain Injury, 17,* 919–930.

Slomine, B.S., Gerring, J.P., Grados, M.A., Vasa, R., Brady, K.D., Christensen, J.R., et al. (2002). Performance on measures of executive function following pediatric traumatic brain injury. *Brain Injury, 16,* 759–772.

Sparrow, S.S., Balla, D.A., & Cicchetti, D. (1984). *Vineland Adaptive Behavior Scales.* Circle Pines, MN: American Guidance Service.

Teasdale, G., & Jennett, B. (1974). Assessment of coma and impaired consciousness. A practical scale. *Lancet, 2,* 81–84.

Index

Note: Information presented in figures and tables is denoted by *f* or *t*.

training for, 55–56, 58, 59–62
types of, 51–52, 53*t*, 54
and user characteristics, 57
Extrafrontal lesions, 341*t*

Facial expressions, 106
Factors, injury, 207*t*
Factors, postinjury, 207*t*
Factors, preinjury, 207*t*
Falls, 89
Falx meningioma, 77
Family, 156–172
and childhood TBI, 225
impact of TBI on, 156–157
psychotherapy for, 158
in support groups, 157–158
Family Assessment Device, 160*t*
Family-centered problem solving
intervention (FPS), 222–224
Family Environment Scale, 162*t*
Family systems theory, 171
FDG-PET, 332
Feedback
and self-awareness, 35–37, 38*t*, 39*t*
Feeding, 16
Femoral nerve, 281*t*
Fentanyl, 283
Fetal alcohol syndrome, 208*t*
F-fluorodeoxyglucose positron emission
tomography (FDG-PET), 332
Finland, 135
Flexor carpi, 282, 288*t*
Flexor digitorum, 282, 288*t*, 297
Florida Affect Battery, 106
fMRI (functional magnetic resonance
imaging), 345. *See also* MRI
and disorders of consciousness, 331
integration with other neuroimaging,
346–347
Focal lesions, 342–343
depth of, 343
Frenchay Arm Test, 287*t*
Frequency of Family Coping Behaviors,
161*t*
Friendship, 88
Frontal cortex, 340
Frontal lesions, 341*t*
Frontal lobe, 121, 208*t*, 340
and behavior, 72–73, 76, 145
and initiation, 78

Frozen shoulder, 18
Frustration, 121
Fugl-Myer Scale, 285*t*
Function, cognitive
and social communication, 109
Functional gains
research demonstrating, 16–18
Functional independence, 17
and cognitive impairments, 47
Functional Independence Measure, 17,
20, 253, 286*t*, 293*t*
Functional magnetic resonance imaging
(fMRI), 345. *See also* MRI
and disorders of consciousness, 331
Functions, executive, 71–84
and ADHD, 221
and behavior, 72–73, 80, 81–83
definition of, 72
and external aids, 78, 79, 80
in mild *vs.* moderate TBI, 241*f*
neurological basis of, 72–73
and problem solving, 74, 75–76, 80–81
problems with, 73
research on, 74–79
and self-awareness, 34–35
vs. self-awareness, 43
and self-regulation, 77
and social communication, 90*t*
testing of, 240*t*

GABAergic system, 298
Gastrocnemius, 282, 297
General Health Questionnaire, 160*t*, 162*t*
Generalization, of research findings, 109–
110, 169
General Responsiveness Score, 315*t*
Germany
early TBI rehabilitation in, 3–4
statistics on employment of veterans in,
5*t*
Gestalt psychology, 4
Glasgow Coma Score, 21, 23, 24, 138,
182
Glasgow Outcome Scale, 120, 135
and age, 237*t*–238*t*
Global Assessment Scale, 287*t*
Goal management training (GMT), 74–75
Goals, 73, 82
Grooming, 16
Groups, support, 157–158

Guns, 249
Gyri, temporal, 345

H ^{15}O PET, 344
Hålstead Impairment Index, 121
Hand Movements Test, 213
Happiness
 and substance abuse, 139–140, 143*f*
Heart rate, 312*t*
Hemiplegia, 275*t*, 281*t*, 296*t*
Hemiparesis, 32, 123
Heterogeneity, among ethnic groups,
 256–257
Heteromodal cortex, 121
Hispanics
 alcohol use among, 254
 heterogeneity of, 256
 income of, and TBI rates, 248
 rates of TBI among, 249
 substance abuse among, 254
Homemaking, 183
Hong Kong, 164
Hospital Anxiety and Depression Scale,
 160*t*
Hospitalization, length of
 effect on, by intensity of intervention,
 19
 and ethnicity, 254
 and severity of injury, 20
Huntington's disease, 31
Hydrocephalus, 208*t*
Hygiene, 16, 317, 319*t*
Hygiene, perineal, 297
Hyperbaric oxygen therapy (HBO), 317,
 320*t*, 321, 329, 330
Hypertonia, spastic, 271–301
 chemodenervation for, 279, 282–283,
 284*t*, 285*t*, 286*t*, 287*t*, 288*t*, 299–
 300
 combination therapies for, 300
 definition of, 271, 298
 duration of, 298
 impact of, 272
 intrathecal therapies for, 283, 289, 290*t*,
 291*t*, 292*t*, 293*t*, 294*t*, 295*t*, 296*t*
 and laboratory assessment tools, 299
 nerve blocks for, 274, 279, 280*t*, 281*t*,
 299
 oral medications for, 273–274, 275*t*,
 276*t*, 277*t*, 278*t*, 299, 300

 physiotherapy for, 300–301
 symptoms of, 271
Hypometabolism, 344
Hypoxia, 291*t*

Implementation intentions, 82
Impulse control, 121
Income
 and ethnicity, 248
 of research participants, 169
Incontinence, 16, 18
Independence, functional, 17
 and cognitive impairments, 47
Independent Observer Report Scale, 93*t*
Individuals with Disabilities Education
 Act, 206
Inference, cross population, 211
Information processing theory, 216
Initiation, 78
Injury factors, 207*t*
Inmates, 139, 141–142
Instruction, strategy-based, 60
Insurance companies, 15
Integrated rehabilitation, 20–21
Intensity, interventional, 19–20
Intentional TBI, 249–250
 and alcohol, 249
 among African Americans, 256
Intentions, implementation, 82
Interpersonal Communication Inventory,
 93*t*, 105
Interpersonal process recall (IPR), 92, 93*t*
Interpersonal Relationship Rating Scale,
 93*t*, 105, 107
Intervention
 cognitive, 214–218
 context sensitivity of, 214–224
 early *vs.* later, 18–19
 intensity of, 19–20
 specificity of, in research, 79–80
Intoxication. *See* Substance abuse
Intracerebral pressure, 320*t*
Intrathecal baclofen, 273, 283, 289,
 290*t*, 291*t*, 292*t*, 293*t*, 294*t*,
 295*t*, 296*t*
Intrathecal baclofen pump implantation,
 291*t*, 292*t*, 293*t*, 294*t*, 295*t*
Intubation, 134
Iowa Recognition Battery, 106
Irritability, 122

CPSIA information can be obtained at www.ICGtesting.com
Printed in the USA
LVOW111929280513

335818LV00003B/7/P